Security Privatization

Oldrich Bures • Helena Carrapico
Editors

Security Privatization

How Non-security-related Private Businesses Shape Security Governance

Springer

Editors
Oldrich Bures
Center for Security Studies
Metropolitan University Prague
Prague, Czech Republic

Helena Carrapico
Department of Politics and International Relations
School of Languages and Social Sciences
Aston University
Birmingham, UK

ISBN 978-3-319-63009-0 ISBN 978-3-319-63010-6 (eBook)
DOI 10.1007/978-3-319-63010-6

Library of Congress Control Number: 2017951117

Printed on acid-free paper

This Springer imprint is published by Springer Nature
The registered company is Springer International Publishing AG
The registered company address is: Gewerbestrasse 11, 6330 Cham, Switzerland

Foreword: "Widening the Debate" and Raising Questions

This volume is a welcome contribution to the debates flourishing in private security studies.[1] The editors rightly underscore that this academic field must keep up with a field of practice undergoing rapid transformations. Their "key aim" to "widen existing debates on security privatisation" beyond PMSCs is therefore to be hailed. Their focus on how non-security-related private business is becoming part of security governance dovetails nicely with ongoing work in this area. Here, I therefore wish to engage the debates this volume opens by highlighting three questions it raises. I do so because these questions are of import not only for private security studies, narrowly or broadly defined, but also beyond. This volume will hopefully contribute to directing sustained attention to them.

The first of these questions is: What is a security function? This volume is centred on how and why non-security companies are taking up security functions. According to the editors, the first ambition of the volume is to map how security is being outsourced. But is that really possible in the kind of world the chapters of this volume describe so well? Are the financial institutions, the telecommunications companies, or the shipping industry really taking over security functions that are outsourced to them and that we can therefore assume to be predefined and pre-existing? For one, why the functions discussed are security rather than military functions? Why is it that in blurring the internal and external boundaries this volume (following of course common academic practice) decides to place the kinds of services on the inside by referring to them as security services rather than on the outside referring to them as military services? Does that not amount to importing a normative bias as it excludes what might be most contentious about these markets? More than this, are these functions (whether we refer to them as "security" or "military") really given to be taken over rather than extension of existing functions of novel creations? Reading through the contributions in this

[1] Abrahamsen, R., & Leander, A. (2016). *Routledge handbook of private security studies*. London: Routledge.

volume, it is not clear that most of these functions existed before companies started to exercise them and therefore also not that they were somehow "outsourced" from states to market actors. So for me, an important question arising from reading these contributions is whether we do not need to more carefully reflect on what security functions are, perhaps abandoning the idea that both security and function are of a fixed nature rather than themselves undergoing profound transformations as "non-security-related private business" engages in them.

The second question is if, how, and with what effects markets transform security functions. If it turns out that both "security" and "function" are themselves undergoing fundamental changes as non-security companies are moving into security, can we say more about how and why? Collectively, the chapters in this volume provide helpful pointers. First, they demonstrate the expanding space of security. For example, the chapter by Prem describes the "blurring" of the PMSC category as it expands into ever novel areas and that by Moreno and Price focuses on the growing "securitisation" of the US state in the post-9/11 period. Second, collectively the chapters also highlight some of the commercial processes at play. They are replete with examples of how commercial considerations merge with security concerns. They also show that this is by no means only because companies lobby for it (though obviously they also do that). Rather, as the chapters on cybersecurity, e.g., highlight with particular lucidity, it is just as often because the market has become the obvious normal place to start. Public regulators therefore not only resort to it but nurture it. Companies get involved "due to the continuous introduction of new legal and technical regulations by public authorities" as the introduction puts it (and often reluctantly I might add). Pointers may no longer suffice though. Perhaps a major task for private security studies is to become far more precise and refined in the analysis of the processes merging commercial logics with security logics and their consequences? For example, how do marketing techniques, commercial priorities written into technical standards or Internet infrastructures, or the focus on cost efficiency in security sector reform shape the way "security functions" are defined and carried out? Do we perhaps need to be more attentive to what place they leave for political processes restraining a "security" increasingly "unbound" as Huysmans puts it?[2] And how indeed is this redefining the gender, race, and space of security? This volume is helpful in that it points to these questions. I wonder if we do not need to do more in terms of answering them.

The third question is if security companies and markets are not also policy-makers doing security. The claim of this volume is that we must recognise that companies are not only policy *takers* but also policy *shapers* as its editors insist. Yet, most (no, all) of the contributions to this volume demonstrate that companies are much more than that; they are policy-*makers*. Giumelli's companies "implement" targeted sanctions, Biaumet's are setting and carrying out a "multi-choice policing" agenda in Burundi, and Procedda's are in the "driver's seat of cybersecurity". Of course, following up on this and acknowledging that companies are not

[2]Huysmans, J. (2014). *Security unbound: Enacting democratic limits*. Abingdon: Routledge.

only shaping but actually making security is uncomfortable. It demands that private security studies go with Foucault and "cut the king's head" to understand politics. Beheadings, needless to say, are no nice affairs. But perhaps much more fundamentally, to move forward in this respect requires acknowledging Bourdieu's insight that the state is an "epistemological problem" inscribed not only in academic practices but also in the practices of the companies/policy-makers observed. Confronting it therefore requires a kind of collective lobotomy which promises to be way more complex, messy, and unpleasant than any relatively neat royal beheading. Therefore, the perhaps most challenging question posed by the contributions to this volume is whether we can go on studying private security and its politics without this discomfort. Do we not end up missing most of what companies and markets do to security functions and as part of the governance of security if we shy away from it? Do we not need to acknowledge that companies are not only shaping but actually making security governance?

What security functions are, through what processes markets transform them, and what political agency companies have are all profoundly political questions of significance not only to scholars of private security studies but also for anyone with a stake in the politics of security and that includes all of us. While these questions are straightforward, posing them and even more answering them is less so. It requires the kind of rupture with the common sense crossing academia and politics that the French philosopher Gaston Bachelard insisted was at the core of any "scientific" endeavour and that has since shaped how most French scholars see their own work. While such ruptures may be creative, they are also profoundly unsettling. They require leaving behind the solid turf and comforting familiarity of the already established for something rather unsettled and uncertain. However, the rewards are commensurate. The ruptures provide not only the satisfaction of discovery but the possibility of remaining practically relevant in and for the rapidly transforming world of private security. We therefore owe it to the editors and contributors to this volume that they encourage us to move in that direction.

Copenhagen Business School
Frederiksberg, Denmark

Anna Leander

Acknowledgments

The editors of this edited volume would like to thank the British International Studies Association for its support in the development of this project, in particular for the funding they offered for a kick-start workshop in June 2015 in London. They would also like to thank all the participants in that workshop for their excellent contributions. In particular, they would like to acknowledge Raphael Bossong, Asne Aarstad and Gilles Biaumet's insightful comments, which considerably contributed to the development of the introductory chapter.

Oldrich Bures would further like to acknowledge research funding provided under internal research scheme VVZ 52-04 of Metropolitan University Prague and the COFUND Senior Research Fellowship which he held at the Institute of Hazard, Risk and Resilience and the Institute of Advanced Study, Durham University from September 2016 till March 2017. The fellowship was awarded under the DIFeREns project, which has received funding from the European Union's Seventh Framework Programme for research, technological development and demonstration under grant agreement no 609412.

Helena Carrapico would also like to mention the invaluable contribution of the Aston Centre for Europe (ACE) towards this project. ACE, which is currently hosting a Jean Monnet Centre of Excellence, funded Helena's fieldwork in Brussels, as well as her participation in a number of conferences, enabling the project to take form and develop into a full-fledged edited volume.

Prague, Czech Republic
Birmingham, UK
April 2017

Oldrich Bures
Helena Carrapico

Contents

Editors and Contributors

Editors

Oldrich Bures is the Head of the Department of International Relations and European Studies and the Center of Security Studies, both at Metropolitan University Prague. He was previously a senior lecturer at Palacky University; a Fulbright Fellow at the Joan. B. Kroc Institute, University of Notre Dame; an External Research Fellow at the Centre for European Security, School of English, Sociology, Politics and Contemporary History, University of Salford; and Marie-Curie COFUND Senior Research Fellow at the Institute of Health, Risk and Resilience at Durham University. His research is focused in the areas of privatisation of security and the EU counterterrorism policy. He was awarded several external research grants, including three multiple-institution grants by the Czech Science Foundation. His work has been published in *Security Dialogue*, *Cooperation and Conflict*, *Terrorism and Political Violence*, *Studies in Conflict and Terrorism*, *International Studies Review*, and *Intelligence and National Security*, among other key journals. He is the author of several monographs, including *EU Counterterrorism Policy: A Paper Tiger?* (Ashgate 2011) and *Private Security Companies: Transforming Politics and Security in the Czech Republic* (Palgrave Macmillan 2015), and (co-)editor of several edited volumes, including *A Decade of EU Counter-terrorism and Intelligence: A Critical Assessment* (Routledge 2016). For a full list of publications, please see http://www.researchgate.net/profile/Oldrich_Bures. Contact: oldrich.bures@mup.cz

Helena Carrapico is a Senior Lecturer in Politics and International Relations at Aston University and she is a co-Director of the Aston Centre for Europe and its Jean Monnet Centre of Excellence. Her research focuses on European internal security, in particular EU organised crime. She holds a doctoral degree in Social and Political Sciences from the European University Institute, where she developed her thesis on the securitisation of organised crime. She has considerable experience publishing on this topic in journals such as the Journal of Common Market Studies, European Foreign Affairs Review, Crime, Law and Social Change, European Security, and Global Crime. She is also co-editor of several edited volumes including *EU Borders and Shifting Internal Security: Technology, Externalization and Accountability*, published with Springer. She has attracted research funding from the European Commission, the Economic and Social Research Council, the British Academy, and the Royal Society. She also has a track record of engagement with policy-making in this field, having advised the UK and Portuguese Governments in matters relating to their organised crime strategies. Contact: h.farrand-carrapico@aston.ac.uk

Contributors

Å.K. Aarstad NorwegianAgency for Quality Assurance in Education, Lysaker, Norway

P. Berenike Research Associate at Witten/Herdecke University, Witten, Germany

G. Biaumet Centre de Recherche en Science Politique (CReSPo), Université Saint-Louis – Brussels, Brussels, Belgium

M.E. Bonfanti ETHCenter for Security Study, Zürich, Switzerland

R. Bossong German Institute for International and Security Affairs (SWP), Berlin, Germany

B. Farrand Warwick School of Law, University of Warwick, Coventry, UK

F. Giumelli Department of International Relations and International Organization, University of Groningen, Groningen, the Netherlands

A. Leander Copenhagen Business School, Frederiksberg, Denmark

K. Moreno Saldivar Long Island University Brooklyn, Brooklyn, NY, USA

M.G. Porcedda Schoolof Law, University of Leeds, Leeds, UK

B.E. Price PublicPolicy & Administration at Medgar Evers College – CUNY, Brooklyn, NY, USA

P. Stefanucci Freelance/independent, Rome, Italy

W. Vlcek School of International Relations, University of St Andrews, St Andrews, UK

B. Wagner Institute for Management Information Systems, Vienna University of Economics and Business, Vienna, Austria

Chapter 1
Private Security Beyond Private Military and Security Companies: Exploring Diversity Within Private–Public Collaborations and Its Consequences for Security Governance

Oldrich Bures and Helena Carrapico

1.1 Introduction to the Activities of the Non-Security Related Private Companies

Experts in several academic disciplines have already investigated the growing role of private companies in the provision of security (Abrahamsen and Williams 2011a, b; Boerzel and Risse 2006; Dunn-Cavelty and Kristensen 2008; Krahmann 2005; Müller-Wille 2004; Parker and Taylor 2010; Petersen 2013; Shearing and Wood 2003; Webber et al. 2004; Wood and Dupont 2006). Empirically, this topic can be found in the recent literature in International Relations, Security Studies, Criminology, and Sociology. A substantial part of this literature, however, focuses only on those private actors that sell various security services for profit as the primary line of their business—e.g. the private military and/or security companies (PMSCs). The usage of PMSCs increased exponentially in the past two decades to complement traditional military forces in conflict scenarios, as well as domestic forces in ensuring law and order. Examples of such PMSCs include, for instance Aegis Defence Services, which was contracted by the United States (US) Department of Defense to provide support in the Iraq and Afghanistan wars (Ortiz 2007), and G4S, whose services are now widely widespread at airports, land borders, ports, financial institutions, governmental institutions, industry, and prisons (Leander 2013). In order to convey an overall impression of the vast scope and scale of private security provision, it is worth noting that the massive use of PMSCs in recent armed

O. Bures (✉)
Center for Security Studies, Metropolitan University Prague, Prague, Czech Republic

Institute of Hazard, Risk and Resilience, Durham University, Durham, UK
e-mail: oldrich.bures@mup.cz

H. Carrapico
Department of Politics and International Relations, School of Languages and Social Sciences, Aston University, Birmingham, UK

O. Bures, H. Carrapico (eds.), *Security Privatization*,
DOI 10.1007/978-3-319-63010-6_1

conflicts prompted one informed observer to conclude that "[t]he private sector is so firmly embedded in combat, occupation and peacekeeping duties that the phenomenon may have reached the point of no return: even the US military would struggle to wage war without it" (Traynor 2003). In other words, the much-cited Weberian definition of the Westphalian state as the only human community that (successfully) claims the monopoly of the legitimate use of physical force within a given territory, no longer reflects the realities of many contemporary armed conflicts. We do not include a comprehensive review of the PMSCs' literature in this introductory chapter as it will be provided in Chap. 3 (authored by Prem), which shows that the contemporary "PMSC industry" is actually an assemblage of extremely diverse and fluid companies whose activities converge and intersect with several parallel non-security industries (for further analyses of PMSCs, also see Avant 2004; Chesterman and Lehnardt 2007; Jäger and Kümmel 2007; Ortiz 2010; Percy 2007; Singer 2003).

As mentioned above, given that the existing literature focuses primarily on those private actors that sell various security services for profit as their primary line of business, it neglects the mushrooming security practices of various non-security related private businesses (e.g. financial institutions, transportation companies, utility services providers, and infrastructure owners/operators), which make profit by selling goods and services that are unrelated to security in the traditional understanding of the term. Thus, the primary aim of this book is to widen the existing debates on security privatization by looking at how and why an increasing number of private actors beyond PMSCs have come to perform various security-related functions. As editors, we believe that adopting a broader perspective, beyond private military companies, contributes to our understanding of the subject by permitting the individual contributors to this edited volume to develop groundbreaking work by, firstly, exploring a range of case studies pointing out the growing presence of the private sector in security-related activities and critical infrastructures, and the consequent transfer of security responsibilities from the public sector to the non-security related private sector. Secondly, we specifically asked the contributors to draw upon their diverse disciplinary expertise and focus on possible ways to approach the conceptualization of the various security roles and practices of non-security related businesses.

In order to ensure unity of purpose, a meeting was held in June 2015 in the context of a one-day workshop at the British International Studies Association annual convention. The objectives of the workshop were to (1) map the extent to which security is being outsourced to private companies beyond PMSCs; (2) assess the social, political and economic consequences of the way security provision is evolving; and (3) explore the plausible conceptual and theoretical frameworks for analysis of the growing rule of non-security related private businesses in security governance. This edited book is the second outcome of those fruitful exchanges, following a special issue in the journal *Crime, Law and Social Change* entitled "Private Security beyond Private Military and Security Companies: Exploring Diversity within Private-Public Collaborations and Its Consequences for Security Governance" (Bures and Carrapico 2017).

This present volume presents the views of a diverse group of scholars in terms of disciplines, primary field of research, epistemological and ontological approaches, academic seniority, institutional affiliation, and nationality, in addition to offering original case studies on the specific roles of non-security related private companies of all sizes, areas of businesses, and geographic origin. The book is composed of 12 chapters, grouped into three parts. The first part explores how public and private security roles are being re-conceptualised within current trends in security governance. By deconstructing the mainstream discourse on the efficiency of public-private collaborations and the slippery nature of the PMSC category, this section underlines the diversity of security governance arrangements, as well as the recurrent absence of shared priorities and strategies between public and private actors. This part is formed of two chapters: Chap. 2, produced by Bures, is titled "Contributions of Private Businesses to the Provision of Security in the EU: Beyond Public-Private Partnerships"; and Chap. 3, written by Prem, is entitled "Who am I? The Blurring of the Private Military and Security Company (PMSC) Category".

The second part maps the expansion of security privatization across different sectors (maritime shipping, financial services, immigration, sanctions implementation and policing) and regions (Africa, America, Europe). It illustrates the diversity in security governance arrangements, which include not only public-private partnerships (PPPs), but also state-based arrangements and fully privatized arrangements, often co-existing within the same territory. The existence of such diversity leads us to re-think the idea that globalization and its impact on the security environment and market have resulted in the homogenization of security governance and the approximation of security actors' practices (Waltz 1999). Furthermore, this second part also analyses the consequences of diverse security arrangements for different areas of activity. In particular, it analyses, firstly, the societal and political outcomes of tasking non-security related businesses with security responsibilities, and, secondly, the consequences of having traditional state sectors become increasingly dependent upon private capabilities and resources. This part is composed of five chapters: Chap. 4, authored by Aarstad, is entitled "Maritime Security and Transformations in Global Governance"; Chap. 5, written by Vlcek, examines the "Privatising Security in Finance: Measures Against the Money Threatening Society"; Chap. 6 by Giumelli analyses the "The Role of For-Profit Actors in Implementing Targeted Sanctions: The Case of the European Union"; Chap. 7 by Saldivar and Price is on "The New (Private) National Security: Social and Political Consequences of Securitization in the U.S. Post 9/11"; and Chap. 8, written by Biaumet, focuses on "The Sentinel and the Rebel: Multi-Choice Policing in Burundi and the State-Centered Approach of Security Sector Reform".

The third part explores the privatization of security in the ever-expanding digital world, which in our view represents the most intriguing sector from the perspective of security governance and public-private relations. This sector is not only one of the most recent fields in the area of security, it is also a field where the private sector has been particularly tasked with governance-related activities. This greater involvement is related namely to the lack of capacity of state institutions to address network and information security problems. The third part not only documents existing PPPs, but it also maps the evolution of these fast-changing relations and asks who is in the driving seat of such arrangements. If the public sector is not rowing, is it at least still steering? This part is consists of five chapters: Chap. 9, authored by Farrand and Carrapico, is entitled "Blurring Public and Private: Cybersecurity in the Age of Regulatory Capitalism"; Chap. 10, written by Bossong and Wagner, offers a "A Typology of Cybersecurity and Public-Private Partnerships in the Context of the European Union"; Chap. 11, produced by Bonfanti and Stefanucci, focuses on "Exploring the New Frontiers of Security Privatisation: Web-Based Social Networking Services and Their Challenging Contribution to Foster Security and Public Safety"; and Chap. 12 by Porcedda is titled "Regulation of Data Breaches in the European Union: Private Companies in the Driver's Seat of Cybersecurity?".

The remainder of this introductory chapter seeks to expand on the main themes and trends of these three sections by starting with an analysis of the sectors and roles that are currently being outsourced to private companies beyond PMSCs. It then turns to how we can begin to conceptualize such trends and concludes with a discussion on the consequences that could emerge from this form of privatization.

1.2 What Is Outsourced to Private Companies Beyond PMSCs?

This book extends the conceptual and theoretical arguments in the emerging body of literature on security provision beyond PMSCs, which indicates that the bulk of private companies' security roles and practices falls under the label of the so-called *critical infrastructure*. While there is still some debate about what makes a particular infrastructure critical to the extent that its incapacity or destruction would have a debilitating effect on national security, there is a consensus that much of it is owned and/or operated by the private sector (Dunn Cavelty 2010). Due to the privatization and deregulation of the public sector since the 1980s and the globalization processes since the end of the cold war, the private sector controls 85% of the critical infrastructure in most Western countries (The National Commission on Terrorist Attacks upon the United States 2004). This concentration is based on two factors: (1) the perception that the private sector is better placed to efficiently manage different sectors of activity, including security ones, thanks to its organizational structure and existing expertise (Braithwaite 2008); and (2) the enlargement of the concept of critical infrastructure, which evolved from being equated with military structures to being associated with more diverse forms of infrastructure such as economic ones (Dunn-Cavelty and Kristensen 2008).

According to O'Rourke (2007), the lists of critical infrastructures have continuously increased since the 9/11 attacks, with key aspects now including agriculture and food systems, energy systems, health care facilities, banking and finance systems, commercial facilities and shipping services, most of which are currently privately owned[1]. As a consequence, representatives of public security agencies in several Western countries have started to increasingly call upon private companies to participate in the management of various national security issues, with an overall political aim of considerably reducing security risk and making the entire society more resilient and resistant to all kinds of threats, natural disasters and man-made catastrophes (Barrinha and Carrapico 2016; Bures, Chap. 2; Farrand & Carrapico, Chap. 9). According to the former US Secretary of Homeland Security Janet Napolitano, for example, "homeland security ... requires not just a 'whole of government', but a 'whole of nation' approach. In some respects, local law enforcement, community groups, citizens, and the private sector play as much of a role in homeland security as the federal government" (cited in Petersen 2013, p. 1).

Several sociology experts consider such statements to be a sign of a larger trend of "responsibilization" whereby individuals, communities, private businesses and other non-state actors "at risk" are increasingly expected to accept substantial responsibility for their own safety and security (Beck 1992; Garland 2001). As such, security becomes more individualized and market-oriented, whereby "responsible individual and corporate behavior entails installing burglar alarms and surveillance systems, engaging the services of a security company, participating in neighbourhood watches, and other forms of non- or quasi-state-related security behavior" (Abrahamsen and Williams 2011a, p. 67). This trend also explains why contemporary criminological analyses commonly point to the fragmentation and blurring of the security sector, where public and private actors interact in the provision of security (Shearing and Wood 2003; Wood and Dupont 2006). While the specifics vary among critical infrastructures, as well as national frameworks, the chapters in this edited volume confirm that some degree of security pluralization is clearly discernible across specific infrastructures, as well as national boundaries.

It is therefore important to clarify at this point what we mean by security provision by non-security companies. Following Bures' contribution to this book, we argue in favor of focusing primarily on those provisions and/or practices of security that are (1) intentional (e.g. not mere by-products of other business activities); and that (2) directly and/or indirectly address the level of (in-)security in a given environment. As in the case of PMSCs, security provision by non-security companies is also inherently political in the sense that it involves activities that impact the perception and/or provision of security, which has been traditionally conceptualized as a public (rather than private or club) good. In contrast to PMSCs, however, not all security provision by non-security companies can be described as voluntary. Moreover, unlike the proactive security engagement that is typical of both public security agencies and PMSCs, non-security companies have several other options at their disposal when it comes to responding to various security threats: (1) Business termination; (2) Taking the security risks and running

[1]Authors such as Bossong (2014), however, critically point out that despite the gradual expansion of the concept of Critical Infrastructures, such expansion has not automatically been reflected in operational programmes.

the business as usual; and (3) Transferring the costs related to the threat's occurrence by purchasing insurance (see Bures, Chap. 2).

1.3 Conceptualizing Private Security Beyond PMSCs: Public-Private Partnerships

In addition to disagreements concerning the impacts and implications of security pluralization in general, and the growing security role of private companies in particular (see below), social sciences experts share a common challenge when it comes to improving the conceptual basis of their positions and arguments. In contrast, public policy-makers have primarily attempted to push for a greater security role of private companies under the rubric of public-private partnerships (PPPs), which have emerged as a particularly popular option in the last decade (Bossong and Wagner, Chap. 10; Bures, Chap. 2; Bures 2013; Bursh and Givens 2012; Farrand and Carrapico, Chap. 9; Verkuil 2007). Albeit originally conceived in the field of administrative reform, in the 1980s, with the dual aim of de-bureaucratize public services and promote privatization (Minow 2003; Ortiz 2010), the concept of PPPs was subsequently utilized within the then new concept of critical infrastructure protection in the 1990s. It was presented as a way to reduce the vulnerability of vital systems to low-probability, yet high-consequence, new security threats (Collier and Lakoff 2008). Since 9/11, the popularity of PPPs has risen to the point that they have been described by public officials as the third leg in counterterrorism—the first two being intelligence and surveillance (or technology) (Petersen 2008, p. 408).

Several chapters in this book, however, suggest that the actual security performance of security-related PPPs is subject to debate. For example, Bures (Chap. 2) argues that PPPs do not always automatically produce the expected win-win solutions, neither for the public nor for the private sector, as there is a dissonance between the "better safe than sorry" logic of public security agencies and the "profit first" logic of private companies. As a consequence, unless imposed by command (via legal and/or technical regulations at both the national and international level which, however, fundamentally contradicts the non-hierarchical nature of PPPs), some private companies are likely to pursue different options from the ones followed by public agencies, which are tasked with ensuring the maximum possible level of security.

The degree of dissonance between the security logic and the market one, however, is not a static one and is bound to vary considerably according to the area under analysis. As Farrand and Carrapico (Chap. 9) argue, the relations established between the public and private sides of PPPs in the field of Network and Information Security have evolved considerably over time and so has the perceived dissonance. Although there is still some concern expressed over such dissonance, the authors clearly indicate that the market logic has spilled over the security one, resulting in the private sector being largely influential within PPPs in this field, which could have serious consequences at the level of their security performance.

Bossong and Wagner (Chap. 10) explore a similar line of enquiry by studying how PPPs are diversely articulated in the area of cyber security. Their article provides a conceptual mapping of the different forms and kinds of PPPs in the area of cybersecurity, especially in so far as it concerns more regular and publicly known forms of cooperation arrangements in this area, differentiating partnerships from other forms of horizontal coordination or co-regulation between public and private actors. Such distinction allows for a more nuanced understanding of PPPs, underlying how different communities of practice are associated to different normative concerns and priorities, thus contributing to a more advanced conceptualization of the relations between public and private actors in the area of cyber security.

Jointly, the three aforementioned Chaps. (2, 9 and 10) in this book suggest that at least within the European Union, the majority of existing examples of genuine public-private cooperation primarily concern cyberspace. This is primarily due to the fact that most cyber security issues transcend not only the public-private divide but also national borders, thus making most of the national/public security governance measures obsolete. As such, in Bourdieu's terms (Bourdieu 1977, 1998), cybersecurity is arguably a rather unique field in terms of the distribution of material, cultural and symbolic capital among public and private actors. Thus, more than in other types of critical infrastructures, where public actors are still often the ones with superior cultural and symbolic capital and thus are able to set the rules of the game via legal and/or technical regulation, their actual performance in cyber security often depends on what Bourdieu (1998, pp. 76–77) called having "the feel for the game", e.g. "the actor's ability to comprehend their place within the field and the relative distribution of forms of capital within it" (Abrahamsen and Williams 2011a, p. 105). According to both Bossong and Wagner (Chap. 10) and Farrand and Carrapico (Chap. 9), private actors in cybersecurity often have the upper hand because when dealing with new or advanced cyber threats, public actors often enter the public-private partnerships as the weaker partner, reliant on specialized IT companies to define both the level of vulnerability and appropriate countermeasures.

1.4 New Security Arrangements and Their Conceptualizations Beyond PPPs

As PPPs appear to underplay the significant costs related to the adoption and implementation of security policies by non-security private companies, academic experts have recently pondered about alternative conceptual frameworks that may be more suitable for explaining the apparent gap between the security-maximizing logic of public security agencies and the profit-maximizing logic of private companies. For example, in the area of counterterrorism, where "[p]revention, detection and reporting are carried out by private partners, while the public partners have an analytic and repressive task," (Verhage 2008, p. 9) several security studies experts suggested that we are witnessing the emergence of new types of security arrangements. Building on Foucault's notion of space,[2] Wesseling described the European Union's fight against terrorism financing as "a network of all private and public, national and international actors that are responsible for standard setting, decision-making, implementing and/or monitoring the EU's measures to combat terrorism finance" (Wesseling 2009, p. 2). Similarly, Parker and Taylor suggested that we are witnessing the emergence of "a new security paradigm in which financial borders and parameters are best understood as a "complex assemblage" in which private financial institutions are in effect, authorized to make security decisions" (Parker and Taylor 2010, p. 953; also see Abrahamsen and Williams 2011a, b).

The chapters included in this book make empirical, conceptual, and theoretical contributions to this growing literature on new security arrangements. In Chap. 2, Bures explores two alternative conceptual frameworks for analyzing the gap between the security-maximizing logic of public security agencies and the profit-maximizing logic of private companies: political corporate social responsibility (PCSR) and resilience. The former comprises a growing number of publications whose authors seek to "normatively prescribe, and positively describe and explain, the political duties and activities of corporations" (Whelan 2012, p. 711). In particular, PCSR highlights the relative decline of political and socio-economic steering capacities of Westphalian territorially-bound nation-states vis-à-vis the (global) business actors, which in turn leads to the blurring of traditional boundaries between the political, economic, and civil spheres of society. The latter concept of *resilience* is a contested one, but it usually takes into account that (1) it is impossible to guarantee the full protection of all critical infrastructure given its sheer size and the enormous costs that it would involve, and (2) even the best security measures sometimes fail. Its proponents therefore argue that more emphasis should be put on the recovery from all kinds of disasters so that the damaged infrastructure can be readily and cost-effectively restored (Pursiainen 2009, p. 728). As such, according to Bures, it may be more acceptable to private companies, whose profit motive makes them very interested in getting their businesses restored and running as soon as possible following any disruption of their production.

In Chap. 3, Prem argues that is it not just the academic literature on the privatization of security that is going beyond PMSCs, but PMSCs themselves stretch conceptual boundaries. Drawing on evolutionary economics and sociological institutionalism, she proposes a co-evolutionary framework for explaining how and why PMSCs in the U.S. "market for force" have evolved over time from

[2]According to Foucault, the notion of "space" does not imply a fixed geographical area, it is rather a constructed transnational "network that connects points and intersects with its own skein" (Foucault and Miskowiec 1986, p. 22).

"kitchen porter" kind of functions to armed security provision, to today's multi-service organizations. Her analysis shows that this evolution reflects both the interests and preferences of the U.S. government, as the single largest client of private military and security services, and the major constraints that the twentieth century norm of the state monopoly over violence has placed on the development of the industry, pushing PMSCs to divest themselves from combat roles and armed security services. Many contemporary PMSCs are therefore multiservice organizations that have expanded dramatically to cover a myriad of service segments that traditionally were not considered as being part of the "PMSC industry".

In Chap. 4, Aarstad challenges several common views regarding current maritime governance arrangements. This author argues that due to several recent shifts in private and public governance capabilities in this domain (primarily related to the proliferation of armed private security provision), public actors nowadays facilitate security governance by carving out privileged spheres for commercial industries through their convening capacities, regulatory infrastructure and legitimizing role. This new role as facilitators signals a departure from the classic governance jargons "rowing" and "steering", as it does not necessarily imply a sense of control and direction. In particular, the agenda-setting capacities of private actors testify to a re-articulated role for public actors that is centered around convening resources, implementing consensual decisions through the existing regulatory infrastructure and casting a shield of legitimacy on the arrangement and the actors involved. Thus, according to Aarstad, the facilitation by public actors of private actors' participation in the governance arrangement surrounding private maritime security denotes both an active and passive reaction to changes in the globalized security environment in order to remain relevant in contemporary security politics.

In Chap. 5, Vlcek argues that the privatization of security in the domain of global finance has emerged over the past three decades out of a process engendered in the production of money laundering as a crime and the increased application of economic sanctions as a tool for maintaining global peace and security. Consequently, financial firms and a variety of non-financial economic actors are now responsible for surveillance against money laundering and terrorist finance, along with the enforcement of economic sanctions, particularly US economic sanctions. There are several consequences stemming from the transfer of the obligation to protect society from public to private actors, including the enforcement costs experienced by financial companies, along with any fines or penalties imposed for the firm's failure to adequately implement the surveillance mechanisms. Vlcek therefore argues that a rational response to state regulatory action pursued by financial companies is to identify those activities and actors that represent a high risk for future sanctions and then to terminate all business with them. This rational action, however, produces an unintended consequence when it forces these activities and actors beyond the scope of the global financial surveillance system. As a result, the privatization of security in the financial domain may be forcing illegality beyond the view of these surveillance mechanisms and thereby circumventing their original objective.

Chapter 6, written by Giumelli, also explores the topic of sanctions, namely looking at the private actors responsible for applying European Union targeted sanctions. Departing from a similar stance as the previous chapter, it highlights that private actors do not always follow the same pattern of behavior where the application of targeted sanctions is concerned. This observation then leads the author to question what the role of the regulatory environment is in shaping the behavior of the private actors involved in this area. To answer this question, the chapter proposes a matrix that explores the interaction between different degrees of regulatory input from State institutions and resulting private actor behavior. The chapter concludes that the capacity of State institutions' to regulate and monitor the private sector's application of targeted sanctions varies considerably. When their instructions are less detailed and their monitoring more limited, the impact of the private actors becomes greater. On the basis of this conclusion, the chapter underlines the need for the EU, not only to develop monitoring capabilities, but also the create mechanisms to train private actors to implement targeted sanctions.

In Chap. 7, Saldivar and Price use Securitization Theory to make sense of the evolution of immigration policies in the United States in the aftermath of the 9/11 terrorist attacks. They argue that securitization was rendered possible through the perceived threat posed by immigration to national identity and security, with increasing numbers of American citizens worrying about the social cohesion of American culture and about potential terrorist attacks. While mostly focusing on the various impacts of the securitization of immigration (see below), these authors also discuss the crucial role of powerful private actors when it comes to their encouraging of a more securitized state (motivated by profit) and their pushing of the public sector towards a growing reliance on the private prison industrial complex.

In Chap. 8, Biaumet offers an intriguing case study of two grassroots policing arrangements in Burundi—the use of informal "sentinels", guarding virtually every commercial and domestic buildings in the capital city, and the reconversion of former bandits into security guards in palm oil fields. Their existence challenges the Western notions of "security governance" and "security sector reform" and suggests that in post-conflict settings, at least two types of "security governance" coexist—a global security assemblage backboned by donors' discourses on state empowerment and involving coordination processes between formal (or growingly formalized) actors of security; and the local self-policing arrangements falling de facto out-of-scope of any public management. While some recent conceptualizations of security sector reform formally depart from state-centered views of security governance, the case study of Burundi suggests that implementation on the ground still resists holistic approaches of security.

In Chap. 9, Farrand and Carrapico argue that critical information infrastructure protection, an area for which the State was traditionally responsible, has become highly dependent on the private sector. This level of dependence is mainly related to the fact that the majority of critical information infrastructures is currently privately owned. As a result, private companies have acquired an expertise that is considered key in the protection of such infrastructures. The chapter explores the topic of security privatization by analyzing how companies, whose main business is related to Internet provision and content hosting, have become responsible for network and information systems security. More specifically, it focuses on how companies such as Internet access providers and online service providers have moved from a passive role, as objects of regulation, to an active one, firstly as actors responsible for adopting regulations, and later as shapers of such regulations.

In Chap. 10, Bossong and Wagner argue that the loosely defined area of "cybersecurity" provides the leading case for involving private actors in transnational security governance, which interacts with the dynamic debate on different models of "internet" or "cyberspace" governance. However, at least within the European Union, official proclamations and the practice of public-private partnerships in cybersecurity remain highly diverse. Bossong and Wagner therefore developed a typology for categorizing different forms of public-private interactions for cybersecurity, only some of which qualify as more regularized and operational "partnership". On this basis, they then surveyed the activities of ENISA and EUROPOL as the two leading agencies of EU cybersecurity. Their conclusions underline the lack of public knowledge and need for critical normative reflection on PPPs in cybersecurity, particularly in so far as they extend to more proactive prosecution of cybercrimes.

In Chap. 11, Bonfanti and Stefanucci contend that social media platforms and services have nowadays become both the object and the instruments of security-oriented initiatives. Their capabilities are exploited by law enforcement, security, and public safety agencies for managing crisis and emergencies, for policing, and/or conducting intelligence activities in the field of counter-terrorism, crime and other threat prevention and response. Bonfanti and Stefanucci review these initiatives, as well as the relevant supranational EU and national-level policy frameworks, governing the employment of social media for security. This chapter underlines that improvements in the governance of the security-related employment of social media can only be achieved through the adoption and implementation of a more coordinated, coherent, comprehensive, and effectively inclusive approach to the matter.

Finally, Chap. 12, written by Porcedda, is also interested in how private companies have come to occupy the driver's seat in cybersecurity. It reaches a similar conclusion as Farrand and Carrapico (Chap. 9), although the analysis is conducted from a different disciplinary perspective. Porcedda conducts a legal analysis of the EU legislation on notification and mitigation of data breaches and identifies its framing logic of risk management and assessment. The author uses this specific case study to ask what are the consequences of such private sector role, and to question whether companies are the most adequate actor to ensure network and information security.

1.5 Consequences of Security Provision Beyond PMSCs

While there appears to be a general agreement across social science disciplines that a pluralization of security is taking place, there is considerable disagreement about its impact and implications. On the one hand, in much of the global governance literature, pluralization of security is presented largely in positive terms as part of a broader shift from government to governance because the traditional hierarchical conceptions of government are seen as inadequate when it comes to capturing the geographically, functionally, normatively and institutionally dispersed structure of security provision (Reinicke and Deng 2000; Brühl 2001). In contrast, various non-hierarchical governance arrangements are viewed positively as presenting numerous opportunities for productive cooperation of multiple actors, including private companies, in the provision of security and other traditionally state-provided goods and services (see Boerzel and Risse 2006 for a literature review). Similarly, in line with the aforementioned claims by public officials, security governance experts have also pointed out that in response to the emergence of recent security threats, there has been a turn towards new modes of security governance that include a hybrid mix of public and private actors, which rest upon non-hierarchical networks, and rely on soft compliance based on instruments such as peer evaluations, best practices or codes of conduct (Gill 2006; Krahmann 2005; Leander 2012, 2016a; Webber et al. 2004). Because of their flexibility, relative independence from national governments, as well as their ability to include a broad range of participants on equal footing, it is generally assumed that these informal policy structures "are more suitable for tackling governance problems or achieving common goals than more hierarchical and formal strategies" (Den Boer et al. 2008, p. 118). Such perceived adequateness usually derives from the conceptualization of emerging security threats as more fluid and networked-based, which makes them less susceptible to traditional State responses (Carrapico et al. 2015).

On the other hand, several security, sociology and criminology experts have expressed a rather negative view of the increasing pluralization of security in general, and of the growing role of private sector actors in particular. Primarily, this is due to concerns about the repercussions on the provision of security, traditionally conceived as a public good provided by states to all citizens, and/or concerns about the lack of public accountability, oversight, and legitimacy of private sector actors (Krahmann 2005; Leander 2010, 2016b; Singer 2003). In the conflict resolution literature, this critical view is pervasive in numerous studies that investigate the role of private companies in contemporary armed conflicts. Their authors almost unanimously conclude that in areas of weak or failing governmental authority, private companies are often contributors to security problems, rather than to their solutions (Ballentine and Sherman 2003; Berdal and Malone 2000; Klare 2001; Musah 2002). Moreover, many of the intriguing questions that have been asked concerning the implications of the increasing utilization of services of private military and/or security companies in the security studies literature are particularly relevant in the context of this book. Namely, how does the growing participation of companies whose primary line of business is not security provision impact on the development and running of security policies? Such question implies concerns about depoliticization and commodification of security: as it becomes a commodity capable of being globally exported as a set of technical capabilities and skills, it is increasingly transformed from a political problem requiring welfare social policy and state intervention to a technical problem amenable to private solutions through the logics of cost efficiency (Abrahamsen and Williams 2011a).

Overall, therefore, the existing literature not only points out the growing presence of the private sector in security related activities and critical infrastructures and the consequent transfer of responsibilities from the public sector to companies—it also underlines the expanding neo-liberal approach to security governance, based on a reduction of risk, a perception of the private sector as being more efficient and adequate to deal with recent security threats, and a responsibilization of all sectors of society for collective security. These issues have been further explored by a growing critical literature on neo-liberalism and its restructuring of security governance (Abrahamsen and Williams 2011a, b; Harvey 2007; Leander 2011; Price 2011). According to this literature, the mainstreaming of neo-liberal economic policies, the consequent commodification of security and the latter's refashioning as an expertise-dominated field have led to the belief that the private sector is better placed to deal with security threats and risks given its high degree of efficiency. Furthermore, private businesses have also emerged as sites of expertise in their own fields, putting them at an advantage, in relation to the State, when dealing with issues of insecurity (Barrinha and Carrapico 2016). This literature voices, however, serious concerns in terms of the private sector's priorities and their incompatibility with the traditional public security and safety priorities of the State (Price 2011).

In this book, the political, economic and social consequences of this transfer of responsibilities from the public sector to the private one are highlighted in very different areas. Farrand and Carrapico (Chap. 9) refer to tangible consequences in the area of cyber security where the privacy and data security of Internet users has been put at risk due to a lack of prioritization of encryption and other security measure. Porcedda (Chap. 12) argues that recent EU-level legislation regarding the processing of personal and impersonal data by private companies is part of a wider infrastructure of risk and security management, which bestows upon private telecommunications companies the processing of sensitive data, thus turning them into active cybersecurity providers. At the moment, the data breaches notification obligation appears to be the only "stick" available to the public actors to ensure the security of critical (information) infrastructure. According to Bonfanti and Stefanucci (Chap. 11), along with the securitization of the Internet and, in a larger perspective, of cyberspace, social media have nowadays become both the object and the instrument of security-oriented initiatives. Their capabilities are exploited by law enforcement, security, and public safety agencies for managing crisis and emergencies, policing, and/or conducting intelligence activities in the field of counter-terrorism, crime or other threats prevention and response. However, the security governance implications of these initiatives are yet to be clarified.

Specifically, Bonfanti and Stefanucci raised the following important, yet largely hitherto unanswered questions: To what extent are providers of social media services accountable for achieving security goals or liable for any ascertained failure or abuse in their conducts? Has the impact generated by the employment of social media for security purposes on society as a whole, and individuals' fundamental rights, been (ex ante or ex post) assessed, and does the applicable policy or regulatory framework acknowledge the results of that assessment?

Beyond the digital world, Vlcek (Chap. 5) discusses the grave consequences of the practice of derisking, whereby private large financial companies terminate en bloc the accounts of remittance transfer firms, whose services are crucial for the well-being of a large proportion of the world's populations in developing countries. Equally serious are the consequences underlined by Giumelli (Chap. 6), who focuses on how private actors are involved in the EU's targeted sanctions regime. His chapter draws our attention to the existence of differing regulatory environments within the same field and to its consequences. In particular, it focuses on the consequences associated with companies' overcompliance and uneven compliance.

Saldivar and Price (Chap. 7) argue that the increasing management of the United States' prison industrial complex by private actors has contributed substantially towards the securitization of immigrants and rendered their integration process more difficult. Having benefitted from the state of exception rationale enabled by the War on Drugs, the private prison system reinforced its own role by lobbying political actors for harsher immigration legislation in view to increasing its profits. Biaumet's case study on Burundi (Chap. 8) suggests that in a transitioning context, where different agents and normativities—namely the government, the police, corporate security actors, donor states and institutions, individuals, transnational norms on (private) security and local dynamics—are intertwined in the provision of security, discrepancies between donor discourses and local dynamics remain at work. To a certain extent, these discrepancies reflect the theoretical debate over the state's role in security governance, particularly in post-conflict contexts where concerns about democratic oversight, the rule of law and accountability abound.

Finally, Bures (Chap. 2) surveyed three key general challenges of the growing role of private businesses in the provision of security—responsibilization, depoliticization, and commodification. These are important reminders that the engagement of private businesses in the provision of security is always bound to raise a number of profound political dilemmas, which imply the need for (re-)consideration of the more traditional regulatory frameworks in order to safeguard important public goods and/or values. Moreover, since private companies can actually decide not to provide particular security goods and/or services if their provision is deemed unprofitable, there is a clear need for public alternatives for the provision of such security goods and/or services available to all citizens at all times.

1.6 Avenues for Future Research

As noted above, the key aim of this book is to widen the existing debates on security privatization by looking at how and why an increasing number of private actors beyond PMSCs have come to perform various security-related functions. It is therefore important to conclude this introduction by acknowledging that there is considerable room for further research going beyond the ground covered in this book, both conceptually and empirically speaking. We would therefore like to encourage further research on the new private actors that are participating in security governance and on the different arrangements that have emerged between those private actors and the public sector. Some of this still to-be-explored ground was covered by other participants in our workshop, at the British International Studies Association annual conference in London. We would therefore like to offer here a summary of these insights regarding (1) the types of actors and areas of security, and the (2) conceptual frameworks covered by these unpublished contributions, as indicators of plausible future avenues of research.

The paper by Hendrik Hegemann explored a number of these avenues for further research. In particular, it looked at the participation of private actors in EU civil security governance via two innovative case studies: the EU security research programme and EU guidelines for integrated risk assessments (Hegemann 2015). The author's research suggested a need to investigate different types of private actor involvement, extending beyond the more traditional concepts delegation, co-regulation and public-private-partnerships. In civil security governance in the EU, where the goal is neither to formally regulate the behavior of private actors nor to award independent security functions to them, but to draw on the specialized experience and knowledge they have gained, this specifically includes consultation, information exchange, and provision of research funding. Conceptually, these arrangements highlight the plausibility of application of concepts of "new" or "experimentalist" governance to the security field with the aim to use the scientific state of art to develop innovative policy solutions that "work" and serve the goal of "better regulation" beyond the intricacies of ideological politics (Nance and Cortrell 2014; Sabel and Zeitlin 2010). The author also suggests that there is a potential value to the concept of "orchestration" given that international organizations often play a special role in these modes of governance: they "orchestrate" private actors based on their cross-national overview of relevant expertise in order to leverage their limited powers and resources and increase their autonomy and authority vis-à-vis skeptical states (see Abbott et al. 2015).

Sarah Komasova explored the concept of airport security and functions of its existing structures at different airports, with primary emphasis on the role, interactions and divergent approaches of public and private actors (Komasova 2015). In the center of her inquiry is the question of how the concept of airport security, including its parts and components, is understood and practiced, and how this understanding and practice are influenced by the presence of private actors. She adopts Marc Salter's understanding of airport security "in terms of passenger, baggage, and airport employees screening; perimeter and sterile area access; and terminal security" (Salter 2008, p. 4). In this view, the important actors of airport security are the following: state, airport company shareholders represented by airport management, state employees and serviceman, private security subcontractors and their employees, relevant airlines personal and travelers, further airport buildings and procedures, technology and ideas of security and risk management. In theoretical terms, Komasova's inquiry primarily builds on actor-network theory and its methodological emphasis on field research, or more precisely, going to the sites of airport security production. In her research project, she is analyzing three cases of existing airports security arrangements, each with different interactions between public and private actors, in order to provide a comparative analysis.

Pawel Frankowski and Irma Słomczyńska explored the growing presence of the private sector in space, building a comparative study between companies in the United States and Europe (Frankowski and Słomczyńska 2015). The conference paper problematized the private sector's approach to data protection and licensing by focusing on privately developed technology such as satellite imagery and satellite remote sensing. The authors also discussed the consequences of this growing presence for global security by asking whether an increased reliance on private capabilities, in a traditional area of state activity, could lead to the emergence of new security threats. One of the particularly interesting aspects of this paper was the mapping of security arrangements in an empirical area that has so far received limited attention. Through their comparison between the US and Europe, the authors uncovered evidence of different security arrangements: in the US, private security companies' shape legislation and policy directly, whereas in Europe, the process is still mainly in the hands of the state sector.

Going beyond this book, there is a considerable range of actors, both private and public worthy of further exploration. It is the case, namely, of international organizations, which play an important role as brokers for many public-private arrangements. The aforementioned concept of orchestration may offer new insights in this respect since it involves IGOs enlisting intermediary actors on a voluntary basis, by providing them with ideational and material support, to address target actors in pursuit of IGO governance goals. Both the intermediary and target actors may include private businesses and via orchestration, the IGO creates, supports and integrates a multi-actor system of soft and indirect governance geared towards shared goals that neither orchestrator nor intermediaries could achieve on their own (Abbott et al. 2015). Furthermore, as this book pointed out, different policy areas are characterized by different arrangements and, as such, this literature would considerably benefit from expanding the limited range of policies covered so far. Although a lot of these arrangements have been referred to as PPPs, their shape and division of labor can vary widely. We would also like to encourage further research on the political, social, and economic consequences of such arrangements and on the conceptual frameworks used to explain these new arrangements. One such framework this new research agenda could engage with is the nodal governance perspective (see Wood and Dupont 2006), which has already been successfully utilized for grappling more explicitly and systematically with the "messy realm of practices and relations" (Garland 1997, p. 199) between public and private actors in criminology. Some of the topics we believe would also be worth expanding upon are the development of private actors' expertise in this field, how it is framed in the context of security governance, and the insights it reveals about the current economic model of neo-liberalism.

References

Abbott, A. W., Genschel, P., Snidal, D., & Zangl, B. (Eds.). (2015). *International organizations as orchestrators*. Cambridge: Cambridge University Press.

Abrahamsen, R., & Williams, M. C. (2011a). *Security beyond the state: Private security in international politics*. Cambridge: Cambridge University Press.

Abrahamsen, R., & Williams, M. (2011b). Security privatization and global security assemblages. *Brown Journal of World Affairs, 18*(1), 171–180.

Avant, D. (2004). *The market for force: The consequences of privatizing security 9*. Cambridge: Cambridge University Press.

Ballentine, K., & Sherman, J. (2003). *The political economy of armed conflict: Beyond greed and grievance*. Boulder, CO: Lynne Rienner Publishers.

Barrinha, A., & Carrapico, H. (2016). The internal, the external and the virtual: The EU and the security of cyberspace. In L. Chappell, J. Mawdsley, & P. Petrov (Eds.), *The EU, strategy and security policy*. London and New York: Routledge.

Beck, U. (1992). *Risk society: Towards a new modernity*. London: Sage.

Berdal, M., & Malone, D. M. (2000). *Greed and grievance: Economic agendas in civil wars*. Boulder, CO: Lynne Rienner.

Boerzel, T. A., & Risse, T. (2006). Public-private partnerships: Effective and legitimate tools of transnational governance. In E. Grande & L. W. Pauly (Eds.), *Complex sovereignty* (pp. 195–216). Toronto: Toronto University Press.

Bossong, R. (2014). The European programme for the protection of critical infrastructures–meta-governing a new security problem? *European Security, 23*(2), 210–226.

Bourdieu, P. (1977). *Outline of a theory of practice*. Cambridge: Cambridge University Press.

Bourdieu, P. (1998). *Practical reason: On the theory of action*. Cambridge: Polity.

Braithwaite, J. (2008). *Regulatory capitalism: How it works, ideas for making it work better*. Cheltenham: Edward Elgar.

Brühl, T. (2001, December 7–8). *The privatization of governance systems: On the legitimacy of environmental policy*. Paper presented at Global Environment and the Nation State, Berlin.

Bures, O. (2013). Public-private partnerships in the fight against terrorism? *Crime, Law and Social Change, 60*(4), 429–455.

Bures, O., & Carrapico, H. (2017). Private security beyond private military and security companies: Exploring diversity within private-public collaborations and its consequences for security governance. *Crime, Law and Social Change, 67*(3), 229–244.

Bursh, N. E., & Givens, A. D. (2012). Public-private partnerships in homeland security: Opportunities and challenges. *Homeland Security Affairs, 8*(18), 1–23.

Carrapico, H., Irrera, D., & Tupman, B. (Eds.). (2015). *Criminals and terrorists in partnership: Unholy alliance*. New York, London: Routledge.

Chesterman, S., & Lehnardt, C. (2007). *From mercenaries to market: The rise and regulation of private military companies*. Oxford: Oxford University Press.

Collier, S. J., & Lakoff, A. (2008). The vulnerability of vital systems: How critical infrastructure became a security problem. In M. D. Cavelty & K. S. Kristensen (Eds.), *Securing 'the homeland': Critical infrastructure, risk and (in)security* (pp. 17–39). Routledge: London.

Den Boer, M., Hillerbrand, C., & Nölke, A. (2008). Legitimacy under pressure: The European web of counter-terrorism networks. *Journal of Common Market Studies, 46*(1), 101–124.
Dunn Cavelty, M. (2010). Cyber-threats. In M. Dunn Cavelty & V. Mauer (Eds.), *The Routledge handbook of security studies*. London and New York: Routledge.
Dunn-Cavelty, M., & Kristensen, K. S. (2008). *Securing 'the homeland': Critical infrastructure, risk and (in) security*. London: Routledge.
Foucault, M., & Miskowiec, J. (1986). Of other spaces. *Diacritics, 16*(1), 22–27.
Frankowski, P., & Słomczyńska, I. (2015). *Outer space and private companies. Consequences for global security*. Conference paper presented at the 2015 British International Studies Association, London.
Garland, D. (1997). 'Governmentality' and the problem of crime: Foucault, criminology, sociology. *Theoretical Criminology, 1*(2), 173–214.
Garland, D. (2001). *The culture of control*. Oxford: Oxford University Press.
Gill, P. (2006). Not just joining the dots but crossing the borders and bridging the voids: Constructing security networks after 11 September 2001. *Policing & Society, 16*(1), 27–49.
Hegemann, H. (2015). *The politics of private actor participation in EU civil security governance: Beyond the 'security-industrial complex'?* Conference paper presented at the 2015 British International Studies Association, London.
Jäger, T., & Kümmel, G. (2007). *Private military and security companies: Chances, problems, pitfalls and prospects*. Wiesbaden: VS Verlag für Sozialwissenschaften.
Klare, M. T. (2001). *Resource wars: The new landscape of global conflict*. New York: Owl Books.
Komasova, S. (2015). *Reassembling airport security: Thesis research proposal*. Conference paper presented at the 2015 British International Studies Association, London.
Krahmann, E. (2005). Security governance and networks: New theoretical perspectives in transatlantic security. *Cambridge Review of International Affairs, 18*(1), 15–29.
Leander, A. (2010). The paradoxical impunity of private military companies: Authority and the limits to legal accountability. *Security Dialogue, 41*(5), 467–490.
Leander, A. (2011). Risk and the fabrication of apolitical, unaccountable military markets: The case of the CIA "Killing Program". *Review of International Studies, 37*(5), 2253–2268.
Leander, A. (2012). What do codes of conduct do? Hybrid constitutionalization and militarization in military markets. *Global Constitutionalism, 1*(1), 91–119.
Leander, A. (2013). Introduction. In A. Leander (Ed.), *Commercialising security in Europe: Political consequences for peace operations. PRIO*. London: Routledge.
Leander, A. (2016a). The politics of whitelisting: Regulatory work and topologies in commercial security. *Environment and Planning D: Society and Space, 34*(1), 48–66.
Leander, A. (2016b). Whitelisting and the rule of law: Accountability in contemporary commercial security. In M. Heupel & T. Reinold (Eds.), *Global governance* (pp. 205–236). London: Palgrave.
Minow, M. (2003). Public and private partnerships. Accounting for the new religion. *Harvard Law Review, 116*(1), 1229–1270.
Müller-Wille, B. (2004, January). *For our eyes only? Shaping an intelligence community within the EU* (Occasional Papers No. 50). Paris: Institute for Security Studies.
Musah, A. F. (2002). Privatization of security, arms proliferation and the process of state collapse in Africa. *Development and Change, 33*(5), 911–933.
Nance, M. T., & Cortrell, M. P. (2014). A turn toward experimentalism? Rethinking security and governance in the twenty-first century. *Review of International Studies, 40*(2), 277–301.
O'Rourke, T. D. (2007). Critical infrastructure, interdependencies, and resilience. *The Bridge, 37* (1), 22–29.
Ortiz, C. (2007). The private military company: An entity at the centre of overlapping spheres of commercial activity and responsibility. In T. Jager & G. Kummel (Eds.), *Private military and security companies: Chances problems, pitfalls and prospects* (pp. 55–58). Wiesbaden: Verlag fur Sozialwissenschaften.

Ortiz, C. (2010). *Private armed forces and global security: A guide to the issues*. Praeger: Santa Barbara, Denver, Oxford.

Parker, M., & Taylor, M. (2010). Financial intelligence: A price worth paying? *Studies in Conflict & Terrorism, 33*(11), 949–959.

Percy, S. (2007). *Mercenaries: The history of a norm in international relations*. Oxford University Press: Oxford.

Petersen, K. L. (2008). Risk, responsibility and roles redefined: Is counterterrorism a corporate responsibility? *Cambridge Review of International Affairs, 21*(3), 403–420.

Petersen, K. L. (2013, April 6–May 30). *The corporate security professional: A hybrid agent between corporate and national security*. Paper presented at the annual meeting of the ISA's 54th Annual Convention, San Francisco, CA, USA.

Price, S. (2011). *Worst-case scenario? Governance, mediation and the security regime*. London, New York: Zed Books Lda.

Pursiainen, C. (2009). The challenge for European critical infrastructure protection. *European Integration, 31*(6), 721–739.

Reinicke, W. H., & Deng, F. (2000). *Critical choices. The United Nations, networks, and the future of global governance*. Ottawa: International Development Research Centre.

Sabel, C. F., & Zeitlin, J. (2010). *Experimentalist governance in the European Union: Toward a new architecture*. Oxford: Oxford University Press.

Salter, M. B. (2008). *Politics at the airport*. Minneapolis: University of Minnesota Press.

Shearing, C., & Wood, J. (2003). Nodal governance, democracy, and the new "Denizens". *Journal of Law and Society, 30*(3), 400–419.

Singer, P. W. (2003). *Corporate warriors. The rise of the privatized military industry*. Ithaca, NY: Cornell University Press.

The National Commission on Terrorist Attacks Upon the United States. (2004, July 22). *The 9/11 Commission Report*. Retrieved November 21, 2008, from http://govinfo.library.unt.edu/911/report/index.htm

Traynor, I. (2003, December 10). *The privatization of war* (Global Policy Forum). Retrieved April 19, 2004, from http://www.globalpolicy.org/security/peacekpg/training/1210privatization.htm

Verhage, A. (2008). Between the hammer and the anvil? The anti-money laundering-complex and its interactions with the compliance industry. *Crime, Law and Social Change, 52*, 9–32.

Verkuil, P. R. (2007). *Outsourcing sovereignty*. Cambridge University Press: Cambridge.

Waltz, K. (1999). Globalization and governance. *PS: Political Science and Politics, 32*(4), 693–700.

Webber, M., Croft, S., Howorth, J., Terriff, T., & Krahmann, E. (2004). The governance of European security. *Review of International Studies, 30*(1), 3–26.

Wesseling, M. (2009, February 15). *New spaces governing the EU's fight against terrorism financing*. Paper presented at the annual meeting of the ISA's 50th annual convention Exploring the Past, Anticipating the Future, New York Marriott Marquis, NY, USA. Retrieved February 21, 2010, from http://www.allacademic.com/meta/p311342_index.html

Whelan, G. (2012). The political perspective of corporate social responsibility: A critical research agenda. *Business Ethics Quarterly, 22*(4), 709–737.

Wood, J., & Dupont, B. (2006). *Democracy, society and the governance of security*. Cambridge: Cambridge University Press.

Part I
Privatization of Security: Terminology, Concepts and Theories

Chapter 2
Contributions of Private Businesses to the Provision of Security in the EU: Beyond Public-Private Partnerships

Oldrich Bures

2.1 Introduction

The European Union (EU) and its Member States have recently called for a greater engagement of the private sector when it comes to countering various contemporary security threats. The 2010 EU Internal Security Strategy, for example, mentions the term "private sector" four times while explicitly stipulating its importance in the prevention of financial crimes, energy shortages, ICT breakdowns and pandemics (European Council 2010, pp. 23–24). References to the crucial role of private sector are also traceable in other recent EU-level security-related strategies and their corresponding action plans (see Table 2.1). The growing role of various private sector actors in the provision of security has also been acknowledged in the academic literature in a number of social sciences. Overall, despite many disagreements about its impact and implications, there appears to be a broad agreement that a pluralization of security is taking place. In fact, in several areas of (inter-)national security, private rather than public entities nowadays shoulder the bulk of the burden in responding to the new security threats, such as terrorism and organized crime. However, in contrast to the burgeoning literate discussing the increasing utilization of services of private military and/or security companies (PMSCs), comparatively little attention has been paid to the other private businesses, which make profit by selling goods and services that have nothing to do with security in the traditional understanding of the term (e.g. financial institutions, transportation companies, utility services providers, and infrastructure owners/operators). This is puzzling because many non-security related private businesses nowadays have to

O. Bures (✉)
Center for Security Studies, Metropolitan University Prague, Prague, Czech Republic

Institute of Hazard, Risk and Resilience, Durham University, Durham, UK
e-mail: oldrich.bures@mup.cz

O. Bures, H. Carrapico (eds.), *Security Privatization*,
DOI 10.1007/978-3-319-63010-6_2

Table 2.1 Private provision of security in EU security strategies

Year of publication and document tittle	Private actors noted	Specific areas of (expected) private sector contributions to the provision of security	Conceptualization of (expected) private sector contributions to the provision of security
2016 European Union Global Strategy	14x	Counterterrorism, cybersecurity	PPPs
2015 European Agenda on Security	4x	Cybersecurity	PPPs, public-private dialogue
2014 EU Maritime Security Strategy	5x	Maritime security	Not specified, only private sector engagement in general
2013 Cybersecurity Strategy of the EU	44x	Cybersecurity	PPPs in general and European Public-Private Partnership for Resilience (EP3R) in particular
2010 Stockholm Programme	6x	Data protection, research and development, cybersecurity, anti-money laundering, tax evasion, corruption	PPPs
2010 Internal Security Strategy for the EU	4x	Money-laundering, energy shortages, ICT breakdowns, pandemics	Resilience
2008 Revised Strategy on Terrorist Financing	10x	Countering terrorist financing, anti-money laundering	Not specified, public-private cooperation, dialogue, and data sharing
2006 Strategy to Combat Illicit Accumulation and Trafficking of Light Weapons	0x	NA	NA
2005 EU Counter-terrorism Strategy	0x	NA	NA
2005 EU Counter-radicalisation Strategy	0x	NA	NA
2005 A Strategy for the External Dimension of JHA: Global Freedom, Security and Justice	0x	NA	NA
2004 The Hague Programme	1x	Crime prevention	PPPs
2003 Strategy against the Proliferation of Weapons of Mass destruction	0x	NA	NA
2003 EU Security Strategy	0x	NA	NA

Source: Author's research

perform at least some security functions due to the continuous introduction of new legal and technical regulations both at the EU and the national level.

Building on a review of key findings from a growing body of social science literatures regarding both the opportunities and challenges of security pluralization, this chapter maps the existing EU level security strategies, their accompanying action plans and implementation reports in order to (a) identify and (b) critically asses the prevailing conceptual frameworks (public-private partnerships and resilience) invoked by EU policy-makers when it comes to the contributions of the private sector in the provision of security. This assessment is then complemented with a succinct overview of a hitherto overlooked conceptual framework that may offer more nuanced ways for understanding the roles of private businesses in the provision of security in the EU (and beyond): political corporate social responsibility (PCSR).

The structure of the chapter is as follows. In the first section, I review a multi-disciplinary body of academic literature that discusses the role of private actors in the provision of security in a broader security pluralization context. In the second section, I survey the official EU security strategies in order to identify specific sub-areas, as well as particular roles and/or contributions (expected) of private businesses in the security field. In the third part of the chapter, I point out the shortcomings of public-private partnerships (PPPs), thus far the most frequently evoked conceptual framework in the EU strategies when it comes to the engagement of the private businesses in the provision of security. Two alternative conceptualizations, resilience and PCSR, are discussed in parts four and five, respectively. The former has already been mentioned in the recent EU documents regarding cybersecurity. The latter has not been entertained thus far, either in EU strategies or in the relevant academic literature. The concluding part of the chapter summarizes both the key challenges of, and the main arguments for, the exploration of alternative conceptual frameworks suitable for the analysis of the currently under-researched area of private security provision beyond PMSCs.

2.2 Pluralization of Security: Challenges and Opportunities

Experts in several academic disciplines have investigated the growing role of private companies in the provision of security. Empirically, this topic can be traced in the recent literature in international relations, security studies, criminology, and sociology, which demonstrates that in several areas of (inter-)national security, private rather than public entities have shouldered the bulk of the burden in responding to the new security threats, such as terrorism and organized crime. Several sociology experts consider this to be a sign of larger trends in "responsibilization" whereby individuals, communities, private businesses and other non-state actors "at risk" are increasingly expected to accept substantial responsibility for their own safety and security (Beck 1992; Garland 2001). As such, security becomes more individualized and market-oriented since "corporate behavior entails installing burglar alarms and surveillance systems, engaging the services of a security company, participating in neighbourhood watches, and other forms of non- or quasi- state-related security behavior" (Abrahamsen and Williams 2011, p. 67). This also explains why contemporary criminological analyses commonly point to fragmentation and blurring of the security sector where public and private actors interact in the provision of security (Shearing and Wood 2003; Wood and Dupont 2006). Similarly, the increasing role of private actors in both national and international security has been acknowledged at least since the end of the cold war in the security studies literature (Krahmann 2005; Webber et al. 2004). However, while there is broad agreement across social sciences that a pluralization of security is taking place, there is considerable disagreement about its impact and implications.

On the one hand, in much of the global governance literature, pluralization of security is presented largely in positive terms as part of a broader shift from government to governance, because the traditional hierarchical conceptions of government are seen as inadequate when it comes to capturing the geographically, functionally, normatively and institutionally dispersed structure of security provision. In contrast, various non-hierarchical governance arrangements are viewed positively as presenting numerous opportunities for productive cooperation of multiple actors, including private companies, in the provision of security and other traditionally state-provided goods and services (see Boerzel and Risse 2006 for a literature review). Similarly, some security governance experts have also pointed out that in response to the emergence of new security threats in the last decade, there has been a turn towards new modes of security governance that include a hybrid mix of public and private actors (Gill 2006; Krahmann 2005; Webber et al. 2004). Because of their flexibility, relative independence from national governments, as well as their ability to include a broad range of participants on equal footing, it is assumed that these non-hierarchical networks "are more suitable for tackling governance problems or achieving common goals than more hierarchical and formal strategies" (Den Boer et al. 2008, p. 118).

On the other hand, several conflict resolution scholars have argued that in areas of weak or failing governmental authority, private companies are often contributors to security problems, rather than to their solutions (Ballentine and Sherman 2003; Berdal and Malone 2000; Klare 2001; Musah 2002). In this context, it is also important to point out the intriguing implications of increasing utilization of services of private military and/or security companies (PMSCs, see Avant 2004; Chesterman and Lehnardt 2007; Jäger and Kümmel 2007; Ortiz 2010; Percy 2007; and Chap. 3), which actually sell various security products services for profit as the primary line of their business. As such, they represent a specific category of private businesses and they are not the primary object of analysis in this chapter. In terms of giving the impression of the vast scope and scale of private security provision, it is nonetheless worth noting that even the US military would nowadays struggle to wage wars without using the services of PMSCs (Singer 2003). This confirms the overall message from the existing academic literature that the much-cited Weberian definition of state as the only human community that (successfully) claims the monopoly of the legitimate use of physical force within a given territory nowadays often does not reflect the realities of security provision on the ground.

Most importantly for this chapter, according to several security, sociology and criminology experts, the increasing pluralization of security in general and the growing role of private businesses in particular is apparent not just in zones of conflict, but also in relatively stable and peaceful countries, including the EU member states (Abrahamsen and Williams 2011; Loader and Walker 2007; Verhage 2008; Verkuil 2007). In this context, three interrelated normative concerns have been raised. Firstly, although security is not necessarily always a classic public good in the sense of being non-excludable and non-rival (Krahmann 2008), it is nonetheless commonly perceived as a special kind of a good due to its significant potential to impact on the life, liberty, and/or property of all people. As a consequence, as two prominent criminologists have argued at length, the idea of security as a public good represents an important part of the "structure of feeling" of citizens of modern polities and the public good of security is the constitutive feature of societies capable of providing a full range of other public goods (Loader and Walker 2007). As such, the idea of security provision by private companies remains normatively controversial because it represents a major challenge to both the public/private divide and the public good perception of security.

Secondly, there is another important question whether one can entrust the protection of life and property to private companies, whose primary motive is always profit, rather than security provision, which implies that private companies can actually decide not to provide particular security goods and/or services if their provision is deemed unprofitable. This in turn highlights the importance of the existence of public alternatives for the provision of security available to all citizens at all times. Even these public alternatives, however, face two additional normative challenges due to the increasing participation of private companies in the provision of security:

1. De-politicization: As security becomes more individualized and market-oriented and less tightly identified with the direct and exclusive authority of state officials, it also is de-politicized and partially transformed from a political problem requiring welfarist social policy and state intervention to a technical problem amenable to private solutions through the logics of security.
2. Commodification: As security becomes a commodity capable of being globally exported as a set of technical capabilities and skills, it ceases in part—but in an important part—to be a quintessentially social and public concern. (Abrahamsen and Williams 2011)

In other words, de-politicization and commodification of security significantly, and the critics would add negatively, affect the answers to all key questions related to the very definition and understanding of security (Krahmann 2008). This is problematic because the security field "refers to the nature and existence of the very polity—with the protection of the territory and the citizenry, to identity and border questions—which are of equal concern and interest for everyone," and as such "they cannot be left to experts or depoliticized decision-making bodies (Eriksen 2011, p. 1183).

Thirdly, greater engagement of the private sector when it comes to the provision of security can at times lead to clashes with other important values and principles, such liberty, privacy, and justice. In different variations, the trade-offs between freedoms and/or/versus security are being made on daily basis in all EU Member States in the search for the most appropriate responses to the new security threats (Bigo et al. 2006), which nowadays almost always and everywhere include active contributions from private companies. Thus, it is crucial to keep in mind not just the economic and legal, but also the social and political consequences of private security provision upon security governance in the EU (and beyond).

2.3 Public-Private Partnerships: The Default Conceptualization?

Even a cursory reading of the recent EU-level security strategies reveals that they are based on a relatively broad understanding of security on both sides of the threats-responses spectrum, which brings them in line with the findings from the aforementioned academic literature. Moreover, as indicated in Table 2.1, almost all EU-level security-related strategies adopted in the last decade have also highlighted the crucial role of the private sector when it comes to countering a wide variety of contemporary security threats. In additions to the threats listed in the 2010 Internal Security Strategy (see above), these include the fight against terrorism, including terrorist financing (European Council 2008, p. 12); terrorist use of internet; acquisition, production and use of explosives and explosive devices; chemical, biological, radiological and nuclear defense; and protection of soft targets (European Council 2011, pp. 6, 16–17, 29). Other recent EU strategies have singled out the role of private sector actors in maritime security, including capability building, risk management, protection of critical maritime infrastructure and crisis response (European Commission 2014, pp. 8–9); crime prevention (European Council 2007, art. 3, 5); private data protection, closing down websites with child abuse content, and the fight against tax evasion and corruption (Council of the European Union 2009, pp. 10, 22–23). Several other official EU documents also call for a greater role of the private sector in research and development in the field of security (European Council 2004, p. 20; Council of the European Union 2009, p. 10) and in July 2012, the European Commission published its Security Industrial Policy (European Commission 2012, p. 2), which stated that "[t]he security industry represents a sector with a significant potential for growth and employment." Most notable, however, is the 2013 Cybersecurity Strategy of the European Union, which mentions the term private sector more than forty-times and which states right in its introduction that "the private sector owns and operates significant parts of cyberspace, and so any initiative aiming to be successful in this area has to recognise its leading role" (European Commission 2013a, p. 2).

The acknowledgement of the key, and sometimes arguably indispensable, role of the private sector represents a remarkable shift from the earlier EU strategic documents that have been traditionally based on the idea of public provision of security. The 2003 European Security Strategy, for example, proclaimed that "[t]he best protection for our security is a world of well-governed democratic states" and argued that "development of a stronger international society, well-functioning international institutions and a rule-based international order" is the key objective of the EU and its Member States (European Council 2003a, pp. 9–10). Five years later, the Report on the Implementation of the European Security Strategy stated that the EU is now "recognized as an important contributor to a better world" although it still needs to be "more capable, more coherent and more active" (European Commission 2008, p. 2). Similar public-security centered language can also be found in some of the older sectoral security strategies, including the 2003 Strategy against the Proliferation of Weapons of Mass Destruction, (European Council 2003b) the 2005 Strategy for the External Dimension of JHA: Global Freedom, Security and Justice, (European Council 2005) and the 2005 EU Counterterrorism Strategy (Council of the European Union 2005). While often recognizing the fact that many contemporary security threats no longer originate from other countries beyond EU borders, the aforementioned strategies failed to entertain the possibility of non-state security responses.

As the most general policy-guiding documents, whose primary goal is to clarify the key strategic objectives, and ideally also prioritize among competing goals and objectives (Parsons 1995, pp. 474–475), the EU security-related strategies listed in Table 2.1 do not (and cannot) offer any specifics regarding the ways leading to the desired greater involvement of private businesses in the provision of security. Thus, for example, the 2010 EU Internal Security Strategy merely stipulates that it is "important for the public and private sectors to work together" without any discussion how this cooperation ought to look like in practice (European Council 2010, p. 29). Most other EU security strategies make only similarly vague calls for dialogue with, and/or further engagement of, the private sector (European Commission 2014, pp. 8–9). Alternatively, they merely state the need to increase and/or enhance cooperation (Council of the European Union 2009, p. 11); facilitate and improve the exchange of information and data (European Council 2008, pp. 9–10, 12); and consult private sector experts (European Council 2004, para 31). In general, this also indicates that in contrast to many academic experts (see above), the authors of the recent EU security strategies tend to perceive the growing role of private businesses in the field of security as a generally desirable development.

Moreover, as indicated in Table 2.2, most EU security strategies have been accompanied with action plans and their implementation has been evaluated in some kind of an implementation report. While in contrast to white or green papers, or legally defined instruments such as common strategies or directives, there is no clear definition of either the form or function of action plans and implementation reports in EU policy-making, it is nevertheless possible to distil some of their

Table 2.2 Private provision of security in action plans and implementation reports

Year of publication and document tittle	Private actors noted	Specific areas of (expected) private sector contributions to the provision of security	Conceptualization of (expected) private sector contributions to the provision of security
2015 European Agenda on Security—State of Play	0x	NA	NA
2015 EU Cybersecurity Strategy: Road Map Development	10x	Improving the network resilience; stimulating trust; awareness raising on the nature of the threats and the fundamentals of good digital practice; addressing cyber threats, creation of policies, strategies and institutions in third countries; capacity building to new technological challenges via innovation, R&D and standardization; developing safeguards that hardware/software produced both in EU/3rd countries, as well as the relevant processes and corresponding infrastructure, meeting necessary levels of security, assurance and protection of personal data; updating on the status of public-private partnerships, in particular involvement of industry and academia.	PPPs, resilience
2014 EU Maritime Security Strategy—Action Plan	2x	Acceleration of technology development; addressing research, development and innovation tasks.	PPPs
2014 Final Implementation Report of the EU Internal Security Strategy 2010–2014	7x	Increasing prevention and resilience in cybersecurity; ensuring respect of fundamental rights; considering the involvement of private sector in the new EU Internal Security Consultative Forum.	PPSs, resilience
2013 Second Report on the Implementation of the EU Internal Security Strategy	3x	Strengthening cybersecurity.	PPPs

(continued)

Table 2.2 (continued)

Year of publication and document tittle	Private actors noted	Specific areas of (expected) private sector contributions to the provision of security	Conceptualization of (expected) private sector contributions to the provision of security
2013 New Approach to the European Programme for Critical Infrastructure Protection	5x	Protection of various critical infrastructures, but only cybersecurity specifically discussed—coordinated prevention mechanisms, improved preparedness and the involvement of the private sector.	Private-public structured dialogues; resilience
2011 First Annual Report on the Implementation of the EU Internal Security Strategy	10x	Combating on-line radicalization; security-related research.	Private-public dialogue
2011 EU Action Plan on Combating Terrorism	7x	Counterterrorism, CBRN, cybersecurity, acquisition, production and use of explosives and explosive devices.	PPPs
2010 Action Plan Implementing the Stockholm Programme	6x	Disrupting the money transfers related to websites with child abuse content; dialogue on illegal online activities related to terrorism and other crimes; improving cybersecurity.	PPPs; private-public dialogue
2008 Report on Implementation of the Hague Programme for 2007	0x	NA	NA
2008 Report on the Implementation of EU Security Strategy	0x	NA	NA
2007 Specific Programme: Preventing and Combating Crime (2007–2013)	2x	Crime prevention.	PPPs
2006 European Programme for Critical Infrastructure Protection	3x	Protection of various critical infrastructures.	Public-private dialogue
2006 EU Action Plan on Combating Terrorism	0x	NA	NA
2005 Action Plan Implementing the Hague Programme	4x	Developing PPPs to improve the prevention and the fight against terrorism, organized crime, cyber crime, and corruption	PPPs

Source: Author's research

ideal-typical characteristics. According to Bossong (2008, p. 29), for example, all EU action plans ought to "include the specification of concrete measures and responsible actors, as well as deadlines for achieving the various steps needed to reach the desired objective." However, when it comes to specification of security contributions of private sector actors, both the EU level action plans and the implementation reports have thus far only stipulated lists of desired policy objectives (see Table 2.2), without almost any discussion regarding their (future) implementation (in case of the action plans), or the lack of it (in case of the implementation reports). Instead, similarly to the strategies that they accompany, these policy-oriented EU documents deflect the expectations for more specific information regarding the engagement of private sector actors in the provision of security by resorting to two relatively well established conceptualizations: public-private partnerships and resilience (also see Table 2.3).

While resilience is a relatively recent addition, thus far mostly limited to the specific subfield of cybersecurity (see below), the former PPPs conceptualization has been invoked in all EU level documents that contain at least some discussion of security contributions from private actors. The Hague Programme, for example, stated that PPPs are "an essential tool" in the fight against organized crime (European Commission 2005, p. 26). In its successor, the Stockholm Programme, the Council explicitly called on the Commission to "take measures for enhancing/ improving public-private partnerships" in the areas of fighting money laundering, internet child pornography and in promoting research and development in the field of security (Council of the European Union 2009, pp. 19, 22–23). According to the 2011 EU Action Plan on Combating terrorism, the Commission has actually already promoted PPPs for countering terrorist use of the internet and called on the Member States to develop PPPs in combating the acquisition, production and use of explosives and explosive devices by terrorists and other criminals (European Council 2011, p. 6). Another area of security where EU documents have often invoked PPPs, is cyber. The 2013 Cybersecurity Strategy of the EU actually offers a rather elaborate discussion about the specifics of the desired cooperation of public authorities and private sector. Specifically, it suggests that the role of the former is to ensure "a free and safe cyberspace," which translates in the following tasks: "to safeguard access and openness, to respect and protect fundamental rights online and to maintain the reliability and interoperability of the Internet" (European Commission 2013a, p. 2). For private sector actors, the strategy claims that they "should continue to play a leading role in the construction and day-to-day management of the Internet," but it also stresses that "the need for requirements for transparency, accountability and security is becoming more and more prominent" (European Commission 2013a, p. 3). Thus, it calls on the private sector to identify causes of cyber incidents and conduct forensic investigations; develop, at technical level, its own cyber resilience capacities; and share best practices across sectors, including the public sector (European Commission 2013a, p. 6).

Cybersecurity is also the only area where PPPs have been actually experimented with at the EU level thus far (also see Chaps. 9 and 10). As a consequence, the few specific examples of public-private cooperation presented in the aforementioned

Table 2.3 Conceptualizations of resilience

Disciplinary roots	Focus	Levels of analysis	Definition
Psychology	Positive adaptation	Individual	The capacity of an individual to positively bounce back from adversity
Criminology	Positive adaptation, process	Individual	A dynamic process encompassing positive adaptation within the context of significant adversity
Engineering	Equilibrium, return to stability	System	About studying the conditions specifying how far a system can be displaced from a fixed point of equilibrium and still return to that equilibrium once the disturbance has passed
Ecology	Disturbance, persistence	System	The capacity of a system to experience disturbance and still maintain its ongoing functions and controls
Socio-ecological	Robustness, reorganisation, stability	System	The amount of disturbance a system can absorb and still remain within the same state, the degree to which the system is capable of self-organisation and the degree to which the system can build and increase the capacity for learning and adaptation
Disaster/ emergency management	Positive adaptation, process of empowering	System/ Community	The capacity of a system, community or society to adapt to disturbances resulting from hazards by persevering, recuperating or changing to reach and maintain an acceptable level of functioning. Resilient capacity is built through a process of empowering citizens, responders, organizations, communities, governments, systems and society to share the responsibility to keep hazards from becoming disasters.

Sources: Compiled by author, drawing on Bourbeau (2013) and Bara and Brönnimann (2011)

EU documents, and thus also in this chapter, primarily concern the cyberspace. Most prominently, with the argument that cybersecurity issues transcend not only the public-private divide but also the national borders, the European Network and Information Security Agency (ENISA) was established in 2004. While in general ENISA aims to become a "the European 'hub' for exchange of information, best practices and knowledge in the field of Information Security," (ENISA 2014a) it has specifically devoted a lot of attention to the concept of PPPs, which it considers to be "essential for the Security and Resilience of Critical Information Infrastructures" (ENISA 2014d). As a consequence, a substantial part of ENISA's efforts has been focused on the analysis and promotion of various PPPs at both the national and European levels. Specifically, ENISA has conducted a study in order to collect the experiences of existing PPPs and to identify best practices at the national level to support those Member States that are establishing a PPP for the first time, or are experiencing barriers and thus are looking for advice. This in turn allowed ENISA to publish a Good Practice Guide with 36 specific recommendations that should "help both public and private stakeholders in their endeavours in setting up and running PPPs in the area of cybersecurity" (ENISA 2014c). Since 2009, pending a request from the European Commission (European Commission 2009), ENISA has also supported the only currently existing security-related EU level PPP—the European Public-Private Partnership for Resilience (EP3R). EP3R is supposed "to build upon national PPPs and engage both the public and private sectors in addressing the pan-European dimension of the resilience of critical EU-wide infrastructure." More specifically, it should:

1. Encourage information sharing and stock-taking of good policy and industrial practices to foster common understanding;
2. Discuss public policy priorities, objectives and measures;
3. Baseline requirements for the security and resilience in Europe;
4. Identify and promote the adoption of good baseline practices for security and resilience. (ENISA 2014b)

Other than the production of three reports (on Terminology Definitions and Categorisation of Assets; Incident Management and Mutual Aid Strategies; and Trusted Information Sharing), it is however difficult to find any information about tangible outcomes of EP3R's hitherto activities.

2.4 Key Challenges of Security-Related Public-Private Partnerships

The concept of PPPs has already been discussed by social scientists from various disciplines. There is neither the space nor the need to offer here even a brief overview of the many different definitions and typologies of PPPs (see Boerzel and Risse 2006; Brinkerhoff and Brinkerhoff 2011; Cabral et al. 2010; Hart 2003; Hodge and Greve 2007; Osborne 2000). For the purposes of this chapter, the most relevant part of this vast and growing literature concerns only the accounts of security-related PPPs. Albeit originally conceived in the field of administrative reform and the concept of *New Public Management* in 1980s with the dual aim of debureaucratization of public services and privatization promotion (Minow 2003; Ortiz 2010), subsequently the concept of PPPs was also utilized within the then new concept of critical infrastructure protection in the 1990s as a way to reduce vulnerability of vital systems to low-probability, yet high-consequence new security threats, such as terrorism (Collier and Lakoff 2008). In the aftermath of 9/11, the topic of PPPs has also been frequently discussed in the US literature on homeland security (Bursh and Givens 2012). In some of the recent counterterrorism literature, the popularity of PPPs has further risen to the point that they have been described as the third leg in counterterrorism (the first two being intelligence and surveillance, see Petersen 2008, p. 408), where the private sector has much to gain from cooperating with the public security agencies:

> [B]ecause they can coordinate their plans in advance regarding evacuation, transportation, and other issues; gain intelligence from law enforcement regarding threats and crime trends, develop relationships so that they will know who to contact for help or to report information; build law enforcement's understanding of corporate needs, such as confidentiality; and boost law enforcement's respect for the security field. (Dempsey 2011, p. 357)

As such, similarly to the many recent EU security-related documents, PPPs have often been presented as win-win solutions to both the public and private sector actors when it comes to responding to the new security threats.

The actual track record of security-related PPPs is, however, subject to debate. The findings of a recent study of the role of private financial institutions in the fight against terrorist financing suggest that PPPs are not always producing the expected win-win solutions either for the public or the private sector due to: (1) disagreements about the definition, scope and methods of analysis of the threat of terrorism to individual private financial institutions; (2) information sharing complications arising from the legal impediments to sharing classified information between public agencies and private companies, as well as the persisting lack of trust among many of their representatives; (3) the dissonance between the "better safe than sorry" logic of public security agencies and the "profit first" logic of private companies. (Bures 2015) The existence of these challenges has also been acknowledged in some the aforementioned EU documents, most notably in the 2013 EU Cybersecurity Strategy. Its authors have acknowledged the first challenge by noting that:

> A high level of security can only be ensured if all in the value chain (e.g. equipment manufacturers, software developers, information society services providers) make security a priority. It seems however that many players still regard security as little more than an additional burden and there is limited demand for security solutions. (European Commission 2013a, p. 12)

Regarding the second and third challenges, they noted that "private actors still lack effective incentives to provide reliable data on the existence or impact of NIS [network and information security] incidents, to embrace a risk management culture or to invest in security solutions" (European Commission 2013a, p. 6).

As a possible remedy to all three challenges, the EU Cybersecurity Strategy suggested the need for adoption of new EU legislation aiming to ensure that private businesses in number of key areas (energy, transport, banking, stock exchanges, and enablers of key Internet services) "assess the cybersecurity risks they face, ensure networks and information systems are reliable and resilient via appropriate risk management, and share the identified information with the national NIS competent authorities" (European Commission 2013a, p. 6). All legislative solutions, however, fundamentally contradict the basic logic underlying the concept of PPPs because they essentially amount to an imposition of "partnership" by command. This is highly problematic because although there are many different conceptualizations of PPPs, arguably none can be stretched to include a top-down hierarchical relationship between public and private actors. In the public management perspective, for example, Linder and Rosenau have defined public-private partnerships as "the formation of cooperative relationships between government, profit-making firms, and non-profit private organizations to fulfill a policy function" (Linder and Rosenau 2000, p. 5). Alternatively, in the global governance perspective, Boerzel and Risse defined transnational PPPs as:

> [I]nstitutionalized cooperative relationships between public actors (both governments and international organizations) and private actors beyond the nation-state for governance purposes. By "governance purposes," we mean the making and implementation of norms and rules for the provision of goods and services that are considered as binding by members of the international community. These can be international regimes with explicit norms, rules and decision-making procedures, but also informal governance arrangements pertaining to specific issue-areas of international life. (Boerzel and Risse 2006, p. 159)

However, according to Boerzel and Risse, PPPs always represent only one particular form of governance where the relations between public and private actors conform to two specific modes of non-hierarchical steering: (1) Governing by incentives, which leave the preferences and identities of actors unaffected, but which are supposed to regulate actors' behavior by changing cost-benefit calculations of utility-maximizing actors; (2) Governing by non-coercive means of persuasion, which involves learning, arguing, and other forms of communicative action geared toward changing actors' interests and even identities (Boerzel and Risse 2006, pp. 157–158). Importantly, both of these non-hierarchical modes ought to be distinguished from hierarchical modes of steering that "are usually reserved to states and public actors who can allocate values authoritatively and enforce rules" and whose top-down nature is incompatible with the concept of PPPs (Boerzel and Risse 2006, pp. 157–158).

The importance of the voluntary principle of public-private cooperation was in the end not lost in the EU Cybersecurity Strategy, which stated that "[l]egal obligations should neither substitute, nor prevent, developing informal and voluntary cooperation, including between public and private sectors, to boost security levels and exchange information and best practices" (European Commission 2013a, p. 6). Nevertheless, the very existence of a discussion of both the legislative and PPPs options in the EU Cybersecurity Strategy reveals that the most daunting challenge of public-private cooperation in the provision of security stems from the difference of the very nature of public and private actors: "Businesses exist to provide a product or service in exchange for fees, thus producing profits. Governments also exist to provide services but also enforce rules, maintain order, and ensure well-being of the people" (Lee 2009, p. 22). Thus, it is important to stress that although private and public actors nowadays indeed often interact in the security field, important difference remains between their primary interests. Private entities are primarily profit, rather than security, maximizers. In the long run, this is arguably the single biggest challenge to involving private businesses in all areas of security provision. Unlike the other aforementioned challenges, it cannot be fixed by improving the data and methodology, or by enhancing the information flow, which may over time also generate a modicum of trust between the relevant public and private sector actors. As a consequence, when it comes to dealing with contemporary security threats, at least some private businesses are likely to pursue different options than the public agencies, which are expected and tasked with ensuring the maximum level of security possible based on the precautionary principle of "better safe than sorry" (Kristensen 2008, p. 77).

Specifically, according to Lee (2009, p. 87), all private companies have the following four options when it comes to addressing security threats:

1. Accept the risk of the threat's actual occurrence, as the costs of countering it may be greater than the potential benefits.
2. Transfer the costs related to threat's actual occurrence, which is usually done with purchasing an insurance policy.
3. Minimize the risk of the threat's actual occurrence by adopting a wide range of measures such as new security policies and procedures, staff training, disaster recovery procedures, physical and logistical controls etc.
4. Terminate activities that are most threatened to eliminate the risk of the threat's actual occurrence all together.

The problem is that concept of PPPs appears ill-suited to make the third of these options more attractive to private businesses due to the significant costs related to the adoption and implementation of security policies. As a consequence, unless imposed by command via legal and/or technical regulations at the national and/or EU level, at least some private companies are likely to pursue different options than option number three, which is normally the only one available to public agencies in matters of national security. All forms of top-down tasking of private businesses by public authorities, however, fundamentally contradict the non-hierarchical nature of PPPs.

2.5 Resilience: The New Conceptualization?

As noted above and illustrated in both Tables 2.1 and 2.2, at least some EU cybersecurity experts appear to be aware of the fact that PPPs have traditionally been conceptualized as efficiency, rather than security, enhancers (Bures 2013). As a consequence, they have begun to explore alternatives that may be more suitable for bridging the apparent gap between the security-maximizing logic of public security agencies and the profit-maximizing logic of private companies. In this context, *resilience* has appeared as the new buzzword in two recent EU security strategies (the 2010 EU Internal Security Strategy (European Council 2010) and the 2013 European Programme for Critical Infrastructure Protection (European Commission 2013b) and, as discussed above, it is also included the title of the only existing security-related EU-level PPP—the European Public-Private Partnership for Resilience (EP3R)—which ought to play a crucial role in EU-wide efforts to protect critical information infrastructures. As such, the nascent EU conceptualization of resilience focuses primarily on infrastructure resilience, which has its roots in the engineering science. This is not surprising—while there is still some debate about what makes a particular infrastructure critical to the extent that its incapacity or destruction would have a debilitating effect on national security (the most frequently listed examples include banking and finance, government services, telecommunications and information and communication technologies, emergency and rescue services, energy and electricity, health services, transportation, logistics and distribution, and water supply (Dunn-Cavelty and Kristensen 2008, pp. 1–2), there is consensus that much of it is owned and/or operated by the private sector. Due to the privatization and deregulation of the public sector since the 1980s, and the globalization processes since the end of the cold war, the private sector controls 85% of the critical infrastructure in most Western countries (The National Commission on Terrorist Attacks Upon the United States 2004, p. 39).

In the current EU conceptualization, resilience is therefore generally understood as the ability of a system to recover from adversity, either back to its original state or an adjusted state based on new requirements. It shifts the attention from security threats to a wide variety of security risks (from natural hazards and the failure of critical infrastructures to terrorist attacks) and from averting, deterring, and protecting from threats to mitigating the consequences once a disaster occurs. These shifts are due to the recognition that (1) it is impossible to guarantee 100% protection to all infrastructure due to both its sheer size and the enormous costs that it would involve, and (2) even the best security measures sometimes fail. Proponents of this understanding of resilience therefore argue that more emphasis should be put on the recovery from all kinds of disasters so that the damaged infrastructure can be readily and cost-effectively restored (Pursiainen 2009, p. 728). As such, this approach also has the benefit of being "substantially less expensive than investments in specific infrastructure upgrades to avoid certain risk scenarios which may or may not occur" (De Bruijne and Van Eeten 2007, p. 24). Herein rests the possibility that the infrastructure resilience approach could be more acceptable to private companies, whose profit motive should make them very interested in getting their businesses restored and running as soon as possible. At least in the area of critical infrastructure protection, the concept of infrastructure resilience may therefore represent a more promising way for involving private businesses in the provision of security.

In this light, the EU's recent emphasis on resilience in some of its strategic documents can be interpreted as a deliberate attempt at a bottom-up "correction" of the hitherto dysfunctional top-down "partnerships" imposed on the private sector via legal regulations by public authorities. Instead of erroneously expecting that private companies will take all necessary steps to ensure maximum security regardless of the related costs, the drafters of these EU documents have embraced the neoliberal form of governmentality that places emphasis on individual adaptability and mobilization of non-state social agents, "which are necessary for governance in a society which is changing fast and where neither the market nor the state seems capable of directing or addressing the changes required" (Joseph 2013, p. 38). On the one hand, this understanding of resilience as a specific type of governance may be more familiar to the business community, albeit under somewhat different terminology. As two senior business security managers argued a recent chapter in the Security Magazine:

> The latest buzzword these days is "Resiliency," which for all intents and purposes is really nothing more than a new term for business continuity planning (BCP) in the private sector and continuity of operations planning (COP) in the public sector. ... After all, the foundation of BCP and COP programs focuses upon the full range and scope of risks the enterprise faces, the potential impacts of those risks and the factors that can be deployed to mitigate those risks. (Brenna and Mattice 2014)

Moreover, the desired end-goal—resuming "business as usual"—is generally in line with the profit-maximizing nature of private companies.

On the other hand, both the engineering and neoliberal conceptualizations of resilience have been challenged on both policy-making and ideational grounds. Regarding the former, the profit-versus-security dilemma of private businesses is unlikely to disappear completely due to "the ever increasing complexity and size of interdependent infrastructure systems make them not only more difficult to protect but also harder [and thus costlier] to get back on line" (Pursiainen 2009, p. 728). In some critical infrastructures, such as the financial systems, an alternative complication arises due to the primary interest of originators of security threats (e.g. terrorists or criminals) in their (ab-)use rather than destruction, which in turn renders the infrastructure-based resilience approach redundant. Regarding the latter, the neo-liberal understanding of resilience as governance "fundamentally challenges the traditional liberal assumptions on which the division of the public and private spheres are based—the private sphere becomes problematised and 'life' becomes the subject of governance (Chandler 2013, pp. 279–280). Other critics have pointed out that in making sense of the rise of resilience as a neo-liberal form of governance, the issue is not so much its newness (i.e. a shift from government to governance), as "the fact that one of the key effects of the discourse of governance is to conceal the continuing reproduction of hierarchical power relations" (Joseph 2013, p. 41). This would in turn suggests that even the drafters of those EU strategic documents that include the term resilience may still operate in the traditional mindset of hierarchical governance and they merely instrumentally employ the term to create an impression of a genuine a bottom-up "correction" of the predominant PPPs approach.

It is nonetheless important to note at this point that there are several alternative conceptualizations of resilience, which stem from various disciplinary and/or ideational roots and thus also differ in the preferred topics, focus and levels of analysis (see Table 2.3). Albeit there is no space here to go into detail (see Bara and Brönnimann 2011; Bourbeau 2013; Walker and Cooper 2011 for literature reviews), it is worth noting at least the community resilience approach that is closely linked to emergency and disaster management, with a specific focus on stress risk awareness, information-sharing, and strengthening of pre-existing resilience patterns at all levels of the society:

> Effective implementation of the four emergency management components [prevention and mitigation, preparedness, response, recovery] should be informed by robustness, redundancy, self-organization, and efficiency, which are key attributes of community resilience. Neither the emergency management components nor the attributes of community resilience should be seen as static end-states. (Bara and Brönnimann 2011, p. 17)

Resilience is therefore understood as an all-encompassing strategy that must be developed on all levels and in all sections of the society, including the private sector. This understanding of resilience has frequently been echoed in the context of homeland security in the US since 9/11, where representatives of public security agencies have increasingly called upon private companies to manage various national security issues with an overall political aim of making the entire society more resistant to all kinds of threats, natural disasters and man-made catastrophes. According to the former US Secretary of Homeland Security Janet Napolitano (cited in Petersen 2013, p. 1), for example, "homeland security ... requires not just a 'whole of government', but a 'whole of nation' approach. In some respects, local law enforcement, community groups, citizens, and the private sector play as much of a role in homeland security as the federal government." While one may also ponder whether this discourse of governance is also not trying to conceal the continuing reproduction of hierarchical power relations, at least one study of the corporate security profession in the United States has provided empirical evidence of voluntary security activities by major companies such as Walmart (Petersen 2013). In either case, there is no doubt that the authors of EU security strategies would benefit from exploring alternative conceptualizations of resilience. Moreover, as discussed in the next section, resilience and PPPs are not the only available conceptualizations of the role of private companies in the provision of security.

2.6 Political Corporate Social Responsibility: The Overlooked Conceptualization?

Taking into account the existence of a vast and ever-growing body of literature on corporate social responsibility (CSR) that has for decades tried to answer the questions of why, when and how private companies engage in various social activities that go beyond profit-making, it is somewhat surprising that none of the drafters of EU security strategies have thus far entertained the idea of exploring CSR as a plausible option for bridging the apparent gap between the security-maximizing logic of public security agencies and the profit-maximizing logic of private companies. There is neither the space nor the need to offer here even a brief overview of the different definitions and understandings of CSR that reflect the numerous views regarding its meaning, practical manifestations, and normative underpinnings (see Ougaard 2010, pp. 24–25; Scherer and Palazzo 2011, pp. 903–906). For the purposes of this chapter, the most relevant part of the CSR literature concerns the recent governance turn, nowadays commonly referred to as "political" CSR. It comprises of a growing number of publications whose authors seek to "normatively prescribe, and positively describe and explain, the political duties and activities of corporations" (Whelan 2012, p. 711).

One influential group of PCSR experts has advanced the concept of *corporate citizenship*. Moon and Crane, for example, argued that due to the effects of globalization, "corporations have tended to partly take over (or are expected to take over) certain functions with regard to the protection, facilitation, and enabling of citizens' rights—formerly an expectation placed solely on governments" (Moon and Crane 2005, p. 171). Alternatively, Moon, Crane, and Matten argued that corporations could reasonably claim to act as if they were metaphorically citizens and contribute to the formulation, construction and administration of various political structures and goods. They also described two levels of political participation of private companies: (1) indirect pressure group activity; and (2) direct participation in governing. In developed political systems, which arguably includes the EU and its Member States, the latter takes the form in the complex relationships that arise in "new governance," where "governments seek to share responsibilities and to develop new modes of operation, whether as a result of overload or of a view that they do not have a monopoly of solutions for society" (Moon et al. 2005, p. 440). Furthermore, to support their claim that the social responsibility of corporations differs from country to country because it reflects the historical institutions of their national business systems, Matten and Moon (2008, p. 405) have also made an important distinction between explicit and implicit PCSR.

While most of the PCSR literature understands PCSR initiatives almost only in *explicit* terms, i.e. as a set of "of voluntary programs and strategies by corporations that combine social and business value and address issues perceived as being part of the social responsibility of the company," in some countries it is also possible to identify *implicit* PCSR that "consists of values, norms, and rules that result in (mandatory and customary) requirements for corporations to address stakeholder issues and that define proper obligations of corporate actors in collective rather than individual terms" (Matten and Moon 2008, p. 409). In other words, PCSR may not only be understood as companies' contributions beyond and above the requirements of the law, but also as "mere" compliance with the law and customary ethics even though the companies do not claim distinctive authorship of these practices (Matten and Moon 2008, p. 410). The concept of implicit PCSR may therefore for example allow for the incorporation of the ever-growing list of counterterrorism measures that various private companies have been both legally and customarily expected to deliver in EU Member States since the 9/11 terrorist attacks, including such far-reaching and citizens' rights and liberties impacting procedures as freezing of all financial assets of persons suspected of terrorism (Bures 2012; also see Chap. 5).

Another group of PCSR authors has advanced a different view of PCSR, according to which companies ought to be seen as political actors that increasingly take over the traditional governmental tasks of political and social regulation, and public goods provision (Scherer et al. 2009; Scherer and Palazzo 2011). This extended view of political CSR highlights the various challenges of globalization upon the political and socio-economic steering capacities of territorially-bound states, which in turn leads to the blurring of traditional boundaries between the political, economic, and civil spheres of society. In this setting, private companies need to go beyond instrumental profit-focused and legal compliance-based arguments for CSR and adopt a new "political" understanding of CSR, which would allow them (along with other civil society actors) to participate in the construction of governance structures that would promote the interest of a globalized society and fill the regulatory vacuum in global governance (Scherer and Palazzo 2011). As such, this strand of PCSR literature offers alternative avenues for analyzing the impact of the blurring of the traditional public-private divide that is not always and everywhere bound to be negative only as commonly implied in the conflict resolution literature (see above).

It is important to note, however, that the PCSR expert community as a whole has thus far not genuinely attempted to extend the scope of their research from low politics issues (e.g. social security, health, education, protection of human rights and/or environment) to the high politics of security provision. A group of German political scientists has nonetheless made the case for "Corporate Security Responsibility" (CSecR) in order to analyze proactive and positive contributions of private companies to conflict resolution efforts in contemporary armed conflicts (Wolf et al. 2007; Deitelhoff and Wolf 2010). Even though they maintained an ideal-type distinction between traditional CSR and their own concept of CSecR by arguing that the latter deals with corporations operating in a violent environment, while the former is concerned with corporations in a peaceful environment (Wolf et al. 2007, p. 301), many of their arguments sound conspicuously similar to those made in the general PCSR literature. Most pertinently here, they argued that the complex demands of contemporary social, market and political environments have altered firms' concerns beyond short-term profit maximization and suggested that only a comprehensive "stakeholder" approach can do justice to this new complex market rationality, which may also include incentives for private contributions to public security (Wolf et al. 2007, p. 299). Furthermore, they claimed that "the private sector could be instrumental in providing security, even as a public good, in a manner similar to the voluntary self-commitments of private corporations in fields such as the environment, health, education or human rights" (Wolf et al. 2007, p. 301). All of these insights highlight the potential for including security provision under the rubric of PCSR.

Going beyond the existing PCSR literature, Wolf et al. (2007) also offered a working definition[1] and typology of corporate contributions to security governance in zones of conflict (see Table 2.4). They also posited several plausible explanations for different types of corporate security activities in contemporary conflict zones (see Table 2.4) and tested them empirically in five case studies of different

[1]They considered only contributions by companies that are (1) political (in the sense that they involve activities that "work towards the creation and implementation of collectively binding rules and norms related to the provision of collective goods"); (2) intentional (e.g. not mere by-products of other business activities); (3) voluntary; and that (4) "directly and/or indirectly address the level of violence in an environment characterized by imminent, on-going or only very recently terminated interactions of physical violence" (Deitelhoff and Wolf 2010, pp. 11–13).

Table 2.4 Types of corporate security activities, key factors influencing their provision, and their impact

	Forms of engagement		Patterns of engagement	Scope of engagement
Types of corporate security activities	• Proactive security engagement • Withdrawal/business termination • Business as usual/taking the security risks • Transferring the costs related to threat's actual occurrence (purchasing insurance)		• Unilateral • Multilateral • PPPs	• Micro-level • Macro-level
Factors influencing corporate engagement in security provision	Company's characteristics	Product(ion) characteristics	Businesses environment	Characteristics of security threat/s
	• Size • Form • Structure	• Product type/ • Production type	• Political • Social • Market	• Causes/issues • Current phase • Intensity
Impact of corporate security activities	Perception of security		Provision of security	Values and principles
	• Public good • Club good • Private good		• Responsibilization • Depoliticization • Commodification	• Liberty • Privacy • Justice

Sources: Compiled by author, drawing on Krahmann (2008), Lee (2009), Deitelhoff and Wolf (2010), and Wolf et al. (2007)

conflict-ridden countries (Rwanda, Congo, Nigeria, Northern Ireland, Israel/Palestine). These case studies in particular highlighted the importance of various indirect costs as a decisive motivation to private companies to engage in security, including reputational costs, consumer boycotts, loss of market share, falling stock prices, and alienation from stakeholders. On the one hand, this contradicts the aforementioned negative view of private companies in the conflict resolution literature by proposing that "most companies prefer stable and secure markets, and only a few profit from conflict or are interested in prolonging it" (Wolf et al. 2007, p. 301). On the other hand, the case studies by Wolf et al. (2007) provide empirical evidence that supports two key arguments made in the PCSR literature. The first concerns the necessity of taking into account the costs of making unhappy various other "stakeholders" than just the company's shareholders and customers. The second concerns the insight from the more recent PCSR scholarship (Matten and Moon 2008) regarding the influence of national political culture and market environment in a company's region of origin on the (lack of) impact of reputational costs of private companies, including the decision to (not) engage in the provision of security.

Notwithstanding its unique contributions towards a more nuanced understanding of the security roles performed by private companies in zones of conflict, the German CSecR concept suffers from two important shortcomings. On the one hand, as acknowledged by Deitelhoff and Wolf (2010, pp. 13–14), their relatively wide understanding of corporate contributions "holds the risk of creating an all-inclusive concept, considering every governance contribution as conflict-relevant which would generally also fit under the CSR umbrella." On the other hand, however, both the definition and the typology of CSecR are too narrow due to their exclusive focus on violent conflicts. As such, CSecR does not, for example, explain the numerous roles that private companies play in countering the new security threats in relatively stable European democracies. Nevertheless, pending their confrontation with several arguments already made in the recent PCSR and security studies literature, it is possible to utilize the other key components of the German CSecR concept even beyond the zones of conflict (see Bures 2015 and Table 2.4).

2.7 Concluding Remarks

The findings presented in the previous sections of this chapter suggest that although the recent EU security-related strategies, as well as their accompanying action plans and implementation reports, duly acknowledge the pluralization of security in general and the growing role of private businesses in particular, the hitherto default EU conceptualization of private-public partnerships may not always represent the best way for understanding the contributions of private businesses in the provision of security. This is primarily due to the profit, rather than security, maximizing nature of private businesses and the traditional conceptualization of PPPs as efficiency, rather than security, enhancers. As a consequence, when it comes to dealing with contemporary security threats, most private businesses are likely to pursue different options than the public agencies, which are generally tasked with ensuring the maximum level of security possible. The authors of future EU security strategies therefore ought to explore alternative conceptual frameworks that offer more nuanced ways for analyzing the role of private companies in the provision of security.

Two such frameworks have been discussed in this chapter in some detail—resilience and political corporate social responsibility. The former has already been incorporated in some of the more recent EU strategic documents concerning security of critical infrastructures, but with a relatively narrow focus on cyberspace and with an apparent neoliberal instrumentality, thus raising questions regarding its suitability as a genuine bottom-up alternative to the prevailing top-down understanding of PPPs. Alternative conceptualizations of resilience are therefore worthy of exploration—although neither of them was originally developed with the aim of theorizing the area of security, they could shed a number of new insights not only in the currently under-researched area of private security provision beyond the much-debated role of private military and/or security companies, but they could also offer a markedly different account than the more traditional public-actors oriented concepts usually utilized in the studies of various aspects of both the EU's internal and external security policies.

Regarding political corporate social responsibility, the key normative challenges of the growing role of private businesses in the provision of security (responsibilization, depoliticization, and commodification) arguably account for both its hitherto absence in the EU strategic documents and the prevailing preference of PCSR scholars for keeping the scope of their research limited to low politics issues only. These challenges are also important reminders that neither resilience nor political corporate social responsibility should be viewed as silver bullets. No matter what conceptual framework one utilizes, the engagement of private businesses in the provision of security is always bound to raise a number of profound dilemmas due to the repercussions on the provision of security traditionally conceived as a public good provided by states to all citizens and concerns about the lack of public accountability, oversight, and legitimacy of private sector actors. In short, the numerous normative challenges highlight the fact that the widening of private companies' roles in the provision of security is not apolitical.

On the one hand, one can therefore agree with those PCSR scholars who argue that in order to address the numerous legitimacy and accountability dilemmas arising from the growing political engagement of private companies, we need to also bring political theory in the debate (Moon et al. 2005; Scherer and Palazzo 2011). Although such a debate would clearly be beyond the remit of EUs security-related documents, its very realization necessitates a multiplicity of conceptual frameworks capable of addressing both the practical and normative aspects of the growing role of private businesses in the provision of security. There may not be too many such frameworks around, but there is certainly more than just PPPs and (neoliberal) resilience.

On the other hand, the very existence of such profound normative dilemmas arising from the provision of security by private actors also implies the need for (re-)consideration of the more traditional top-down regulatory frameworks in order to safeguard important public goods and/or values. The search for alternative conceptual frameworks suitable for bridging the apparent gap between the security-maximizing logic of public security agencies and the profit-maximizing logic of private companies should therefore not degenerate in the search for rhetorical devices suitable for anchoring core public values in privately operated and/or owned critical infrastructures. Instead, the analysis presented in this chapter suggests the need for a careful case-by-case assessment of the comparative advantages and disadvantages of both the traditional top-down hierarchical governance instruments and the more flexible non-hierarchical alternatives in different areas of security provision in the EU (and beyond).

References

Abrahamsen, R., & Williams, M. C. (2011). *Security beyond the state: Private security in international politics*. Cambridge: Cambridge University Press.

Avant, D. (2004). *The market for force: The consequences of privatizing security*. Cambridge: Cambridge University Press.

Ballentine, K., & Sherman, J. (2003). *The political economy of armed conflict: Beyond greed and grievance*. Boulder, CO: Lynne Rienner Publishers.

Bara, C., & Brönnimann, G. (2011). *Resilience: Trends in policy and research*. Focal Report 6, Crisis and Risk Network, (CRN). Accessed July 23, 2013, from http://mercury.ethz.ch/serviceengine/Files/ISN/134314/ipublicationdocument_singledocument/39e12b8c-34e1-4fd0-a9a4-45a260c21b22/en/CRN-Focal-Report-6-Resilience.pdf

Beck, U. (1992). *Risk society: Towards a new modernity*. London: Sage.

Berdal, M., & Malone, D. M. (2000). *Greed and grievance: Economic agendas in civil wars*. Boulder CO: Lynne Rienner.

Bigo, D., Bonelli, L., Guittet, E., Olsson, C., & Tsoukala, A. (2006). *Illiberal practices of liberal regimes: The (in)security games*. Paris: L'Harmattan.

Boerzel, T. A., & Risse, T. (2006). Public-private partnerships: Effective and legitimate tools of transnational governance. In E. Grande & L. W. Pauly (Eds.), *Complex sovereignty* (pp. 195–216). Toronto: Toronto University Press.

Bossong, R. (2008). The action plan on combating terrorism: A flawed instrument of EU security governance. *Journal of Common Market Studies, 46*(1), 27–48.

Bourbeau, P. (2013). Resiliencism: Premises and promises in securitisation research. *Resilience: International Policies, Practices and Discourses, 1*(1), 3–17.

Brenna, J., & Mattice, L. (2014, May 1). How to add resiliency to your risk management strategy. *Security Magazine*. Accessed June 26, 2014, from http://www.securitymagazine.com/articles/85461-how-to-add-resiliency-to-your-risk-management-strategy

Brinkerhoff, D. W., & Brinkerhoff, J. M. (2011). Public-private partnerships: Perspectives on purposes, publicness, and good governance. *Public Administration and Development, 31*(1), 2–14.

Bures, O. (2012). Private actors in the fight against terrorist financing: Efficiency versus effectiveness. *Studies in Conflict and Terrorism, 35*(10), 712–732.

Bures, O. (2013). Public-private partnerships in the fight against terrorism? *Crime Law and Social Change, 60*(4), 429–455.

Bures, O. (2015). Political corporate social responsibility: Including high politics? *Journal of Business Ethics, 129*(3), 689–703.

Bursh, N. E., & Givens, A. D. (2012). Public-private partnerships in Homeland Security: Opportunities and challenges. *Homeland Security Affairs, 8*(18), 1–23.

Cabral, S., Lazzarini, S. G., & Furquim de Azevedo, P. (2010). Private operation with public supervision: Evidence of hybrid modes of governance in prisons. *Public Choice, 145*(1-2), 281–293.

Chandler, D. (2013). International statebuilding and the ideology of resilience. *Politics, 33*(4), 276–286.

Chesterman, S., & Lehnardt, C. (2007). *From mercenaries to market: The rise and regulation of private military companies*. Oxford: Oxford University Press.

Collier, S. J., & Lakoff, A. (2008). The vulnerability of vital systems: How critical infrastructure became a security problem. In M. D. Cavelty & K. S. Kristensen (Eds.), *Securing 'the Homeland': Critical infrastructure, risk and (in)security* (pp. 17–39). London: Routledge.

Council of the European Union. (2005). *European counter-terrorism strategy*. Accessed January 27, 2007, from http://register.consilium.europa.eu/pdf/en/05/st14/st14469-re04.en05.pdf (European Union).

Council of the European Union. (2009). *The Stockholm programme - An open and secure Europe serving and protecting the citizens*. Accessed February 1, 2010, from http://www.se2009.eu/polopoly_fs/1.26419!menu/standard/file/Klar_Stockholmsprogram.pdf

De Bruijne, M., & Van Eeten, M. (2007). Systems that should have failed: Critical infrastructure protection in an institutionally fragmented environment. *Journal of Contingencies and Crisis Management, 15*(1), 18–29.

Deitelhoff, N., & Wolf, K. D. (2010). *Corporate security responsibility: Corporate governance contributions to peace and security in zones of conflict*. Basingstoke: Palgrave Macmillan.

Dempsey, J. S. (2011). *Introduction to private security*. Belmont, CA: Wadsworth.

Den Boer, M., Hillerbrand, C., & Nölke, A. (2008). Legitimacy under pressure: The European web of counter-terrorism networks. *Journal of Common Market Studies, 46*(1), 101–124.

Dunn-Cavelty, M., & Kristensen, K. S. (2008). *Securing 'the Homeland': Ciritical infrastructure, risk and (in)security*. London: Routledge.

ENISA. (2014a). *About ENISA*. Accessed June 24, 2014, from http://www.enisa.europa.eu/about-enisa

ENISA. (2014b). *European public private partnership for resilience (EP3R)*. Accessed June 24, 2014, from http://www.enisa.europa.eu/activities/Resilience-and-CIIP/public-private-partnership/european-public-private-partnership-for-resilience-ep3r

ENISA. (2014c). *Good practice guide on cooperative models for effective PPPs*. Accessed June 24, 2014, from http://www.enisa.europa.eu/activities/Resilience-and-CIIP/public-private-partnership/national-public-private-partnerships-ppps/good-practice-guide-on-cooperatve-models-for-effective-ppps

ENISA. (2014d). *Public private partnerships (PPPs)*. Accessed June 24, 2014, from http://www.enisa.europa.eu/activities/Resilience-and-CIIP/public-private-partnership/public-private-partnerships-ppps

Eriksen, E.O. (2011). Governance between expertise and democracy: The case of European Security. *Journal of European Public Policy, 18*(8), 1169–1189.

European Commission. (2005). *The Hague Programme: Ten priorities for the next five years*. Accessed June 24, 2014, from http://europa.eu/rapid/pressReleasesAction.do?reference=MEMO/05/153&format=HTML&aged=0&language=EN&guiLanguage=en (European Union).

European Commission. (2008). *Report on the implementation of the European security strategy*. Accessed April 14, 2014, from http://www.consilium.europa.eu/ueDocs/cms_Data/docs/pressdata/EN/reports/104630.pdf. S407/08.

European Commission. (2009). *Protecting Europe from large scale cyber-attacks and disruptions: Enhancing preparedness, security and resilience*. Accessed April 14, 2014, from http://eur-lex.europa.eu/LexUriServ/LexUriServ.do?uri=COM:2009:0149:FIN:EN:PDF. COM(2009) 149 final.

European Commission. (2012). *Security industrial policy*. Accessed April 14, 2014, from http://eur-lex.europa.eu/LexUriServ/LexUriServ.do?uri=COM:2012:0417:FIN:EN:PDF. COM(2012) 417 final.

European Commission. (2013a). *Cybersecurity strategy of the European Union*. Accessed April 14, 2014, from http://ec.europa.eu/dgs/home-affairs/e-library/documents/policies/organized-crime-and-human-trafficking/cybercrime/docs/join_2013_1_en.pdf. JOIN(2013) 1 final.

European Commission. (2013b). *New approach to the European programme for critical infrastructure protection*. Accessed May 30, 2014, from http://ec.europa.eu/energy/infrastructure/doc/critical/20130828_epcip_commission_staff_working_document.pdf

European Commission. (2014). *For an open and secure global maritime domain: Elements for a European Union maritime security strategy*. Accessed April 14, 2014, from http://eur-lex.europa.eu/legal-content/EN/TXT/PDF/?uri=CELEX:52014JC0009&from=EN. JOIN(2014) 9 final.

European Council. (2003a). *European security strategy*. Accessed April 14, 2014, from http://www.consilium.europa.eu/uedocs/cmsUpload/78367.pdf

European Council. (2003b). *Strategy against the proliferation of weapons of mass destruction*. Accessed April 14, 2014, from http://register.consilium.europa.eu/pdf/en/03/st15/st15708.en03.pdf. 15708/03.

European Council. (2004). *EU drugs strategy (2005–2012)*. Accessed April 14, 2014, from http://europa.eu/legislation_summaries/justice_freedom_security/combating_drugs/c22569_en.htm
European Council. (2005). *Strategy for the external dimension of JHA: Global freedom, security and justice*. Accessed April 14, 2014, from http://eur-lex.europa.eu/legal-content/EN/TXT/PDF/?uri=CELEX:52005DC0491&from=EN. COM/2005/0491 final.
European Council. (2007). *Specific programme: Preventing and combating crime (2007–2013)*. Accessed April 14, 2014, from http://eurlex.europa.eu/LexUriServ/LexUriServ.do?uri=CELEX:32007D0125:EN:NOT
European Council. (2008). *Revised strategy on terrorist financing*. Accessed April 14, 2014, from http://register.consilium.europa.eu/doc/srv?l=EN&f=ST%2011778%202008%20REV%201. 11778/1/08.
European Council. (2010). *Internal security strategy for the European Union*. Accessed April 14, 2014, from http://www.consilium.europa.eu/uedocs/cms_data/librairie/PDF/QC3010313ENC.pdf
European Council. (2011). *EU action plan on combating terrorism*. Accessed April 14, 2014, from http://register.consilium.europa.eu/doc/srv?l=EN&f=ST%2015893%202010%20REV%201. 15893/1/10.
Garland, D. (2001). *The culture of control*. Oxford: Oxford University Press.
Gill, P. (2006). Not just joining the dots but crossing the borders and bridging the voids: Constructing security networks after 11 September 2001. *Policing & Society, 16*(1), 27–49.
Hart, O. (2003). Incomplete contracts and public ownership: Remarks, and an application to public-private partnerships. *Economic Journal, 113*(486), 69–76.
Hodge, G., & Greve, C. (2007). Public-private partnerships: An international performance review. *Public Administration Review, 67*, 545–558.
Jäger, T., & Kümmel, G. (2007). *Private military and security companies: Chances, problems, pitfalls and prospects*. Wiesbaden: VS Verlag für Sozialwissenschaften.
Joseph, J. (2013). Resilience as embedded neoliberalism: A governmentality approach. *Resilience: International Policies, Practices and Discourses, 1*(1), 38–52.
Klare, M. T. (2001). *Resource wars: The new landscape of global conflict*. New York: Owl Books.
Krahmann, E. (2005). Security governance and networks: New theoretical perspectives in transatlantic security. *Cambridge Review of International Affairs, 18*(1), 15–29.
Krahmann, E. (2008). Security: Collective good or commodity? *European Journal of International Relations, 14*(3), 379–404.
Kristensen, K. S. (2008). 'The absolute protection of our citizens': Critical infrastructure protection and the practice of security. In M. D. Cavelty & K. S. Kristensen (Eds.), *Securing 'the Homeland': Critical infrastructure, risk and (in)security* (pp. 63–83). London: Routledge.
Lee, E. (2009). *Homeland security and private sector business: Corporation's role in critical infrastructure protection*. New York: CRC Press.
Linder, S. H., & Rosenau, P. V. (2000). Mapping the terrain of the public-private policy partnership. In P. V. Rosenau (Ed.), *Public-private policy partnerships*. Cambridge: MIT Press.
Loader, I., & Walker, N. (2007). *Civilizing security: Policing and political community in a global era*. Cambridge: Cambridge University Press.
Matten, D., & Moon, J. (2008). "Implicit" and "explicit" CSR: A conceptual framework for a comparative understanding of corporate social responsibility. *Academy of Management Review, 33*(2), 404–424.
Minow, M. (2003). Public and private partnerships. Accounting for the new religion. *Harvard Law Review, 116*(1), 1229–1270.
Moon, J., & Crane, A. (2005). Corporate citizenship: Toward an extended theoretical conceptualization. *Academy of Management Review, 30*(1), 166–179.
Moon, J., Crane, A., & Matten, D. (2005). Can corporations be citizens? Corporate citizenship as a metaphor for business participation in society. *Business Ethics Quarterly, 15*(3), 429–453.
Musah, A.-F. (2002). Privatization of security, arms proliferation and the process of state collapse in Africa. *Development and Change, 33*(5), 911–933.

Ortiz, C. (2010). *Private armed forces and global security: A guide to the issues*. Santa Barbara, Denver, Oxford: Praeger.
Osborne, S. P. (2000). *Public-private partnerships: Theory and practice in international perspective*. London: Routledge.
Ougaard, M. (2010). Introducing business and global governance. In M. Ougaard & A. Leander (Eds.), *Business and global governance* (pp. 1–36). Abingdon: Routledge.
Parsons, W. (1995). *Public policy: An introduction to the theory and practice of policy analysis*. Northampton, MA: Edward Elgar.
Percy, S. (2007). Morality and regulation. In S. Chesterman & C. Lehnard (Eds.), *From mercenaries to market: The rise and regulation of private military companies* (pp. 11–28). Oxford: Oxford University Press.
Petersen, K. L. (2008, September). Risk, responsibility and roles redefined: Is counterterrorism a corporate responsibility? *Cambridge Review of International Affairs, 21*(3), 403–420.
Petersen, K. L. (2013). *The corporate security professional: A hybrid agent between corporate and national security*. Paper presented at the annual meeting of the ISA's 54th Annual Convention, San Francisco, CA, USA, April 6, 2013. Retrieved May 5, 2013, from http://files.isanet.org/ConferenceArchive/41b0823857654c71ae63da45c4d6c257.pdf
Pursiainen, C. (2009, November). The challenge for European critical infrastructure protection. *European Integration, 31*(6), 721–739.
Scherer, A. G., & Palazzo, G. (2011). The new political role of business in a globalized world: A review of a new perspective on CSR and its implications for the firm, governance and democracy. *Journal of Management Studies, 48*(4), 899–931.
Scherer, A. G., Palazzo, G., & Matten, D. (2009). Introduction to the special issue: Globalization as a challenge for business responsibilities. *Business Ethics Quarterly, 19*(3), 327–347.
Shearing, C., & Wood, J. (2003). Nodal governance, democracy, and the new "Denizens". *Journal of Law and Society, 30*(3), 400–419.
Singer, P. W. (2003). *Corporate warriors: The rise of the privatized military industry*. Ithaca and London: Cornell University Press.
The National Commission on Terrorist Attacks upon the United States. (2004). *The 9/11 Commission report*. Accessed November 21, 2008, from http://govinfo.library.unt.edu/911/report/index.htm
Verhage, A. (2008). Between the hammer and the anvil? The anti-money laundering-complex and its interactions with the compliance industry. *Crime Law Social Change, 52*, 9–32.
Verkuil, P. R. (2007). *Outsourcing sovereignty*. Cambridge: Cambridge University Press.
Walker, J., & Cooper, M. (2011). Genealogies of Resilience: From systems ecology to the political economy of crisis adaptation. *Security Dialogue, 42*(2), 143–160.
Webber, M., Croft, S., Howorth, J., Terriff, T., & Krahmann, E. (2004). The governance of European security. *Review of International Studies, 30*(1), 3–26.
Whelan, G. (2012). The political perspective of corporate social responsibility: A critical research agenda. *Business Ethics Quarterly, 22*(4), 709–737.
Wolf, K. D., Deitelhoff, N., & Engert, S. (2007). Corporate security responsibility: Towards a conceptual framework for a comparative research agenda. *Cooperation and Conflict, 42*(3), 294–320.
Wood, J., & Dupont, B. (2006). *Democracy, society and the governance of security*. Cambridge: Cambridge University Press.

Chapter 3
Who Am I? The Blurring of the Private Military and Security Company (PMSC) Category

Berenike Prem

3.1 Introduction

While scholarly attention has long focused on Private Military and Security Companies (PMSCs), there is now an emerging body of literature on private security provisions beyond PMSCs. Implicit in this mushrooming debate is the assumption that PMSCs and 'non-security related businesses' are different species possessing different capabilities and performing different activities. PMSCs, in particular, are treated as stand-alone entities whose defining feature is that they sell various military and security services as their *primary line of business*. This chapter sets out to investigate the validity of this assumption. It argues that what we commonly refer to as 'the PMSC industry' escapes the designation and treatment as private military and/or security companies. First, various firms labeled PMSCs have their roots in other, non-security related sectors from where they have expanded into the proper military business. Second, even those PMSCs that have gained prominence through their involvement in 'traditional' security assignments in Iraq/Afghanistan and the global war on terror disguise almost any involvement in security work in favor of more innocuous activities. Third, many of today's industry players have diversified into new lines of business so that their actual involvement in military and security work has become almost imperceptible.

The conceptual confusion surrounding the industry is well established. It is reflected in the old scholarly debate about how to categorize PMSCs and the critique of existing definitions that tend to divide the PMSC market into ideal-typical companies based on their relationship to the battlefield and the level of force used in performing their services (Kinsey 2006, pp. 11–33; McFate 2014, pp. 15–18; Singer 2008, pp. 91–100). Implicit in such categorizations is the idea

B. Prem (✉)
Witten/Herdecke University, Alfred-Herrhausen-Straße 50, 58455 Witten, Germany
e-mail: Berenike.Prem@uni-wh.de

O. Bures, H. Carrapico (eds.), *Security Privatization*,
DOI 10.1007/978-3-319-63010-6_3

that, similar to the military, a PMSC's position is fairly fixed within a continuum of force in that it either provides lethal force at the front/trains other to do so ("tooth"), or undertakes logistical and administrative work at the rear ("tail") (McFate 2014, p. 18; Singer 2008, p. 91). This assumption, however, is somewhat misleading since most companies move across the lethal/non-lethal, combat/non-combat, offensive/defensive divide implicit in these taxonomies (Avant 2005, p. 17; Dunigan 2011, p. 13; Joachim and Schneiker 2014, pp. 1–2). They can span everything from combat and combat support, training advice and consulting, logistics and technical support, armed security services, intelligence/reconnaissance/surveillance, demining and humanitarian services, to security sector reform (SSR). It is along this service spectrum that the great variety of the PMSC industry unfolds. While the literature agrees on the dynamic nature of the PMSC industry, it pays less attention to the conditions and factors that may account for the direction of its past, current and future evolution. *How can we explain the multi-faceted nature of the industry?*

To be sure, scholars have examined several *structural conditions* that can account for the recent boom of the PMSC industry such as the end of the Cold War and ensuing changes in the supply and demand of security, transformations in the nature of warfare (Avant 2005; Singer 2008), and the diffusion of neoliberal norms into the realm of security (Cutler 2010; Leander and van Munster 2007), but none of these explanations specifically relates to why PMSCs take the shape they do. Percy (2012, 2007) and Petersohn's (2014) historical account of the post-cold war evolution of the industry is a notable exception in that regard. They trace the transition from combat-oriented Private *Military* Companies (PMCs), such as Executive Outcomes and Sandline International, to Private *Security* Companies (PSCs) of a more defensive posture, to (changes in) the anti-mercenary norm which prohibits violent market actors from participating in combat. In contrast, a second strand of literature has come to focus more on the role of PMSC-*agency* by investigating how these companies actively construct their public image through self-promotion and self-legitimation. PMSCs, it is argued, have not only shown that they are increasingly flexible in terms of what they offer, but they have also invested in continuously reshaping their identity in public discourse (Østensen 2011b, p. 8; Pingeot 2014). Repeated attempts to vindicate the industry's reputation against charges of mercenarism by purveying a feel-good image as "new humanitarians" (Joachim and Schneiker 2012) are the most visible sign that PMSCs are actively seeking to influence public perceptions about what or who they 'really' are—and what not (see also Joachim and Schneiker 2014; Leander 2005).

While these studies point out a number of important reasons for the industry's diversity (normative pressures, market-driven factors, active PMSC-entrepreneurship and the industry's structural power), these 'stories' remain largely disconnected from one another and therefore fail to account for the bigger picture of change in the industry. First, they tend to narrowly focus on structural constraints (e.g. norms, changes in demand and supply) *or* firm-level strategies. Implicit in such reasoning is a deterministic, one-directional causality that either treats PMSCs as passive 'dopes' that simply conform to outside pressures or, conversely, puts disproportionate emphasis on the ability of PMSCs to dominate and shape our understandings and perceptions of the industry. Second, they miss out on the fact that PMSCs operate in heterogeneous environments where they face incongruent, conflicting expectations from clients, regulators, and society at large. This, as I will argue, is an important factor that accounts for the multi-faceted and chameleon-like nature of today's PMSCs.

Thus, the aim of this chapter is to systematize our understanding of the industry's fragmentation. Drawing on evolutionary economics and sociological institutionalism, this chapter advances a theoretical framework for explaining how and why firms in the PMSC industry evolve and develop over time. While putting emphasis on different logics for change, material and ideational, both approaches recognize that organizations are embedded within and co-evolve with their external environment in order to survive. They rest on the premise that those organizations that do adapt, anticipate or even push for changes in their environment will have a much better chance at achieving their mission and performing well. Thus, in order to understand why the PMSC industry is in a perpetual process of adaptation, never really rigid or fixed, we need to follow both changes in its environment *and* firm-level strategies. This contribution discusses these dynamics largely with respect to PMSCs in the United States (U.S.). Although the U.S. is just one among a variety of global, national, and local markets (Abrahamsen and Williams 2011; Dunigan and Petersohn 2015), this chapter spells out a theoretical framework that makes explanations and findings drawn from the U.S.-case study amenable to comparative, cross-national analysis.

The chapter is structured as follows. The first section spells out a co-evolutionary framework to explain how and why change unfolds in organizations like PMSCs. Against this backdrop, the second section will trace the co-evolution of the PMSC industry from the 1990s until today. The analysis will focus on the selection pressures that PMSCs face from their economic and normative environments (outside-in perspective) as well as on firm-level strategies to respond to these changes (inside-out perspective). I will argue that the protean nature of the industry is the result of shifting and sometimes incongruous demands and expectations emanating from its broader social and normative environment on the one hand and from the U.S. government as major public consumer of private military and security services on the other. The last section condenses the main findings of my analysis and discusses its validity beyond the U.S. market for force.

3.2 PMSCs and Their Environment: A Co-Evolutionary Framework

Explaining how and why organizations change is a recurrent theme for management and organizational scholars. In pursuing this line of inquiry, they have borrowed many concepts and theories from other disciplines, including evolutionary biology. In fact there is a large body of literature in the social sciences that has harnessed evolutionary theory to study human behavior, media, and markets (see, for instance, Baum and Singh 1994; Blyth et al. 2011; Schmid and Wuketits 1987; van de Ven and Poole 1995). When applied to the world of organizations, evolutionary theory represents "a manner of reasoning" (Hodgson 2013, p. 979) about organizations as living organisms. Like any living system, organizations are presumed to exist in and be "open" to a wider environment on which they depend for the satisfaction of various needs (Morgan 2006, p. 38; Pfeffer and Salancik 2003) zonetary or physical resources as well as information and social legitimacy. This embeddedness view of organizations has important consequences for their operation and well-being. Since they are not 'closed' or self-contained but, to a certain degree, dependent on their environment for various resources, organizations must achieve an appropriate relationship with that environment if they are to survive. As Pfeffer and Salancik's (2003, p. 43) note, "[o]rganizations could not survive if there were not responsive to the demands from their environments". Hence, one of the major concerns of every organization is to achieve a 'good fit' with the world around, i.e. to adjust to pressures from an independent selection environment.

In using the analogy of an organism in constant exchange with its environment, we are encouraged to take an open and flexible view of PMSCs. From that perspective, PMSCs are adaptive entities that evolve as a function of forces external to themselves. Evolutionary theories, as (Dosi and Marengo 2007, p. 492) rightly point out, "share the methodological imperative 'dynamics first!'". That is, the explanation for why certain organizational characteristics take the value they do rests on "a process account of how [they] became what [they are]" (Dosi and Marengo 2007, p. 492). This 'open systems approach' to PMSCs means that in order to understand the multi-faceted nature of the industry, we need to direct our attention to the interactions between the industry and its environment. In theorizing how organizations and environments co-evolve, scholars have put emphasis on different kinds of mechanisms (Lewin and Volberda 1999; Volberda and Lewin 2003)—a tension that mirrors the long-standing agency-structure debate in international relations theory. The so called population-ecology (*outside-in*) view focuses on the *selection pressures* that organizations face from their environment. The main criticism of this perspective is directed to what is perceived as its external determinism—the idea that organizations are mainly passive in the sense that they do not actively seek to adjust to their environment (Volberda and Lewin 2003, p. 2116). Instead, variations are viewed to emerge by blind or random change initiatives (Volberda and Lewin 2003, p. 2116). In the end, it is the environment 'choosing' which firms will persist and which will die. Adaptation theories, by contrast, take a more optimistic (*inside-out*) view on the role of agency and firm-level strategies. Indeed, this is where social sciences have left their deepest imprint on evolutionary theory. Once one adds intelligence into the equation, variations become more deliberate and intelligent-based (Blyth et al. 2011, p. 304). From that perspective, organizational change is "a highly rational, proactive process involving specific elements such as setting goals, monitoring units, assessing unit capabilities, searching for and evaluating alternative actions and developing plans to achieve organizational goals" (Volberda and Lewin 2003, p. 2120f.).

This chapter benefits from a combination of both perspectives, something which is mostly missing from the existing PMSC literature. While the outside-in view directs our attention to the major external constraints and opportunities that confront PMSCs in their *selection environments*, the inside-out view sheds light onto *how* PMSCs navigate through this universe, i.e. by transforming from one kind of company into another, by shifting from a declining niche into a more profitable one, or by actively shaping that environment rather than conforming to it. In other words, change in the PMSC industry is the *joint* outcome of environmental selection *and* managerial action. With this in mind, the remainder of the section will identify two major approaches to conceptualizing 'the world around organizations', with evolutionary economics highlighting the material aspects of companies' environment (markets, resources, and competition) and sociological institutionalism focusing on its ideational aspects (meanings, beliefs, and norms) (for a comprehensive overview of theories of adaptation and selection see Volberda and Lewin 2003). It will then discuss firm-level adaptation strategies that oscillate between mere compliance to external demands and the active manipulation of PMSCs' environment.

3.2.1 Evolutionary Economics: Economic Fitness and Competitiveness

Evolutionary economists conceive of markets as primary selection environments in which companies compete for scarce material resources (Dosi and Nelson 1994, p. 162). In this immediate "task" or "business environment", competitiveness and efficiency are the main selection criteria that create pressures towards adaptation. Firms possessing superior technologies, routines and strategies, and offering products or services that fit the demands of their customers better than the goods, services, and commodities of their competitors will stand a good chance of receiving more resources (e.g. money, equipment, personnel) (Dosi and Marengo 2007, p. 492; Geels 2014, p. 263). Firms with a lower degree of fitness, in turn, receive fewer resources and may ultimately face 'extinction'. In both cases, the market provides performance feedback, positive and negative, which encourages successful firms to retain or reproduce their strategies and routines while also weeding out those companies with less successful policies and structures.

It is important to note that PMSCs' task environment can be either enabling or constraining: opening up new business opportunities or foreclosing certain options. While market pressures and opportunities can take various forms, this chapter will focus on those emanating from the demand and supply side in the U.S. private military and security market. Changes in supply and demand in the "market for force" have been already identified as necessary factors to the *emergence* of the PMSC industry (Avant 2005, pp. 30–38; Singer 2008, pp. 49–60). They have been less systematically explored, though, for their effect on the specific *contours* that the sector has taken on since its emergence in the 1990s, which is the object of this chapter. What makes the U.S. 'market for force' a particularly interesting case to study is not only the fact that the U.S. is headquarters to some of the largest PMSCs worldwide (DeWinter-Schmitt 2013, p. 17). Its private military and security market is also of longer standing than in the rest of the OECD world which allows for a long-term analysis of the most significant developments in the organizational ecology of U.S.-based PMSCs. While the client base of American PMSCs includes international organizations, humanitarian organizations and companies in the extractive and shipping sectors (DeWinter-Schmitt 2013, p. 18), the U.S. PMSC market remains largely government-driven (DeWinter-Schmitt 2013, p. 20; Krahmann 2016). Therefore, the ways PMSCs have developed in the U.S. are likely to reflect the needs of their primary client, the U.S. government.

3.2.2 Sociological Institutionalism: Social Fitness and Legitimacy

Evolutionary economics' dynamic notion of organizational trajectories offers a useful way to conceptualize change in the PMSC industry. It has been criticized, though, for its emphasis on efficiency as the main selection criterion and its neglect of environments other than markets (Geels 2014, p. 264). This is where sociological institutionalism comes in. The new institutionalists in sociology argue that in order to survive and thrive in their *social* environment, organizations "also need social acceptability and credibility" (Scott 2008, p. 59; see also Hall and Taylor 1996). Central to this approach is thus the question of what confers 'legitimacy' or 'social appropriateness'. Legitimacy denotes "a generalized perception or assumption that the actions of an entity are desirable, proper, or appropriate within some socially constructed systems of norms, values, beliefs and definitions" (Suchman 1995, p. 574). In other words, a company deserves the predicate 'legitimate' to the degree that it operates within the bounds and norms of society. This 'social fitness' is as essential to a company's ability to function as is the acquisition of finance, goods or commodities. "Organizations", as DiMaggio and Powell (1983, p. 150) explain, "compete not just for resources and customers, but for political power and institutional legitimacy, for social as well as economic fitness". From a resource-dependency or social-exchange point of view, failure to live up to broader societal norms may have severe consequences for organizational survival. Key audiences such as clients, shareholders, decision-makers, regulators, special interests groups and citizens may withdraw their support and impose 'sanctions' through termination of contracts, burdensome regulation, boycotts or other disruptive actions (Ginzel et al. 2004, p. 230; Herbst 2013). This creates an isomorphic pressure in the direction of a better fit with the company's normative environment because "nonoptimal forms are selected out of a population of organizations or because organizational decision makers learn appropriate responses and adjust their behavior accordingly" (DiMaggio and Powell 1983, p. 149). This means that many of the institutional forms that modern organizations, or PMSCs, take do not (only) stem from an imperative to advance their efficiency, but from a desire to enhance their social legitimacy (Hall and Taylor 1996, p. 949; Suchman 1995, p. 571).

As Scott (2008, p. 61) points out, there are different bases for legitimacy. He distinguishes regulative, normative, and cultural-cognitive sources (Scott 2008, pp. 50–59). A *regulative* conception emphasizes conformity to rules, laws and regulations.[1] The *normative* view, which will inform the theoretical reasoning of this chapter, conceives of values, norms and role expectations as the major base for acquiring legitimacy. From that point of view, organizations embrace specific institutional forms or practices because the latter are widely valued within a broader normative environment. Finally, organizations can derive legitimacy by conforming to preconscious *cultural-cognitive* models of reality, mental maps, and frames of reference that are widely shared within an organization or organizational field.

From a normative standpoint, gaining legitimacy is an uphill struggle for PMSCs since there is a strong normative presumption against the use of private commercial force. This aversion finds expression in what is commonly known as the anti-mercenary norm and the norm of the state monopoly on the legitimate use of violence (Krahmann 2013; Percy 2007; Petersohn 2014). Krahmann (2013, p. 58) defines the norm of the state monopoly on violence as "the generalized expectation that sovereign governments or rulers should be the only actors who may legitimately use collective armed force" and that their citizens hold the sole right to wield it as members of national armies (Krahmann 2013). She argues that the latter is a "foundational norm" which has not only informed national and international law, but also the more specific norm against mercenary use (Krahmann 2013, p. 58). The latter prohibits self-interested and wholly independent market actors from using force (Percy 2007; Petersohn 2014). Both norms share the ideal of centralized state

[1]Of course, this presupposes the availability of tools to oversee, regulate and, if necessary, sanction the activities of PMSCs should they be found to be in contravention of existing laws (Herbst 2013, p. 283). The problem with these companies, however, is that it is often unclear which laws, if any, apply to them and who is legally responsible for their conduct (Pattison 2014, p. 144; Schreier and Caparini 2005, p. 56). In that regard, it is important to note the push for more (self-)regulation of the industry which has been a constant endeavor since the 1990s when the UK government first published a Green Paper setting out different options for regulating the activities of PMSCs. With the Green Paper process under way, PMSCs had to fear no less than the end of their enterprise should a ban on their activities materialize. Since 2009, however, the UK government has veered towards a lighter regulatory framework, encompassing a government-backed system of self-regulation to control the activities of UK-based PMSCs (FCO 2009; Hague 2010; Simmonds 2012). There is a consensus in both the U.S. and U.K. in favor of some kind of *permissive control* of the industry which is currently embodied in initiatives such as the Montreux Document, a restatement of the existing international legal obligations and good practices of states pertaining to the use of PMSCs in conflict zones, and the International Code of Conduct for Security Service Providers (ICoC) in which PMSCs, by singing, voluntarily agree to abide by the principles of international human rights law and codes of good practice for the responsible provision of security services.

control over the *means* of violence and the *political decision* to raise, maintain, and use armed force, which has rendered illegitimate any violent actor not incorporated into the state structure (Petersohn and Dunigan 2015). It is therefore hardly surprising that the PMSC industry's standing in security governance rests on a somewhat precarious position: They are private actors paid to do what is traditionally seen as the exclusive hallmark of the modern nation-state. That being said, scholars have observed a change in the norm against mercenarism in that its prohibitive content has been progressively narrowed down to include actors serving in a *combat* role while leaving open the private use of force for *defensive* purposes (Krahmann 2013; Petersohn 2014). This normative shift, as sociological institutionalism would lead us to expect, is likely to be followed by major transformations in the industry's make-up. In fact, Percy (2007, p. 225) sees the millenarian shift of combat-oriented PMCs to PSCs that eschew combat as a sign that the anti-mercenary norm, even if altered, is alive and well. Yet this account can neither explain the persistence of armed security contractors even in the face of overriding evidence that they have de facto become engaged in direct hostilities nor the resurgence of PMSCs in quasi-combat roles.

Now that we have a better idea of the nature of PMSCs' selection environments, we can turn to firm-level adaptation strategies.

3.2.3 Company Responses

As outlined above, organizations are not quite so passive and powerless as the outside-in perspective might suggest (Ashforth and Gibbs 1990; Oliver 1991; Pfeffer and Salancik 2003; Suchman 1995). Oliver (1991), for instance, takes a more optimistic (inside-out) view on the role of agency and firm-level strategies. She rejects that firms are invariably conforming to their institutional environment at any time. Instead, co-evolution is conceived of as a highly strategic and proactive process in which organizations enjoy considerable room for maneuverability in responding to institutional pressures and expectations, including the "latitude to alter or control the environment in accordance with organizational objectives" (Oliver 1991, p. 150). This echoes the burgeoning PMSC-literature which has begun to scrutinize the power and agency of these companies (Joachim and Schneiker 2012; Leander 2005; Østensen 2011a).

The inside-out view redirects our attention to the issue of firm-level adaptation. Adaptation is defined to have occurred if an organization changes its "strategies, structures, procedures or other core attributes, in anticipation or response to a change in its environment" (Hodgson 2013, p. 980), including attempts to change that environment. I assume that adaptation strategies can take three major forms: conformance, decoupling, and manipulation. Figure 3.1 locates these strategies along a continuum, ranging from *conformance/compliance* to PMSCs' economic (task) and social environment at the far end of the continuum, to *decoupling* located midfield, to *manipulation* of their environment at the other end. This gradation

Fig. 3.1 Firm level-adaptation strategies

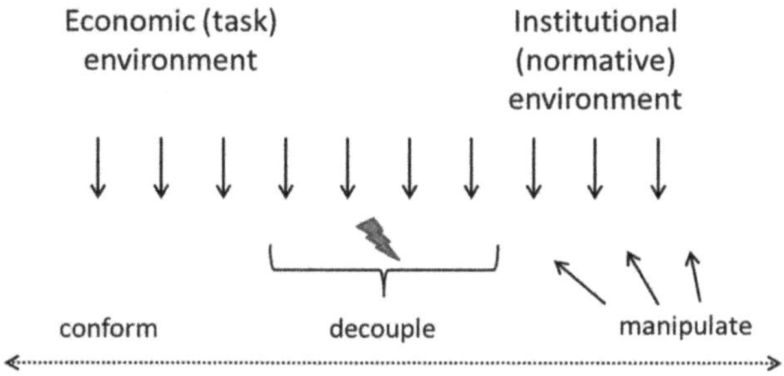

reflects different assumptions about the relative force of structure versus agency in determining the evolution and make-up of the industry. The force of structure is most intensely felt at the compliance-end where PMSCs' economic and normative environment exerts one-directional pressure to which companies conform on order to enhance their legitimacy and/or economic position. Yet compliance is not only enacted in response to external *pressure*, but it can be also based on the conscious exploitation of new market *opportunities*.

However, "organizations cannot survive by responding completely to every environmental demand", as Pfeffer and Salancik (2003, p. 43) note. Particularly in fragmented and heterogeneous environments, where corporations are confronted with a multitude of expectations from consumers, shareholders, employees, NGOs or activists, compliance may not be feasible (Scherer et al. 2013). For example, accommodation to normative pressures for shutting down a controversial service line such as armed security may contradict economic reason. Neo-institutional research into organizations holds that, under such conditions, organizations frequently de-couple talk and action to resolve conflicts between incongruent demands and expectations (Brunsson 2002 [1989]; Krasner 1999; Suchman 1995). Rather than changing their structures and actions, organizations can cynically devise symbols to give off a false appearance of conformity to societal norms. Thus, decoupling is a strategic and somewhat manipulative response that enables organizations to gain legitimacy while simultaneously maintaining enough flexibility to address economic exigencies.

Manipulation strategies, by contrast, presuppose that PMSCs will shape their environment in their own image. Typically, manipulation of a company's *economic* environment can be achieved by means of influencing consumer tastes and demands, e.g. through product advertisement. This strategy relies on the socially constructed nature of particular offerings. According to Einstein and Rollins (2010, p. 14), "products [here: services] aren't necessities and they aren't about physical attributes; they are about the stories, the fables, the brand mythologies created around them. It is these stories we purchase." By playing on those stories, fables and brand mythologies, PMSCs are able to mold external assessments of the desirability and suitability of particular offerings (Suchman 1995, p. 591). Just as PMSCs' economic environment is, at least to some extent, malleable and "negotiated" (Morgan 2006), the industry's *institutional/normative* surrounding can turn into a battleground for certain norms and ideas (Geels 2014, p. 269; Petersohn 2014), a 'struggle' in which PMSCs take an active part as they try to advance new understandings or interpretations of the surrounding normative order. Here, companies take on the role of norm entrepreneurs not only in initiating new norms but also in changing them (Petersohn 2014).

3.3 Private Military and Security Companies Now and Then

3.3.1 Formation and Consolidation of the Industry (1998–2008)

To make sense of the startling diversity of 'the' PMSC industry, Percy (2012) suggests to follow the historical evolution of these firms and examine the various manifestations the industry has taken over time. Along these lines, this section gives a brief account of core business change in the PMSC industry from the 1990s until 2008.

Historically speaking, American PMSCs are originated in the logistic and engineering sector, where the majority of companies is still located today (Huskey and Sullivan 2012, p. 337; Kinsey 2006, p. 98; McFate 2014, p. 22f.). Thus, many of the companies that we commonly refer to as PMSCs aren't strictly speaking *military* and *security* companies, but longer established corporations that have pushed into the PMSC market by carrying diverse non-military support services into the public sector. DynCorp International, for example, began as California Eastern Airways in 1946, set up by two former Second World War II pilots, transporting spare parts for the armed forces. During the first Gulf War, DynCorp technicians provided maintenance for the helicopter forces deployed in forward areas. In a similar vein, the Pentagon contracted out the provision of diverse non-military support services to the U.S. forces stationed in the Balkans to the oil-pipe engineering company Brown and Root Services (BRS which became later part of Kellogg, Brown and Root, a Halliburton subsidiary) under the first Logistics Civil Augmentation Program (LOGCAP)[2] contract in 1992. This type of PMSC can be referred to as the KP-model, which is shorthand for kitchen porter, the 'foot soldier' in the restaurant kitchen brigade that you never see. Akin to the kitchen porter, KP-type of PMSCs are auxiliary forces that offer less visible but nevertheless important rear echelon support tasks (transport, catering, laundry, sanitation, setting up of bases and camps) that have rendered them essential players in the deployment and maintenance of U.S. forces in conflict regions like the Balkans or Iraq, more recently.

[2]The Logistics Civil Augmentation Program (LOGCAP) is the prime tool for managing the DoD's use of contractors in full-spectrum logistical support of contingency operations.

The origins of this new company type can be traced to two momentous dynamics—one market-driven, the other normative—which have exerted uniform pressure upon would-be PMSCs. First, downsizing of the military at the end of the Cold War, growing defense budget-saving pressures and the changing nature of increasingly asymmetric warfare have created new demands for skills, qualifications and expertise that many Western militaries had difficulty supplying or fostering on their own (Avant 2005; Kinsey 2006; Kruck 2013; Singer 2008). Specifically, the U.S. as one of the countries more regularly involved in protracted and equipment-intensive military operations (Taylor 2004, p. 196) had become more reliant on transport, catering, laundry and sanitation services, as well as on specialists to operate weapons and information systems on the battlefield (Kruck 2013; Singer 2008, p. 62).

The diffusion of neoliberal norms into the realm of security (Cutler 2010, pp. 163–164; Kruck 2013, pp. 7–9; Singer 2008, pp. 66–70) underpinned and reinforced this dynamic. According to Kruck, "decisions by states in favour of PMSC use [...] are not taken in an ideational vacuum", but they are shaped by "prior ideational contexts". Against this backdrop, the advancing belief in the superiority of the private sector as the more effective and less costly alternative to the state-based provision of public services can explain why alternative supply side options have been sidelined. It provided the normative rationale for privatizing a number of previously 'untouchable areas' of government, from prisons to postal systems to security. The armed forces, too, were now expected to focus exclusively on their inherent or core competencies, as a series of congressional and governmental initiatives in the 1990s evidenced. The Commission on Roles and Missions of the Armed Forces, set up in 1995 by the Clinton administration to examine the potential for reducing the scope of the government in the realm of security, recommended the military to focus on its "core competencies" and rid itself of "commercial type" functions, including warehousing, the maintenance of weapon systems and property management (Roles and Missions Commission of the Armed Forces 1995). In a similar vein, the Quadrennial Defense Review (QDR) of 2001 asserted that "[o]nly those functions that must be performed by DoD should be kept by DoD" (DoD 2001, p. 53). It declared that the 'DoD will assess all its functions to separate core and non-core functions. The test will be whether a function is directly necessary for war fighting." (DoD 2001, p. 53). In areas not linked to warfighting, the DoD would seek to privatize or outsource entire functions (DoD 2001, p. 54). As a result, the template for the armed forces began shifting from the 'self-sufficient' to the 'core competency' model (Petersohn 2010; Taylor 2004).

Early entrants into the PMSC market seized the opportunity offered by this altered business environment by carrying services that were already part of their corporate portfolio to the public sector (such as DynCorp International) or by establishing new firms specifically designed to meet the demand of the U.S. government. The company Military Professional Resources Incorporated (MPRI) is a case in point. The retired American military officers who founded MPRI in 1987 as a provider of training reported thinking of this emerging gap as "a chance to capitalize on their skills and connections to profit by supplying non-core services to the US military" (cited in Avant 2005, p. 35). According to company officials, "[i]n the new, downsized Army, soldiers [...] don't do KP anymore. We don't need to spend all that money and effort training a fine combat soldier and have him peeling potatoes." Thus, the elaboration of the KP-model, the supply of a wide range of defense-related rear echelon tasks, can be viewed as the result of *strategic reorientation/conformance* as (would-be) PMSCs took advantage of both the U.S. government's retreat from functions now deemed 'non-core' and a permissive normative environment which valued a reduced role for the state in the provision of services.

The relative success of the KP-model can be contrasted with the short-lived business experience of another PMSC-kind in the late 1990s: companies like Executive Outcomes (EO) and Sandline International which reaped their first major contracts in Angola, Sierra Leone and Papua New Guinea. What was new and controversial about EO and Sandline was both companies' readiness to deploy in a combat role. The ability and willingness to literally 'pull the trigger', if required, had become Sandline and EO's generic 'trade mark'. Unlike the KP-type of PMSCs, the "beans and broccoli providers", as a Sandline representative put it, "real PMCs" did not hesitate to "dirty their hands" and were "ready to fire" (Grunberg 2004).[3] However, Sandline's insistence of being one of the few active PMCs that were ready to deploy in a combat role and pull the trigger ultimately proved counterproductive. It failed to align with the strong normative presumption against using private contractors in combat roles. In particular, major states like the U.S. and U.K. were adamant about defending their monopoly over the use of violence, i.e. the provision of offensive military force.[4] This 'red line' or privatization barrier had been repeatedly upheld in U.S. policy prohibiting outsourcing of inherently governmental functions.[5] The Office of Management and Budget (OMB) Circular A-76, for example, advised governmental agencies to avoid privatization in areas where the "provider is more likely to use force, especially deadly force" (OBM 2003).[6] In its 1996 report "Improving the Combat Edge through Outsourcing", the DoD followed this line. It categorically opposed

[3]"Sandline ist das einzige eingetragene Unternehmen, das sich öffentlich zu echten Kampfeinsätzen bekennt. Unser Interesse war stets der operative Einsatz. All die anderen Aufgaben, die das Militär jetzt an Private abtritt Lagerverwaltung, Küchendienste, Nachschub, Reparaturen, haben mit dem Militärischen kaum etwas zu tun. Militärische Dienstleistungen im engeren Sinne, echte PMF so wie wir, erleben zwar durch den Irak-Krieg einen ungeheuren Schub. Aber es ist Unsinn, uns, die wir die Drecksarbeit wirklich mit der Waffe in der Hand erledigen, mit all den Bohnen-und Brokkoli-Lieferanten gleichzusetzen." (Grunberg 2004).

[4]The fact that the U.S. also acted as potential consumer of PMSC services added to this normative pressure.

[5]The Federal Activities Inventory Reform Act (FAIR) of 1998 defines inherently governmental functions as "so intimately related to the public interest as to require performance by Federal Government employees", specifically if it can "significantly affect the life, liberty, or property of private persons" (1998).

[6]However, the circular does explicitly not prohibit contracting for guard services, convoy security services, or the operation of prison or detention facilities.

outsourcing of those functions that affected the military's core capabilities, i.e. the offensive use of force (DoD 1996, p. 4). The state's monopoly on violence worked as a selection mechanism, sanctioning those firms that overstepped the line. Thus, in 1998, EO was forced to shut down its business, followed by Sandline in 2004. Sandline's homepage declared that the main reason behind the decision to close was a "general lack of governmental support for Private Military Companies" (Sandline International 2004). Sandline's failure to adapt had proven a 'death knell' for the active PMSC experiment. By contrast, KP-PMSCs seemed to act within the market's normative boundaries. They 'merely' took over a 'supporting role' in 'ancillary' areas such as training, cleaning, construction and base support while leaving the military's core, understood as the application of offensive force, untouched.

But while the PMC project had failed, PMSCs have sought opportunities of a similar kind. Following the attacks on 11 September 2001, the economic outlook for the industry has, in fact, never looked better. The attacks placed security on top agenda of the U.S. and its allies which have become embroiled in a time- and energy-consuming global war on terror. With open-ended military commitments unfolding in Iraq and Afghanistan, the U.S. soon came to realize that it possessed insufficient capacities to sustain and 'win' either mission. This made contracting an attractive answer—it has become "a stopgap, in lieu of sending more US troops to fill the lack of significant allied support" (Singer 2008, p. 247), raising a larger army or calling up more reservists.

Again, the industry had proven nimble reaction by accommodating to this changing business (task) environment (*conformance*). New upstarts were pushing into the PMSC market to fill the gap. Many of these firms were small "Mom and Pop concerns created [...] overnight, often by retired military personnel operating out of their homes and equipped with a Rolodex of contacts and not much else" (Isenberg 2009, p. 67). They offered services lying noticeably far away from the industry's traditional role of logistical support. Christopher Beese (2004, p. 1), then director of the U.S. PMSC ArmorGroup, put forward a template for this new PMSC specie: "Private Security Companies (PSCs) offer protective services in a defined area (e.g. an installation, an embassy or a refinery) or for defined persons (e.g. reconstruction engineers). Although they may be armed [which puts them apart from the KP-model] they have nothing in common with Private Military Companies [...] who engage in, or support, offensive combat operations that may seize ground and try to change the prevailing balance of power in a foreign country." These companies were not given combat responsibilities, but their mission was defined in defensive terms: protect government facilities and personnel. They soon gained a foothold in the U.S. foreign and security policy. As reconstruction in Iraq began, armed security became the fastest-growing item among the types of contingency services drawn from the PMSC sector since the security situation in Iraq had begun to deteriorate, forcing armies to divert substantial resources to protect the reconstruction efforts (Huskey and Sullivan 2012, p. 338; McFate 2014, p. 18f.). "Men with guns", as a commentator observed, "are the new dotcoms" (Lynn 2006).

Yet PMSCs did not simply conform to functional needs on the market for force, but they took an active part in shaping and *manipulating* that demand. They framed societal issues in a particular way—a securitizing way[7]—that enabled them to link their know-how and their services with previously identified sources of insecurity. According to them, we live in dangerous world, "a nasty place, full of insecurity" (Messner 2007) and "crises" (Control Risks 2014a) where states and people are faced with "an ever-increasing set of risks", such as "[g]lobal terrorism" (CusterBattles 2005), and "instability and breakdown in government authority" (Blackwater 2007). The modality of permanent threat justified the use of extraordinary means to handle them: the implementation of privatized security measures. On the supply side, PMSCs stressed the lack of reasonable alternatives by casting their role as one of making up for an ineffective and expensive state sector that was incapable of meeting its security responsibilities. According to Brooks, founder of the industry organization ISAO, the private sector is "faster, better and cheaper compared to past state efforts" (Brooks 2004). Blackwater even contended that "[t] here is no alternative except through contracts" (Prince 2007).

PSCs like Aegis, Blackwater, Custer Battles, Erinys International, Olive Security, or Triple Canopy gave the industry a whole new imprint. They frequently possessed lethal capabilities, bringing them closer to the warfighting capabilities than the activities of their unarmed KP-brethren in logistics and base support. While these companies insisted that their work was merely "defensive in nature" (Brooks 2006, pp. 2–3; Howell 2007; Prince 2007), a string of high profile scandals, involving armed guards shooting indiscriminately at civilians seemed to prove the exact opposite. Among the most notorious incidents were the 'Nisoor Square massacre' in 2007 when Blackwater employees opened fire in a Baghdad traffic circle, killing seventeen civilians, and Aegis contractors shooting randomly at civilian cars in Baghdad to the music of Elvis Presley's 'Runaway Train' (Human Rights First 2008). Such 'incidents' represented a major challenge to the twentieth century norm of the state monopoly over violence which has become synonymous with a prohibition of the private use of armed force for purposes other than self-defense (Krahmann 2013). This concern was echoed by NGOs. They warned that the U.S. government, by tasking PMSCs to protect a military object against an enemy, "virtually ensures that they will engage in combat" (Human Rights First 2008, p. 21). The use of force, even if deployed in a defensive capacity, could amount to a "direct participation in hostilities" (Beerli 2012) in asymmetric conflict environments like those in Iraq and Afghanistan: These conflicts were fought without a clear front and moved closer to highly populated areas which would make a distinction between offensive/defensive, combat/non-combat hard to sustain.

Since then, PMSCs were confronted with contradictory demands from their economic and institutional environments. While consumer preferences called for

[7]According to the Copenhagen school, policy issues are securitized if they are turned into existential threats that require extraordinary responses (Buzan et al. 1998).

PSC-kind of firms with a strong armed presence in the field, there were also considerable normative reservations against the use of such companies, whether their mission was defined as defensive or not. PMSCs responded with a *decoupling* strategy, hiding in plain sight. Even if they continued competing for lucrative security contracts and maintained their armed security portfolio, they played down their actual stakes in this business niche. Being among the three private security firms employed by the State Department to protect its personnel in Iraq beside Blackwater and Triple Canopy, DynCorp has been careful about not being lumped together with 'other' private security contractors: "While this service represents a small piece of what we do—in fact, it is less than two percent of our business—the high profile and intense scrutiny this business generates has a disproportionate impact on how we are perceived." (Ryder 2010, p. 3) Company representatives were eager to point out that DynCorp was "not a security company" at all, but provided "sophisticated aviation, knowledge-transfer, logistics, humanitarian and operational solutions" (DynCorp International 2012). As we will see later, today's PMSCs disguise almost any involvement in security work in favor of more legitimate vocations: from "cleaning toilets" to "serving food in the mess hall" (Brooks 2010, p. 4; Messner 2007, p. 24). Even Blackwater, now renamed Academi, lists security under "life support" along with other, more innocuous items such as laundry, waste management and food (Academi 2017). Today, neither combat nor armed security are seen as legitimate vocations which explains why these services are notably absent from the PR material of the industry. Decoupling enables PSCs to engage in 'business as usual' even in the light of continued criticism, which, at least in the short-term, enhances the survival prospect of the PSC-model. In that regard, it is particularly insightful to reflect on Sandline's failed business attempt. In the end, the *open* provision of combat was simply too controversial and international distaste for private offensive force helped push EO and Sandline out of business. By contrast, *rhetorical divestment* of an otherwise illegitimate service line enables PMSCs to conduct business as usual.

3.3.2 The Post-Iraq and Afghanistan Phase (2008 Onwards)

As the conflicts that had helped consolidate the PSC-model winded down, firms were forced yet again to adapt. They have diversified into new lines of business so that their actual involvement in military and protective security work has become almost imperceptible. The acquisition of ArmorGroup by G4S in 2008 was a foretaste of what was to come. While the initial 'gold rush' in Iraq and Afghanistan had offered ample business opportunities for PMSCs, competition got fierce once demand for lucrative Iraqi and Afghan security contracts dampened. With nearly half of its turnover being derived from private security services in Iraq, ArmorGroup was particularly vulnerable to such market pressure, making the takeover by the industry giant G4S an attractive option (Power 2008). Size matters for two main reasons. First, consolidation and concentration gives these companies a strong position vis-à-vis smaller competitors due to the U.S. government's preference for open-ended and long-term contracts which requires PMSCs to supply services in unspecified quantities and large numbers of service personnel (Krahmann 2016, p. 37). Second, it enables PMSCs to offer a wider range of military and security services than single-service firms (Pingeot 2012, p. 12). As I am going to discuss below, this lineup is a convenient way for governments to purchase the full plate of services when operating in complex environments where war-making, humanitarian aid and development often overlap. In sum, the post-Iraq and Afghanistan period has favored *large and diversified PMSCs*, either as stand-alone companies or as attractive candidates for buyout and consolidation, at the expense of smaller 'niche firms' that have thrown their eggs exclusively into one basket (Spearin 2008, p. 369). Thus, many of today's PMSCs have become veritable 'one stop shop' organizations that offer "integrated" and "comprehensive solutions" (Ballhaus 2009a, p. 1; b, p. 1; DynCorp International 2013c; Constellis 2017). According to industry figure Doug Brooks (2011, p. 34), "the scale and diversity of the industry has vastly expanded [...]" with PMSCs doing everything from the delivery of humanitarian assistance, development work, maritime security, and the operation and maintenance of unmanned aerial vehicles (UAVs or drones). G4S is an emblematic case in that respect. Years of extension and takeovers have tuned the company into an outright 'all-rounder', as an NGO representative points out:

> "[...] a huge problem we are facing is that their expertise outside are [sic!] being marketed internally to privatize other state sectors. G4S, for example, now has private banks, private prisons. It is privatizing the police service, privatizing welfare programs. So this industry has gone from being used externally in wars to being used very much internally in privatizing all state functions. [...] they are megaprojects that are privatizing every aspect of the state." (Interview#6 2014)

In a similar vein, Blackwater (now named Academi) joined forces with rival private security companies Triple Canopy, Edinburgh International, and Olive Group to form Constellis Holdings in 2014. With this merger, Constellis has not only become one of the largest PMSCs in the U.S. market, but the fusion moves the operations of the company far beyond protective security. Constellis operates across commercial sectors, spanning everything from insurance, manufacturing, maintenance of critical national infrastructures, to diplomacy and international development. This is also reflected in the new company name. Derived from the word 'Constellation', a grouping of stars on the celestial sphere perceived as one coherent figure or design, Constellis is represented as a 'family of businesses' that "take[s] multiple elements and connect[s] them to create something greater than the sum of [its] parts" (Constellis 2017).

Diversification can be seen a strategic response to the new demand requirements the industry faces: the wish of states for integrated security solutions (Spearin 2008). This desire has been well articulated by the Obama administration. During her Senate confirmation hearing on January 13, 2009 former Secretary of State Hillary Clinton explicitly called for "the need to elevate *diplomacy* and *development* alongside *defense*—the 'smart power' approach to solving global problems"

(Clinton 2010, p. 13; emphasis mine); a doctrine which has been subsequently embraced by President Obama. In his famous 2011 speech on the Middle East and North Africa, he called for a 'smart power' strategy which would incorporate development and diplomacy, in addition to defense, to meet twenty-first century security challenges (Obama 2011).

In this sense, co-evolution implies *conforming* to the needs of the industry's single biggest client: the U.S. government. The profitability of international development contracting coupled with the growing competition in the market for protective services has attracted PMSCs. They have taken advantage of this emerging market opportunity by amending and expanding their capabilities and task specialization, often through outright acquisition of international development firms, to bid on new contracts that may not be directly related to their traditional area of expertise (Nagaraj 2015). L-3 Communications, for example, a leading defense contractor of the U.S. government, acquired International Resources Group (IRG) in 2008 (L-3 Communications 2008). IRG is a Washington-based international development contractor and was among the first companies being awarded a contract under the U.S. agency for international development (USAID) for reconstruction and humanitarian aid in Iraq (International Resources Group 2003). Commenting on this deal, L-3's President Carl E. Vuono explained that "[t]ogether we will now be able to offer government agencies, international organizations and foreign nations *comprehensive solutions* to the most complex requirements of development, institutional capacity building and stability operations" (L-3 Communications 2008; emphasis mine). Likewise, DynCorp International has sealed its expansion into the international development sector by acquiring Casals & Associates, a well-known international development contractor that had supported U.S. development programs and IOs for decades (DynCorp International 2010). Diversification into the development sector has left these companies ideally placed to satisfy the U.S. government's demand "for defense, diplomacy and international development" (DynCorp International 2013d). By virtue of their broad service portfolio, they are able to deliver "total mission", "holistic", "end-to-end", "seamless", "integrated", "full-spectrum" and "self-sustaining" solutions (Academi 2013a; Blackwater 2009; Constellis 2017; Control Risks 2014b; DynCorp International 2013a, b, c, e): surge capacity prior to and during the conflict (platform, aviation, logistics, and equipment) as well as development and post-conflict stability in its aftermath. They profit equally from "making war, talking peace, engaging in post-war reconstruction and development" (Nagaraj 2015, p. 611).

Thus, corporate portfolio expansion and diversification follow a strategy of total *alignment* with client interests and are explicitly framed in such a way. As DynCorp's CEO Ballhaus stresses, its "international program footprint and focus closely align with the emphasis placed by the Administration of President Obama on the use of 'smart power' as a vital means of advancing U.S. national security and foreign policy interests" (2009a, p. 2). The lobby group ISOA adds that the industry's primary mission is to "represent[...] the U.S. Government, and subsequently U.S. government policy objectives, around the world". PMSCs "serve—willingly in all locations and conditions" (DynCorp International 2013g), "no matter how difficult, no matter how dangerous, no matter how remote" and "with anything it [the U.S. government] may need to be successful" (Rosenkranz 2007). Underlying such mission statements is the industry's claim to act as an 'agent of the state'. PMSCs convey an impression of being a "useful tool" which is "utilized principally by [...] governments in the furtherance of their policies" (Brooks and Chorev 2008, p. 122). Their main functions is "to serve" (Academi 2011; Ballhaus 2009a, p. 2; Brooks 2007, p. 2; Xe Services 2009), "assist" (Blackwater 2007; DynCorp International 2013f; Roitz 2009; Rosenkranz 2007, p. 3) and "support" (Ballhaus 2009b, p. 1; DynCorp International 2013a; IPOA 2007; Roitz 2009, p. 6; Rosenkranz 2007, p. 2; Ryder 2010, p. 9) the state's foreign policy objectives in Iraq, Afghanistan, and elsewhere. Identification with the goals and interests of the U.S. government gives these companies an appearance as quasi-public actors and dilutes the fact that they have an independent agency and interests that might differ from those of their state client: making profit first and foremost.

Besides economic positioning, diversification is a legitimizing tool to get rid of the disliked Rambo image that has haunted the industry post-Nisour Square. It allows PMSCs to signal allegiance to the prevailing normative order, which has placed major constrains on the open provision of combat and armed security services, by diverting attention away from such controversial activities. PMSCs are not (only) soldiers, but "aid workers", "diplomats", "IT professionals", "educators", "instructors" "technical experts" and "political advisers" (Academi 2013b; Constellis 2017; IDS International 2017). This multifaceted, chameleon-like nature prevents them from being typecast as unequivocally bad or illegitimate. It helps them to remain undefined and stay 'aloof' of their critics because "if nobody knows exactly what you do, then it's hard to protest to or object to what you do" (David Isenberg in an interview with Hagedorn 2014, p. 213). This blurring follows the rationale of *decoupling*—it results in a "practical and discursive obfuscation of the role of PMCs" (Leander 2010, p. 482) which tends to veil the fact these companies still provide military services. Indeed, PMSC have resurfaced in quasi combat roles: as cyber warriors and operators of drones.

With the decision of the Obama administration to expand the drone war and the increasing importance of the cyberspace as the fifth domain of warfare PMSCs have rushed to fill two new profitable gaps: as intelligence, surveillance, and reconnaissance (ISR) specialists tracking suspected terrorists by analyzing surveillance data gathered by drones flying over war zones and as 'cyber soldiers'. Since these assignments are usually beyond their ordinary skill-set, PMSCs have either leveraged their existing know-how, e.g. from defending themselves against hacking attacks, or acquired that expertise by buying up other firms in the IT-sector (Hennigan 2015). DynCorp International, for example, has partnered with the drone manufacturer Textron in 2012 to compete for a 1 billion USD contract with the U.S. Air Force to maintain Predator and Reaper drones (McGarry 2012). Given the presumed strength of the norm of the state monopoly over violence, it is surprising that this development has gone mostly unnoticed and unchallenged. While removed from the actual scene of fighting, ISR provision can be as integral to the use of force as actually pulling the trigger since the assessments passed on by analysist may affect whether someone on the ground is perceived as a threat, giving rise to so-called "kinetic situations"—those that entail the use of force (Fielding-Smith et al. 2015). Similarly, the provision of military and security services in the cyber domain makes the assertion that PMSCs refrain from offensive operations no longer tenable (Liu 2015). Indeed, cybersecurity firms are involved with 'active defense', which includes launching pre-emptive or retaliatory strikes (Harris 2014).

According to Liu "we are blinded to [those] new activities that PMSCs now engage in" (2015). This is because the industry, by decoupling, can cloud its actual involvement in the 'robust' business segment in favor of more benign activities. NGOs effectively caution that it has become more difficult to campaign against these companies since they "take on more and more roles, anything from catering which obviously isn't a problem and hotel security right down to being [...] armed on ships in the Indian Ocean and work in conflict zones" (Interview#9 2014). As long as some of their tasks qualify as "innocuous" (CAAT 2013, p.§21), objections against the legitimacy of the industry are hard to sustain. This means that one of the few (normative) barriers that have been erected against the provision of private force may be circumvented by giving the false impression of conforming to the existing normative order. Whenever there is a demand in the marketplace, PMSCs will step up to the plate.

3.4 Conclusion

The preceding analysis has shown that the multi-faceted and protean nature of the industry can be traced to companies' ability to adapt to and manage diverse selection pressures from their tasks and institutional environment. Not unlike chameleons, PMSCs have coevolved to reflect the goals and interests of their most attractive client, the U.S. government, and overall societal expectations about what constitutes a legitimate security provider. As to the direction of the industry's evolution, market demand and supply have functioned as an enabling structure, providing companies with ever-expanding business opportunities: from the so-called kitchen porter-PMSC that would supply non-core functions to the U.S. military (basically logistical supply), to the archetypical private security company that guards government facilities and protects government personnel in Iraq and Afghanistan, to today's multiservice organizations that have expanded dramatically to cover myriad service segments that traditionally were not considered as being part of this industry. By contrast, PMSCs' institutional environment has mainly confronted these companies as a constraining force by effectively limiting the range of activities to be taken on by PMSCs. Today, neither combat nor armed security are regarded as appropriate vocations as they run afoul of the state monopoly over violence.

Yet my analysis suggests that PMSCs have found a non-orthodox way of responding to such limitations. Since the failed PMC experiment—the *open* provision of combat services—, they have learned to decouple from a more or less restrictive normative environment by adopting practices that mask or distract attention away from controversial activities. This leads to the paradoxical situation that many of today's companies that we refer to as PMSCs seem to escape this designation altogether while, *formally,* they have neither discarded the offensive nor the protective business niche fully. Rather, the continuing profitability of such services has left companies with the dilemma of conforming to diverging expectations simultaneously.

The proposed co-evolutionary framework allows us to identify those situations in which conflicting environmental demands may lead PMSCs to develop hybrid organizational forms. In departure from existing single-factor explanations of the industry's diversity, it provides a 'big picture perspective' that does not only take into account the directionality and interactions between external influences that companies face from both their task *and* institutional environment, but also firms' ability to adapt through shifting their capabilities across different corporate sectors and identities.

To what extent are these findings valid beyond the Anglo-Saxon world? Kinsey cautions that PMSCs remain tightly associated with their national contexts (2006, p. 97) which makes it rather unlikely that PMSCs outside the U.S. follow a similar evolutionary path. This is, first of all, owing to the fact that U.S.-based companies have mainly evolved with an eye toward the U.S. government which has played an important consumer role in the market and whose choices have had a large impact on the industry's ecology. The situation is arguably different in other countries where PMSCs work for a more varied clientele. As a result, the evolution and lookout of non-American PMSCs is presumably very different. The same goes for societal expectations about who should be responsible for the direction and management of the means of violence. According to Finnemore and Sikkink, "international norms must always work their influence through the filter of domestic structures and domestic norms, which can produce important variations in compliance and interpretation" (1998, p. 893). Continental European countries such as Germany or France, for example, have a more conservative understanding of the state's monopoly over violence (Krahmann 2010; Kruck 2013) which leads us to suspect a dominance of KP-kind of PMSCs compared to their more robust brethren. That being said, the same selection mechanisms would still apply (economic and social fitness). The co-evolutionary framework spelled out in this chapter therefore offers a reasonable template to compare the evolution of PMSCs across world regions.

References

Abrahamsen, R., & Williams, M. C. (2011). *Security beyond the state. Private security in international politics*. Cambridge: Cambridge University Press.

Academi. (2011). *Leading training and security services provider Xe services announces name change to ACADEMI*. Accessed March 11, 2013, from http://academi.com/press_releases/1

Academi. (2013a). *Recruit highly skilled personnel*. Accessed March 13, 2013, from http://academi.com/pages/assess/assess-overview/recruit-highly-skilled-personnel

Academi. (2013b). *Training cadre*. Accessed March 11, 2013, from http://academi.com/pages/train/train-overview/training-cadre

Academi. (2017). *Managed support services*. Accessed Feburary 24, 2017, from https://www.academi.com/pages/managed-support-services

Ashforth, B. E., & Gibbs, B. W. (1990). The double-edge of organizational legitimation. *Organization Science, 1*(2), 177–194.

Avant, D. (2005). *The market for force: The consequences of privatizing security*. Cambridge: Cambridge University Press.

Ballhaus, W. L. (2009a). *Statement by William L. Ballhaus, President and CEO of DynCorp International LLC, before the commission on wartime contracting*. Accessed July 01, 2013, from http://www.dyn-intl.com/media/590/cwc_ii_draft_statement_for_the_record_9_14_2009.pdf

Ballhaus, W. L. (2009b). *Statement by William L. Ballhaus, President and CEO of DynCorp International, before the commission on wartime contracting*. Accessed July 01, 2013, from http://www.dyn-intl.com/media/593/8-11-09_cwc_hearing_ballhaus_statement_for_the_record.pdf

Baum, J. A. C., & Singh, J. V. (1994). *Evolutionary dynamics of organizations*. Oxford: Oxford University Press.

Beerli, C. (2012). *A humanitarian perspective on the privatization of warfare*. Accessed October 15, 2013, from http://www.icrc.org/eng/resources/documents/statement/2012/privatization-war-statement-2012-09-06.htm

Beese, C. (2004). *Regulation – An armorgroup perspective (private security companies)*. Accessed November 06, 2015, from http://web.archive.org/web/20061024012650/http://www.armorgroup.com/mediacentre/publications/?year=2004

Blackwater. (2007). *Global stabilization*. Accessed March 03, 2013, from http://web.archive.org/web/20070925092502/http://www.blackwaterusa.com/securityconsulting/Global_Stable.asp

Blackwater. (2009). *Supply chain management*. Accessed March 12, 2013, from http://web.archive.org/web/20090120042440/http://blackwaterusa.com/mobility_logistics/ML_supply_chain.html

Blyth, M., Hodgson, G. M., Lewis, O., & Steinmo, S. (2011). Introduction to the Special Issue on the Evolution of Institutions. *Journal of Institutional Economics, 7*(3), 299–315. doi:10.1017/S1744137411000270.

Brooks, D. (2004). *The challenges of African peace keeping*. Accessed April 25, 2012, from http://commdocs.house.gov/committees/intlrel/hfa96360.000/hfa96360_0f.htm

Brooks, D. (2006). *Congressional testimony by Doug Brooks before the committee on government reform, subcommittee on national security, emerging threats, and international relations*. Accessed July 17, 2013, from http://web.archive.org/web/20061002231637/http://ipoaonline.org/en/gov/ipoa-shays.pdf

Brooks, D. (2007). *IPOA testimony before the house armed services committee, subcommittee on oversight and investigation. Security sector reform in Iraq: Enhancing the role of the private sector*. Accessed July 17, 2013, from https://lapa.princeton.edu/conferences/military07/restricted/brooks_april_military07.pdf

Brooks, D. (2010). Are contractors military? Terminology matters, especially in international regulations and law. *Journal of International Peace Operations, 5*(5), 4.

Brooks, D. (2011). A decade in stability. ISOA's rise from Sierra Leone to Washington D.C. and around the world. *Journal of International Peace Operations, 6*(5), 4–34.

Brooks, D., & Chorev, M. (2008). Ruthless humanitarianism. Why marginalizing private peacekeeping kills people. In M. Caparini, D.-P. Barker, & A. Alexandra (Eds.), *Private military and security companies: Ethics, policies and civil-military relations* (pp. 116–131). New York: Routledge.

Brunsson, N. (2002 [1989]). *The organization of hypocrisy: Talk, decisions and actions in organizations* (Reprinted ed.). Oslo: Copenhagen Business School Press.

Buzan, B., Weaver, O., & de Wilde, J. (Eds.). (1998). *Security: A new framework for analysis*. Boulder: Lynne Rienner.

CAAT. (2013). *Submission from the campaign against arms trade to the defence committee's inquiry "Towards the next Defence and Security Review"*. Accessed June 02, 2014, from http://www.caat.org.uk/resources/publications/government/def-com-next-sdsr-april2013.pdf#page=4&zoom=auto,-82,720

Clinton, H. R. (2010). Leading through Civilian power. Redefining american diplomacy and development. *Foreign Affairs, 89*(6), 13–24.

Constellis. (2017). *Who we are*. Accessed Feburary 10, 2017, from https://constellis.com/who-we-are/overview

Control Risks. (2014a). *Ethical and independent*. http://www.controlrisks.com/AboutUs/Pages/EthicalAndIndependent.aspx

Control Risks. (2014b). *Travel security services*. http://www.controlrisks.com/Services/Security/TravelSecurity/Pages/Home.aspx

CusterBattles. (2005). *About us*. Accessed Feburary 24, 2017, from http://web.archive.org/web/20050206170821/http://www.custerbattles.com/aboutus/index.html

Cutler, C. (2010). The legitimacy of private transnational governance: Experts and the transnational market for force. *Socio-Economic Review, 8*(1), 157–185.

DeWinter-Schmitt, R. (Ed.). (2013). *Montreux five years on: An analysis of state efforts to implement montreux document legal obligations and good practices*. Washington, DC: Center for Human Rights & Humanitarian Law, American University.

DiMaggio, P. J., & Powell, W. W. (1983). The iron cage revisited: Institutional isomorphism and collective rationality in organizational fields. *American Sociological Review, 48*(2), 147–160. doi:10.2307/2095101.

DoD. (1996). *Improving the combat edge through outsourcing*. Accessed May 18, 2015, from http://www.defense.gov/Speeches/Speech.aspx?SpeechID=890

DoD. (2001). *Quadrennial defense review report*. U.S. Department of Defense. Accessed May 18, 2015, from http://www.comw.org/qdr/qdr2001.pdf

Dosi, G., & Marengo, L. (2007). On the evolutionary and behavioral theories of organizations: A tentative roadmap. *Organization Science, 18*(3), 491–502. doi:10.1287/orsc.1070.0279.

Dosi, G., & Nelson, R. R. (1994). An introduction to evolutionary theories in economics. *Journal of Evolutionary Economics, 4*(3), 153–172. doi:10.1007/bf01236366.

Dunigan, M. (2011). *Victory for hire: Private security companies' impact on military effectiveness*. Stanford: Stanford Security Studies.

Dunigan, M., & Petersohn, U. (2015). *The markets for force: Privatization of security across world regions* (1st ed.). Philadelphia: University of Pennsylvania Press.

DynCorp International. (2010). *Casals & associates joins dyncorp international*. Accessed October 31, 2014, from http://www.casals.com/2010/01/casals-associates-joins-dyncorp-international/

DynCorp International. (2012). *DynCorp response to report raising human rights concerns over its operations*. Accessed July 16, 2013, from http://www.business-humanrights.org/Links/Repository/1013843/jump

DynCorp International. (2013a). *Aviation*. http://www.dyn-intl.com/what-we-do/aviation.aspx

DynCorp International. (2013b). *Collection & analysis*. http://www.dyn-intl.com/what-we-do/training-intelligence-solutions/intel-training-solutions/collection-analysis.aspx

DynCorp International. (2013c). *Contingency operations*. http://www.dyn-intl.com/what-we-do/contingency-operations.aspx

DynCorp International. (2013d). *Overview*. http://www.dyn-intl.com/about-us/overview.aspx

DynCorp International. (2013e). *Security services*. http://web.archive.org/web/20120914222028/http://dyn-intl.com/what-we-do/security-services.aspx

DynCorp International. (2013f). *Training & mentoring*. http://www.dyn-intl.com/what-we-do/training-intelligence-solutions/training-mentoring.aspx

DynCorp International. (2013g). *Values & code of conduct*. http://www.dyn-intl.com/about-us/values-code-of-conduct.aspx

Einstein, M., & Rollins, J. (2010). Introduction: Market. *Women's Studies Quarterly, 38*(3/4), 13–20.

FAIR. (1998). *The federal activities inventory reform act of 1998*, Pub L No 105-270 § 5(2)(A), 112 Stat 2382.

FCO. (2009). *Public consultation on promoting high standards of conduct by private military and security companies (PMSCs) internationally: Summary of responses*. Accessed April 02, 2014, from http://psm.du.edu/media/documents/national_regulations/countries/europe/united_kingdom/united_kingdom_fco_consultation_standards_conduct_pmsc_internationally_summary_2010.pdf

Fielding-Smith, A., Black, C., Ross, A., & Ball, J. (2015, July 30). Revealed: Private firms at heart of US drone warfare. *The Guardian*.

Finnemore, M., & Sikkink, K. (1998). International norm dynamics and political change. *International Organization, 52*(4), 887–917. doi:10.1162/002081898550789.

Geels, F. W. (2014). Reconceptualising the co-evolution of firms-in-industries and their environments: Developing an inter-disciplinary triple embeddedness framework. *Research Policy, 43* (2), 261–277. doi:10.1016/j.respol.2013.10.006.

Ginzel, L. E., Kramer, R. M., & Sutton, R. I. (2004). Organizational impression management as a reciprocal influence process: The neglected role of the organizational audience. In M. J. Hatch & M. Schultz (Eds.), *Organizatiobal identity. A reader* (pp. 223–261). Oxford: Oxford University Press.

Grunberg, M. (2004, May 3). Mit einem Fuß im Grab. *Der Spiegel* (p. 142).

Hagedorn, A. (2014). *The invisible soldiers: How America outsourced our security*. New York: Simon & Schuster.

Hague, W. (2010). *Written ministerial statement. Promoting high standards of conduct by private military and security companies internationally*. Accessed January 15, 2014, from http://psm.du.edu/media/documents/national_regulations/countries/europe/united_kingdom/united_kingdom_written_ministerial_statement_standards_pmscs_2010.pdf

Hall, P. A., & Taylor, R. C. R. (1996). Political science and the three new institutionalisms. *Political Studies, 44*(5), 936–957. doi:10.1111/j.1467-9248.1996.tb00343.x.

Harris, S. (2014, November 12). The Mercenaries. *Slate*.

Hennigan, W. J. (2015, January 21). Defense contractors see opportunity in cybersecurity sector. *Los Angeles Times*.

Herbst, K. (2013). Searching for legitimacy - Private military and security companies (PMSCs). Overcoming ingrained stereotypes. *Security Journal, 26*(3), 280–293.

Hodgson, G. M. (2013). Understanding organizational evolution: Toward a research agenda using generalized Darwinism. *Organization Studies, 34*(7), 973–992. doi:10.1177/0170840613485855.

Howell, A. (2007). *Prepared statement by Andrew G. Howell for the committee on oversight and government reform*. Accessed April 09, 2013, from http://www.gpo.gov/fdsys/pkg/CHRG-110hhrg36546/html/CHRG-110hhrg36546.htm

Human Rights First. (2008). *Private security contractors at war. Ending the culture of impunity*. Accessed June 9, 2013, from http://www.humanrightsfirst.org/wp-content/uploads/pdf/08115-usls-psc-final.pdf

Huskey, K., & Sullivan, S. (2012). United States: Law and policy governing private military contractors after 9/11. In M. Sossai & C. Bakker (Eds.), *Multilevel regulation of military and security contractors: The interplay between international, European and domestic norms* (pp. 331–380). Oxford: Hart.

IDS International. (2017). *Who we are*. Accessed Feburary 24, 2017, from http://www.idsinternational.net/who-we-are

Interview#6. (2014, May 16). NGO representative. *Personal Interview*. London.
Interview#9. (2014, May 29). NGO representative. *Telephone Interview*.
IPOA. (2007). *IPOA endorsement of MEJA expansion and enforcement act*. Accessed July 17, 2013, from http://web.archive.org/web/20110123164053/http://ipoaworld.org/eng/press/133-20071002mejaexpansionact.html
IRG Selected to Implement Key Post-War Reconstruction. (2003, March 13). *PR Newswire*.
Isenberg, D. (2009). *Shadow force. Private security companies in Iraq*. Westport, CT.: Praeger Security International.
Joachim, J., & Schneiker, A. (2012). New humanitarians? Frame appropriation through private military and security companies. *Millennium: Journal of International Studies, 40*(2), 365–388.
Joachim, J., & Schneiker, A. (2014). All for one and one in all: Private military security companies as soldiers, business managers and humanitarians. *Cambridge Review of International Affairs*, 1–22. doi:10.1080/09557571.2013.867300.
Kinsey, C. (2006). *Corporate soldiers and international security: The rise of private military companies*. London: Routledge.
Krahmann, E. (2010). *States, citizens, and the privatization of security*. Cambridge: Cambridge University Press.
Krahmann, E. (2013). The United States, PMSCs and the state monopoly on violence: Leading the way towards norm change. *Security Dialogue, 44*(1), 53–71.
Krahmann, E. (2016). Choice, voice, and exit: Consumer power and the self-regulation of the private security industry. *European Journal of International Security, 1*(01), 27–48. doi:10.1017/eis.2015.6.
Krasner, S. D. (1999). *Sovereignty: Organized hypocrisy*. Princeton, NJ: Princeton University Press.
Kruck, A. (2013). Theorising the use of private military and security companies. A synthetic perspective. *Journal of International Relations and Development, 17*, 112–141. doi:10.1057/jird.2013.4.
L-3 Communications. (2008). *Press release*. L-3 Acquires International Resources Group Ltd. Accessed December 22, 2016, from http://www.defense-aerospace.com/articles-view/release/3/100396/l_3-acquires-international-resources-group.html
Leander, A. (2005). The power to construct international security: On the significance of private military companies. *Millennium: Journal of International Studies, 33*(3), 803–826.
Leander, A. (2010). The paradoxical impunity of private military companies: Authority and the limits to legal accountability. *Security Dialogue, 41*(5), 467–490.
Leander, A., & van Munster, R. (2007). Private security contractors in the debate about darfur: Reflecting and reinforcing neo-liberal governmentality. *International Relations, 21*(2), 201–216.
Lewin, A. Y., & Volberda, H. W. (1999). Prolegomena on coevolution: A framework for research on strategy and new organizational forms. *Organization Science, 10*(5), 519–534.
Liu, H.-Y. (2015). *Cybersecurity and cyberwarfare as emerging gaps in private military and security company regulation: Thoughts for the UN working group on the use of mercenaries*. Accessed Feburary 24, 2017, from http://www.ohchr.org/Documents/Issues/Mercenaries/WG/Event2015/HinYanLiu.pdf
Lynn, M. (2006, November 2). Men with guns are the new dotcoms. *The Spectator*.
McFate, S. (2014). *The modern mercenary: Private armies and what they mean for world order*. Oxford: Oxford University Press.
McGarry, B. (2012, December 18). Retired veterans beat textron for nearly $1 billion military drone contract. *The Washington Post*.
Messner, J. J. (2007). What's in a name? The importance of language for the peace and stability operations industry. *Journal of International Peace Operations, 2*(6), 24.
Morgan, G. (2006). *Images of organization*. Thousands Oaks: SAGE.

Nagaraj, V. K. (2015). 'Beltway Bandits' and 'Poverty Barons': For-profit international development contracting and the military-development assemblage. *Development and Change, 46*(4), 585–617. doi:10.1111/dech.12164.

Obama, B. H. (2011). *Remarks by the president on the Middle East and North Africa*. Accessed July 13, 2013, from http://www.whitehouse.gov/the-press-office/2011/05/19/remarks-president-middle-east-and-north-africa

OBM. (2003). *Performance of commercial activitites, circular No A-76 revised*. White House Office of Management and Budget.

Oliver, C. (1991). Strategic responses to institutional processes. *Academy of Management Review, 16*(1), 145–179. doi:10.5465/amr.1991.4279002.

Østensen, Å. G. (2011a). In from the cold? Self-legitimating the market for private security. *Global Change, Peace & Security, 23*(3), 369–385.

Østensen, Å. G. (2011b). *UN use of private military and security companies. Practices and Policies*. Accessed.

Pattison, J. (2014). *The morality of private war: The challenge of private military and security companies*. Oxford: Oxford University Press.

Percy, S. (2007). *Mercenaries. The history of a norm in international relations*. Oxford: Oxford University Press.

Percy, S. (2012). Regulating the private security industry: A story of regulating the Last War. *International Review of the Red Cross, 94*(887), 941–960.

Petersohn, U. (2010). Sovereignty and privatizing the military: An institutional explanation. *Contemporary Security Policy, 31*(3), 531–552.

Petersohn, U. (2014). Reframing the anti-mercenary norm: Private military and security companies and mercenarism. *International Journal: Canada's Journal of Global Policy Analysis, 69* (4), 475–493. doi:10.1177/0020702014544915.

Petersohn, U., & Dunigan, M. (2015). Introduction. In M. Dunigan & U. Petersohn (Eds.), *The markets for force. Privatization of security across world regions* (pp. 1–19). Philadelphia: University of Pennsylvania Press.

Pfeffer, J., & Salancik, G. R. (2003). *The external control of organizations: A resource dependence perspective (Stanford business classics)*. Stanford: Stanford Business Books.

Pingeot, L. (2012). *Dangerous partnership. Private military & security companies and the UN*. New York: Global Policy Forum.

Pingeot, L. (2014). *Contracting insecurity. Private military and security companies and the future of the United Nations*. Accessed April 23, 2014 from http://www.globalpolicy.org/images/pdfs/GPFEurope/PMSC_2014_Contracting_Insecurity_web.pdf

Power, H. (2008, March 21). Troubled ArmorGroup secures sale to G4S. *The Daily Telegraph*.

Prince, E. (2007). *Statement by Erik D. Prince, chairman and CEO of Blackwater USA, for the house committee on oversight and government reform*. Accessed April 11, 2013, from https://house.resource.org/110/org.c-span.201290-1.1.pdf

Roitz, F. (2009). *Statement by Fred Roitz, executive vice president of contracts and sales of Xe Services LLC, before the commission on wartime contracting in Iraq and Afghanistan*. Accessed April 09, 2013, from http://cybercemetery.unt.edu/archive/cwc/20110929220814/http://www.wartimecontracting.gov/docs/hearings/20091218/Statement_of_Exec_VP_Fred%20Roitz_Xe_Services.pdf

Roles and Missions Commission of the Armed Forces. (1995, May 24). *Directions for defense. Report to congress, the secretary of defense, and the chairman of the joint chiefs of staff*. Accessed December 30, 2016, from http://web.archive.org/web/20130702134600/http://www.fas.org/man/docs/corm95/di1062.html

Rosenkranz, R. B. (2007). *Statement by Robert B. Rosenkranz, president government services division of DynCorp International, before the subcommittee on management, investigation, and oversight committee on Homeland Security*. Accessed July 02, 2013, from http://web.archive.org/web/20130301235110/http://dyn-intl.com/media/596/increasing_border_patrol.pdf

Ryder, D. J. (2010). *Statement by Ronald J. Ryder, Vice President and Program manager of DynCorp International LLC, before the commission on Wartime Contracting*. Accessed Feburary 12, 2016, from http://cybercemetery.unt.edu/archive/cwc/20110929215906/http://www.wartimecontracting.gov/docs/hearing2010-06-21_testimony-Ryder.pdf

Sandline International. (2004). *Closure of Sandline's operations*, 04/16/2004. Accessed May 14, 2013, from http://www.sandline.com/comment/list/comment48.html

Scherer, A. G., Palazzo, G., & Seidl, D. (2013). Managing legitimacy in complex and heterogeneous environments: Sustainable development in a globalized world. *Journal of Management Studies, 50*(2), 259–284. doi:10.1111/joms.12014.

Schmid, M., & Wuketits, F. M. (1987). *Evolutionary theory in social science*. Dordrecht: D. Reidel Publishing Company.

Schreier, F., & Caparini, M. (2005). *Privatising security: Law, practice and governance of private military and security companies*. Occasional Paper No. 6, Geneva Centre for the Democratic Control of Armed Forces (DCAF).

Scott, W. R. (2008). *Institutions and organizations: Ideas, interests and identities* (3rd ed.). Los Angeles: Sage.

Simmonds, M. (2012). *Written ministerial statement. Private security companies*. Accessed August 21, 2013, from http://psm.du.edu/media/documents/national_regulations/countries/europe/united_kingdom/uk_2012_fco-statement_adoption_of_asis-psc1.pdf

Singer, P. W. (2008). *Corporate warriors: The rise of the privatized military industry*. Ithaca: Cornell University Press.

Spearin, C. (2008). Private, armed, humanitarian? States, NGOs, international private security companies and shifting humanitarianism. *Security Dialogue, 39*(4), 363–382.

Suchman, M. C. (1995). Managing legitimacy: Strategic and institutional approaches. *The Academy of Management Review, 20*(3), 571–610.

Taylor, T. (2004). Contractors on deployed operations and equipment support. *Defence Studies, 4* (2), 184–198. doi:10.1080/1470243042000325896.

van de Ven, A. H., & Poole, M. S. (1995). Explaining development and change in organizations. *The Academy of Management Review, 20*(3), 510–540. doi:10.2307/258786.

Volberda, H. W., & Lewin, A. Y. (2003). Co-evolutionary dynamics within and between firms: From evolution to co-evolution. *Journal of Management Studies, 40*(8), 2111–2136.

Xe Services. (2009). *International training*. Accessed March 01, 2013, from http://web.archive.org/web/20090801032443/http://xecompany.com/Adv.Training.html

Part II
The Continuous Expansion of Security Privatization: Industry and Geographical Trends

Chapter 4
Maritime Security and Transformations in Global Governance

Åsne Kalland Aarstad

4.1 Introduction

On the International Maritime Organization's (IMO) web page, the organization's evolving position on the issue of private armed security for the purpose of protecting vessels, carriage and crew is briefly outlined (IMO (2015) Private Armed Security). From 'strongly discouraging' the carrying and use of firearms in 1993 and 2009, the organization's current position as of 2016 'tacitly acknowledge that the deployment of armed security personnel on board ships has become an accepted industry and flag state practice in certain circumstances' (IMO (2015) Private Armed Security). The outline testifies to a change in perception, and mirrors a change in practice, by which private armed security solutions have gone from being shunned to becoming an integrated part of maritime security provision. The change is most notably linked to the increasing growth in attempted and successful piracy attacks in the Gulf of Aden from 2007 onwards. Within 1 year (2011), the share of armed transits through the Gulf of Aden was estimated to have risen from 10 to 50% (Dutton 2013, p. 108).[1]

Whereas much has been written on the reason why armed private security was deemed necessary by ship-owners in the critical period from 2007 onwards, less has

The article was originally published while the author was affiliated with Aarhus University, Department of Political Science. The article reflects the opinions of the author and does not represent NOKUT.

[1]It is important to stress that the use of armed guards is not a new feature in the maritime industry. However, the official recognition of the practice is new (Roundtable of International Shipping Associations 2011), and this very recognition and following legalization created a measurable increase in the number of armed transits as documented by Dutton (2013, p. 108). It is difficult, however, to say exactly how widespread the practice was before the 2010–2012 official recognition (see Cullen 2012).

Å.K. Aarstad (✉)
The Norwegian Agency for Quality Assurance in Education (NOKUT), Oslo, Norway
e-mail: asne.kalland.aarstad@nokut.no

O. Bures, H. Carrapico (eds.), *Security Privatization*,
DOI 10.1007/978-3-319-63010-6_4

been written on how the demand for private security came to alter the widespread international consensus against the utilization of armed private security. This is an important task, since the shift in perception and practice involves a vast number of the world's largest maritime nations, a major international organization, and the global shipping industry. In a short period of time stretching from 2010 to 2012, international guidelines were issued, industry guidelines were re-written and national laws were changed for the purposes of enhancing maritime security through armed private security provision. As for most maritime issue areas, the governance of private maritime security cuts across public/private and global/local division, because of global shipping's enormous economic impact and transnational nature. Making sure that global shipping can be carried out in a secure manner is an obvious interest to the shipping industry itself, but also by states whose economic lifelines are dependent upon unhindered trade-lines. The governance of private maritime security requires regulation at, at a minimum, two levels in order to ensure effectiveness. Ships are always registered in nationally anchored registers and subject to national legislation. National action is, however, dependent upon international harmonization of standards and practices, since a ship from state A might travel from state B to state C on a route through the territorial waters of state D, F, and G.

It is exactly the mixture between public and private and global and local interests and implications that make the maritime domain a highly relevant domain for the study of contemporary global governance dynamics. Analyses of complex global relationships beyond the realm of bi/multilateral state interaction is an important exercise in a global political landscape increasingly characterized by actors and practices which defy and challenge the boundaries between the public and the private, and between the local and global spheres of action (Walker 1993; Agnew 1994; Owens 2008; Leander 2010; Williams 2010). Although not unique, the governance of maritime security encapsulates these in-between positions in a condensed and illustrative manner. The interdependency of both public and private economic interests and national and international regulatory dynamics substantiates the working assumption that maritime governance is an important indicator of broader governance dynamics. The main purpose of this chapter is therefor to tap into the governance arrangement surrounding the resort to armed private security in the maritime domain for the purpose of casting new light on the 'who governs' question (Avant et al. 2010). What, if anything, can maritime governance tell us about contemporary roles and responsibility sharing between public and private governing actors?

What at first sight could appear to be a 'business solution' to the problem of piracy reveals itself as a political and consensual move, involving deliberate choices about the necessity of private security by a vast array of stakeholders across public and private sectors. Through an empirical analysis of the processes that led to the reliance on private maritime security, the chapter argues that the governance arrangement was driven forward by maritime, insurance and private security industry representatives, and that it is business-oriented at its core in that it favours high degree of corporate autonomy and self-regulation. However, this process was *facilitated* by public actors through the IMO, most notably the IMO's Maritime Security Committee (IMO MSC), which carved out privileged spheres for the maritime, insurance and private security industries through their convening capacities, legitimizing roles, and regulative infrastructures. Hence, public actors' re-articulated role is best characterized as governance facilitators, in turn contributing to their own continued relevance and influence in global governance through the dual process of both mobilizing and accepting knowledge and power resources from private stakeholders (inspired by Jessop 2002, p. 199, quoted in Bieling 2007, p. 14). The role of public actors in the governance of private maritime security can therefore be understood with reference to 'the globalization paradox' (Behr 2008). This refers to the observation that public actors respond to deterritorialised politics by resorting to means which themselves further deterritorialises politics (ibid.). The facilitation *by* public actors *of* private actors therefore denotes a relationship that can hardly be settled on the premises of a zero-sum game, as it is both a role undertaken by choice, and a role assigned by default.

A secondary and more implicit contribution of this chapter is to bring global shipping (back) into the study of global politics. In the same way that shipping is largely invisible to the public as an industry (despite affecting us all), the global shipping industry is rendered largely invisible in the study of global politics despite being fuelled by, and fuelling, globalization. The governance of maritime affairs, including issues such as flag state registration, seafarers' working conditions, and environmental protection, are largely dealt with in specialized maritime journals by economists, natural scientists, historians, anthropologists and geographers, and only occasionally by scholars of global politics (Cutler 1999; Steinberg 2001, 2009; Cowen 2014). This chapter aims to show how maritime affairs are part and parcel of broader political dynamics as observed through the governance of armed private security.

The chapter starts by first presenting the evolving literature on private security governance with a specific eye to the maritime domain, and frames the chapter's research in terms of time, space, actors, and empirical data. The following analytical section chronologically outlines the processes that led to the adoption of international documents that expresses a new consensus vis-à-vis the usage of armed private security in the maritime domain. This processes is then subject to a discussion around the 'who governs' question, drawing upon key insights from the governance literature.

4.2 Maritime Governance and Private Security: Linking the Literatures

The understanding of maritime affairs as reflecting broader political dynamics is not new. Colas and Mabee point to the eighteenth century's practices of piracy and privateering and show how the functioning of diplomacy and trade were 'reliant on the combination of private and public mobilizations of force, authority, manpower and resources' (Colás and Mabee 2010, p. 85). Until the nineteenth century, the enmeshment of public and private actors characterized the ways in which sea powers such as the UK, France and the Netherlands both waged war and conducted trade (Thompson 1994; Colás and Mabee 2010; Leira and de Carvalho 2010). However, the dual processes of state consolidation, which increased financial and military capacities and the authority exercised over citizens, and the economic shift from mercantilism to capitalism, which necessitated free and unhindered sea trade, sharpened the separation between private and public activities at sea. Privateering, understood as state-sanctioned seaborne violence, was made illegal and largely eroded as an activity, commerce was made private and largely left to private companies, and warfare became consolidated as a public responsibility (Ritchie 1997; Colás and Mabee 2010). The separation between public and private was never absolute, but the construction of two separate spheres of engagement became institutionalized as an ideal in both theory and, largely, in practice, with an assumed division between private companies responsible for commercial shipping, and public authorities such as coast guards and naval forces responsible for guaranteeing security at sea (see Florquin 2012; Murphy 2009; Berube and Cullen 2012; Petrig 2014; the Roundtable of International Shipping Associations 2011).

This historical understanding of public and private roles and responsibilities as bound in time and space draws upon a growing body of research arguing that the increasing presence of private actors in the performance of functions previously associated with the state is linked to structural, technological and ideational transformations of societies across the globe (Hall and Biersteker 2002; Cutler 1997, 2003; Sassen 2003, 2006; Owens 2008; Avant et al. 2010; Abrahamsen and Williams 2011; Williams 2010). Most notably this refers to the fragmentation (de-nationalisation and actor pluralization) of previously public competencies related to neo-liberal modes of governing (Dupont 2004; Avant et al. 2010). However, both causes and consequences of the above-sketched developments remain contested. Most influential, perhaps, are the discussions surrounding the power-balance between public and private actors within the new governance structures, illustrated by recent IR publications such as Avant et al.'s *Who Governs the Globe?* (Avant et al. 2010), Guzzini and Neumann's *The Diffusion of Power in Global Governance* (Guzzini and Neumann 2012) and Best and Gheciu's *The Return of the Public in Global Governance* (Best and Gheciu 2014).

Within the domain of security governance, the above discussion has received additional fuel by the widespread perception of security as an inherent public good (see Wood and Shearing 2006 and Loader and Walker 2007 for different stances), and the theoretical Weberian conception of a state monopoly on violence (see Colás and Mabee 2010). However, amidst the theoretical-normative tensions, a range of contributions acknowledge that Avant et al.'s question is indeed highly relevant for a wide spectre of security governance arrangement across the globe (see, for example, Abrahamsen and Williams 2007, 2009, 2011; Biaumet, Chap. 8; Bures, Chap. 2; Berndtsson and Stern 2011; Hönke 2013; Salter 2009; Schouten 2014). A major implication raised by these studies is that the analytical lenses traditionally employed when studying security-related issues require revision. Most notably, actors and spheres of action, i.e. national/global, must be assessed empirically, rather than theoretically, attempting to avoid misleading juxtapositions about both public and private roles and subsequent power positions in contemporary security governance deriving from the symbolic and theoretical assumptions about the state's tight association, or even conflation, with security provision (inspired by Green 2014, p. 5). This chapter picks up on the 'who governs' question forwarded by Avant et al. by taking a detailed look into the global security governance arrangement surrounding private maritime security provision. Based upon a case study of maritime governance, the chapter questions which roles and responsibilities are undertaken by which actors, and how we can make sense of them.

To accomplish this, the chapter targets a compilation of agenda-setting guidelines and standards, which in turn constitute (1) a global consensus surrounding the appropriateness of private armed security, (2) international guidelines providing frameworks of action for how to deal with private armed security provision, and (3) soft law providing regulatory standards for private maritime security companies. The chapter is not concerned with the more concrete, nationally-anchored frameworks that flag-states have developed amidst these global guidelines and standards, although it is recognized that the global and national governance frameworks are two sides of the same coin. National frameworks trigger developments at the international arena and vice-versa. Furthermore, and as already mentioned, in order to function effectively, maritime regulatory frameworks require implementation both at the national and the global level.

Compared to nationally-anchored governance arrangements, the global governance arrangement surrounding private maritime security arrangement is (even) looser in its institutional structure, and consists of interplays between public and private actors across the national and global levels of analysis. Although not exhaustive, the actors identified as most relevant are the United Nations agency International Maritime Organization (IMO), in turn composed of national governments; the shipping industry, composed of individual shipping companies and their industry associations, most importantly the International Chamber of Shipping (ICS) and the Baltic and International Maritime Council (BIMCO); maritime underwriters and insurance companies, most notably Lloyd's of London's Joint War Committee (JWC); security/risk consultancies such as Aegis; and maritime security companies and their industry associations such as the Security Association for the Maritime Industry (SAMI) and the Security in Complex Environments Group (SCEG). More specifically, the consensus, framework for action, and soft law are based upon several key documents that were implemented through efforts by a mixture of the above-mentioned actors: (1) the maritime industry's Best Management Practices 4 (BMP4), which is supported by virtually all international stakeholders of shipping, insurance and public/private security; (2) the IMO's Interim Guidelines on private maritime security personnel in the High Risk Area from 2011 and 2012 (IMO 2011, 2012a, b, c); and (3) the international self-regulatory efforts, most notably the Guardcon standardized contract and the ISO/PAS 28007 standard.

The analysis looks at the agenda-setting and implementation capacities performed by the various actors in the realization of these key documents, drawing upon the documents themselves, interviews with key stakeholders, media sources and secondary scholarly sources. Actors were identified on the basis of a pre-reading of the IMO Maritime Safety Committee's reports from the sessions in which the interim guidelines were developed, which contained multiple references to agenda setting activities by a range of public and private actors. Semi-structured background interviews were conducted in London in September 2014 with four key stakeholders in the maritime and security industries, which are referred to by names and institutions throughout the text. The primary objective of these interviews was to gain an understanding of the process itself, and secondarily to hear some of the involved actors' perspectives on the processes they had been engaged in. Due to the incompleteness of the list of interviews, their function in the chapter has been limited to that of casting light on written material derived from other publicly accessible sources.

4.3 Maritime Security Governance in Practice

Piracy—or more specifically the threat posed by piracy to global shipping—moved up on the international security agenda following a reported upsurge beginning in 2007 and a corresponding series of high-profile hijackings. According to the specialized division International Maritime Bureau (IMB) of the International Chamber of Commerce, consistently cited as the most thorough source on piracy attacks (Struett et al. 2013, p. 100), the upsurge was geographically limited to piracy activities surrounding the Horn of Africa, and predominantly conducted by Somali-based pirates. Whereas Somali-based piracy comprised 22 out of 239 actual or attempted attacks in 2006, roughly 9% of the total share, it rose to comprise 237 out of 439 attempted or successful piracy attacks, roughly 54%, of the total share in 2011, as reported by the IMB (2007, 2012). Thus, despite piracy having persisted as an endemic problem to seafarers throughout history, it was transformed into an international security issue through the involvement of a range of international actors, including the UN Security Council, and increasing public attention from 2007 onward (Oliveira 2013). One of the responses to the threat posed by piracy to the maritime infrastructure was the identification, use, recognition and regulation of private armed security by maritime stakeholders as a counter-piracy measure.

Although some ship owners used private security guards on their ships before 2011 (see Cullen 2012, p. 33), the pattern of usage was scattered and unsystematic and there was no overall consensus regarding the acceptability of such individual actions. Both academics and industry representatives claimed that the prospects of utilizing private security in the maritime domain blurred established public/private responsibilities, and there was a general agreement among both industry representatives and governments that private security was an undesirable option (Petrig 2014; Roundtable of International Shipping Associations 2011). From 2011, however, attitude changes quickly manifested in practice. For example, since 2011,

13 out of the 15 most important European flag states have authorized the use of private armed security onboard ships flying their flags (ibid.). The oft-repeated quote that 'no ship has been hijacked with armed personnel on board' (Kraska 2013; Pristrom et al. 2013) has yet to be disproven, despite the equally oft-repeated reminder that absence of evidence does not mean evidence of absence.

4.3.1 Raising Private Security on the Agenda

The attitude change vis-à-vis the armed private security option was first made visible in the shipping industry. Despite the presence of naval forces in the Gulf of Aden and in the Indian Ocean, the number of reported piracy attacks grew steadily until 2012, with more than 400 attacks annually in 2009, 2010 and 2011 (see IMB's reports 2007–2014). The seeming inability of existing solutions to secure against piracy attacks, such as the patrolling of naval forces and strict adherence to the then-applicable industry BMPs, is put forward as the most important reason why the international shipping industry softened its previously negative attitude towards the use of private armed guards on ships (Stawpert 2014; see Dutton 2013, pp. 129–130). In February 2011, the chairman of the ICS, 'the world's principal umbrella shipping organization' (Pittney and Levin 2013, p. 38), acknowledged the use of armed private security and argued that 'ship operators must be able to retain all possible options' in the face of the piracy threat (Dutton 2013, pp. 129–130).

The tacit acceptance by the shipping industry associations was an important move in order to get the issue—armed private security—on the political agenda in a concerted manner. Representing the bulk of the world's ship owners and operators, their attitudes matter greatly vis-à-vis individual ship owners, national ship owners' associations and their governments, and the IMO. The latter point is underscored by the long list of shipping industry associations accredited as NGOs with consultative status at the IMO. The acceptance of armed private security by the world's leading maritime industry associations had multiple practical outcomes. One was the issuing of industry guidelines for the use of private maritime security contractors by BIMCO, the ICS, INTERCARGO, INTERTANKO, OCIMF, and IG P&G Clubs, which in turn were submitted to the IMO's Maritime Safety Committee's 89th session in order to assist the preparations with IMO guidance for ship-owners in the selection of companies (Safety4Sea 2011; SAMI 2014). Another was the issuing of the 2011 4th revised version of the highly influential industry Best Management Practices—the BMP4—which stated that whether to use armed guards 'is a matter for individual ship operators to decide following their own voyage risk assessment and approval of respective Flag States' (BMP4 2011). Falling short of an encouragement, this statement represents a break with the silence (see BMP3 2010) and expressed opposition of the past (Kraska 2013).

Individual shipping companies had, however, reached the conclusion about the necessities of using armed private security companies prior to the industry association's position change. That numerous shipping companies were already making use of armed private maritime security solutions before any international consensus had emerged was shown in a survey of private security companies' websites conducted between June and October 2010 by Cullen (2012). The survey indicated that 'over half a dozen claim to be providing as many as 40 such *armed* anti-piracy transits through the Gulf of Aden and elsewhere on a monthly basis since 2008 or 2009' (Cullen 2012, p. 33, my emphasis). Regarding the decision to acknowledge armed private security as a counter-piracy measure, Stawpert at the ICS argued along similar lines when he stated that ship owners were already making use of these private security services, so the ICS had to respond to a factual, not a hypothetical, situation (Stawpert 2014). The demonstrated inadequacy of existing piracy remedies (naval forces and BMPs) in countering the surge in piracy experienced from 2008–2011 go a long way in explaining the industry associations' shift in position, but the practical decision to make use of the burgeoning market for private security had *already* been made by individual shipping companies, and in some instances it had already been acknowledged and acted upon by national industry associations. This choice stems largely from the increased economic threat faced by the companies, the physical and psychological threat faced by their employees, and the less well-known increased insurance costs faced by individual companies.

In 2008, the Lloyd's Joint War Committee (JWC) designated the Gulf of Aden as a 'war-risk area', a designation that is translated into the more subtle 'High Risk Area' in common usage among representatives from the insurance, maritime and security industries. The logic behind such listings is that areas found to present a higher risk of war, strikes, terrorism and related perils infer higher insurance premiums for ships transiting the area (Brown 2012). The zone was extended in 2010 to cover an even larger area, reflecting the belief that the practice of turning hijacked ships into so-called motherships had increased the range of Somali-based piracy (JWC JW2010/009). Although not a formalized practice, underwriters elsewhere normally follow the JWC's lead. Hence, based on the JWC's threat level assessments, the areas requiring extra premiums were massively extended among war risk insurers. However, many underwriters came to offer reduce premiums for ships that hired private security. As put forward by Brown (2012), 'in some cases, underwriters will not issue kidnap and ransom insurance unless a ship hires armed guards' (see also Cullen 2012; Lobo-Guerrero 2008; Miller 2009). This practice gives private insurance and underwriter bodies considerable influence over individual shipping companies' conduct, and, in effect, over the recognition of the very same conduct by their industry associations and, in turn, by national governments (for an elaboration of this argument, see Lobo-Guerrero 2008).

The importance of the insurance industry and its practices also makes it relevant to highlight the role of the providers of intelligence upon which insurance threat levels are based. The JWC draws its recommendations in large part from the British-registered private security company Aegis. The above-mentioned 2010 extension of the war-risk zone was based, according to the JWC's own report, exclusively on an Aegis security assessment (JWC JW2010/009). Aegis is furthermore credited with the now-infamous JWC decision to designate the Straits of Malacca as a war-risk area in 2005 (Liss 2009). Although the latter was short-lived, both of these decisions raised the insurance premiums that ship owners were required to pay when their vessels transited the areas (ibid.). In addition to offering intelligence assessment, Aegis also offers technical solutions to maritime insecurities, 'from operating and managing Early Warning Systems (MEWS) to establishing physical security measures' (see Aegis (2015) Services - aegis maritime). Aegis therefor performs a double-hatted role offering both risk assessment and risk abatement (Carmola 2010, p. 73), a not uncommon mixture by private security companies in the contemporary security environment (see Bures and Carrapico, Chap. 1). Aegis became, however, an industry giant already back in 2004 through its contract with the US Department of Defence to assist, among other undertakings, with the Iraqi reconstruction process (Pfeifer 2009). Therefore, the Aegis example also shows how the private market for maritime security services is a continuation of an already existing market for land-based security services, displaying similar dynamics such as the presence of former military personnel, the provision of multiple services by the same company, and the global character of companies with reference to operations, employees and customers. That a private security industry was already in place when piracy in the Gulf of Aden increased from 2007 provided shipping companies with an alternative security strategy that only a decade earlier had not been an option. With the upsurge in piracy from 2007 and onwards, Aegis was capable of drawing upon already existing resources to establish itself as an important stakeholder in the maritime security domain through its advisory role vis-à-vis the JWC.

The industry associations' revised positions in early 2011 were quickly reflected at the IMO, as illustrated above. In the preparations for the IMO Maritime Security Committee's (MSC) 89th session in May 2011, a range of proposals aiming to put armed private security on the agenda were submitted. Flag states such as the Cook Islands, Singapore, the Philippines, Liberia, Bahamans, the Marshall Islands, industry associations, and the Contact Group on Piracy off the Coast of Somalia (CGPCS) (the latter presented through BIMCO) asked for private security to be put on the agenda and/ or proposed draft guidelines for the employment of private armed security (MSC 2011 89/25; Kraska 2013). According to the minutes from the 89th session the MSC 'accepted that the guidelines received from the joint submission by BIMCO, the ICS, INTERCARGO, INTERTANK, OCIMF, and IG P&G Clubs could be used to inform the deliberations of the MSPWG' (the IMO Working Group on Maritime Security including Piracy and Armed Robbery against Ships) (MSC 2011 89/25, p. 80), which testifies to the influential position held by the shipping and insurance industry at the IMO, and the proactive manner by which the industry was able to set the agenda for discussion through its private security experience stemming from its members/ clients. As an outcome of the 89th session, the IMO's MSC issued a set of interim guidelines in May and September 2011, and another set of interim guidelines in May 2012. Here, the IMO provided guidance for the use of private security for ship owners, ship operators and shipmasters, flag states, port and coastal states, and, finally, guidelines targeting the private maritime security industry.

4.3.2 *Implementation: Guiding and Regulating the Usage of Private Security*

The issuing of IMO guidelines constituted the recognition by the IMO, and hence by its member states, that the usage of armed private security was a factual development that would benefit from standardized guidelines (Pristrom and Madsen 2014; see also IMO (2015) Private Armed Security). According to Pristrom and Madsen, Technical Officers at the maritime security section at the IMO, the guidelines acknowledge the fact that armed private security was well in use in 2011, and that arms carried on board pose a risk to seafarers who are not security professionals. Issuing voluntary guidelines became a way by which the IMO could encourage its members to minimize risk, while leaving the matter on whether or not to allow for private security entirely in the hands of the flag state (Pristrom and Madsen 2014; see also Pristrom et al. 2013). The May 2011 guidelines on the use of privately contracted armed security personnel on board ships in the High Risk Area advised ship owners, ship operators and shipmasters and flag states. These guidelines were later revised (IMO—International Maritime Organization 2012b, c) and followed by the issuing of another set of guidance in May 2012, which advised port and coastal states (IMO—International Maritime Organization (2011)) and, finally, the private maritime security industry itself (IMO—International Maritime Organization (2012a)). Although the guidelines are entirely voluntary in nature, they are frequently mirrored in national regulations, and cross-referenced in industry guidelines such as the BMP4. The guidelines are careful to note that the decision on whether or not to authorize the usage of private security companies is a decision left fully to each flag state, followed up with a particularly weak and indicative set of guidance targeting the flag state level (IMO—International Maritime Organization (2012b)). In contrast, the guidelines targeting private industries, i.e. ship owners, ship operators and shipmasters (IMO—International Maritime Organization (2012c)) and the private maritime security industry (IMO—International Maritime Organization (2012a)), are rich, detailed, and contains operational recommendations (Klinkenberg 2013). The distinction between the two sets of guidelines in terms of clarity testifies to the obstacles of delivering guidance to flag states with vastly different legal regimes but with an equal right to maritime operations in the very same space. IMO legislation is plagued by non-uniform implementation across the world (Grewal 2008, p. 30), triggered by flag states being well aware of the negative effects of ship owners 'flagging out' to countries of with more lenient regulatory frameworks, often referred to as Flags of Convenience (FOCs) (International Transport Federation (2015)). As documented by Van Hespen (2014), the most relevant FOCs, including the Marshall Islands, Liberia and Panama, do not have specific legislation in place regarding the usage of private security in their registered fleets, and largely leave the responsibility for authorization and use up to the individual ship owners, operators and masters. Furthermore, the IMO guidance targeting the shipping industry, i.e. the 'richest' set of guidelines, was essentially drafted by the shipping industry. Pristrom and Madsen share the assumption that the majority of the input to the MSC.1/Circ.1405 came from industry representatives (Pristrom and Madsen 2014; see also Pristrom et al. 2013). Together with the 77 other NGOs with consultative status at the IMO, the big shipping industry associations such as the ICS and BIMCO enjoy no voting power at the IMO. However, effectively they can support and assist the drafting of documents, and propose agenda points ahead of meetings (Pristrom and Madsen 2014; Cook 2014; Stawpert 2014; see IMO-MSC webpage). The already advanced industry-developed guidelines existing prior to the MSC meetings help explain the advanced outcome of the MSC.1/Circ.1405, where the industry was able draw upon accumulated experience from both formally and informally advising their own members and clients on the usage of maritime private security.

However, the set of guidelines issued by IMO carry no obligations, and cannot be considered regulatory beyond that of expressing an ideal of streamlined conduct. The IMO's official stance is that the decision on whether or not to make use of maritime private security is a matter that only flag states can decide upon; hence regulation is also considered to be a flag state responsibility. As country after country came to explicitly or implicitly authorize the usage of armed private security onboard their registered fleet in a domino-like fashion (see van Hespen 2014), a variety of national regulatory models were implemented. Flag state regulation, however, carries along severe loopholes as it allows for varying standards across jurisdictions, a problem elevated by the inherently global and mobile nature of both the shipping industry and the private security industry, which can both easily re-register in the country found to have the most favourable working conditions. Therefore, in the absence of 'hard' regulatory standards at the international level, and with poor prospects for future developments in this direction at the IMO (Pristrom et al. 2013; MSC briefing 2012), important industry self-regulatory initiatives have been developed to address the contracting of private security companies by shipping companies. Some of the initiatives refers to already existing documents and standards developed for the land-based private security industry, such as the Montreux Document and the International Code of Conduct. Maritime security specific initiatives include, most importantly, the standard Guardcon contract provided by BIMCO, and the development of an international company standard targeting the private maritime security industry through the International Organization for Standardization (ISO). ISO, the world's largest developer of voluntary international standards, was referred to by the IMO to develop an internationally recognized standard for the certification of private maritime security companies in 2012 (Pristrom et al. 2013). The ISO/ PAS 28007 standard which was presented in late 2012, requires private maritime security companies to demonstrate compliance with a range of requirements identified to enhance the standards of the company and to make it suitable for the task at hand (ISO—International Organization for Standardization (2013)). To obtain the standard, companies must adhere to strict contractor selection requirements, documentation procedures of incidents, and criteria regarding armament, to mention a few (Pittney and Levin 2013, p. 106). Compliance is ensured through independent certification bodies, and currently three companies are undertaking certification, having received accreditation by the UK Accreditation Service (UKAS) to do so. As of early 2015, 42 private maritime security companied had received ISO/PAS 28007 certification, approximately half of them based in Britain (SCEG—Security in Complex Environments Group (2015)).

The ISO/PAS 28007 standard was presented at the IMO in November 2012, and welcomed—but not officially endorsed. Individual countries argued against a collective endorsement, expressing concern for lowering the flexibility of flag states and highlighting the priority of nationally-anchored standards (MSC 2014 94/21). Hence, the ISO/ PAS 28007 serve as an example of some paradoxical characteristics of contemporary global security governance, both in procedure and outcome. The former refers to the initial referral to the ISO by the IMO MSC, in where an international public body referred the task of developing a standard recognized as key to more effective regulation to private body, thereby largely writing itself out of the process of drafting. The core drafting team behind the ISO standard involved actors from the shipping and the maritime security sectors, with BIMCO and ICS representing the former, and the British industry association Security in Complex Environments Group (SCEG) and SAMI representing the latter (Stawpert 2014; Cook 2014; Gibson 2014; see also Lloyd's Register LRQA 2014). In addition to the expressed wishes from the involved industry actors to improve the regulatory frames surrounding private maritime security, the standard also serves a clear and undisputable business imperative, namely to proactively confront the very realistic prospects of having a range of national certification requirements that would create hiccups for the global operations of the private maritime shipping and security industries. Regarding the outcome, concerns of international 'overrule' have so far prevented the ISO standard to live up to its potential as a global regulative mechanisms, as it would require streamlined national implementation. This, in turn, renders the regulation of the (maritime) market for force incomplete, unable to effectively respond to the global character of both the issue area and the involved stakeholders.

4.4 Who Governs Private Maritime Security?

The chain of actors involved in the governance arrangement surrounding armed private security stretches far beyond the traditional perception of security as bound to the public sphere, and signifies a fragmentation of the capacity to determine what and who is a threat, the 'price' of the threat, and how/when to eliminate the threat and through which means. A mixture of actors, predominantly from various industry sectors, raised the issue of armed private security on the political agenda, and were instrumental in the making of a global consensus surrounding the necessity of armed private maritime security, the implementation of international guidelines and regulatory initiatives. Interesting public/private dynamics can be observed in the relationship between the IMO, national governments and a range of industries, most notably the shipping industry, the insurance industry and the private security industry.

In the light of the above points, the role of the maritime shipping, insurance and security industry can hardly be overemphasized when assessing the consensus-creation, implementation of standards, guidelines and regulatory initiatives in the governance of private maritime security. Both the placing of private maritime security on the global agenda and the concrete drafting of guidelines and standards have been undertaken by a combination of private industry actors, involving not only ship owners' associations, but also the insurance industry and private security industry. This assessment makes it tempting to claim that maritime governance provides one of the few examples of the classical economist's 'perfect competition' model at work. New challenges—regardless of their nature—are solved within the existing business imperative, bearing in mind the cost-sensitivity of the shipping industry.

However, this picture overlooks a number of important features represented by public authorities in the governance of private maritime security. First and foremost, states—more specifically flag states—remain a key role, vested with the authority to choose whether or not to authorize private force. The rigor of such authorizations, understood as the degree of regulation and oversight accompanying them, is left at the discretion of the state. In some instances, such as in Germany, the state has carved out a tight space within which the German private security industry may operate, mandating that German-flagged ships have to employ private maritime security companies licensed by the German government (Siebels 2014). Furthermore, Germany has been one of the advocates for nationally-anchored standardizations schemes (MSC 2014, p. 94/21). In other countries, such as Denmark or Britain, the governments have carved out larger spaces for the maritime industry and the private security industry (Dutton 2013). In contrast to the German example, neither Denmark nor Britain ensures public oversight of the vetting process for guards and/ or companies (ibid). In FOCs such as Liberia, the space carved out for the shipping industry is virtually unrestricted with reference to the use of private security (ICS 2013; Maritime Security Advisory 3/ 2011).[2] In all these cases, private maritime security companies operate within, and not outside, the regulatory frameworks provided by the state, and are, in turn, considered to be legitimate and collaborating actors in the nationally anchored governance arrangement.

At the international level, it is possible to interpret the role of the IMO within the governance arrangement of maritime security along the lines of national public actors with reference to the IMO's convening capacities and legitimating powers. Regarding the former, not only does the IMO convene states, but, as argued by Hansen, the IMO has played a crucial role in assisting the maritime industry to

---

[2]For comprehensive overview of flag-state regulations, see the overview provided by the ICS (2013).

overcome large coordination problems, facilitating the development of the very first industry BMPs from 2008 an onwards (Hansen 2012, p. 565). This was further illustrated by the plethora of draft guidelines presented to the IMO in advance of its 89th MSC session in 2011. In the governance of private maritime security, the IMO was a key target for the shipping industry, the insurance industry and the private maritime security industry seeking to influence the drafting of guidelines within the organization (Stawpert 2014; Cook 2014; Gibson 2014; see MSC 2011 89/25, p. 80). For stakeholders without observer status at the IMO, such as SAMI, a different route to the inside was provided through a security-consultancy partnership with the Marshall Islands since February 2011. Using SAMI as an example, the associations' desire to pursue objectives through the IMO signals a clear ambition to influence the drafting of key-documents. However, it also testifies to a recognized need for synthesized guidelines among all stakeholders and the IMO's corresponding facilitating capacities, and, furthermore, a recognition of the legitimacy that the IMO carries (SAMI 2014; Cook 2014). In particular for an actor like SAMI, shunned by a range of stakeholders for only a few years ago (SAMI 2014), having formal ties to public actors not only provides access to policy-making processes but furthermore signal a good and respectable profile. A similar patter can be observed in the wording of the relationship between the between the ISO/PAS 28007 standard and the IMO as described at the web pages of the various private security companies that by now have received ISO accreditation, where the IMO association figure as close and important (i.e. 'The ISO was tasked by the IMO...'/ 'The ISO/PAS 28007 is backed by the IMO...'/ '...the IMO-backed ISO/ PAS 28007...'). Although the lack of consensus among member states on developing a mandatory instrument at the IMO was the main reason for the referral of the task to the ISO (Pristrom et al. 2013, p. 689), the ISO is nevertheless presented as the IMO's preferred choice regardless with no references to institutional obstacles. For the private maritime security industry, IMO association appears important due to its legitimating powers.

The intelligence accumulation and analysis that determines the need for armed private maritime security in the first place, the incentives to make use of private maritime security through cost/ risk insurance calculations, the actual drafting of standards and guidance, and the ensuring of quality standards in the private security sectors are, by and large, matters where private actors have left heavy fingerprints. However, this happened with the explicit or implicit authorization and encouragement by a range of public bodies, which gives rise to the understanding of the public actors involved in the governance of private maritime security as governance *facilitators*. To be a facilitator, in this context, signals a departure from the classic governance jargons 'rowing' and 'steering', as it does not necessarily imply a sense of control and direction. Rather, it signals an intended effort to assist in a process in which ones' competencies are instrumental for achieving a consensual goal. Or, to borrow a formulation by Jessop (2002) it signals a reordering of public actors' general function towards that of being responsible for 'organizing the self-organization of social forces'. The competencies in question, and as discussed above, refer most importantly to the convening capacities, regulatory infrastructures and legitimizing powers of public actors. Already in 1992 Hirst and Thompson, making references to changes experienced in national economic regulation, argued that whereas 'technical macro-economic management is less important, [. . .] the role government as a facilitator and orchestrator of private economic actors remains strong' (Hirst and Thompson 1992, p. 371; see also Aarstad 2016). As such, the referral to public actors as governance facilitators is not new. However, more than 20 years later, it is argued that the facilitating label also denotes the re-articulated role of public actors in the context of security based upon observations from the governance arrangement surrounding private maritime security.

How does the facilitator argument implicate the contested question of the relationship between public and private actors in the governance of security? To what extent do the increasingly important role of private actors and the corresponding facilitating role undertaken by public actors signal a strengthening of the former at the extent of latter? Arguably, the answer depends largely upon the normative importance attached to the state's role in security provision. If the role of the state is partly defined upon its provision of security, then 'the state is either the ultimate security actor, or an insufficient actor' (Mabee 2003, p. 147), and the role as facilitator appears as a straightforward weakening of the state's key role. However, the answer can be shaped by an equally normative view of public actors as occupying the central space in governance, where the increasing governance capacities of private actors is seen as a way to 'enhance the state's capacity to project influence and secure its objectives by mobilizing knowledge and power resources from influential non-governmental partners or stakeholders', as argued by Jessop (2002, p. 199). From this point of view, the increasing importance of private actors is not synonymous with public actors being diminished, but indicative of an increase in the relative weight of governance. In between these two positions lies the recognition that objections against armed private security are also based upon the concern that mechanisms in order to ensure the public, understood as non-discriminatory, enjoyment of security might become weakened as a consequence of the commercialization of security as a service. These objections are less normative, and are concerned with the practical dimension of changes in public/private roles and responsibilities. Furthermore, Jessop's optimistic account regarding the instrumental usage by public actors of private actors only take into account an active and 'mobilizing' reaction to the confrontation by 'influential non-governmental partners or stakeholders', thereby neglecting the theoretical possibility that knowledge and power resources can also be met in a far more passive and 'accepting' manner depending both on the issue area in question, and the positions held by public and private actors.

In the specific governance arrangement under the loop, it is difficult to persuasively argue that public actors became undermined as a consequence of the important presence of private actors in the very same arrangement. From the point of view of the IMO, the production of interim guidelines testifies to a trend towards a growing inclusion of a variety of stakeholders beyond that of states, which in itself has contributed to a better implementation of safety regulations due to 'the increasing accessibility of participatory mechanisms at the supranational level' (Barrows

2009, p. 198). From the point of view of national governments, key maritime nations have facilitated a private alternative to state-based security provision in a context where state-security provision had already been ruled out by the very same governments (e.g. Great Britain, Denmark, the United States, Norway). However, the question whether the relationship between public and private actors both at the international and national level are best characterized by public actors' active 'mobilization' of private governance capacities or, conversely, by public actors' passive 'acceptance' of private governance capacities is answered differently depending upon the actor in question. To be a governance facilitator, therefore, can both be conceptualized as a role of choice and a role by default, and, arguably most accurately, as a combination of both (see also Carrapico and Farrand, Chap. 9). This counter-intuitive point is underscored by Behr, who argues that the great 'paradox of globalization' is that states are required to react towards deterritorialised politics by overcoming their traditional principles off territorial politics and further develop deterritorialising politics (Behr 2008, p. 376). The paradox is best exemplified in the governance arrangement surrounding private maritime security in the way that the IMO, through its MSC, came to provide interim guidelines for the usage of private maritime security. Arguably, the interim guidelines institutionalized the global consensus on the necessity of private maritime security provision, despite the insistence by the IMO that it does not have an official position vis-à-vis armed private security and the many references to the issue as a flag-state responsibility.

The paradox of globalization poses two main challenges. First, Behr points to the structural challenge related to the practical task of organizing and monitoring such solutions as outlined above (Behr 2008, p. 376). How to preserve, for example, the rule of law and desired principles of democracy in global (security) governance arrangements? The second, and related, challenge is intellectual, referring to the epistemological problem of envisioning other forms of political organization than state-based, public actor-centred forms (Behr 2008, p. 377). This challenge is exaggerated, in turn, by the corresponding problem that existing tools for regulation such as national and international laws are both state-centric in scale and scope—made by states for states. In the governance arrangement surrounding private maritime security, both challenges can be exemplified with an eye to the capacity witnessed by the JWC to establish War Risk Zones with implications throughout the security chain, which essentially is taking place in the complete absence of a public platform for debate on the accuracy of such a highly political move. Here, the crucial issues to discuss is both of a structural nature, related to the accountability of the JWC for undertaking such a political function, and the corresponding intellectual issue related to the invisibility of the JWC due to perceptions of economic and political action as separate spheres of activities (Cutler 1999), and the remaining strong association of (political) power with the formal competencies of the state (Leander 2010; see also Bures, Chap. 2).

4.5 Conclusion

'Who governs' in maritime affairs? This chapter has argued that private actors from the shipping, industry and private security industries were instrumental in establishing the global consensus surrounding the appropriateness of armed private security, international guidelines providing frameworks of action for how to deal with armed private security provision, and soft law providing regulatory standards for private maritime security companies. However, these actors did not arise, nor operate, in a vacuum. The governance arrangement unfolded with the explicit or implicit authorization and encouragement by various public actors, which carved out privileged spheres for the maritime, insurance and private security industries. This in turn gives rise to the understanding of the public actors involved in the governance of armed private security as governance facilitators. To be a facilitator, in this context, signals a departure from the classic governance jargons 'rowing' and 'steering', as it does not necessarily imply a sense of control and direction. In particular the agenda-setting capacities by private actors testifies to a re-articulated role for public actors more centred around convening resources, implementing consensual decision through the existing regulatory infrastructure and casting a shield of legitimacy on the arrangement and the actors involved. The facilitation *by* public actors *of* private actors denotes a role undertaken by choice, i.e. as an active mobilization of private governance capacities, and by default, i.e. as a passive acceptance of private governing capacities.

The idea that activities at sea, such as armed private security provision, could be an extension of political dynamics at land is a largely unexplored matter by scholars of global politics. The recent surge in maritime security both as a policy doctrine and as a buzzword for the discipline (Bueger 2015) provides an intriguing possibility to investigate the extent to which theories and concepts employed in the study of global politics are waterproof in the face of maritime issues, actors and dynamics. The fluid maritime domain and the inherently global shipping industry, in turn accelerated by the confrontation from private security provision, make the surrounding governance arrangement appear as a paradigmatic case of global transformations in global governance in which de-nationalisation and actor pluralisation are key components. The relevance of approaching global shipping as a domain where global politics play out is pertinent in a time when politics not only grows out of our theoretical-intellectual categories, as argued by Behr (2008), but also because these territorial perceptions of power and politics themselves keep the globalizing impact and inherently transnational nature of maritime activities in the dark.

References

Aarstad, Å. K. (2016). Who governs Norwegian maritime security? Public facilitation of private security in a fragmented security environment. *Cooperation and Conflict*. doi:10.1177/0010836716652425.

Abrahamsen, R., & Williams, M. C. (2007). Security the city: Private security companies and non-state authority in global governance. *International Relations, 21*(2), 237–253.

Abrahamsen, R., & Williams, M. C. (2009). Security beyond the state: Global security assemblages in international politics. *International Political Sociology, 3*, 1–17.

Abrahamsen, R., & Williams, M. C. (2011). *Security beyond the state*. Cambridge: Cambridge University Press.

Aegis. (2015). *Services – aegis maritime*. Accessed December 01, 2014, from http://www.aegisworld.com/service/maritime/

Agnew, A. (1994). The territorial trap: The geographical assumptions of international relations theory. *Review of International Political Economy, 1*(1), 53–80.

Avant, D. D., Finnemore, M., & Sell, S. K. (2010). *Who governs the globe?* New York: Cambridge University Press.

Barrows, S. (2009). Racing to the Top. . .at Last: The regulation of safety in shipping. In W. Mattli & N. Woods (Eds.), *The politics of global regulation* (pp. 189–210). Princeton: Princeton University Press.

Behr, H. (2008). Deterritorialisation and the transformation of statehood: The paradox of globalisation. *Geopolitics, 13*(2), 359–382.

Berndtsson, J., & Stern, M. (2011). Private security and the public-private divide: Contested lines of distinction and modes of governance in the Stockholm-Arlanda security assemblage. *International Political Sociology, 5*, 408–425.

Berube, C., & Cullen, P. (Eds.). (2012). *Maritime private security. Market responses to piracy, terrorism, and waterborne security risks in the 21st century*. London: Routledge.

Best, J., & Gheciu, A. (Eds.). (2014). *The return of the public in global governance*. New York: Cambridge University Press.

Best Management Practice 3. (2010). *Best management practice 3. Piracy off the coast of Somali and Arabian Sea area. Version 3, June 2010*. Edinburgh: Witherby Seamanship International Ltd..

Best Management Practice 4. (2011). *Best management practices for protection against Somali based piracy. Version 4, August 2011*. Edinburgh: Witherby Seamanship International Ltd..

Bieling, H.-J.. (2007). On the other side of the coin: Conceptualizing the relationship between business and the state in the age of globalisation. *Business and Politics, 9*(3), article 5.

Brown, J. (2012, September). *Pirates and privateers: Managing the Indian oceans private security Boom*. Lowy Institute for International Policy. Accessed October 5, 2014, from http://www.lowyinstitute.org/files/brown_pirates_and_privateers_web.pdf

Bueger, C. (2015). What is maritime security? *Marine Policy, 53*, 159–164.

Carmola, C. (2010). *Private military companies and new wars: Risk, law & ethnics*. London: Routledge.

Colás, A., & Mabee, B. (2010). The flow and ebb of private seaborn violence in global politics: Lessons from the Atlantic World, 1689–1815. In A. Colás & B. Mabee (Eds.), *Mercenaries, pirates, bandits and empires: Private violence in historical context* (pp. 83–106). New York: Columbia University Press.

Cook, P. (2014). SAMI - The security association for maritime industries. *Interview, 2*(09), 14.

Cowen, D. (2014). *The deadly life of logistics*. Minneapolis: University of Minnesota Press.

Cullen, P. (2012). Surveying the market in maritime private security services. In C. Berube & P. Cullen (Eds.), *Maritime private security. Market responses to piracy, terrorism, and waterborne security risks in the 21st century* (pp. 25–37). London: Routledge.

Cutler, C. A. (1997). Artifice, ideology, and paradox: The public/private distinction in international trade law. *Review of International Political Economy, 4*(2), 261–285.
Cutler, C. A. (1999). Private authority in international trade relations: The case of maritime transport. In C. A. Cutler, V. Haufler, & T. Porter (Eds.), *Private authority and international affairs* (pp. 283–332). Albany: State University of New York Press.
Cutler, C. A. (2003). *Private power and global authority*. Cambridge: Cambridge University Press.
Dupont, B. (2004). Security in the age of networks. *Policing & Society, 14*(1), 76–91.
Dutton, Y. (2013). Gunslingers on the high seas: A call for regulation. *Duke Journal of Comparative & International Law, 24*(1), 107–160.
Florquin, N. (2012). Escalation at sea: Somali piracy and private security companies. In Small Arms Survey (Ed.), *Small arms survey 2012: Moving targets* (pp. 190–217). Cambridge: Cambridge University Press.
Gibson, P. (2014). SCEG - The security in complex environments group. *Interview, 1*(09), 14.
Green, J. F. (2014). *Rethinking private authority: Agents and entrepreneurs in global governance*. Princeton: Princeton University Press.
Grewal, T. (2008). International ship safety regulations. In W. Talley (Ed.), *Maritime safety, security and piracy*. London: Informa Law.
Guzzini, S., & Neumann, I. (Eds.). (2012). *The diffusion of power in global governance*. Basingstoke: Palgrave Macmillan.
Hall, R. B., & Biersteker, T. J. (Eds.). (2002). *The emergence of private authority in global governance*. Cambridge: Cambridge University Press.
Hansen, S. J. (2012). The evolution of best management practices in the civil maritime sector. *Studies in Conflict & Terrorism, 35*(7–8), 562–569.
Hirst, O., & Thompson, G. (1992). The problem of "globalization": International economic relations, national conomic management and the formation of trading locks. *Economy and Society, 21*, 357–396.
Hönke, J. (2013). *Transnational companies and security governance: Hybrid practices in a postcolonial world*. London and New York: Routledge.
ICS—International Chamber of Shipping. (2013). *Comparison of flag state laws on armed guards and arms on board*. Accessed January 10, 2015, from http://www.ics-shipping.org/docs/default-source/Piracy-Docs/comparison-of-flag-state-laws-on-armed-guards-and-arms-on-board3F9814DED68F.pdf?sfvrsn=0
IMB—International Maritime Bureau. (2007). *Piracy and armed robbery against ships, report for the period 1 January–31 December 2006*. London: ICC International Maritime Bureau. Accessed October 31, 2014, from https://www.icc-ccs.org/piracy-reporting-centre/request-piracy-report
IMB—International Maritime Bureau. (2012). *Piracy and armed robbery against ships, report for the period 1 January–31 December 2011*. London: ICC International Maritime Bureau. Accessed October 31, 2014, from https://www.icc-ccs.org/piracy-reporting-centre/request-piracy-report
IMO—International Maritime Organization. (2011). *Interim recommendations for port and coastal states regarding the use of privately contracted armed security personnel on board ships in the high risk area*. IMO Doc.MSC.1/Circ.1408. London: IMO.
IMO—International Maritime Organization. (2012a). *Interim guidance to private maritime security companies providing privately contracted armed security personnel on board ships in the high risk area*. IMO Doc.MSC.1/Circ.1443. London: IMO.
IMO—International Maritime Organization. (2012b). *Revised interim guidance for flag states regarding the use of privately contracted armed security personnel on board ships in the high risk area*. IMO Doc.MSC.1/Circ.1406/Rev.2. London: IMO.
IMO—International Maritime Organization. (2012c). *Revised interim guidance to ship owners, ship operators and ship masters on the use of privately contracted armed security personnel on board ships in the high risk area*. IMO Doc. MSC.1/Circ.1405/Rev2. London: IMO.

IMO—International Maritime Organization. (2015). *Private armed security*. Accessed December 30, 2015, from http://www.imo.org/en/OurWork/Security/PiracyArmedRobbery/Pages/Private-Armed-Security.aspx
International Transport Federation. (2015). Defining FOCs and the problems they pose. Accessed January 3, 2015, from http://www.itfseafarers.org/defining-focs.cfm
ISO—International Organization for Standardization. (2013). *Ships and marine technology – Guidelines for private maritime security companies (PMSC) providing privately contracted armed security personnel (PCASP) onboard ships (and pro forma contract)*, ISO/PAS 28007. Geneva: ISO.
Jessop, B. (2002). Globalization and the national state. In S. Aaronowitz & P. Bratsis (Eds.), *Paradigm lost: State theory reconsidered* (pp. 185–220). Minneapolis: University of Minnesota Press.
JWC—Joint War Committee. (2010, December 16). *Increased range of Somali-based piracy*. JW2010/009. Accessed January 3, 2015, from http://www.lmalloyds.com/LMA/CMDownload.aspx?ContentKey=2e87ba17-4c5f-4318-aaa2-9b0011b7e86c&ContentItemKey=a80d3f67-9693-4d7b-9247-3eedfa741d46
Klinkenberg, I. K. (2013). *Pirates versus private security companies – A road to safety or insecurity at sea*. Unpublished MA dissertation. Department of Nograric, Norwegian University of Life Sciences.
Kraska, J. (2013). International and comparative regulation of private maritime security companies employed in counter-piracy. In D. Guildfoyle (Ed.), *Modern piracy: Legal challenges and responses* (pp. 19–249). Cheltenham: Edward Elgar Publishing Limited.
Leander, A. (2010). Practices (Re)producing orders: Understanding the role of business in global security governance. In M. Ougaard (Ed.), *Business and global governance* (pp. 57–78). Abingdon: Routledge.
Leira, H., & de Carvalho, B. (2010). Privateers of the North Sea: At worlds end. In A. Colás & B. Mabee (Eds.), *Mercenaries, pirates, bandits and empires: Private violence in historical context* (pp. 55–82). New York: Columbia University Press.
Liss, C. (2009). Privatization of maritime security in Southeast Asia. In T. Jäger & G. Kümmel (Eds.), *Private military and security companies: Chances, problems, pitfalls and prospects*. Wiesbaden: Springer.
Lloyd's Register LRQA. (2014). *Your guide to implementing ISO/PAS 28007*. Coventry: Lloyd's Register Quality Assurance Limited.
Loader, I., & Walker, N. (2007). *Civilizing security*. Cambridge: Cambridge University Press.
Lobo-Guerrero, L. (2008). "Pirates," stewards, and the securitization of global circulation. *International Political Sociology, 2*(3), 219–235.
Mabee, B. (2003). Security studies and the 'Security State': Security provision in historical context. *International Relations, 17*(2), 135–151.
Miller, J. (2009). Piracy causes changes in routes, insurance. *The Wall Street Journal, 9* April.
MSC—Maritime Safety Committee. (2011). *Report of the maritime safety committee on its eighty-ninth session*. MSC 89/25, 27.05.11. London: IMO.
MSC—Maritime Safety Committee. (2012). *Guidance for private maritime security companies agreed by IMO's Maritime Safety Committee*. Briefing: 17, 25.05.12. Accessed January 20, 2015, from http://www.imo.org/MediaCentre/PressBriefings/Pages/17-msc-90-piracy.aspx#.VMv8EC4YG5I
MSC—Maritime Safety Committee. (2014, November 26). *Report of the maritime safety committee on its ninety-fourth session*. MSC 94/21. London: IMO.
Murphy, M. (2009). *Small boats, weak states, dirty money: Piracy and maritime terrorism in the modern world*. London: Hurst and Company.
Oliveira, G. C. (2013). 'New Wars' at sea: A critical transformative approach to the political economy of Somali piracy. *Security Dialogue, 44*(1), 3–18.
Owens, P. (2008). Distinctions, distinctions: 'Public' and 'private' force. *International Affairs, 84* (2), 977–990.
Petrig, A. (2014). *Human rights and law enforcement at sea: Arrest, detention and transfer of piracy suspects*. Leiden: Koninklijke Brill.

Pfeifer, S. (2009, April 21). Aegis sets sights on foiling pirates off Somali coast. *Financial Times.*
Pittney, J. J., Jr., & Levin, J. C. (2013). *Private anti-piracy navies: How warships for hire are changing maritime security*. Lanham: Lexington Books.
Pristrom, S., Li, K. X., Yang, Z., & Wang, J. (2013). A study of maritime security and piracy. *Maritime Policy & Management, 40*(7), 675–693.
Pristrom, S. & Madsen, H. (2014, September 1) IMO – The international maritime organization. *Interview.*
Ritchie, R. C. (1997). Government measures against piracy and privateering in the Atlantic area, 1750–1850. In D. J. Starkey, E. S. van Eyck van Heslinga, & J. A. de Moor (Eds.), *Pirates and privateers: New perspectives on the war on trade in the eighteenth and nineteenth centuries.* Exeter: University of Exeter Press.
Roundtable of International Shipping Associations. (2011). *Letter for secretary-general Ban Ki-Moon.* Accessed November 28, 2014, from https://www.bimco.org/~/media/About/Press/2011/Letter_to_Ban_Ki-Moon_-_Piracy.ashx
Safety4Sea. (2011). *Industry guidelines regarding the use of private maritime security contractors,* May 20, 2011. Accessed April 20, 2015, from http://www.safety4sea.com/industry-guidelines-regarding-the-use-of-private-maritime-security-contractors--4073
Salter, M. (Ed.). (2009). *Politics at the airport.* Minneapolis: University of Minnesota Press.
SAMI—Security Association for the Maritime Industries. (2014). *The evolution of the security association for the maritime industry (SAMI) and piracy in the Indian Ocean.* Lessons from Piracy. Accessed September 10, 2014, from http://www.lessonsfrompiracy.net/files/2014/06/DRAFT-The-Evolution-of-the-Security-Association-for-the-Maritime-Industry-8-May-14.pdf
Sassen, S. (2003). Globalization or denationalization. *Review of International Political Economy, 10*(1), 1–22.
Sassen, S. (2006). *Territory, authority, rights: From medieval to global assemblages.* Princeton: Princeton University Press.
SCEG—Security in Complex Environments Group. (2015). *Accredited certification for PSC1/ISO 18788 and ISO 28007.* Accessed August 5, 2014, from https://www.adsgroup.org.uk/pages/95837038.asp
Schouten, P. (2014). Security as controversy: Reassembling security at Amsterdam airport. *Security Dialogue, 45*(1), 23–42.
Siebels, D. (2014). International standards for the private security industry. *The RUSI Journal, 159*(5), 76–83.
Stawpert, J. (2014, October 02). ICS – The international chamber of shipping. *Interview.*
Steinberg, P. (2001). *The social construction of the ocean.* Cambridge: Cambridge University Press.
Steinberg, P. (2009). Sovereignty, territory, and the mapping of mobility: A view from the outside. *Annals of the Association of American Geographers, 99*(3), 467–495.
Struett, M., Carlson, J. D., & Nance, M. (Eds.). (2013). *Maritime piracy and the construction of global governance*. New York and London: Routledge.
Thompson, J. (1994). *Mercenaries pirates and sovereigns.* Princeton: Princeton University Press.
Van Hespen, I. (2014). Protecting merchant ships from maritime piracy by privately contracted armed security personnel: A comparative analysis of flag stat legislation and port and coastal state requirements. *Journal of Maritime Law & Commerce, 45*(3), 361–400.
Walker, R. B. J. (1993). *Inside/Outside: International relations as political theory.* Cambridge: Cambridge University Press.
Williams, M. C. (2010). The public, the private and the evolution of security studies. *Security Dialogue, 41*(6), 1–8.
Wood, J., & Shearing, C. D. (2006). *Imagining security.* Devon: Willan Publishing.

Chapter 5
Privatising Security in Finance: Measures Against the Money Threatening Society

William Vlcek

5.1 Introduction

Financial firms (and a variety of non-financial economic actors) have been responsible for surveillance against money laundering and (since 2001) terrorist finance for over two decades.[1] This responsibility has effectively privatised aspects of national and international security from state governments to economic actors, arguably because they are closest to the economic activity that may be suspected of criminality. As explained in one of the earliest reports of the Financial Action Task Force (FATF), financial firms are responsible for the initial identification of a suspicious financial transaction and reporting it to law enforcement (FATF 1990a).[2] J.C. Sharman has observed that 'AML [anti-money laundering] policy is exceptional in the degree' to which it has been delegated to private actors (Sharman 2011). Additionally, since the 2008 financial crisis there has been increased activity against financial institutions over their failure to maintain anti-money laundering (AML) compliance procedures and to enforce US-specific economic sanctions against Iran and Sudan, among others. The extent of the fines applied over the

[1]My thanks for the feedback shared with me by the editors and other participants in the 2015 BISA Innovation Workshop, 'Private Security beyond Private Military and Security Companies: Practices and Governance', along with my St Andrews colleagues Javier Argomaniz and Faye Donnelly. All errors remain my responsibility.

[2]The FATF was created to identify the methods used in money laundering in order to create mechanisms to counter the money laundering associated with illegal drugs trafficking. The story of its origins and the evolution of an international regulatory regime against first money laundering and later terrorist financing is well rehearsed (Gilmore 2004; Sharman 2011; Jakobi 2013). The elements of that story relevant for the following analysis will emerge in the next section.

W. Vlcek (✉)
School of International Relations, University of St Andrews, Arts Faculty Building, The Scores, St Andrews, Fife KY16 9AX, Scotland, UK
e-mail: wbv2@st-andrews.ac.uk

O. Bures, H. Carrapico (eds.), *Security Privatization*,
DOI 10.1007/978-3-319-63010-6_5

past several years may not yet have reached a size comparable to the imputed profits of these firms from the illicit activities they are accused of performing over previous years (see the chart in Barrett et al. 2014b). Nonetheless, the fines served to reduce corporate profitability in the present moment, agreements made with regulators involve additional on-going costs for increased compliance staff and third-party auditors, along with potential damage to corporate image (Rothfeld et al. 2010). As a natural consequence from updated internal cost/benefit analyses, these firms are increasingly concluding that the profit to be gained from operations in some business sectors may not be sufficient to offset the increased cost arising from the risks identified in those sectors. In turn the result is the decision by the firm to reduce risk by reducing business in them.

At the centre of this analysis are the unintended consequences (side-effects) from US financial sanctions and its punishment of foreign multinational financial firms. The actions of the US represent one aspect in a financial governance regime created to suppress the money laundering associated with illegal drugs trafficking (Jakobi 2013). Central to the evolution of this global governance regime has been the role of the US dollar as global reserve currency and the application of 'dollar hegemony' by the US government to achieve global enforcement of its national economic sanctions regime (Norrlof 2014).[3] When speaking of dollar hegemony here, the concern is not with its sources, origins, or continued longevity (see, e.g. Prasad 2014; Cohen 2015). It is simply accepted as given, because the concern is rather with the coercive application of dollar hegemony by the United States' regulatory agencies and the consequences for both intended and unintended victims (Matthews 2015). Combined with the transfer of responsibility for financial surveillance against money laundering and terrorist finance to private sector financial actors, one unintended consequence has been the practice of 'derisking' (Financial Conduct Authority 2016; FATF 2014a). This term is used to identify the rational actor response of financial firms to reduce their exposure to clients, customers, firms, and consumers that may pose a risk for involvement in suspicious (illicit or illegal) transactions. These sources for risk are at the same time sources for potential disciplinary action by the state's regulatory agencies, particularly those regulating the US financial market. It is one motivation for a financial firm's desire to reduce its exposure to sources of risk, and any potential future regulatory action that might be taken against them. Other motivations include concerns over profitability, impact to the firm's reputation, and corporate retrenching after the 2008 financial crisis.

The following exploration of these circumstances is situated in an understanding of structural power in global finance following Susan Strange (1994). The application here of the concept of structural power in global finance provides a framework in which to appreciate the role and influence of the US financial system and the US

[3]It is further interesting to note that a Google Scholar search with the term 'dollar hegemony' results in a large number of Chinese academic publications on the topic. Unfortunately they are beyond the language skills of the author.

dollar as an international reserve currency on the decision-making processes of non-US financial firms. The next section outlines the contours of structural power and some of the mechanisms deployed to operate it. Two case studies are provided in the third section to demonstrate the impact of this structural power as experienced by financial firms performing cross-border monetary transfers. In turn the response of regulatory bodies to this derisking activity is outlined. The final section explores some of the implications of derisking from the privatisation of financial surveillance before concluding the chapter.

5.2 Privatising Financial Surveillance

The first point to understand about the privatisation of security in the financial domain is that it is not simply the transfer of responsibility from the state to private actors. More importantly, it is because the private actors involved did not willingly take up the responsibility to perform the security function delegated to them by the state (White 2014; Eckert 2008; Shaughnessy 2002). The US banking community, for example, lobbied against attempts to increase its tasks and responsibility for anti-money laundering surveillance in the late 1990s, arguing that the costs far outweighed any benefits (Eckert 2008). Consequently, the privatisation of financial security is not privatisation as seen with other examples like privatising state assets or industries, e.g. gas, electricity, water or railroads (Megginson 2005). In the latter cases, the private actors expected to receive compensation from their investment generating income and profits from the private provision of formerly public goods and services. Rather, in this case of privatised security, the financial and designated non-financial firms involved had been identified by the FATF and were forced to undertake the activity, at their own expense.[4] Moreover, these firms must absorb all costs associated with heightened regulatory compliance and the provision of surveillance in support of the security obligations of the state. The cost for achieving compliance is not minor and now accounts for 10 percent of the staff employed by large multinational banks (Ensign and Colchester 2015; Bussey 2007; KPMG International 2014; Halliday et al. 2014; Millman and Rubenfeld 2014). Financial institutions have become in the language of some authors, 'reluctant partners' in the efforts of the state to expose and prosecute money laundering (Favarel-Garrigues et al. 2011).

A second point to understand about the privatisation of financial security is the nature of the power resting behind this 'soft law' form of global governance (Jakobi 2013). It may be encapsulated through a recognition that 'the unilateral activities of the United States were subsequently internationalized in the FATF' (Jakobi 2013). In other words, the power and influence exercised by international organisations to

[4]See the list of 'designated non-financial businesses and professions' and the list identifying 'financial institutions' in the glossary of (FATF 2012).

privatise financial surveillance followed the lead of the US, which had already privatised financial surveillance domestically with the Bank Secrecy Act in 1970 (Adams 2000). But given the transient nature of capital, particularly following the end of capital controls in most national economies, the US recognised the need to internationalise the process. Or, in the terminology of Rainer Hülsse, to 'problematise' money laundering as an issue of global concern and one that required a global solution (Hülsse 2007). Yet in Hülsse's analysis the process was one of persuasion in which the US first persuaded other states that money laundering did, in fact, exist as a global problem requiring internationally coordinated action to tackle it. And having done so, the persuasion involved convincing these same states of the need to construct an international organisation to craft the means and mechanisms to determine the modalities of money laundering. After determining those modalities, the FATF turned to the production of guidelines, or Recommendations as they are known, for national legislation to criminalise money laundering as an illicit economic activity (Hülsse 2007; see also FATF 2012).

Absent from this 'radical constructivist' account for the origins of the FATF and the international criminalisation of money laundering is the role of power, in the creation of the FATF as much as in the production of money laundering as a global problem.[5] It is that power, exercised through the sinews of the global financial system and enforced by agencies of government at multiple levels in the United States, that undergirds the operation of global AML activity. In the twenty-first century, the FATF has evolved to occupy the centre of a network of FATF-style regional bodies which replicate its functions and practices at the regional level (Lewis 2016). In 2001 the scope of the FATF's responsibilities was expanded to include terrorist financing, further elevating its role in global financial governance. Its position as a global authority on the measures to implement against money laundering and terrorist financing was established with UN Security Council Resolution 1617, which directed UN member states to implement the FATF's Forty Recommendations (United Nations Security Council 2005; FATF 2012). Yet without the extraterritorial enforcement action performed by the US, it may be assumed that non-US financial firms would circumvent local AML legislation as demonstrated by the charges made against non-US firms in recent years for past AML and economic sanctions circumvention activity *outside of US territory* (Barrett et al. 2014b). The next subsection interrogates the nature of US financial power to first problematise money laundering (and since 2001 terrorist financing), while the second subsection identifies the mechanisms in operation to enforce the international rules on money laundering and terrorist finance.

[5]Rainer Hülsse does, however, briefly refer to the power deployed by the FATF itself when identifying non-compliant jurisdictions (Hülsse 2007).

5.2.1 The Nature of Financial Power

In *States and Markets* Susan Strange described a model for power in the world economy consisting of four interacting structures: finance, production, security, and knowledge (Strange 1994). By exercising power through these structures a state exercised power in and through the world economy. With regards to criminal finance, two structures of power are in operation, first the knowledge structure to produce the problem of criminal finance and then second the finance structure to enforce the remedies devised to counter and control criminal finance. The operation of the knowledge structure was described above as the problematisation of money laundering. The operation of the finance structure to enforce the anti-money laundering and counter terrorist finance remedies operates in great part through the hegemonic status of the US dollar and the US financial market in global finance. For each of these four structures, the structural power itself resides with those possessing the position and/or means 'to exercise control' which Strange located for the finance structure in the means to control 'the supply and distribution of credit' (Strange 1994). The elucidation of the finance power structure in the privatisation of security for the financial domain reproduces one of the conclusions offered by Strange. It is the conclusion that, contrary to the arguments current at the time that the US had lost hegemonic power in the world economy (and reflected in the late and unlamented hegemonic stability theory then popular in American international political economy), the structural power analysis she offered demonstrated the continued presence and operation of US hegemonic power. In this instance, that power resides in the US financial system and capital markets as much as with the US dollar as world currency (Strange 1987, 1994; see further, Norrlof 2014; Cohen 2015; Germain 2016).

The finance structure of power in the world economy is described in depth in Chap. 5 of *States and Markets*. The succinct definition provided for the financial structure is 'the sum of all the arrangements governing the availability of credit plus all the factors determining the terms on which currencies are exchanged for one another.' (Strange 1994) For the context of dollar hegemony today and its utilisation to maintain a system of privatised financial surveillance it is the weight of the deep and liquid financial market of the US in combination with the position of the US dollar as world currency which positions them at the centre of the financial structure of the world economy. For Carla Norloff, this situation was demonstrated in Fig. 1 of her article with its graphical presentation for the distribution of monetary capabilities of other states vis à vis the US (Norrlof 2014). To some extent the literature on global financial governance is indifferent to this situation, accepting the assumption of benevolence on the part of the US with regards to the dollar as world currency (e.g., Norrlof 2014). Which is not to say that any embedded belief that the US represents a benign hegemon is not challenged. In part that assumption of US benevolence was one factor motivating Susan Strange in her work investigating the operation and conduct of international currency markets (Strange 1994).

Jonathan Kirshner summarised Strange's conceptualisation of structural power with a Woody Allen reference—that 90% of the structural power of a hegemonic state is simply 'showing up' (Kirshner 2009). In other words, the material capacity of the hegemon without explicit coercion or deployment of that material power suffices to produce most of the structural power described by Strange. For the finance dimension of structural power, Kirshner agreed that the primacy of the dollar is the context in which any discussion of international monetary relations would occur. And he acknowledged that 'structural power can also be quite purposeful', but purposeful through shaping the agenda rather than through coercive practices (Kirshner 2009). The privatisation of financial surveillance, however, operates in that 10% space, and beyond simply shaping the agenda (at the FATF) it involves the coercive enforcement of the agenda. Hence, similar terms present in the literature analysing international monetary relations and the role of the US dollar in the world economy, such as 'exorbitant privilege', are not employed here because it is the deployment of coercion to maintain and enforce the privatised mechanisms of financial surveillance in 'purposeful' operation that is central. At one extreme the coercion may be so frank as to be little less than a declaration of 'our way or the highway' as reflected in demands from the New York Department of Financial Services for bank staff to be punished by the firm with their firing (Barrett et al. 2014a).[6]

This discussion of structural power in the world economy, focused through the medium of US financial power in the global economy and global financial governance, is a factor in the presentation below because it influences the cost/benefit analysis conducted by the financial firm. The deployment of structural power as a tool by the US government, and 'a weapon in the war on terrorism', represents a significant potential cost element for the financial firm (Taylor 2007; see also Zarate 2013). The nature of that cost and its influence on corporate decision-making processes will be demonstrated in the next sub-section.

5.2.2 Mechanisms of Enforcement

The experience of BNP Paribas in 2014 offers a clear example for the coercive structural power of finance in operation. Accused by a collection of US regulatory bodies and law enforcement agencies with circumventing US sanctions imposed on Cuba, Iran, and Sudan between 2002 and 2012, the firm agreed to a fine of US$8.97 billion, to enter a guilty plea to one charge of violating the US's International Emergency Economic Powers Act, and to accept a 2 year ban on transactions to

[6]Another example was the statement of Lanny Breuer, as head of the criminal division of the US Justice Department in 2012 in the context of money laundering activity at HSBC's Mexican subsidiary, 'Our goal here is not to bring HSBC down' but 'the "sword of Damocles" hung above the bank if it did not follow through on its commitments.' (Braithwaite 2012)

clear US dollars on behalf of its clients (Barrett et al. 2014b). This French multinational financial firm was simply the most prominent, because of the size of its fine, among a number of multinational financial firms to accept a deferred prosecution agreement accompanied by a large fine. Other firms included Barclays, Credit Suisse, HSBC, Standard Chartered and UBS, and several investigations were reopened in subsequent years for similar or related accusations of financial malfeasance (Scannell and Arnold 2014; Protess and Silver-Greenberg 2014). The appearance of a focus by US regulatory agencies on foreign multinational financial firms, suggested by this roster of investigated banks, was criticised strongly by French government ministers with the Governor of the Bank of France observing that BNP Paribas had not violated either French or European laws (Stothard 2014; Horobin and Gauthier-Villars 2014; see also Scannell and Braithwaite 2012 for the case of Standard Chartered in 2012). Moreover, the agreement to pay a fine to US government agencies and enter a deferred prosecution agreement is not the end for the case. The deferred prosecution agreement will include provisions outlining the corrective measures the firm is expected to take, along with the presence of an independent monitor embedded in the firm to evaluate compliance. In 2012, HSBC paid a US$1.9 billion fine and accepted a deferred prosecution agreement related to charges that it had failed to identify more than $881 million in illegal drugs money laundered through its offices along with charges it had facilitated the evasion of US financial sanctions on Iran, Libya, and Sudan. Subsequent media reports highlighted the deficiencies found by the monitor, including the slow pace of change in 'corporate culture' to reform its AML practices (Ehreriene and Patrick 2016; Ensign and Viswanatha 2015).

These apparently aggressive extraterritorial efforts by US regulators to punish multinational financial firms for failing to maintain adequate measures against money laundering and US economic sanctions must be understood within a historical context. The FATF was established in 1989 to investigate and determine the modalities of money laundering related to illegal drugs trafficking. After completing that task, it produced the first version of its Forty Recommendations on money laundering in 1990 (FATF 1990b). Initially the Forty Recommendations were implemented by just the member states of the organisation. After several years, the FATF member states identified topics that required further explanation in order to effectively implement the Recommendations, leading to the production of Interpretive Notes. This initial implementation experience also revealed gaps in coverage that were addressed by a revision released in 1996, including the introduction of the concept of a predicate crime to money laundering (Recommendation 4) and extending the coverage of the Recommendations beyond simply banks to include 'financial activities undertaken by businesses or professions which are not financial institutions' (FATF n.d.). In addition to evaluating the progress and extent of implementation of the Forty Recommendations among member states (through a process of mutual evaluation) the organisation sponsored a series of 'typologies' studies. The reports produced by these studies identified additional methods used to accomplish money laundering as illegal actors sought to evade the AML measures initially implemented by financial firms and related businesses (see e.g. FATF 2006b, 2009).

A greater challenge for the FATF was identified in 1999, when it was discovered in the New York City financial sector that money laundering had not only shifted to different methodologies, but it also had relocated to non-FATF member jurisdictions (Minority Staff of the Permanent Subcommittee on Investigations 2001; General Accounting Office 2000). The response of the FATF was to produce a 'blacklist' comprised of non-member jurisdictions, and the member states of the FATF were to follow the guidance contained in Recommendation 21. It meant that the jurisdictions identified in this list of 'non-cooperative countries and territories' (NCCT) were to be subjected to increased scrutiny by the member states' financial sectors (FATF 2000). Essentially all cross-border economic transactions with one of the listed jurisdictions were to be treated as 'potentially criminal' until such time when the FATF would determine that the jurisdiction had sufficiently modified its legislation and enforcement practices to be considered 'cooperative'. The process lasted for several years with the final jurisdiction delisted by the FATF in 2006, ending the NCCT process (FATF 2006a).[7]

The NCCT process at the FATF ended in part because it was politically contentious, using the financial power of its member states to impose the rules of the club (FATF) on jurisdictions that were not members of that club (Sharman 2009; see also Tsingou 2015). The initial solution to the concern over global compliance with the Forty Recommendations involved convincing the International Monetary Fund (IMF) to include them as a component in the IMF suite of financial surveillance evaluations. This change was achieved through lobbying pressure from some IMF members to increase the organisation's efforts against money laundering combined with an IMF-internal perception that it would provide a more balanced and objective assessment than that produced by the NCCT process. Significantly for the states evaluated by this process the IMF does not undertake punitive actions when a jurisdiction is assessed as non-compliant (Gordon 2010). In turn the lack of an enforcement mechanism at the IMF meant the FATF was only able to continue for a short period of time without resuming its practice of publicly identifying jurisdictions that in its assessment were deficient in anti-money laundering enforcement. The initial jurisdiction of concern was Iran in 2007 and the FATF publicly advised member states that they should ensure their financial institutions conducted 'enhanced due diligence' on any transaction with Iran (FATF 2007a). Updating its list of jurisdictions is now a regular feature of the FATF's semi-annual plenary meeting; in October 2016, for example, Iran and North Korea were listed as subject to 'counter-measures to protect the international financial system' from AML and terrorist financing risks while Afghanistan, Bosnia and Herzegovina, Iraq, Laos, Syria, Uganda, Vanuatu, and Yemen were identified as having 'strategic AML/CFT deficiencies' which they have committed to resolve under the continued monitoring of the FATF (FATF 2016b).

[7]The experience of the Philippines with the NCCT is discussed in (Vlcek 2012).

Notwithstanding the appearance for collective action success provided by the FATF against money laundering and terrorist finance, even in these multilateral forums the structural power of the US remains present and functioning. As a leading member of the FATF, the role performed by the US dollar as world currency, global reserve currency, and the location of US capital markets as a source for investment capital, all give weight and credibility to the actions and sanctions desired by the US. In turn that role encourages cooperation with these desires behind the closed doors of the FATF plenary meetings, beyond simply influencing the shape and contents of the organisation's agenda. The impact of the finance structure of power exercised by the US, and the unilateral actions of its regulatory agencies, encourages private financial actors to respond by acting to avoid risky customers when confronted with US structural power in global finance.

5.3 Mitigating the Risky Customer

In response to the evolving requirements of AML legislation over the past several decades financial institutions hired compliance staff, provided AML training to all staff and underwent third-party compliance audits to verify implementation. Administering AML compliance was part of the cost of doing business, though apparently it did not always have high visibility among a firm's senior management, given that the objective for a multinational financial firm is to generate a profit for its shareholders. In 2004 the authors of KPMG's now annual *Global Anti-Money Laundering Survey* observed that 'unprecedented activity by governments, regulators, and supra-national bodies in the AML sphere' over the preceding 5 years meant that 'AML has become a key issue for senior management' (KPMG International 2004). Nonetheless, the level of attention paid to this 'key issue' by the multinational financial firm's senior management increased significantly in the face of the acts by US regulatory officials against large foreign multinational banks. As noted in the foreword to KPMG's 2014 survey report, 'AML has never been higher on senior management's agenda, with regulatory fines now running into billions of dollars, regulatory action becoming genuinely license threatening, and threats of criminal prosecution against banks and individuals.' (KPMG International 2014)

The process to identify named individuals and groups or to prevent transactions with a specific territory had become increasingly complex as these lists grew in size (Amicelle and Jacobsen 2016). It involves verification checks on transactions and customer identification details against these lists through the use of database software (Favarel-Garrigues et al. 2011; Liss and Sharman 2015). Increasingly a commercially available software system is used and thus financial firms are relying on additional private actors to maintain the currency of their verification systems. It is a situation that led Liss and Sharman to observe that a private actor 'sets the specific content of AML policy for many of the world's most important private financial institutions.' (Liss and Sharman 2015) These verification procedures succeed only when there is data accompanying the financial transaction to identify who is sending it and who is receiving it. The charges made against BNP Paribas and others over the past decade have included wilful negligence and 'data stripping' to conceal and remove the identity of customers named on a sanctions list (Horobin and Gauthier-Villars 2014; Rothfeld et al. 2010). Confronted by a situation in which foreign actors (state as well as private) are failing to support the economic sanctions component of its foreign policy, the US has claimed extraterritorial jurisdiction and taken unilateral action (Hong 2015). As a result of the heightened US regulatory attention financial firms in turn have engaged in risk mitigation activities that have become known as 'derisking'. It is a process to identify and close the account held by any individual or firm with a risk profile suggesting a higher than acceptable potential for suspicious transactions in the future.[8]

Financial regulatory agencies in the US actively enforce domestic requirements imposed on the financial sector. In this environment, the practice of derisking migrated from the large national banks to the regional banks and then down to state and community banks. The derisking activity focused in particular on the money service businesses (MSBs) largely responsible for remittance transfers and also believed by some people as facilitating terrorist financing. For example, in March 2014, the Bell State Bank in Fargo, North Dakota closed the accounts of MSBs supporting migrant remittances because of the increased costs of compliance and potential fines if the bank was determined to be non-compliant (Kolpack 2014). In November 2014, the North Dade Community Development Federal Credit Union in Miami Gardens, Florida, was fined US$300,000 by the Financial Crimes Enforcement Network (FinCEN). This bureau of the US Treasury Department is the regulatory agency enforcing the Bank Secrecy Act and it is the Financial Intelligence Unit (FIU) for the US.[9] In that capacity it fined the Florida credit union for failing to maintain adequate AML controls on the accounts it provided to MSBs (Ensign 2014a). Yet it was a rather contradictory action because only two weeks earlier FinCEN released a statement 'on Providing Banking Services to Money Services Businesses' (FinCEN 2014). In that statement, FinCEN acknowledged that MSBs, 'play an important role in a transparent financial system' and the organisation expected them to be treated in the same manner as any other customer 'on a case-by-case basis.' (FinCEN 2014)

Nonetheless, several months later a headline on the BBC News website read, 'Somalia criticises US bank's move to halt remittances' (BBC News 2015). The story involved the Merchants Bank of California and its move to close the accounts it provided to remittance agents responsible at that point in time for an estimated 89% of the transfers to Somalia from the US. The bank decided that it was unable to comply with the guidance of the regulator to correct what the Office of the

[8]This derisking activity also extends to expatriate US citizens, when banks close their accounts in order to reduce their reporting obligations to the US government as required by the Foreign Account Tax Compliance Act (FATCA) legislation (Saunders 2014; see further Palan and Wigan 2014).

[9]See https://www.fincen.gov/what-we-do

Comptroller of the Currency (OCC) had identified as deficiencies in the bank's anti-money laundering procedures (BBC News 2015). In a statement reported by the *Los Angeles Times,* the OCC indicated that it did not support derisking, but rather it expected banks 'to assess the risks posed by customers on a case-by-case basis' (Reckard and White 2015). There is a tension, however, between a regulatory agency's publicly declared expectation for the bank to perform a discrete risk analysis for each individual customer, and the bank's expedient and cost effective solution to derisk by closing the accounts for an entire business sector. Moreover, when announcing its action against Merchants Bank the OCC's deputy comptroller for compliance operations and policy stated 'The Somali situation is a terrible human tragedy that cannot be solved by bank regulators; rather, it requires an international government and private-sector effort' (Tracy 2015). In other words, the consequences elsewhere in the world that result from our actions as regulators to protect against a risk in our banking industry are not our problem.

The challenge with sending remittances to Somalia is not limited to those Somalis residing in the US. In the UK, derisking practices in the retail banking sector hit newspaper headlines in 2013 when a large Somali remittance transfer firm resisted the closure of its account by Barclays Bank. Dahabshiil has been identified as one of the largest remittance firms operating in Somalia and it was among the 250 firms affected in May 2013 when Barclays announced its intention to close all such accounts by 10 July 2013. At the time Barclays was the last licensed bank in the UK providing accounts to money service businesses and it had provided Dahabshiil with an account for 15 years (Flood 2013; M. Arnold 2014). The explanation for the action, not from Barclays but attributed to 'a person with knowledge of the situation' was that

> Many money-service businesses just don't have proper checks in place to spot criminal activity and, therefore, unwittingly facilitate money laundering and terrorist financing. It is reasonable for banks to only want to bank those that can filter out criminal transactions. (Masters 2013)

Dahabshiil persisted in challenging Barclays' decision, leading to a court case and a court injunction against the closure of its account (Tran 2013). Ultimately the court case enabled the development of an alternative banking relationship allowing Dahabshiil to remain legitimate in the UK as a major remittance transfer service provider for Somalia (M. Arnold 2014). But beyond the remittance transfer business there are a variety of financial services provided by small firms, including prepaid card providers and online payment processing services, similarly impacted by the closure of their accounts with Barclays and other large UK banks (Masters 2013). The risk assessment performed by these banks sought to limit their exposure to any customer group that could be involved in money laundering.

The remittance transfer firms and other small financial activities now finding themselves without an account at a licensed bank in the United Kingdom are also in a regulatory trap. The Financial Conduct Authority (FCA) requires them to 'safeguard' or protect funds received from a customer in a payment service transaction if those funds are held overnight or for a longer period of time. Such funds are to be segregated from the firm's operating capital and protected in the event of the firm's insolvency (Financial Conduct Authority 2013). Fundamentally, the safeguard process serves to protect the customer from fraud, and two methods are approved for safeguarding customer funds, either with a form of insurance policy or with a 'safeguard' account maintained with an 'authorised credit institution' (Financial Conduct Authority 2013). The authorised credit institution is a financial institution authorised and licensed to accept deposits. Thus, firms providing financial services that do not require them to possess a retail bank license as a deposit accepting firm must either maintain an insurance policy or a guarantee with an authorised insurer, or it must maintain an account with a licensed deposit accepting firm in order to comply with the safeguard requirements of the FCA as the regulator for firms covered by the Payment Services Regulations 2009. Without an account at Barclays or some other authorised credit institution these remittance firms are non-compliant with the guidance regulating their business, and as a result they were left 'in limbo' by the closure of their account (Masters 2013).

Beyond the OCC and FinCEN in the US and the FCA in the UK, the problem of derisking emerged as an agenda item at the October 2014 Plenary of the FATF (FATF 2014a, b). The agenda item text reflected a concern that derisking would 'drive illicit markets and financial exclusion.' (FATF 2014b) And the announcement for the meeting agenda included a link to a speech by the then current FATF President on that concern, delivered to the 6th Annual International Conference on Financial Crime and Terrorism Financing. In his speech, the FATF President touched on the factors producing the tension in privatised financial surveillance that leads to derisking. With regards to the substantial fines imposed on large multinational financial firms he noted that they had 'concentrated the minds of financial organisations' and that the fines served to demonstrate 'the power and reasoning of regulators when they are intent on acting.' (Wilkins 2014) Rather than concur, however, that derisking represents a rational response by those large banks the FATF President attempted to make the case that derisking was in fact an *incorrect* response. First, it was incorrect because the act of derisking broad categories of customers produces a 'reputational risk' for the bank. Second, it was incorrect because there is a 'commercial risk' for the large bank from abandoning the financial business of 'a large proportion of the world's populations'. And third, it was an incorrect response to regulatory action because of the presence of a 'business risk' for these large banks from 'failing to harness new ways of doing banking', such as with mobile banking. Essentially, the argument offered was that the process of derisking will lead to these banks leaving 'a significant amount of "money on the table"' for other firms to profit from in the future (Wilkins 2014). This viewpoint is substantially at odds with the views expressed by the banks that are derisking in response to regulatory fines or the threat of a fine should the bank fail to significantly improve its compliance practices. And critically, as discussed in the next section, customers denied access to formal banking services will resort to informal banking practices.

The perspective offered by the FATF President in 2014 is consistent with an earlier FATF initiative to produce a 'risk-based approach' for implementing its recommendations for privatised financial security against money laundering and terrorist finance. Yet it is interesting to observe that the FATF's initial document for introducing the risk-based strategy in 2007 (*FATF Guidance on the Risk-Based Approach to Combating Money Laundering and Terrorist Financing: High Level Principles and Procedures*) did not specify a definition for 'risk' or 'a risk'. The document's purpose is to 'support the development of a common understanding of what the risk-based approach involves', but it does so without specifying risk (FATF 2007b). Nonetheless, when identifying challenges for the implementation of a risk-based approach the document notes it 'requires that financial institutions have a good understanding of the risks and are able to exercise sound judgement.' (FATF 2007b) The overall impression from reading the FATF document is a belief that what comprises a risk for this environment is recognised and understood by the financial community without further delineation. And while the application of a risk-based approach to this problem domain involves an assessment for whether a particular customer represents a 'risk' for money laundering, or not, the precise mechanism for determining that risk is not specified. At the same time, the document designates three categories of risk: country/geographic risk, customer risk, and product/service risk. Possible determining factors for each category are provided, but without the suggestion that this is a comprehensive list and leaving the final decision on the risk assessment with the operational practices and procedures of the firm (FATF 2007b).

Unfortunately, the risk-based approach as implemented by major multinational financial firms (rather than state actors) produced yet further problems for the FATF and its mission to combat money laundering and terrorist finance at a global level. As demonstrated by the FATF President's speech, the mechanisms of a privatised financial surveillance regime followed a business-oriented agenda rather than a security-oriented agenda as desired. In part, it is an understandable situation because the risk-based approach was developed as a collaboration between the FATF and participants drawn from a cross-section of the international banking and securities industry (FATF 2007b). Yet the lack of clear defining criteria to determine what is, and is not, a risk in this context may make it difficult to identify low-risk cases for reduced surveillance (De Koker 2009). The risk-based approach offered regulators and financial firms with flexibility in determining risk levels and implementing reduced surveillance for low-risk customers. However, confronted with the extraterritorial application of US financial power, these firms also found it easier to deal with high-risk customers through derisking, rather than investing in a detailed assessment of each individual customer.

The challenges raised by derisking are not limited to these examples from the US and UK. Wider international attention on the problem developed with the investigation initiated by the FATF. The FATF sought to demonstrate that its evaluation of national AML implementation, and US enforcement action against large multinational financial firms, were not solely responsible for derisking. The statement released following the October 2014 Plenary meeting emphasised that there were a number of factors behind derisking, including 'concerns about profitability, prudential requirements, anxiety after the global financial crisis, and reputational risk. It is a misconception to characterise derisking exclusively as an anti-money laundering issue.' (FATF 2014a) A discussion paper prepared for that Plenary meeting, however, was not so broad in its identification of the causal influences for derisking in the financial sector. Rather, it emphasised the role played by the increased attention given to a bank's performance in meeting its surveillance obligations to police financial crime. It noted the increased weight given to risk assessments reducing the firm's exposure to a customer or business sector with potential high risks. The expansion of anti-money laundering beyond simply identifying the money of illegal drugs traffickers to include a range of other criminal activities, terrorist financing, nuclear proliferation, and the enforcement of economic sanctions had necessarily increased the complexity of risk assessments. The discussion paper further noted the complex regulatory environment in which the multinational financial firm operates, with differences among regulators and their enforcement of the local implementation of international standards (De-risking: Global Impact and Unintended Consequences for Exclusion and Stability 2014).

Surveys conducted by the Finance and Markets Global Practice staff at the World Bank gathered data on the derisking experience in correspondent banking relationships and the 'remittance market', otherwise known as MSBs (Finance and Markets Global Practice 2015a, b). Reasons behind the closure of accounts did include items other than regulatory enforcement and money laundering risk, such as industry consolidation, nonetheless risk assessment and risk mitigation (derisking) remained a prominent explanation for those answering the surveys. The position of a report released by the Commonwealth, on the other hand, situated the role of regulatory action as the cause of derisking in the title for its report on the problem. In *Disconnecting from Global Finance: The Impact of AML/CFT Regulations in Commonwealth Developing Countries*, this report reviewed data gathered from a survey of Commonwealth member states, most of whom are developing economies. From this survey it then developed a set of policy solutions and recommendations for their implementation to deal with the problems created by derisking in Commonwealth countries. The derisking experience was framed in the report as an unintended consequence from international AML regulations, and the increased cost to businesses from complying with them (Hopper 2016). While derisking may be an unintended consequence, the practice in turn produces further unintended consequences for the privatised security regime intended to identify suspicious money in the financial system.

5.4 Implications for Privatised Financial Surveillance

Irrespective for the variety of factors identified by the FATF as motivating derisking practices, the argument here is that US structural power in global finance is a significant driver behind derisking. The World Bank report on derisking in correspondent banking notes in its Introduction that 'stories and anecdotes have been circulating in media and international policy fora' and they attributed efforts by international banks to limit their risk exposure for the derisking practice. One important issue for all of these studies was the consequences of derisking, both for the customers being isolated from the formal financial system and for the efficacy of the financial surveillance regime itself when those most at risk for money laundering are now isolated from regulated finance. Ten years ago the drive was to formalise the informal, to move informal remittance transfer agents and firms into a regulated formal financial environment. In that regulated environment, they would participate and operate in and with a financial surveillance regime monitoring for terrorist finance, and simultaneously for any suspected money laundering activity. In this fashion, these remittance agents and money service businesses would support the wider security agenda. At that time, some academic observers, including this author, questioned the efficacy of the process to bring informal remittance networks into the structures of retail banking (Vlcek 2008, 2010; Atia 2007; Ballard 2005; de Goede 2003). We have now come full circle, having convinced these firms to formalise and operate through accounts with a licensed retail bank, they are now being rejected and abandoned by those banks. The derisking process motivated by financial surveillance enforcement actions against financial institutions in turn convinced them to reduce the presence of 'risky' clients throughout their customer base.

Identifying the existence and nature of a problem is the first step in dealing with the problem and its consequences. For the process of derisking by financial firms in the privatised financial surveillance domain the existence of the problem is clearly recognised, and to some extent the nature of the problem has been understood. But at the same time the inherent internal contradiction produced by the state regulatory agencies enforcing the legislation that privatised financial surveillance in the first place has not been accepted by them. As stated by a senior executive at Standard Chartered (a major multinational financial firm operating in a number of emerging markets), 'We are supposed to police that our counterparties and clients are not money laundering, and if when we are policing we have a lapse, we don't get treated like a policeman who's had a lapse, we are treated like a criminal' (White 2014). Treated by regulatory agencies in this fashion the rational response on the part of the bank is to avoid any and all potentially risky clients (De-risking: Global Impact and Unintended Consequences for Exclusion and Stability 2014). This response in turn leaves the desired objects for financial surveillance outside the oversight provided by the privatised structures of financial surveillance constructed over the past three decades. Acknowledging this situation, as in the case, for example, of the 'departing undersecretary of the Treasury for terrorism financial intelligence' who declared in January 2015, 'We are concerned about … the possibility that financial institutions are terminating or restricting an entire class of business relationships simply to avoid perceived regulatory risk, not in response to an assessment of the actual risk posed by individual MSBs', is not at the same time accepting responsibility for it (Rubenfeld 2015).

The impact from derisking reaches beyond migrant remittances and similar small financial service providers (e.g. internet payment processors). In 2012, the

FATF-style regional body, Asia/Pacific Group on Money Laundering, released a new typologies report investigating the modalities of trade-based money laundering and updating the FATF's earlier study of the issue (Asia/Pacific Group on Money Laundering 2012; FATF 2006c; see also, FATF 2008). The proposition that money laundering may be accomplished via cross-border trade in goods and services had been raised at least since the 1980s and is similar to practices of transfer pricing (FATF 2006c; see Cassara 2015). A public statement made at an anti-money laundering conference highlighted what law enforcement agencies recognised as a trend toward increased trade-based money laundering (Ensign 2014b). And the use of trade for money laundering by illegal drug traffickers was demonstrated by US law enforcement in September 2014 when a massive raid on a number of businesses in the Los Angeles Fashion District led to nine arrests and the seizure of US$65 million (Audi 2014). Again, the rational response by the large multinational banks is to move out of the trade finance business sector, an activity reported in the media in 2014 (Fleming 2014; see also CGD Working Group 2015). This news article referred to a study produced by the International Chamber of Commerce (ICC) which noted the large 'material fines' imposed on multinational banks and the impact of their derisking practices for the smaller firms facilitating trade and export finance services (ICC 2014b). Yet another 2014 study by the ICC provided the specific details gathered in a survey from 'trade finance banking members of the participating organizations' with a total of 298 survey responses representing 127 jurisdictions (ICC 2014a). For the questions addressing the derisking practices of banks, more than a third of the respondents reported their correspondent banking relationships had been terminated in 2013 and two thirds reported that transactions had been declined for regulatory compliance reasons (ICC 2014a). Moreover, 41 percent of the respondents reported that 'complying with sanctions restricted trade finance operations in 2013 to a greater extent than in previous years.' (ICC 2014a) It is yet another aspect to derisking, where the relevant regulatory agencies identified a potential risky client sector and the banks responded by withdrawing from existing customer relationships and abandoning future business activity involving trade finance in order to avoid potential involvement in trade-based money laundering or economic sanctions violations.

Finally, the problem of derisking was recognised beyond the forums that engage directly with money laundering and terrorist finance, to include those focused on the role and purpose of financial sanctions, including the prevention of nuclear proliferation. The *Bulletin of the Atomic Scientists* published an opinion piece on its website in January 2015 titled 'Big banks and their game of risk' (A. Arnold 2015). In this piece, the author reviewed the fines imposed on large multinational banks, the role of economic sanctions against Iran as part of the negotiating strategy over Iran's nuclear programme, and the emergence of derisking among the large multinational banks. The objective of the article was to identify the potential consequences from derisking on the multinational efforts to identify and suppress the financing behind nuclear proliferation activity. Actions that encourage the growth of alternative financial transaction networks not subject to the international regime of privatised financial surveillance serves to 'decrease transparency' and weakens the leverage created by financial sanctions against Iran (A. Arnold 2015). The concern that derisking by financial institutions could in time weaken the impact of economic sanctions by encouraging the creation of alternative mechanisms also is now being recognised (The pros and cons of a SWIFT response 2014; Tett and Farchy 2015). Aggressive enforcement of regulations against the financial industry is progressively producing a privatised financial security regime observing those customers whose money does not represent a threat to society, while those engaged in money laundering, terrorist finance and the evasion of US economic sanctions operate elsewhere using other means.

The structural power of the US dollar and financial market provide US regulatory authorities with the leverage needed to gain the cooperation of foreign firms to abide by US domestic laws and national economic sanctions. Government agencies pursue national anti-money laundering/terrorist financing goals by directly investigating any financial firm with a demonstrated nexus to their scope of jurisdiction. Thus, any firm desiring access to US financial markets or conducting business in US dollars may be subjected to investigation, prosecution and subsequent penalties and fines. This situation represents an enforcement capacity that essentially is beyond the capability of any other state's financial regulatory authorities. No other national financial system possesses the weight or attractiveness required to produce the leverage necessary to achieve extraterritorial enforcement action. Yet, following the superhero trope that 'with great power comes great responsibility' (attributed to Spiderman's Uncle Ben), by utilising its structural power in this fashion the agencies of the US government have not accepted their responsibility for influencing the cost/benefit analysis of foreign financial firms that led to their derisking practices. This process of derisking serves to reduce the extent of oversight provided by this privatised security system to state law enforcement agencies investigating potential money laundering or terrorist financing. Over time, US enforcement action against privatised security actors has effectively reduced the security provided by them, a problem acknowledged with the release of a 'Joint Fact Sheet on Foreign Correspondent Banking: Approach to BSA/AML and OFAC Sanctions Supervision and Enforcement' by the US Treasury Department and Federal Banking Agencies in August 2016 (U.S. Treasury and Federal Banking Agencies 2016).

5.5 Conclusions

The practice of derisking involves the identification by multinational financial firms of customers that potentially may represent a risk in the future as a target of US regulatory enforcement action. For these firms, it is more expedient and cost-effective to remove an entire group of customers operating in a particular business activity than it is to investigate each one in sufficient depth to assure the customer is not engaged in any transactions which may be money laundering, terrorist finance, or evading economic sanctions. This risk mitigation is carried out on a large scale by financial firms not simply because the cost to assure compliance may exceed any profit generated by the business relationship. Also, there are the costs from any US regulatory determination that the firm is non-compliant, direct costs including fines and long-term, indirect costs from the potential denial of access to the US financial markets. In other words, these firms are responding to the influence of US structural power in the operation of the global financial system. After guiding the construction of the privatised financial surveillance regime, the US has increasingly and aggressively been enforcing over the past few years the obligations the regime imposes on financial firms. For domestic financial firms, it is clearly an exercise of government authority, while for multinational financial firms it is an exercise of the structural financial power possessed by the US as a result of dollar hegemony.

From a US government perspective, part of its foreign policy objective has been achieved and that achievement is demonstrated by the derisking process itself—firms desist from facilitating the means for individuals, firms, and states subject to US financial and economic sanctions to circumvent them. One national security goal has been achieved, with regards to transactions operating in the formal sector. At the same time this success encourages the use of informal economy practices and the production of an alternate international payments system using a currency other than the US dollar (The pros and cons of a SWIFT response 2014; Tett and Farchy 2015). The operation of the privatised financial surveillance regime produced under the guidance of the FATF over the past three decades is increasingly avoided when potentially risky customers are denied access by the regulated firms. And regulatory agencies have come to recognise this unintended consequence from their enforcement actions, emphasising that the risk-based approach expects the firm to assess risk on a case-by-case basis (FATF 2014a, 2016a; Szubin 2015). Nonetheless, they also recognise it is a business decision by a private actor (Ensign 2015). After successfully privatising financial surveillance, the regulatory agencies have found that their ability to influence actual practice is constrained by the conduct of the neo-liberal market when firms operate as rational actors, and prevent potentially risky customers from entering the realm under surveillance in the first place.

References

Adams, T. E. (2000). Tacking on money laundering charges to white collar crimes: What did congress intend, and what are the courts doing? *Georgia State University Law Review, 17*(2), 531–573.

Amicelle, A., & Jacobsen, E. K. (2016). The cross-colonization of finance and security through lists: Banking policing in the UK and India. *Environment and Planning D: Society and Space, 34*(1), 89–106. doi:10.1177/0263775815623276.

Arnold, M. (2014, April 16). Barclays and remittance group reach deal on Somalia services. *Financial Times*.

Arnold, A. (2015). Big banks and their game of risk. Accessed January 23, 2015, from http://thebulletin.org/big-banks-and-their-game-risk7941

Asia/Pacific Group on Money Laundering. (2012). APG typology report on trade based money laundering. Sydney, Australia: Asia/Pacific Group on Money Laundering Secretariat.

Atia, M. (2007). In whose interest? Financial surveillance and the circuits of exception in the war on terror. *Environment and Planning D, 25*, 447–475.

Audi, T. (2014, September 10). Federal agents raid Los Angeles garment businesses allegedly linked to drug cartels. *Wall Street Journal*.

Ballard, R. (2005). Coalitions of reciprocity and the maintenance of financial integrity within informal value transmission systems: The operational dynamics of contemporary hawala networks. *Journal of Banking Regulation, 6*(4), 319–352.

Barrett, D., Bisserbe, N., & Johnson, A. R. (2014a, May 30). U.S. Wants Firings at France's BNP. *Wall Street Journal*.

Barrett, D., Matthews, C. M., & Johnson, A. R. (2014b, June 30). BNP Paribas Draws Record Fine for 'Tour de Fraud'. *Wall Street Journal*.

BBC News. (2015). Somalia criticises US bank's move to halt remittances. Accessed February 18, 2015, from http://www.bbc.co.uk/news/world-africa-31168615

Braithwaite, T. (2012, December 11). DoJ holds 'sword of Damocles' over HSBC. *Financial Times*.

Bussey, J. (2007, February 15). Anti-money laundering compliance sparks debate. *The Miami Herald*.

Cassara, J. A. (2015). *Trade-based money laundering: The next frontier in international money laundering enforcement*. Hoboken, NJ: Wiley.

CGD Working Group. (2015). *Unintended consequences of anti-money laundering policies for poor countries*. Washington, DC: Center for Global Development.

Cohen, B. J. (2015). *Currency power: Understanding monetary rivalry*. Princeton and Oxford: Princeton University Press.

de Goede, M. (2003). Hawala discourse and the war on terrorist finance. *Environment and Planning D, 21*(5), 513–532.

De Koker, L. (2009). Identifying and managing low money laundering risk: Perspectives on FATF's risk-based guidance. *Journal of Financial Crime, 16*(4), 334–352.

De-risking: Global Impact and Unintended Consequences for Exclusion and Stability. (2014). Accessed January 28, 2017, from https://classic.regonline.com/custImages/340000/341739/G24%20AFI/G24_2015/De-risking_Report.pdf

Eckert, S. E. (2008). The US regulatory approach to terrorist financing. In T. J. Biersteker & S. E. Eckert (Eds.), *Countering the Financing of Terrorism* (pp. 209–233). London and New York: Routledge.

Ehreriene, E., & Patrick, M. (2016, March 29). Iranian Miniskirts, bags of cash raise doubts over controls at HSBC. *Wall Street Journal*.

Ensign, R. L. (2014a, November 25). Florida credit union fined over controls on MSB customers. *Wall Street Journal*.

Ensign, R. L. (2014b, September 29). Money laundering moving to smaller banks, Trade. *Wall Street Journal*.

Ensign, R. L. (2015, March 30). Banks, regulators reach impasse over risky account closures. *Wall Street Journal*.

Ensign, R. L., & Colchester, M. (2015, January 12). HSBC struggles in battle against money laundering. *Wall Street Journal*.

Ensign, R. L., & Viswanatha, A. (2015, April 1). HSBC monitor says bank's compliance progress too slow. *Wall Street Journal*.

FATF. (1990a). Financial action task force on money laundering report. Accessed March 21, 2002, from http://www.fatf-gafi.org/

FATF. (1990b). The forty recommendations of the financial action task force on money laundering. Accessed March 21, 2002, from http://wwwfatf-gafi.org

FATF. (2000). Review to identify non-cooperative countries or territories: increasing the worldwide effectiveness of anti-money laundering measures. Accessed March 21, 2002, from http://www.fatf-gafi.org/

FATF. (2006a). Chairman's summary, Vancouver plenary, 9–13 October 2006. Accessed February 19, 2007, from http://www.fatf-gafi.org/
FATF. (2006b). Report on new payment methods. Accessed November 28, 2006, from http://www.fatf-gafi.org/
FATF. (2006c). Trade based money laundering. Accessed July 18, 2006, from http://www.fatf-gafi.org/
FATF. (2007a). Chairman's summary, Paris plenary, 10–12 October 2007. Accessed October 17, 2007, from http://www.fatf-gafi.org/
FATF. (2007b). Guidance on the risk-based approach to combating money laundering and terrorist finance: High level principles and procedures. Accessed July 17, 2007, from www.fatf-gafi.org
FATF. (2008). Best practices paper on trade based money laundering. Accessed August 4, 2008, from http://www.fatf-gafi.org/
FATF. (2009). Vulnerabilities of casinos and gaming sector. Accessed May 2, 2009.
FATF. (2012). International standards on combating money laundering and the financing of terrorism & proliferation: The FATF recommendations. Accessed February 27, 2012, from http://www.fatf-gafi.org/
FATF. (2014a). FATF clarifies risk-based approach: Case-by-case, not wholesale de-risking. Accessed November 15, 2014, from http://www.fatf-gafi.org/
FATF. (2014b). Meeting of the FATF plenary, Paris 22–24 October 2014. Accessed November 15, 2014, from http://www.fatf-gafi.org/
FATF. (2016a). Guidance on correspondent banking services. Accessed December 30, 2016, from http://www.fatf-gafi.org/
FATF. (2016b). Outcomes of the Plenary meeting of the FATF, Paris, 19–21 October 2016. Accessed February 2, 2017, from http://www.fatf-gafi.org/
FATF. (n.d.). The forty recommendations. Accessed February 6, 2002, from http://www.fatf-gafi.org/
Favarel-Garrigues, G., Godefroy, T., & Lascoumes, P. (2011). Reluctant partners?: Banks in the fight against money laundering and terrorism financing in France. *Security Dialogue, 42*(2), 179–196.
Finance and Markets Global Practice. (2015a). *Report on the G20 survey on de-risking activities in the remittance market*. Washington, DC: World Bank Group.
Finance and Markets Global Practice. (2015b). *Withdrawal from correspondent banking: Where, why, what to do about it*. Washington, DC: World Bank Group.
Financial Conduct Authority. (2013). The FCA's role under the Payment Services Regulations 2009: Our approach.
Financial Conduct Authority. (2016). Derisking: Managing money laundering risk.
FinCEN. (2014). *FinCEN statement on providing banking services to money services businesses*. Washington, DC: U.S. Department of the Treasury.
Fleming, S. (2014, June 19). ICC flags up concerns over effect of money-laundering laws. *Financial Times*.
Flood, Z. (2013, July 4). Barclays set to exit remittance business. *Financial Times*.
General Accounting Office. (2000). Suspicious banking activities: Possible money laundering by U.S. corporations formed for Russian entities. *Report to the Ranking Minority Member, Permanent Subcommittee on Investigations, Committee on Governmental Affairs, United States Senate* (p. 12). Washington, DC: General Accounting Office.
Germain, R. (Ed.). (2016). *Susan Strange and the future of global political economy: Power, control and transformation* (RIPE Series in Global Political Economy). London and New York: Routledge.
Gilmore, W. C. (2004). *Dirty Money: The evolution of international measures to counter money laundering and the financing of terrorism* (3rd ed.). Strasbourg: Council of Europe Publishing.
Gordon, R. K. (2010). The international monetary fund and the regulation of offshore centers. In A. P. Morriss (Ed.), *Offshore financial centers and regulatory competition* (pp. 74–101). Washington, DC: The AEI Press.

Halliday, T., Levi, M., & Reuter, P. (2014). Global surveillance of dirty money: Assessing assessments of regimes to control money-laundering and combat the financing of terrorism (pp. 61). Champaign, IL: Center on Law and Globalization.

Hong, N. (2015, March 25). Sanctions law a powerful tool for prosecutors. *Wall Street Journal.*

Hopper, R. (2016). Disconnecting from global finance: The impact of AML/CFT regulations in commonwealth developing countries. London: Commonwealth Secretariat.

Horobin, W., & Gauthier-Villars, D. (2014, May 23). Top French Banker Defends BNP Paribas. *Wall Street Journal.*

Hülsse, R. (2007). Creating demand for global governance: The making of a global money-laundering problem. *Global Society, 21*(2), 155–178.

ICC. (2014a). Global survey 2014: Rethinking trade and finance (pp. 144). Paris: International Chamber of Commerce.

ICC. (2014b). ICC trade register report 2014 – Summary (pp. 56). Paris: International Chamber of Commerce.

Jakobi, A. P. (2013). *Common goods and evils? The formation of global crime governance.* Oxford: Oxford University Press.

Kirshner, J. (2009). After the (relative) fall: Dollar diminuation and the consequences for American power. In J. Kirshner & E. Helleiner (Eds.), *The future of the dollar* (pp. 191–215). Ithaca and London: Cornell University Press.

Kolpack, D. (2014, March 5). North Dakota bank dumps money service businesses. *Washington Times.*

KPMG International. (2004). Global anti-money laundering survey 2004: How banks are facing up to the challenge. Accessed November 13, 2004, from http://www.kpmg.hr/dbfetch/52616e646f6d4956cb229f447c30ce0928bbb20d4bed0ebd/antimoney_laundering_survey_2004.pdf

KPMG International. (2014). Global anti-money laundering survey 2014. Accessed January 25, 2015, from http://www.kpmg.com/Global/en/IssuesAndInsights/ArticlesPublications/global-anti-money-laundering-survey/Pages/default.aspx

Lewis, D. (2016). Speech on the importance of the FATF Global Network. Accessed January 13, 2017, from http://www.fatf-gafi.org/

Liss, C., & Sharman, J. C. (2015). Global corporate crime-fighters: Private transnational responses to piracy and money laundering. *Review of International Political Economy, 22*(4), 693–718.

Masters, B. (2013, June 12). Lenders pull banking facilities from small financial groups. *Financial Times.*

Matthews, C. M. (2015, February 25). Lawsky proposes new cybersecurity, money-laundering rules for banks. *Wall Street Journal.*

Megginson, W. L. (2005). *The financial economics of privatization.* New York: Oxford University Press.

Millman, G. J., & Rubenfeld, S. (2014, January 15). Compliance officer: Dream career? *Wall Street Journal.*

Minority Staff of the Permanent Subcommittee on Investigations. (2001). Report on correspondent banking: A gateway for money laundering. Washington, DC: U.S. Senate Committee on Government Affairs.

Norrlof, C. (2014). Dollar hegemony: A power analysis. *Review of International Political Economy, 21*(5), 1042–1070.

Palan, R., & Wigan, D. (2014). Herding cats and taming tax havens: The US strategy of 'Not In My Backyard'. *Global Policy, 5*(3), 334–343.

Prasad, E. S. (2014). *The Dollar Trap: How the U.S. dollar tightened its grip on global finance* (Paperback ed.). Princeton and Oxford: Princeton University Press.

Protess, B., & Silver-Greenberg, J. (2014, October 30). Prosecutors suspect repeat offenses on wall street. *New York Times*, p. A1.

Reckard, E. S., & White, R. D. (2015, February 5). Money transfers cut off to Somalia. *Los Angeles Times.*

Rothfeld, M., Enrich, D., & Solomon, J. (2010, August 17). Barclays in Sanctions Bust. *Wall Street Journal*.

Rubenfeld, S. (2015, January 14). Officials Extoll Money-Service Businesses Amid 'De-risking' Drive. *Wall Street Journal*.

Saunders, L. (2014, September 11). Expats left frustrated as banks cut services abroad. *Wall Street Journal*.

Scannell, K., & Arnold, M. (2014, August 18). StanChart faces fresh $300m US settlement. *Financial Times*.

Scannell, K., & Braithwaite, T. (2012, August 7). Size of StanChart problem U-turn dependent. *Financial Times*.

Sharman, J. C. (2009). The Bark *is* the bite: International organisations and blacklisting. *Review of International Political Economy, 16*(4), 573–596.

Sharman, J. C. (2011). *The money laundry: Regulating criminal finance in the global economy*. Ithaca and London: Cornell University Press.

Shaughnessy, P. (2002). The new EU money-laundering directive: Lawyers as gate-keepers and whistle-blowers. *Law and Policy in International Business, 34*, 25–44.

Stothard, M. (2014, June 2). French outcry over threat to BNP Paribas of $10bn US fine. *Financial Times*.

Strange, S. (1987). The persistent myth of lost hegemony. *International Organization, 41*(4), 551–574.

Strange, S. (1994). *States and markets* (2nd ed.). London and New York: Contiuum.

Szubin, A. (2015). Remarks of acting under secretary for terrorism and financial intelligence Adam Szubin at the ACAMS anti-money laundering and financial crime conference. Accessed April 14, 2015, from http://www.treasury.gov/press-center/press-releases/Pages/jl9998.aspx

Taylor, J. B. (2007). *Global financial warriors: The untold story of international finance in the post-9/11 world*. New York & London: W. W. Norton & Company.

Tett, G., & Farchy, J. (2015, January 23). Russian banker warns west over Swift. *Financial Times*.

The pros and cons of a SWIFT response. (2014, November 22). *The Economist*.

Tracy, R. (2015, February 4). Bank to close accounts related to Somalia. *Wall Street Journal*.

Tran, M. (2013, September 30). Somalia remittances: Barclays gives further reprieve to money-transfer firm. *The Guardian*.

Tsingou, E. (2015). Club governance and the making of global financial rules. *Review of International Political Economy, 22*(2), 225–256.

U.S. Treasury, & Federal Banking Agencies. (2016). Joint fact sheet on foreign correspondent banking: Approach to BSA/AML and OFAC sanctions supervision and enforcement. Accessed September 1, 2016, from https://www.treasury.gov/press-center/press-releases/Documents/Foreign%20Correspondent%20Banking%20Fact%20Sheet.pdf

United Nations Security Council. (2005). Resolution 1617 (2005). *S/RES/1617 (2005)*.

Vlcek, W. (2008). Development vs. terrorism: money transfers and EU financial regulations in the UK. *British Journal of Politics and International Relations, 10*(2), 286–302.

Vlcek, W. (2010). Alongside global political economy – A rhizome of informal finance. *Journal of International Relations and Development, 13*(4), 429–451.

Vlcek, W. (2012). Power and the practice of security to govern global finance. *Review of International Political Economy, 19*(4), 639–662.

White, L. (2014, August 7). StanChart executive – Banks treated like 'criminals' for anti-money laundering lapses. *Reuters*.

Wilkins, R. (2014). The danger of driving both illicit markets and financial exclusion. Accessed November 9, 2014, from http://www.fatf-gafi.org/

Zarate, J. (2013). *Treasury's war: The unleashing of a new era of financial warfare*. New York: Public Affairs.

Chapter 6
The Role of For-Profit Actors in Implementing Targeted Sanctions: The Case of the European Union

Francesco Giumelli

6.1 Introduction

The evolution of sanctions from comprehensive to targeted has favored the inclusion of for-profit actors[1] in the policy process. When financial restrictions are imposed, banks and financial institutions play a key role in ensuring that implementation is done according to *De l'Esprit des Lois* (the spirit of the law). When an economic boycott is decided, then it is trading companies and producers that are directly responsible for not delivering and selling certain goods to listed individuals and entities. Targeted sanctions are disciplined via public regulations and for-profit actors are central to the achievement of the policy objectives that inspired the adoption of sanctions. As a foreign policy instrument "between wars and words" in the international system (Wallensteen and Staibano 2005), sanctions are normally used to deal with security challenges. As such, for-profit actors play a central role in the provision of security, which is also in line with a general trend that has been recognized and discussed in the literature. In domestic politics, for instance, private actors have been used to provide security (Johnston 1992; Shearing and Stenning 1987), to administer prisons (Hart et al. 1997) and to protect critical infrastructures (Dunn Cavelty and Kirstensen 2008; Lee 2009). In external affairs, most of the attention was devoted to the study of for-profit actors that were dealing directly with security matters, such as the case of private military and security companies (PMSCs) in military operations (Avant 2005; Kinsey 2006). However, less attention has been paid to 'less-spectacular' for-profit actors (Abrahamsen and

[1]For-profit actors are defined as firms and companies. They will be referred to as private actors and non-state actors in the text, but they will be treated as synonyms of actors for-profit.

F. Giumelli (✉)
Department of International Relations and International Organization (IRIO), University of Groningen, Oude Kijk in 't Jatstraat 26, 9712 EK Groningen, The Netherlands
e-mail: f.giumelli@rug.nl

O. Bures, H. Carrapico (eds.), *Security Privatization*,
DOI 10.1007/978-3-319-63010-6_6

Williams 2009; Bures and Carrapico Chap. 1), such as banks and trading companies, which are central to the implementation of sanctions.

This chapter intends to investigate the role of for-profit actors in the implementation of sanctions. More specifically, this chapter suggests a typology of regulatory environments that facilitates explaining and understanding the behavior of for-profit actors in implementing targeted sanctions. The typology of regulatory environments, defined in terms of formal institutions only, is constituted by the quality of instructions provided by state authorities and their capacity to monitor the implementation of such decisions. This typology presents two advantages: first, it allows us to consider the transnational nature of the role of for-profit actors in the provision of security in general, and in implementing sanctions in particular; second, it permits us to identify problems and challenges that can emerge through the involvement of non-state actors in implementing public regulations across policy areas. The chapter argues that there are four types of regulatory environments—*enforceable implementation, implementation by persuasion, enforceable delegation of implementation,* and *delegation of implementation by persuasion*— and that each of these regulatory environment is likely to create problems of overcompliance, uneven and lack of compliance. The theoretical framework is tested on the case study of the restrictive measures of the European Union (EU). The EU has adopted a targeted sanctions approach (European Union 2013) whose particular institutional architecture forces the EU to adopt domestic legislations to regulate the behavior of firms and companies within its own borders. The regulations also have effect beyond EU borders. The imposition of sanctions is motivated by security concerns, and its hybrid nature of domestic as well as international dimension makes it a most typical case study to test the typology proposed in this chapter. The data for this chapter was collected through semi-opened interviews and focus groups held in Brussels from 2013 to 2015.[2]

The chapter is divided into five sections. The first one presents the academic debate on the role of non-state actors in the provision of security. The second section presents the typology of regulatory environments that can be used to analyze the behavior of for-profit actors in implementing public regulations. The third part introduces the targeted sanctions policy of the European Union. The fourth one analyzes each of the four types applied to EU targeted sanctions. Finally, the chapter ends with a discussion on the usefulness of the typology and it suggests some venues for future research.

[2]Interviews were held in different phases. First, I participated in two focus groups with EU officials and private sector representatives in two workshops held in Brussels in July and October 2013. The focus groups took place as background activity for writing 'The effectiveness of EU sanctions. An analysis of Iran, Belarus, Syrian and Myanmar', a report that I co-authored with Paul Ivan and which was published by the European Policy Centre in November 2013. Additionally, a total of thirteen interviews were held with EU officials in Brussels between March 2010 and February 2015. Sparse email communications took place with companies between 2013 and 2015, but only one is used in this chapter. The interviews were held under anonymity; therefore only the position, date and role of the interviewees are indicated whenever necessary.

6.2 Non-State Actors and the Provision of Security

The provision of public goods very often depends on the role and the activities of private actors, such as firms, individuals, non-governmental organizations, and enterprises. As a departure from the understanding of the Westphalian system, wherein states are the main security providers within their own borders and of their own borders, the growing complexity of the international system has brought about two main changes that need to be pointed out. First, borders became more permeable to external security threats. At the same time, security threats evolved from states and state-sponsored to a more hybrid and molecular nature, facilitating their enacting from distant geographical locations. In an attempt to enhance their role as security providers, states have gradually involved non-state actors in the protection of their borders and the management of distant and non-state based security threats.

The growing reliance of states on private actors did not start with the provision of security, as properly emphasized by the literature on New Public Management and on Regulatory Capitalism (Braithwaite 2008; Gilardi 2008; Levi-Faur 2005). Although states became service providers following the industrial revolution in the nineteenth century, the growing complexity of a globalized world incentivized their evolution to further extend their range of services at the same time as reducing their costs (Olsen 1988; Lane 2000). In order to diversify the governance of service provisions, states took the initiative to involve private actors (Kettl 1993; King 2007). Since the 1970s, the state has shifted towards becoming a regulatory entity rather than a direct provider of public goods (Majone 1994, 1996). Although this transformation initially regarded mostly non-security related sectors—Knill and Lehmkuhl refer to the regulation of internet domain names, the standardization of digital copyright and the internet content registration (2002, pp. 53–57), while other studies mention environment policy, and labor practices (Vogel 2010, p. 68)—security has also been gradually included in this process (Abrahamsen and Williams 2009; Avant 2005; Hall and Biersteker 2002; Leander and van Muster 2007). Especially relevant to this chapter, the link between business and security has been investigated as well (Bailes and Frommelt 2004; Bures and Carrapico Chap. 1). Such link regards non-explicit security tasks—such as the protection of critical infrastructure (Lee 2009; Dunn Cavelty and Kristensen 2008) and the monitoring of money laundering (Allidge 2008; Levi 2010; Favarel-Garrigues et al. 2011)—and explicit security tasks—such as combat support and other tasks performed by PMSCs (Singer 2003; Kinsey 2006).

The provision of security is the product of a collaboration between state and non-state actors, either in voluntary or mandatory terms. For instance, state and non-state actors, and therefore for-profit as well, can decide to engage in public-private partnerships (PPPs) (Donahue and Zeckhauser 2006; Schaferhoff et al. 2009). In other cases, firms decide to act out of feelings of responsibility for the social implications of their behavior defined as Corporate Social Responsibility (CSR) (Garriga and Mele 2004; Petersen 2008; Bures 2015). Furthermore, states have also taken the lead and regulated, or tried to, the behavior of business actors for the provision of security. For instance, there is a flourishing literature on the role played by non-state actors in countering money laundering[3] (Allidge 2008; Levi 2010; Favarel-Garrigues et al. 2011) and terrorist financing (Biersteker and Eckert 2007). This approach is often resisted by private actors, who lament that they have to perform tasks that, in fact, should be carried out by public institutions (Bergstrom et al. 2011, p. 1049; Bures 2013, p. 443; Lee 2009; Jordana and Levi-Faur 2004; Bull and McNeill 2007).

In any case, regulations require that for-profit actors behave in specific ways implementing the policy according to the spirit of the law. This opens a debate about the conditions under which for-profit actors comply with public regulations (Peters 1999; Scott 2001, as cited by Parker and Lehmann Nielsen 2011, p. 18). First, enterprises and firms comply because of specific motives. The original assumption was that companies are motivated by economic gains, therefore firms and companies fear the imposition of penalties and fines. However, the debate was subsequently extended beyond this assumption as other motivations were explored. For instance, Winter and May (2001) argue that firms are driven by social motives, namely the need to earn the respect of other actors, whether they are consumers, other peers or regulators. In other words, for-profit actors are afraid of reputational costs as well. Alternatively, companies also comply for normative reasons, meaning that firms conform to a broader sense of what's the right thing to do in given circumstances. Others claim that companies comply *when they can*. This set of motivations regards the specific organizational peculiarities of companies, such as the size of the company, the types of products/services they are providing and the markets where they operate. This is also affected by the organizational culture, the decisions of their management and/or their employees. For instance, companies differ because of 'their economic resources, technical knowhow, knowledge about the law and managerial capacity and oversight' among others (Parker and Lehmann Nielsen 2011, p. 15). Finally, companies do not operate in a vacuum and, therefore, they are subject to influence of external factors. These factors are the formal and informal institutions that 'dictate, limit and also enable certain actions'. Accordingly, institutions are classified in regulative (laws), normative (norms and values) and cultural cognitive (administration practices). In other words, the quality of the regulation explains why private actors comply, or not, with public regulations.

However, these explanations do not fully account for the special nature of a regulatory environment in international security. First, the international system is characterized by the absence of institutions that can enforce common rules. Second, while regulations on non-security related issues are based on 'hard' facts, security is characterized by 'soft' facts, namely it is managed through assumptions and risk assessments. On the one hand, the rule of law is weak in the international system and, on the other hand, security operates in a realm of uncertainties. In this context,

[3]Money laundering can be security related, for instance if the activity is carried out by international criminal organizations, and non-security related, for instance in case of tax evasion.

understanding and explaining the role of for-profit actors becomes central to understanding and explaining the implementation of targeted sanctions. The next section suggests a typology hat enhances the understanding of the effects of formal rules on the behavior of for-profit actors when they are asked to contribute to the provision of security.

6.3 The Regulatory Environment and the Implementation of Sanctions

As mentioned above, this chapter intends to contribute to the debate on regulating the behavior of for-profit actors to deal with security challenges in the international system. This chapter argues that given that international and domestic systems are different *in nature* from one another and that dealing with security challenges means dealing with uncertainties, there is the need for wider analytical frameworks undertaking comparisons across time, space and policy areas. In this analysis, the assumption is that focusing on regulatory environments provides the necessary analytical perspective to identify recurrent problems when for-profit actors are requested to implement public policies via regulations. A regulatory environment is the set of formal institutions—such as laws and institutional actors instructing, monitoring and enforcing public regulations—in which for-profit actors operate. Certainly, regulatory environments could be defined more extensively and, therefore, they could include other defining characteristics. However, the focus in this chapter is on formal institutions and, therefore, informal institutions and other variables are not considered.

The regulatory environment is determined by the clarity of instructions provided by the regulations adopted by public authorities and by the monitoring/enforcing capacities of public authorities. When it comes to enacting legislation, state authorities need to have at least as much knowledge as private actors. Knowledge allows state authorities to provide private actors with specific guidelines on what needs to be done. However, private actors can have more knowledge than state institutions. This can occur for several reasons. For instance, the growing complexity of technological innovations allow firms and companies to draw from market forces and rely on specific expertise that state institutions, being less flexible and unable to acquire competences in each policy area, cannot afford. Additionally, non-state actors are often closer to the daily activity of their customers, therefore they are exposed to dynamics that state institutions are not witnessing (Dunning 1999 also see Chaps. 9–12 in Part III of this book).

The objective of public regulations is to ensure that for-profit actors carry out specific actions, such as implementing targeted sanctions as investigated in this chapter. In order to *implement* targeted sanctions, for-profit actors need to be provided with specific instructions regarding what they have to do. If for-profit actors do not receive such information and, instead, are provided only with vague instructions, then public authorities are *delegating* the implementation of sanctions to for-profit actors. In such a case, private actors are asked to make substantive decisions about specific situations that states cannot make (Cherednychenko 2016). At the same time, for-profit actors can embark on deviant behavior and refuse to implement sanctions. In such a case, public authorities can be either in a position to *enforce* implementation, for instance by monitoring and imposing fines on deviant behavior, or to *persuade* implementation, for instance by convincing for-profit actors to implement sanctions by reasons other than coercion such as reputational costs, sense of justice, etc.

The intersection of the two variables constitutes a typology of regulatory environments of formal institutions that allows to account for both the domestic/international divide, as well as security/non-security policies. Thus, four types of regulatory environments can be identified: (1) *enforceable implementation* (type A), which is when governments can specifically outline what private actors are supposed to do and also monitor their behavior in order to enforce the regulation; (2) *implementation by persuasion* (type B), wherein public authorities can provide detailed regulations, but monitoring cannot be properly done. This could be a situation in which specific actions are forbidden, but public authorities cannot act because the violations occur beyond their reach (and knowledge sometimes); (3) *enforceable delegation of implementation* (type C), regards those situations wherein public authorities do have the power to monitor the behavior of non-state actors, but clear and specific instructions cannot be provided. For instance, this would occur in security-related matters in domestic systems, wherein strict coordination between private and public actors replaces the state in providing public goods; and (4) *delegation of implementation by persuasion* (type D) which refers to situations in which private actors do not know exactly what they have to do to comply and public authorities cannot monitor what they do. For instance, this is a security-related challenge in the international system. Table 6.1 summarizes the 2×2 matrix of the four regulatory environments.

If regulatory environments influence the behavior of private actors, then specific patterns of behavior should be expected when applied to concrete cases of security governance. This chapter proceeds inductively and it applies the theoretical framework to a case study in order to observe whether there are regularities in behavioral patterns that can be identified with for-profit actors. This chapter does not intent to discuss the role of non-state actors regarding the effectiveness of a public policy, but it aims to identify regularities in private actors' behaviors. The targeted sanctions of the European Union (EU) is the case study for this research. First, sanctions are inherently a security topic. Second, the evolution from comprehensive

Table 6.1 A typology of regulatory environments

	Detailed instructions	Vague instructions
High monitoring capacity	Type A: enforceable implementation	Type C: enforceable delegation of implementation
Low monitoring capacity	Type B: implementation by persuasion	Type D: delegation of implementation by persuasion

to targeted sanctions has increased the need to involve private actors in the implementation of sanctions. Finally, the case of the EU is also relevant as the level of formalization reached in Europe further emphasizes the importance of guidelines needed by companies to implement public regulations. The next section introduces the case of the targeted sanctions of the European Union.

6.4 Targeted Measures and the Case of the EU

The EU imposes sanctions as one of its foreign policy instruments under its Common Foreign and Security Policy (CFSP).[4] The EU became a political entity with the entry into force of the Maastricht Treaty and, since then, EU member states began to act on foreign policy matters[5] with Decisions by the Council of Ministers, which find their inspiration in European Council conclusions (Portela 2010; Eriksson 2010; Giumelli 2011, 2013). As economic sanctions also affect the functioning of the common market, the Commission had to be involved in receiving the decisions of the member states and in transposing them into EU legislation that would be binding for everyone in the common market. As such, the case of targeted sanctions constitutes a complex private-public security governance structure that involves transforming the way in which firms and companies ought to operate.

Sanctions are adopted on the basis of article 29 of the Treaty of the European Union, which allows the Council of ministers to adopt foreign policy decisions by consensus. There are three main documents that discipline the utilization of sanctions by the EU. First, sanctions are imposed according to tenets illustrated in the "Basic Principles" adopted in 2004 (European Union 2004). Second, sanctions are designed and imposed according to the ideas listed in the "Guidelines", whose latest versions were adopted in 2013 (European Union 2013). This document states that the European Union has adopted a "targeted" approach, meaning that sanctions were designed to minimize the impact on civilians while increasing the burden on certain actors, namely targeted individuals, political parties, and governmental leaders. Finally, given that imposing sanctions on individuals is extremely detailed, the third document indicates "Best Practices" to overcome implementing problems and to favor the homogenous implementation of EU decisions across member states (European Union 2015).

The adoption of the "Best Practices" document was necessary because the implementation of sanctions is shared between the Council and member states. The Council is responsible for measures that alter the functioning of the common

[4]The Lisbon Treaty included a distinction between imposing sanctions on third parties (CFSP) and imposing sanctions on terrorist groups that operate within the borders of the European Union (art. 75 of the Treaty on the Functioning of the European Union). The latter is considered a measure related to internal security (Area of Freedom, Security and Justice) and, therefore, it will not be considered in this chapter.

[5]Formerly also with 'Common positions'.

market, such as economic boycotts and financial restrictions. Economic boycotts entail the prohibition to sell specific products or services to a targeted country, region, company and/or individual. Financial sanctions include the freezing of assets and the prohibition of providing loans and making payments. Article 215 of the Treaty on the Functioning of the European Union (TFEU) grants the Council with implementing powers regarding sanctions. The pre-Lisbon framework foresaw this possibility for the Commission with 'Commission Regulations', while article 215 transferred this implementing power to the Council. Additionally, the Treaty of Lisbon also grants further implementing power to the Council which, in foreign policy matters (article 24 TUE), can exercise powers to implement legislative acts (article 291). When the Council exercises such power, the legal documents are headed with 'Council Implementing Regulations'. The contours of Article 291 have been also subject to the attention of the Court of Justice of the European Union (Case C-440 P-14 National Iranian Oil Company v Council, see European Union 2016). EU regulations have immediate effect for everyone in the European Union and, therefore, firms and companies have to comply with them.

Member states are responsible for the implementation of arms embargoes and travel bans, which are still under their competence despite the numerous treaties signed since 1957. Arms embargoes prohibit the sale of weapons and dual-use technologies to specific political actors. Although the EU has produced a list of dual-use goods in 2009 to facilitate the coordination among EU members, it is still up to the latter to monitor and enforce trade in this area as provided by a clause added to the Treaty of Rome indicating that the trade of weapons directly affects the security of member states. Travel bans, which restrict access to the territories of the member states for security reasons, are also implemented by member states.

This means that the EU sanctions process is triggered by the European Council, decided by the Council of Ministers, and implemented either by member states or by the EU, but the implementation involves the regulation of the behavior of firms and companies. Private businesses are important players in the sanctioning process since firms are the first ones to come into contact with targeted entities or potential ones. Indeed, private businesses have extensive knowledge of their partners while public authorities do not. Thus, private actors become central in guaranteeing an effective implementation of restrictive measures. For instance, financial sanctions are often directly implemented by banks and financial institutions, since it is their tasks to freeze accounts, and block payments to/from listed individuals. Sometimes decisions are taken independently, other times private actors consult with public institutions on the best course of actions to undertake. Economic boycotts become truly effective when companies make further efforts to prevent certain technologies, services, finances and goods from becoming available to targeted individuals. EU regulations are binding for firms and companies that are based in the EU even when they operate abroad. In practice, this means that the monitoring and the enforcement capacities of EU institutions (also including member states) are relevantly affected by the lack of reach of public authorities. The next section analyses the four regulatory environments of EU targeted sanctions.

6.5 Regulatory Environments, Sanctions and For-Profit Actors

By analyzing the behavior of for-profit actors through a regulatory environments lens, it may be possible to predict when the implementation of sanctions by private actors will produce the consequences desired by policymakers. Indeed, there are four recurrent problems that correlate with specific regulatory environments. For instance, for-profit actors can either over comply with public regulations or they can disregard them. Additionally, the behavior of for-profit actors may depend on their geographical location in the EU and on their characteristics, such as size. This section summarizes the evidence on for-profit actors collected through interviews and desk-research between 2013 and 2015.

6.5.1 Type A of Regulatory Environment: Enforceable Implementation

Enforceable implementation occurs when public regulators provide clear instructions to for-profit actors and have the capacity to monitor and enforce the regulation. In the area of sanctions, this occurs when EU regulations are applied to firms and companies that are based and operate in the EU, and when the guidelines are very specific. For instance, financial transactions originating in the EU that are directed at targeted individuals in the EU would fall under this category. There are many regimes (Ukraine, Syria, etc.) that include a number of individuals to whom banks cannot provide financial support. Financial resources should not be made available to such individuals, and/or their bank accounts should be frozen. The regulation is specific about the required behavior and for-profit actors' actions can be monitored by national competent authorities because the transaction takes place within the borders of a EU member state. There is also enforceable implementation regarding high-value transactions, with public authorities retaining the final word in their authorisation. For instance, article 30 of the regulation 267/2012 on Iran requested financial transactions above 40,000 euros to be authorized by the competent authorities of member states (European Union 2012). Cases of *enforceable implementation* are characterized neither by the anarchy of the international system nor by the uncertainties of governing security as indicated above, therefore they will not be discussed further.

6.5.2 Type B of Regulatory Environment: Implementation by Persuasion

Implementation by persuasion is defined by the fact that for-profit actors are given instructions on what to do, but public authorities lack institutions that can monitor and control the behavior of for-profit actors. Sanctions regulations do provide a number of detailed information, for instance the correct spelling of the target's name, his/her date of birth and his/her passport number (among others), which enable financial institutions to identify targeted individuals. However, assessing the level of compliance is extremely problematic when monitoring is weakened by the transnational nature of the transactions. For instance, EU regulations are quite specific regarding the listing of entities in the Russian regime, but financial institutions operating outside of one's jurisdiction do pose a problem of monitoring and, therefore, enforcing the regulation. For instance, the Austrian Raiffeisen Bank is under scrutiny for having lent $183 million to VEB, a Russian bank that has been included in the list of sanctions by the EU Council in the July 2014 round (Corcoran et al. 2014). Discerning whether these loans are in violation of sanctions depends directly on the degree of knowledge that the ownership of the foreign subsidiaries in Russia had about these transactions. In other words, it would be easier to investigate such operations had they taken place within the EU since their extra-EU nature makes it more difficult to adjudicate what has happened. EU regulations are clear and provide the necessary details, but operating beyond EU borders provides non-state actors with greater leeway than what they would otherwise have.

Lacking and/or uneven monitoring further exacerbates the collective action problem, especially within the EU architecture, and this creates the problem of incoherent application of targeted sanctions.[6] This occurs not just in cases when the guidelines are not clear (see type C), but also when EU member states do not devote the same attention to the monitoring and enforcement of sanctions. EU regulations list the competent authorities that are supposed to be responsible for each member state, but a comparative analysis shows that not all EU members place equal effort into providing contacts of competent authorities. There are at least three different responses. First, there are the sanction-diligent states, which provide information to economic operators about the type of sanctions and the point of contacts for each of them in case of necessity. States such as the UK, Germany and the Netherlands would belong to this group. The second group is composed of those who do the minimum in providing information to operators, usually indicating the general point of reference in the ministry of foreign affairs and the ministry of finance. This would be the case of states such as Poland, Cyprus and Portugal. Finally, the third group is composed of those states that provided incorrect information about the national competent authorities, therefore making it intelligible to know who

[6]Interview with private stakeholders on sanctions in Brussels, 5 July 2013 and 22 October.

monitors the implementation of sanctions in certain member states. States in this category are Malta and Spain.[7]

Another instance of this problem occurs when dual-use goods cannot be sold to targeted entities. For instance, the decision of the Council to impose a ban on dual-use goods on Russia can be quite specific. Dual-use goods, whose system has been highly criticized for lack of clarity in the past, are now identified by a Council decision (European Union 2009). When the transaction takes place within the domain of one of the member states of the EU, and the good is listed as a dual-use good, then private companies have to decide whether to submit the request for export to a competent public authority. Given the lack of knowledge in this area, the decision depends very much on the extent to which that companies cooperate with public authorities and/or assess the risk of complying against the risk of non-complying.

As EU members do not devote the same attention to the enforcement of sanctions, firms can decide to relocate to other EU members and continue their business with targeted individuals and other targets. The behavior of for-profit actors in implementing public regulations is dependent more on their geographical location rather than on the spirit of the law.

6.5.3 Type C of Regulatory Environment: Enforceable Delegation of Implementation

Enforceable delegation of implementation refers to a situation where the delegation of sanction implementation can be enforced by public authorities. This means that while detailed instructions are not provided, monitoring and enforcing mechanisms are in place to favor compliance. This can be a strategic choice that is formulated through so-called 'constructive ambiguities'. These are formulations whose aim is to raise for-profit actors' attention regarding certain aspects of their activities in order to increase the system's resilience to threats. However, for-profit actors need to make sense of these constructive ambiguities and public authorities have the possibility to enforce the regulation.

This is the case, for instance, when regulations require financial institutions to block all 'suspicious transactions' (Art. 31, par. 1(d) of Regulation 267/2012 on Iran) without specifying what a 'suspicious transaction' is. Another example is the Regulation on the Crimea crisis, where Art. 2 par. 1 of Council Regulation 269/2014 demands that 'No funds or economic resources shall be made available, directly or indirectly, to or for the benefit of natural persons or natural or legal persons, entities or bodies associated with them listed in Annex I'. What does 'indirectly' mean? Who are the 'associated' bodies, legal persons or entities? In

[7] Author's own research, May 2014, based on Council Regulation No 325/2013 of 10 April 2013 on Syria.

most of the cases these decisions are left to the actors who are directly involved with the implementation of the restrictive measures, often private actors.

In the EU context, this means that even different EU states can interpret the regulation differently[8] as shown in the case of Valvitalia. Valvitalia is an Italian company that concluded an agreement for the export of valves to Iran in 2010, when sanctions still allowed such shipments. It obtained the export license from the Italian government, but the export and payment procedure was done via Germany. As the latter had a different interpretation of EU regulations, it froze the payment from the Iranian company to Valvitalia (A typology of regulatory environments 2012). Other major business groups indicated that different levels of implementation cause market distortion between EU companies.[9] As a consequence, the location of companies determines the behavior of for-profit actors.

As mentioned above, 'constructive ambiguities' have been monitored and enforced by public authorities. Enforcement actions have originated mostly from the United States (see Vlcek Chap. 5), but given the lack of response from the EU and EU member states authorities, it can be assumed that the EU accepted the extra-territorial claim of the US. As one EU member state official put it when asked if the EU is doing enough to monitor how sanctions are implemented within its territory: 'We do what we can, then we ask the Americans'.[10] Indeed, the activity of EU members in sanctions enforcement has not received the same attention as the one given to US actions. According to the report on the application of EU law, the EU does not take an active role in monitoring and enforcing the implementation of sanctions as there are no initiatives for late transpositions of sanction regulations. With the exception of Germany, which is publicly active in investigating sanctions' busting activities (Charbonneau 2010; Chambers 2012), it is assumed that EU members prefer to take a less spectacular approach, so implementation takes place on a one-to-one discussion between public authorities and individual firms.[11] Whereas a lack of, or only a few, fines can be interpreted as a sign of perfect compliance (Weingast and Moran 1983), the interviews carried out with individuals from the private sector suggest that the lack of fines is actually interpreted as a lack of interest on the side of the EU.[12] In any case, US authorities are mainly responsible for setting the tone of the international sanctions regime by imposing fines on several non-state actors. The first target of the Office for Foreign Assets Control (OFAC) was the UK-based bank Lloyds Banking Group for USD350 million in 2009. The list also includes banks from Germany (Deutsche Bank for USD258 million in 2013), the Netherlands (e.g. ING Bank for USD619

[8]This is not new, for instance it applies to the diverging categorization of conflicts across EU member states in Asylum policy (UNHCR 2007).

[9]Phone interview with firm, 14 January 2014.

[10]Interview with official from EU member state, February 2015.

[11]Interview with official from EU member state, February 2015.

[12]Interview with private stakeholders on sanctions in Brussels, 5 July 2013 and 12 November 2013.

million in 2012) and Italy (e.g. Intesa Sanpaolo for USD2.9 million in 2013) among others. OFAC's highest settlement took place with BNP Paribas in 2013, with the bank agreeing to pay USD8.9 billion to US authorities for violations of sanctions in Sudan, Cuba, Myanmar/Burma and Iran. Non-financial institutions have been hit as well. For instance, companies from Sweden (Stena bulk and KTM group), the Netherlands (Aviation Services International, CWT and Fokker Services), the UK (Balli Group PLC and Balli Aviation), Luxembourg (Weatherford International Holdings), Denmark (Maersk) and France (Schlumberger and CGG Services) settled with US authorities as a response to accusations of sanctions busting activities (Giumelli and Levi 2016).

The situation, in which companies are unsure about how to proceed, although they feel that their actions can be sanctioned, is likely to lead to overcompliance. This is a well-known problem in the sanctions field and has already been identified in counter-terrorism measures (Bures 2012). Over-compliance occurs when private actors avoid the risk of violating public regulations on restrictive measures by choosing to adopt extremely cautious behavior towards any transaction to and from targeted countries to such an extent that targeted sanctions become, in fact, comprehensive sanctions. Certainly, firms and companies based in the EU were affected by the dynamism of OFAC in enforcing sanctions. The result is, as recorded in Iran, that the behavior of for-profit actors turned sanctions from targeted to comprehensive (for instance, for the case of Iran see Giumelli and Ivan 2013). Banks and financial institutions did it because they were 'afraid of the consequences' as the reputational costs 'would be too high for our interests'.[13] The same situation has occurred with Syria where the increasing uncertainties scared private businesses away, adding to the already limited opportunities offered by this market. Given the growing uncertaintines and the risk of incurring into fines, compliance officers have preferred to advise firms and companies not to have contacts with countries that host sanctioned individuals or targets.

6.5.4 Type D of Regulatory Environment: Delegation of Implementation by Persuasion

Finally, *delegation of implementation by persuasion* refers to a situation wherein public authorities do not provide precise instructions and are not in the position to monitor and enforce the regulation. This is more frequently the case when economic boycotts are imposed. Although anti-money laundering policies in the last two decades have created an international regime with instruments to monitor the movement of capital, nothing comparable is yet in place when it comes to monitoring the trade of goods and services. Constructive ambiguities as indicated above

[13]Interview with private stakeholders on sanctions in Brussels, 5 July 2013 and 12 November 2013.

(type C) are therefore harder to monitor. For instance, art 15 par. D of Regulation 267/2012 does not specify whether machinery falls under the technical assistance linked to gold, precious metals and diamonds as specified in annex VII. When such transaction involves companies operating outside of the EU, then public authorities encounter problems to monitor and enforce the regulation.

The first problem of enforcement by persuasion is lack of compliance. Lack of monitoring combined with the possibilities of companies to interpret the spirit of public regulations explains why, sometimes, sanctions are perceived to be harmless. For instance, arms embargoes are notorious for the inability to prevent weapons from reaching conflict torn areas (Brzoska and Lopez 2009). While OFAC has been active in censoring the violation of financial sanctions, public institutions have been less keen on pursuing sanctions' busters in this area.

In other occasions, restrictive measures created the incentive for targeted entities to profit even further from the situation. It was reported that a sanctioned businessman in Myanmar managed to exploit the favorable fiscal regimes for import/export with the EU from neighboring countries.[14] This phenomenon is caused by for-profit actors exploiting the loopholes of vague instructions and it is made possible by the lack of monitoring mechanisms that characterises the activity of the EU in the area of targeted sanctions.

A further problem of d*elegation of implementation by persuasion* is that different companies respond differently to the same *persuasion* effort. Empirical research shows that the imposition of sanctions increases the possibilities of illegal trade for certain companies as sanctions regimes almost systematically involve busting activities (Naylor 2001; Early 2015). However, it appears that not all actors respond similarly to sanctions. The various interviews with firms and companies in the EU revealed that smaller companies are more likely to engage in sanctions busting activities than bigger ones. Smaller size companies take longer to adjust to EU sanctions because they are less sensitive to reputational costs than larger companies.[15] In such a case, public regulations alter the incentive structure of firms and companies according to their size.

Table 6.2 summarizes the classificatory typology of regulatory environments with the examples discussed above. The typology is relevant because it enhances the understanding of problems and challenges in regulating for-profit actors regarding the implementation of targeted sanctions. This typology contributes to explaining the (lack of) impact that EU regulations have when implementing sanctions on third parties by taking into account that for-profit actors can be central to the policy process.

[14]Interview with EU official in March 2010.

[15]Email exchange with private firm, 05 September 2014.

Table 6.2 A typology of regulatory environments

	Detailed instructions	Vague instructions
High monitoring capacity	Type A: Enforceable implementation Problem: not considered	Type C: Enforceable delegation of implementation Problem: overcompliance
Low monitoring capacity	Type B: Implementation by persuasion Problem: behavior depends on location of company	Type D: Delegation of implementation by persuasion Problem: lack of compliance, behavior depends on type of company

6.6 Conclusions

The Council of Ministers of the European Union frequently relies on targeted sanctions to deal with foreign policy challenges. In the tradition of the changing nature of state institutions and their relations to the use of force, the implementation of targeted sanctions takes place with regulations that rely on for-profit actors to implement targeted sanctions. The role of for-profit actors in the provision of security was thus far mainly studied in the context of private military and security companies, while less 'spectacular' actors have been largely neglected. The analysis presented in this chapter, however, demonstrates that implementation of targeted sanctions often relies on these less 'spectacular' actors.

The analysis was carried out by developing a classificatory typology that highlighted the importance of regulatory environments to determine (or make more likely) the behavior of for-profit actors. By looking at the clarity of instructions and the capacity of monitoring and enforcing public regulations, whose absence would depict the area of international security, the four ideal-types of regulatory environments highlight how different decisions may lead to different problems. For instance, overcompliance takes place in a situation of uncertainty wherein public regulators have demonstrated their capacity to enforce public regulations. The inability to monitor and enforce the behavior of for-profit actors, for instance by imposing targeted sanctions way beyond the borders of the EU, may be a guarantee of lack of impact. Finally, either the inability to provide clear instructions or to monitor the behavior of private actors creates a situation in which either the location or the type of companies/firms produces an uneven implementation of the regulation.

Several theoretical implications can be derived from this investigation. In particular, regulatory environments as permissive contexts could be further refined with the inclusion of more descriptive/qualifying variables, such as the quality of connections or the type of trade that is occurring between targeted entities and the rest of the world. The regulatory environment framework also presents the opportunity to investigate the micro-level, for instances by investigating the specific effect of companies' location, size and motivations on sanctions compliance.

At the same time, the findings of this analysis also bear several policy implications. First, the non-existent monitoring structure of the European Union is alarming. For-profit EU based actors are exposed, on the one hand, to extremely harsh US actions and, on the other hand, to the inaction of EU institutions and EU member states. New institutional developments, such as the adoption of the Panel of Experts' model that proved to be quite successful for United Nations sanctions, could ensure that for-profit actors would take EU regulations more seriously. Second, a monitoring mechanism would allow the EU to acquire independent and accurate information, which in turn would facilitate the design of sanctions by making the guidelines for implementation more specific. Finally, since the role of for-profit actors is indispensable in contemporary politics of sanctions, EU institutions should consider developing mechanisms to involve, train and prepare private actors to implement targeted sanctions. Whether this is done in the form of an open consultation or within a more dedicated forum, public institutions and private actors should engage in discussions on cross-cutting themes and issues, such as coordination across EU member states and drafting of general guidelines that can be used by for-profit actors to reduce the uncertainties to engage in business deals with actors located in states where certain individuals were hit by EU sanctions. This would also strengthen the resilience of the system against foreign threats and reduce the expectation/reality gap between *De l'Esprit de Lois* of regulations and their policy outcomes.

References

Abrahamsen, R., & Williams, M. C. (2009). Security beyond the state: Global security assemblages in international politics. *International Political Sociology, 3*(1), 1–17.

Allidge, P. (2008). Money laundering and globalization. *Journal of Law and Society, 35*(4), 437–463.

Avant, D. D. (2005). *The market for force: The consequences of privatizing security*. Cambridge, UK: Cambridge University Press.

Bailes, A. J. K., & Frommelt, I. (2004). *Business and security. Public-private sector relationships in a new security environment*. Stockholm: Stockholm International Peace Research Institute.

Bergstrom, M., Helgesson, K. S., & Morth, U. (2011). A new role for for-profit actors? The case of anti-money laundering and risk management. *Journal of Common Market Studies, 49*(5), 1043–1064.

Biersteker, T. J., & Eckert, S. E. (2007). *Countering the financing of terrorism*. New York: Routledge.

Braithwaite, J. (2008). *Regulatory capitalism: How it works, ideas for making it work better*. Cheltenham: Edward Elgar.

Brzoska, M., & Lopez, G. A. (Eds.). (2009). *Putting teeth in the tiger: Improving the effectiveness of arms embargoes*. Bingley, UK: Emerald Books.

Bull, B., & McNeill, D. (2007). *Development issues in global governance: Public–private partnerships and market multilateralism*. London: Routledge.

Bures, O. (2012). Private actors in the fight against terrorist financing: Efficiency versus effectiveness. *Studies in Conflict & Terrorism, 35*(10), 712–732.

Bures, O. (2013). Public-private partnerships in the fight against terrorism? *Crime, Law and Social Change, 60*(4), 429–450.

Bures, O. (2015). Political corporate social responsibility: Including high politics? *Journal of Business Ethics, 129*(3), 689–703.

Chambers, M. (2012, 15 August). Germany arrests four men suspected of busting Iran embargo. *Reuters.com*. Available at http://www.reuters.com/article/2012/08/15/us-germany-iran-embargo-idUSBRE87E0IT20120815

Charbonneau, L. (2010, 20 May). German arrests over Iran sale anger Russia-envoys. *Iran Focus: News and Analysis*.

Cherednychenko, O. O. (2016). Cooperative or competitive? Private regulators and public supervisors in the post-crisis European financial services landscape. *Policy and Society, 35*(1), 103–114.

Corcoran, J., Groendahl, B. & Katz, A. (2014). Raiffeisen draws sanctions scrutiny for Russia bond sale. *Bloomberg.com* (New York).

Donahue, J. D., & Zeckhauser, R. J. (2006). Public-private collaboration. In M. Moran, M. Rein, & R. E. Goodin (Eds.), *The Oxford handbook of public policy*. Oxford: Oxford University Press.

Dunn Cavelty, M., & Kirstensen, S. K. (2008). *Securing 'the Homeland'. Critical infrastructure, risk and (in)security*. London: Routledge.

Dunning, J. H. (Ed.). (1999). *Governments, globalization, and international business*. Oxford: Oxford University Press.

Early, B. R. (2015). *Busted sanctions. Explaining why economic sanctions fail*. Stanford: Stanford University Press.

Eriksson, M. (2010). *Targeting peace: Understanding UN and EU targeted sanctions*. Farnham, UK: Ashgate.

European Union. (2004, June 7). *Basic principles on the use of restrictive measures (Sanctions)*. The Council of the European Union. Available at http://register.consilium.europa.eu/doc/srv?l=EN&f=ST%2010198%202004%20REV%201

European Union. (2009). *Council Regulation (EC) No. 428/2009 of 5 May 2009 setting up a Community regime for the control of exports, transfer, brokering and transit of dual-use items*. Brussels: The Council of the European Union.

European Union. (2012, March 23). *Council Regulation (EU) No 267/2012 of 23 March 2012 concerning restrictive measures against Iran and repealing Regulation (EU) No 961/2010*. The Council of the European Union. Available at http://eur-lex.europa.eu/legal-content/EN/TXT/PDF/?uri=CELEX:32012R0267&from=EN

European Union. (2013, June 20). *Guidelines on implementation and evaluation of restrictive measures (sanctions) in the framework of the EU Common Foreign and Security Policy*. The Council of the European Union. Available at http://data.consilium.europa.eu/doc/document/ST-11205-2012-COR-2/en/pdf

European Union. (2015, March 24). *Restrictive measures (Sanctions) update of the EU best practices for the effective implementation of restrictive measures*. The Council of the European Union. Available at http://data.consilium.europa.eu/doc/document/ST-7383-2015-REV-1/en/pdf

European Union. (2016, March 1). *C-440/14 P – National Iranian Oil Company v Council*. Court of Justice of the European Union. Available at http://curia.europa.eu/juris/liste.jsf?language=en&num=C-440/14

Favarel-Garrigues, G., Godefroy, T., & Lascoumes, P. (2011). Reluctant partners? Banks in the fight against money laundering and terrorism financing in France. *Security Dialogue, 42*(2), 179–196.

Garriga, E., & Mele, D. (2004). Corporate social responsibility theories: Mapping the territory. *Journal of Business Ethics, 53*(1–2), 51–71.

Gilardi, F. (2008). *Delegation in the regulatory state: Independent regulatory agencies in western Europe*. Cheltenham, UK/Northampton, MA: Edward Elgar.

Giumelli, F. (2011). *Coercing, constraining and signalling. Explaining and understanding UN and EU sanctions after the Cold War*. Colchester: ECPR Press.

Giumelli, F. (2013). *The success of sanctions. Lessons learned from the case of the European Union*. Farnham: Ashgate/Routledge.

Giumelli, F. & Ivan, P. (2013, November). *The effectiveness of EU sanctions—An analysis of Iran, Belarus, Syria and Myanmar (Burma)* (EPC Report N. 76).

Giumelli, F. & Levi, G. (2016, June 3). Sanzioni: alle imprese europee la multa arriva dagli Usa. *LaVoce.info*. Available at http://www.lavoce.info/archives/41389/sanzioni-alle-imprese-europee-la-multa-arriva-dagli-usa/

Hall, R. B., & Biersteker, T. J. (Eds.). (2002). *The emergence of private authority in global governance*. Cambridge: Cambridge University Press.

Hart, O., Shleifer, A., & Vishny, R. W. (1997). The proper scope of government: Theory and an application to prisons. *The Quarterly Journal of Economics, 112*(4), 1127–1161.

Johnston, L. (1992). *The rebirth of private policing*. London: Routledge.

Jordana, J., & Levi-Faur, D. (Eds.). (2004). *The politics of regulation: Institutions and regulatory reforms for the age of governance*. Cheltenham, UK/ Northampton, MA: Edward Elgar.

Kettl, D. (1993). *Sharing power: Public governance and private markets*. Washington, DC: The Brookings Institution.

King, R. (2007). *The regulatory state in an age of governance*. London: Macmillan.

Kinsey, C. (2006). *Corporate soldiers and international security: The rise of private military companies*. London: Routledge.

Knill, C., & Lehmkuhl, D. (2002). Private actors and the state: Internationalization and changing patterns of governance. *Governance, 15*(1), 41–63.

Lane, J.-E. (2000). *New public management*. London: Routledge.

Leander, A., & van Muster, R. (2007). Private security contractors in the debate about Darfur: Reflecting and reinforcing neo-liberal governmentality. *International Relations, 21*(2), 201–216.

Lee, E. (2009). *Homeland security and private sector business: Corporations' role in critical infrastructure protection*. New York: CRC Press.

Levi, M. (2010). Combating the financing of terrorism: A history and assessment of the control of threat finance. *British Journal of Criminology, 50*(4), 650–669.

Levi-Faur, D. (2005). The global diffusion of regulatory capitalism. *The Annals of the American Academy of Political and Social Science, 598*, 12–32.

Majone, G. (1994). The rise of the regulatory state in Europe. *West European Politics, 17*(3), 77–101.

Majone, G. (Ed.). (1996). *Regulating Europe*. London: Routledge.

Massaro, F. (2012, July 17). Le sanzioni all Iran? Colpiscono il made in Italy. *Corriere della Sera*.

Naylor, T. R. (2001). *Economic warfare: Sanctions, embargo busting, and their human cost*. Boston: Northeastern University Press.

Olsen, J. P. (1988). Administrative reform and theories of organization. In C. Campbell & G. Peters (Eds.), *Organizing governance: Governing organizations*. Pittsburgh, PA: University of Pittsburgh Press.

Parker, C., & Lehmann Nielsen, V. (Eds.). (2011). *Explaining compliance: Business Responses to Regulation*. Cheltenham, UK/ Northampton, MA: Edward Elgar.

Peters, G. B. (1999). *Institutional Theory in Political Science: The 'New Institutionalism'*. New York: Pinter.

Petersen, K. L. (2008). Risk, responsibility and roles redefined: Is counterterrorism a corporate responsibility? *Cambridge Review of International Affairs, 21*(3), 403–420.

Portela, C. (2010). *European Union sanctions and foreign policy. When and why do they work?* Abingdon: Routledge.

Schaferhoff, M., Campe, S., & Kaan, C. (2009). Transnational public-private partnerships in international relations: Making sense of concepts, research frameworks and results. *International Studies Review, 11*(3), 451–474.

Scott, R. W. (2001). *Institutions and Organizations*. Thousand Oaks: Sage.

Shearing, C. D., & Stenning, P. C. (Eds.). (1987). *Private policing*. London: Sage Publications.

Singer, P. W. (2003). *Corporate warriors: The rise of the privatized military industry*. Ithaca: Cornell University Press.

UNHCR. (2007). *Asylum in the European Union. A study of the implementation of the qualification directive*. Brussels: UNHCR.

Vogel, D. (2010). The private regulation of global corporate conduct. Achievements and limitations. *Business and Society, 49*(1), 68–87.

Wallensteen, P., & Staibano, C. (Eds.). (2005). *International sanctions: Between wars and words in the global system*. Frank Cass: London.

Weingast, B. R., & Moran, M. J. (1983). Bureaucratic discretion or congressional control? Regulatory policymaking by the federal trade commission. *Journal of Political Economy, 91* (5), 765–800.

Winter, S., & May, P. J. (2001). Motivation for compliance with environmental regulations. *Journal of Policy Analysis and Management, 20*, 675–698.

Chapter 7
All in the Name of National Security: The Profiting from Xenophobia by Private Corporations in the Trump Era

Karina Moreno and Byron Eugene Price

7.1 Introduction

In June 2015, Donald Trump rode down an escalator at Trump Tower in New York City to announce his candidacy for president in a truly unconventional fashion, with an hour-long speech in which he called Mexican immigrants in the United States "criminals" and "rapists". This was the moment he first introduced his promise to build a "great, great wall on our southern border, and have Mexico pay for that wall." The speech proceeded with Donald Trump stating, "Mark my words. Nobody would be tougher on ISIS than Donald Trump." People laughed in amusement and jokes spread quickly throughout social media.

Trump's presidential campaign was run on a critical cornerstone piece, a crackdown on Mexican immigrants; footage of his political rallies throughout the country showed large crowds in attendance emphatically cheering for the U.S.–Mexico wall. Mexico was a regular talking point of the Trump campaign, as it is deemed responsible for a lagging economic recovery in the United States (U.S.) due to international trade deals, as well as a serious symbolic threat to American values, culture, and identity through the large numbers of Mexican immigrants that reside in the U.S. Along with these talking points on the immigration threat, Trump also regularly discussed the terror threat, linking counterterrorism to immigration enforcement. In December of 2015, he issued a press release calling for a "total

K. Moreno (✉)
Long Island University Brooklyn, 1 University Plaza, Brooklyn, NY 11201, USA
e-mail: karina.moreno@liu.edu

B.E. Price
Medgar Evers College of the City University of New York, 1650 Bedford Avenue, B-2015H, Brooklyn, NY 11225, USA
e-mail: bprice@mec.cuny.edu

O. Bures, H. Carrapico (eds.), *Security Privatization*,
DOI 10.1007/978-3-319-63010-6_7

and complete shutdown of Muslims entering the United States" following the San Bernadino attacks in California.

Though initially not taken seriously, Trump won more state contests than any of the other initial 17 Republican candidates in the presidency race. He became the Republican frontrunner and formally won the GOP nomination in July 2016. In a stunning development, he beat Democratic candidate Hillary Rodham Clinton and won the presidency November 8, 2016. Trump won because voter turnout in swing states that had previously voted for President Barrack Obama now voted in favor of the Republican's right wing populist candidate. Large numbers of Americans fervently responded to his rhetoric on immigration and terrorism. The Pew Research Center reported about 80% of Trump supporters considered illegal immigration a very big problem, and that about 86% viewed the immigration situation in the U.S. as one that had gotten worse since 2008. This strand of right wing party populism denounces immigrants and trade deals as outsourcing valuable American jobs. Trump capitalized on this sentiment, winning over a large number of Americans who believed he could "Make America Great Again."

7.2 Securitization of Immigration: Adding Private Corporations

We use the Trump illustration (though plenty of international examples exist, such as the UK's Leave Campaign that resulted in "Brexit," and the role of far-right political parties in the most recent national elections and referenda in Switzerland, Denmark, and France, for example) as an illustration to showcase how the securitization of immigration has become prevalent and largely accepted throughout the U.S., and even provides political gains for those who most loudly endorse these ideas. The securitization of immigration is "a process through which Western political elites—governments, leading political parties, and associated policy networks—rhetorically frame immigration as a security threat" (Chebel d'Appollonia 2015, p. 3). Since the horrific attacks of September 11th, it is observable how governments on both sides of the Atlantic have produced an escalating number of public policies that justify the expansion of state powers at the expense of democracy and individual civil liberties. In the U.S., the War on Terror continues to grow based on the magnitude of its inputs and activities and based on the amount of government financial, personnel, and technological resources devoted to protecting national security (Chebel d'Appollonia 2012).

However, we propose that this securitization picture, where governments, political parties, and associated policy networks are the key players, is incomplete by not including interests of private entities that are an integral part of the power elites responsible for encouraging an increasingly securitized approach to immigration. We also argue that this story is one the U.S. knows all too well, because it is history repeating itself. The War on Terror is strikingly similar to the U.S.'s previous War on Drugs, which led to a boom in mass incarceration disproportionately devastating African Americans and their families. Most notably, however, is the fact that the War on Drugs and the tough on crime movement were facilitated by the powerful private prison industrial complex. Meaning, the industry that scored the lucrative and coveted government contracts to incarcerate felons *created* those felons through lobbying for harsher criminal justice laws and longer mandatory minimum sentencing laws, which they sponsored and drafted. Through millions of lobbying dollars donated to both political parties, the private prison industrial complex was able to write the laws that resulted in an influx of prisoners, amassing unprecedented levels of profits (Price 2006).

Similarly, as the securitization of immigration has grown in size and scope in the U.S., governments at all levels have turned to private contracts to keep up with the exponential increase in demand for detention facilities (Doty and Wheatley 2013). Due to "liberal economic policies in general and privatization in particular, [privatization] has spread around the globe in recent decades" (Bortolotti et al. 2003, p. 95). Neoliberal ideology has driven privatization across the globe steadily since its inception in the 1970s by advocating the only way to meet macroeconomic objectives is by privatizing public enterprise (Schmitt 2011).

As this edited volume points out, traditional state sectors are now increasingly dependent on the private sector's capabilities and resources. As a result, market-like mechanisms are now embedded into what was traditionally public domain. This is more and more a popular occurrence internationally, as Bures (Chap. 2) corroborates and illustrates through his research on public-private partnerships (PPP) and the growing promotion of privatization. This is the current context of immigration enforcement in the U.S., and, as this book points out, little research has been done on how private businesses have come to manage the security sector. Our specific chapter aims to reinforce Bures' contribution (Chap. 2) in which he explains that the process of providing what was traditionally a public good, security, is inherently a political one; the reality of politics cannot be removed from the companies that constitute this immigration enforcement sector. Privatization has grown rapidly since 9/11, which has serious implications for how immigration enforcement is implemented through numerous private entities.

Our previous research study (2015) showed that the prison industrial complex is also involved in immigration detention as a result of rigorous lobbying, policymaking, managing private contracts, and in the running of immigration detention centers themselves. Our initial exploratory study illustrated how the prison industrial complex industry has turned to immigration detention as a new untapped market for more profits, with private prisons spending most (over 90%) of their lobbying dollars in states that have proposed harsher and more stringent immigration laws, like Arizona's infamous Senate Bill (S.B.) 1070. Official statements eventually revealed the extent to which the private prison industry was involved with this legislation; lobbyists themselves had directly drafted the bill (Sullivan 2010a, b). Ultimately, this creates financial returns and higher profits for them (Moreno Saldivar and Price 2015; Cohen 2015).

7.3 Research Question

Building upon this line of research, the present chapter argues that the ability of private actors to push for a more securitized approach to immigration state (motivated by profit-seeking, see Hodia 2012) negatively impacts the groups that it disproportionately targets, such as Latinos, immigrants, Muslims in the U.S., and anyone socially perceived as a "foreigner." Our research question is *what is the social and political impact of securitization of immigration in the U.S. on racial, ethnic minorities and immigrants*? To answer this question, we turn to the existing lines of inquiry on prison privatization (Aman and Greenhouse 2014; Bortolotti and Siniscalo 2004; Burkhardt and Conner 2016; Feely 2002; Jing 2010; Kim and Price 2014; Seidenstat 1996), its role in growing mass incarceration (motivated by profit-seeking) (Ashton and Petteruti 2011; Berg and Huebner 2011; Hirschi 1969; Laub and Sampson 2003; Mauer 2016; Smith and Hattery 2011; Western 2006), and its social and political effects on minorities in the U.S. because we believe these research areas overlap in a number of ways. First, we review the social, political, and economic effects of mass incarceration on racial and ethnic minorities in the U.S., which were the direct result of private interests shaping key legislation, as is currently the case of immigration and security. Then, we run a series of quantitative analyses using hierarchical regression models to test nationally representative data from 2013 and compare our dependent variables measuring social and political elements across different social groups; our findings show that Latinos and immigrants in the U.S., which represent the groups most vulnerable to securitization, are worse off compared to whites and African Americans, even when controlling for education, income, and age in *both* social and political aspects.

A key interpretation, which is also stated by Farrand and Carrapico in Chap. 9, emerged from our analysis. It emphasizes that market logic applied to security likely results in very serious consequences. Our paper's findings illustrate just how serious these consequences (spurred by private entities) can be for racial, ethnic minority groups and immigrants in the U.S. as it relates to their social and political standing. Specifically, social consequences that result from applying a market logic to a securitized immigration sector leads to problems of integration and assimilation, to alienation in social and political spheres, and affects the social capital and networks of these groups. Political consequences include reduced participation of members of groups most affected by securitization in electoral structures, which is a direct measure of democracy, as all as limited trust in government entities, law enforcement, and government efficacy. Both social and political dimensions are also critical to community development.

7.4 Background

Our initial analysis (Moreno Saldivar and Price 2015) showed evidence of how the private prison industrial complex has adapted and updated their business strategy from the War on Drugs to the current War on Terror, with very similar causal mechanisms

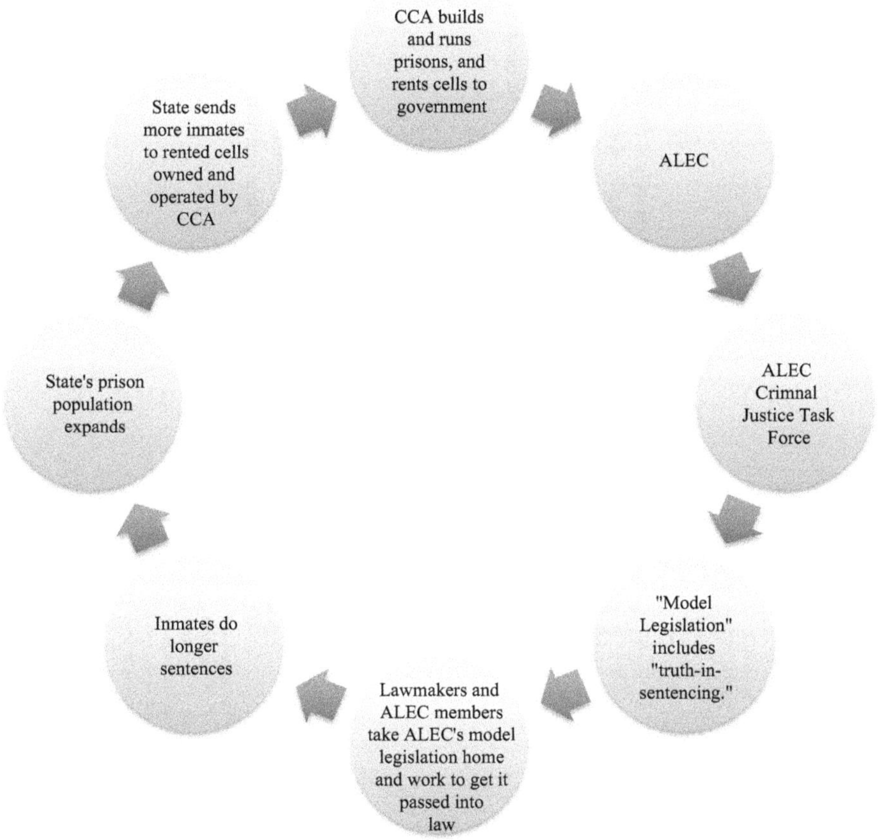

Fig. 7.1 Original model, private prisons' role in growing mass incarceration. Note: This model was used by Price (2006) from Biewen (2002)

in place to shape legislation and increase profit (please see Figs. 7.1 and 7.2 for visual illustrations of these similar cycles). As the political actors are the same and their actions are similar, we predict this new and unique line of research will tell a similar story to that of how the private prison industrial complex, driven by profit-seeking, grew mass incarceration and resulted in a detrimental impact on African Americans in the U.S., with weakened social, political, and economic structure participation that perpetually hinders democracy and promote social inequality. Thanks to the extensive literature that has carefully documented the detrimental effects of the War on Drugs on Black and Brown families throughout America (Ackerman and Furman 2013; Price 2006; Alexander 2010), we focus on juggling the anomalies of the securitization of immigration to push together lines of research that will provide a more comprehensive and complete picture of how the securitization of immigration has impacted immigrant and minority groups in the U.S. This is presented in the context of private corporate interests being, to some extent, responsible for the social and political impact on groups most vulnerable to securitization.

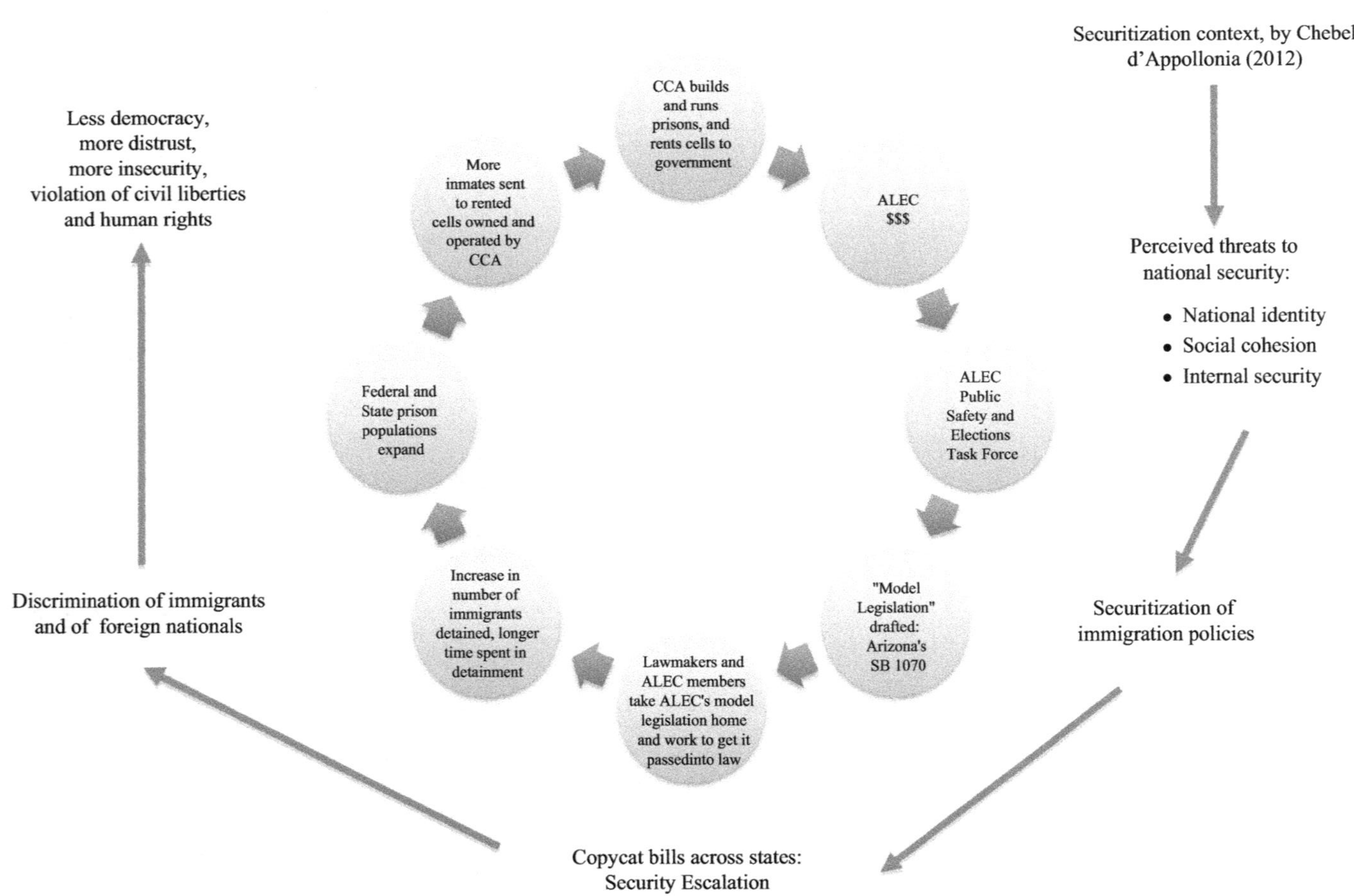

Fig. 7.2 Updated model by Moreno Saldivar and Price (2015)

This area of inquiry, which combines interdisciplinary research produced by scholars on the impact of the securitization of immigration, the political economics associated with markets, and the prison industrial complex's role in facilitating government legislation that prioritizes profit at the expense of democracy and social equality remains understudied. The topic, as it becomes increasingly prevalent, is of grave importance, especially in the given political climate, with more and more Americans worrying about the social cohesion of American culture and potential terrorist attacks. The *New York Times* referred to the 2016 presidential election as a national security one, as issues of immigration and security took center stage as the most important concerns to voters of both political parties.

Previous research relevant to our specific research question has largely focused on four key areas: (1) the evolution of immigration policies and politics post 9/11 as exclusionary and xenophobic (Schein 2008a, b; Fraga 2009; Mavelli 2013); (2) the securitization process, consisting of discourse and speech acts (Buzan et al. 1998; Balzacq 2005; Huysmans 2002; Stritzel 2007; Watson 2012); (3) integration and social incorporation of immigrants in host societies, arguing security-driven policies have become barriers to these processes post 9/11 and lead to alienation (Mollenkopf and Hochshild 2009; Hochschild et al. 2013; Mollenkopf 2013; Mollenkopf and Hochschild 2010); and, finally, (4) how ethno-racial groups manage intergroup competition, social and symbolic boundaries, and shape their political responses according to institutions and national ideologies (Chebel d'Appollonia 2015, p. 5; Lerman and Weaver 2014b).

Although these lines of research make for a greater understanding of immigrant processes and potential responses to an evolving securitized sector of immigration, they fail to include the political economy perspective. These lines of research do not mention that immigrant processes are affected by private corporations, questioning the normative reach and scope of what in theory has traditionally been public sector domain; that the detention of immigrants is a new market for the private prison industry, generating profits by capitalizing on the political discourse that actively reinforces immigrants as a security threat, and shaping subsequent public policies that disproportionately target and burden immigrants, Latinos, and Muslims in the U.S. Finally, these existing lines of research fail to address that although 9/11 marks the beginning of a new security paradigm, the War on Terror can learn from revisiting the social and political outcomes that resulted from the War on Drugs for racial and ethnic minorities, in attempts to learn from and correct perverse causal mechanisms that damage democracy. These items are all addressed here. We contend that in order to enforce accountability of the state, we should also weigh the effects of its outsourcing to private contractors and what this means for democracy, social equity, due process, fairness, and civil liberties. We link the social and political outcomes of securitization to private prisons, as governments increasingly defer to these in the immigration enforcement sector.

This chapter consists of two parts: part one summarizes the social, political, and economic effects that the War on Drugs had on Black and brown communities in the U.S.; the War on Drugs was a state initiative that represented private moneyed interests, especially the private prison industrial complex, and generated vast profits for these corporations through the mass incarceration boom created by the implementation of harsh legislation the corporations themselves wrote, sponsored, and lobbied for. Part two presents an empirical analysis that provides us with a profile of racial and ethnic minorities' and immigrants' current social and political standing. Although a limitation of the empirical analysis is to isolate the effects of securitization, given the complexity of the data available, we look at social and political variables of minorities and immigrants using nationally representative data from 2013, a year by which securitization is in full force in America. We find that those individuals who were disproportionately targeted by securitization and the War on Terror, specifically immigrants and Latinos, have lower levels of social and political capital. We conclude by predicting that the War on Terror will have marginalizing, disenfranchisement effects just as the War on Drugs had on Blacks in America; however, our findings also suggest a divergence in *the response* of those targeted. While African Americans were able to politically mobilize and protest against veiled attempts to undermine their civil rights (currently, this is visible through the #BlackLivesMatter movement), our findings show a much bleaker picture when it comes to Latinos and immigrants.

7.5 This Story Is Not New: The Role of Markets and Private Interests in the War on Drugs

It is imperative to consider, due to the existing parallels, the effects the War on Drugs had on those it targeted, which were disproportionately Black and Brown men. Due to its interest in further expanding its profits, the prison industrial complex played a key role in the proliferation of tougher sentencing laws and increasing incarceration rates (Fulcher 2012). Private prisons were key to growing mass incarceration in the U.S., which makes it difficult to distinguish public and private actors in the War on Drugs, as privatization processes allowed private prisons to obtain government contracts and interact with public agencies on a very large scale (Price 2006). A similar pattern has been observed regarding the securitization of immigration; private contractors (a lot of them the same actors as in the War on Drugs) proliferated through the political economy of security and immigration, with more and more private enterprises involved, shaping, and profiting from technology, transportation, and detainment practices that are now becoming standard practices in the securitization of immigration. In this section, we summarize the economic, political, and social impact of prison privatization and mass incarceration on racial and ethnic minorities.

According to Price and Morris, "the past four decades have witnessed a worldwide movement toward the privatization of goods and services traditionally, provided, produced, and delivered by government" (2012, p. 1). The contemporary roots of private prisons can be traced back to the "tough on crime" movement, which served as the impetus for the incarceration boom, in the late 1960s, early 1970s. The late 1970s and early 1980s were characterised by the War on Drugs campaign with the Rockefeller Drug Laws being the most infamous of all the policy changes related to drug policy. Hattery and Smith (2014) explain that other key changes to drug laws, such as mandatory minimums (Meierhoefer 1992), longer sentences for crack cocaine possession (King and Mauer 2006), felony drug offenses (King and Mauer 2006), and three-strikes laws (Haney and Zimbardo 1998) all contributed to the U.S. incarcerating more than 2.3 million citizens, approximately 1.3 million in state and federal prisons and another million in local jails, according to the Bureau of Justice Statistics. Concomitant with the increasing incarceration rate, "practically overnight the budgets of federal law enforcement agencies soared. Between 1980 and 1984, FBI antidrug funding increased from $8 million to $95 million. Department of Defense antidrug allocations increased from $33 million in 1981 to $1042 million in 1991. During that same period, DEA antidrug spending grew from $86 million to $1026 million, and FBI antidrug allocations grew from $38 to 181 million" (Alexander 2010, p. 49). Ironically, during the same period, public agencies in the preventative and rehabilitative areas of government that focused on drug treatment, prevention and education had their operational budgets severely slashed. For instance, the National Institute of Drug Abuse's budget was cut from $274 million to $57 million from 1981 to 1984 (Alexander 2010), and antidrug funds awarded to the Department of Education were cut from $14 million to $3 million.

Before proceeding, it is important to highlight the social and political ease with which political leaders in the U.S. not only gain financial campaign support from private corporations (Herman and Chomsky 2002), but also gain political support and legitimacy from their constituents (Schneider and Ingram 1997), is possible because of the social construction of knowledge that justifies punitive measures by the state. African Americans were socially portrayed (and still are) as "undeserving," as "deviants" by elected officials and the mass media, and actively linked to criminality. This backdrop is no coincidence (Schneider and Ingram 1997). It allows for the political economy reality of the punitive measures, which created mass incarceration in the U.S. and which disproportionately devastated the lives of Black and Brown men and their families, to be politically advantageous and an opportunity for those that endorse them in office (i.e. Bill Clinton's Welfare Reform of the 1990s). Furthermore, as the U.S. state is firmly grounded in neoliberal ideology, which encourages private contracting in general, this perpetual cycle of social manipulation of images and stigma towards "deviants" also makes for a financially sustainable business since it is based on the demand government itself created and is politically rewarded by visibly addressing it. Blessett (2012, p. 13) explains that Nixon's declaration against crime gave credibility to the public's unwarranted perceptions of crime and violence, particularly to their perceptions of African Americans as dangerous and deviants. He also claims that the Republican strategy was successful thanks to the use of coded anti-black campaign rhetoric (Blessett 2012, citing Beckett and Sasson 2005), which appealed to deep-rooted institutional racial bias in the U.S. Similar parallels exist in which Latino immigrants in the U.S. are socially constructed as "deviant" and are presented as an economic and symbolic threat to the U.S.'s national identity and social cohesion by political elites, who then facilitate state punitive action against them (Saldivar 2012).

The campaigns associated with the tough on crime and the War on Drugs movements, along with President Reagan's push to permanently reduce the role and scope of government created a ripe economic environment for private prisons to thrive. The "ascendant market-oriented conservatism, which painted government as inept and inefficient and held up the private sector as a superior service provider" (Chi and Jasper 1998, p. 78; President's Private Sector Survey on Cost Control 1983) was a key driving force in the rise of the government's use of privatization. The more recent impetus to privatize has been characterized by Megginson and Kay as both a political act and an "ideological and symbolic break with a history of state control over a country's productive assets" (2000, p. 14). Schmitt (2011) explains "liberal economic policies in general and privatization in particular have spread around the globe in recent decades" (p. 95). Scholars agree that neoliberal ideas have been the impetus behind increased privatization with their emphasis on government as ineffective in its responses to market failure.

Private prison corporations were quick to seize the opportunity and exploit this environment, which began to deemphasize restorative justice and concentrate on punishment as a very lucrative for-profit industry. This led to a number of societal deficiencies. For example, "the for-profit prisons have transformed into a vast industrial system at the expense of education in many states. The police, lawyers, court staff, lobbyists, convicts, long-distance phone service providers, and prison personnel all are a part of this growing business behemoth that generates billions of dollars for the for-profit prisons" (Price 2006, p. 111).

Furthermore, a review of a report on prisoners in 2010 (Guerino et al. 2011) shows that 30 states maintain a degree of privatization and seven states house more than a quarter of their prison population in for-profit prison facilities.

> In 2010, private prisons held 128,195 of the 1.6 million state and federal prisoners in the United States, representing eight percent of the total population. For the period 1999–2010, the number of individuals held in private prisons grew by 80%, compared to 18 percent for the overall prison population. While both federal and state governments increasingly relied on privatization, the federal prison system's commitment to privatization grew much more dramatically. The number of federal prisoners held in private prisons rose from 3828 to 33,830, an increase of 784%, while the number of state prisoners incarcerated privately grew by 40%, from 67,380 to 94,365.

Table 7.1 illustrates the point with respect to how private prisons have expanded their market.

To further help their cause and take advantage of this prison boom, private prison companies provided substantial financial support to the American Legislative Exchange Council (ALEC). This organization is reputable for championing privatization initiatives and advocating harsher sentencing and detention laws, such as mandatory sentencing statues and drafting model legislation on privatization (ACLU 2011). According to the Justice Policy Institute (2011), "At a time when many policymakers are looking at criminal and juvenile justice reforms that would safely shrink the size of our prison population, the existence of private prison

Table 7.1 Change in private prison populations, 1999–2010

Jurisdiction	Number in private prisons		Percent change (%)	Percentage of population (%)		Percent change (%)
	1999	2010		1999	2010	
Alabama	0	1024		0	3.2	
Alaska	1387	1873	35	35.1	33.5	−5
Arizona	1392	5356	285	5.4	13.3	146
Arkansas	1224	0	−100	10.7	0	−100
California	4621	2170	−53	2.8	1.3	−54
Colorado		4498			19.7	
Connecticut	0	883		0	4.6	
Delaware	0	0		0	0	
Florida	3773	11796	213	5.4	11.3	109
Georgia	3001	5233	74	7.1	10.6	49
Hawaii	1168	1931	65	23.8	32.7	37
Idaho	400	2236	459	8.3	30.1	263
Illinois	0	0		0	0	
Indiana	936	2817	201	4.8	10.1	110
Iowa	0	0		0	0	
Kansas	0	0		0	0	
Kentucky	1700	2127	25	11.1	10.4	−6
Louisiana	3080	2921	−5	9	7.4	−18
Maine	22	0	−100	1.3	0	−100
Maryland	131	70	−47	0.6	0.3	−50
Massachusetts	0	0		0	0	
Michigan	301	0	−100	0.6	0	−100
Minnesota	80	0	−100	1.3	0	−100
Mississippi	3429	5241	53	18.8	24.9	32
Missouri	0	0		0	0	
Montana	726	1502	107	24.6	40.4	64
Nebraska	0	0		0	0	
Nevada	561	0	−100	5.9	0	−100
New Hampshire	0	0		0	0	
New Jersey	2517	2841	13	8	11.45	43
New Mexico	1873	2905	55	38.6	43.6	13
New York	0	0		0	0	
North Carolina	1395	208	−85	4.5	0.5	−89
North Dakota	0	0		0	0	
Ohio	0	3038		0	5.9	
Oklahoma	6228	6019	−3	27.8	22.9	−18
Oregon	0	0		0	0	
Pennsylvania	0	1015		0	2	
Rhode Island	0	0		0	0	
South Carolina	0	17		0	0.1	

(continued)

Table 7.1 (continued)

Jurisdiction	Number in private prisons 1999	2010	Percent change (%)	Percentage of population (%) 1999	2010	Percent change (%)
South Dakota	46	5	−89	1.8	0.1	−94
Tennessee	3476	5120	47	15.4	18.7	21
Texas	11653	19155	64	7.1	11	55
Utah	248	0	−100	4.6	0	−100
Vermont	0	562		0	27	
Virginia	1542	1560	1	4.8	4.2	−12
Washington	331	0	−100	2.3	0	−100
West Virginia	0	0		0	0	
Wisconsin	3421	25	−99	16.8	0.1	−99
Wyoming	281	217	−23	16.4	10.35	−37
Federal	3828	33830	784	2.8	16.1	475
State	67380	94365	40	5.5	6.8	24
Total	71208	128195	80	5.2	8	54

companies creates a countervailing interest in preserving the current approach to criminal justice and increasing the use of incarceration" (p. 2). The system has been preserved, and an entire commercial correctional complex has been developed concomitant with the expansion of detention driven by profit-seeking. Pager (2003) found that "in terms of policy implications, this research has troubling conclusions. In our frenzy of locking people up, our 'crime control' policies may in fact exacerbate the very conditions that lead to crime in the first place" (p. 961).

7.6 The Economic Result from the Private Prison Industry Growing Incarceration

Mass incarceration, as a direct result of the private prison industry's powerful lobby, eroded economic prospects for Black and Brown men by charging offenders with fees and a criminal record. These fees are then used to support the expansion and growth of private prisons. Pager (2003) emphasized that the "research consistently shows that finding quality steady employment is one of the strongest predictors of desistance from crime" (Shover 1996; Sampson and Laub 1993; Uggen 2000). Ultimately, "the fact is that a criminal record severely limits employment opportunities—particularly among blacks" (Pager 2003, p. 961; Holzer et al. 2013)." Social networks are also compromised by incarceration and further exacerbate the inability to find legal employment; even worse, it forces ex-offenders to develop new social networks, which may make criminal activity more likely. American legislatures "deny convicted offenders the right to enter into contracts, automatically dissolving their marriages, and barring them from a wide variety of jobs and benefits" (Travis 2005, p. 18). Additional adverse impacts of felony disenfranchisement laws are the "denial of public housing, welfare benefits, the mobility necessary to access jobs that require driving, child support, parental rights, the ability to obtain an education, and in, the case of deportation, access to opportunities that brought immigrants to this country" (Travis 2005, p. 18). The combination of cost shifting and the inability to find stable employment leaves the formerly incarcerated unable to meet the obligations of supporting their families and stabilizing their home life. Another impediment to reform that can challenge the growth of private prisons is the fact that these facilities are now tied to local employment and economic development among a number of states and to a substantial number of counties and municipalities.

7.7 The Social Result from the Private Prison Industry Growing Incarceration

Loury (2014) built on Alexander's research by connecting detention, democracy, and inequality with marginalization and disconnectedness. Research documents that incarceration has an adverse impact on those it incarcerates as well as on adult children of incarcerated parents (Lee 2015). They find that "the adult children of incarcerated parents are less civically engaged than other children of similar backgrounds" (Lee 2015). This study attributes this behavior to the parents who were not civically engaged themselves; "prisoner's offspring, in turn, end up being less likely to be registered to vote, less likely to have voted in the last president election, and less likely to engage in community service" (Lee 2015). The authors also find that the children of incarcerated parents report less trust in government and perceive more discrimination.

Muller and Schrage (2014) also found a correlation between weakened family structures, the ability to find stable employment, achievement of economic security, and incarceration. They believe Americans' high rates of imprisonment have the ability to erode Americans' trust in the government. Byproducts of this growing distrust are social movements to reduce the number of people in prison and a "self-reproducing cycle whereby growing distrust leads to more punishment and more punishment leads to more distrust" (Muller and Schrage 2014, p. 141).

Because of the U.S.'s hyper-incarceration, "a person can cease to have economic value in capitalism if they cannot be deployed productively" (Hattery and Smith 2014, p. 131). As this devaluing takes place, there is a disengagement from society and an erosion of social bonds precisely in the communities with the direst need of stability. Given the social costs associated with incarceration, at what point do policy makers reform the current system? "Prison expansion is expensive in the costs it imposes on both those who serve time behind bars and in absorbing tax dollars. Policy discussion should be informed by the limitation of the fact that prison expansion, beyond a certain point, will no longer serve any reasonable purpose. It seems that that point has been reached" (Liedka et al. 2006, p. 247). Although prisons have reached their marginal diminishing returns, the incentive to reform them is thwarted because of the lobbying dollars they provide to both political parties, which are critical to finance political campaigns, and ensuring that any changes that would cut into private prisons' profit dollars are not politically feasible.

7.8 The Political Result from the Private Prison Industry Growing Incarceration

The U.S. incarcerates more people than any other nation in the world and a by-product of this mass incarceration is the marginalization of large segments of the African American and Latino community: "Like Jim Crow, mass incarceration marginalizes them physically (in prisons, jails, and ghettos), and then authorizes discrimination against them in voting, employment, housing, education, public benefits, and jury service" (Alexander 2010, p. 11). Loury finds that "a fundamental source of contemporary inequality in punishment is the alienation of local urban populations from the exercise of democratic controls over the apparatus of punishment" (Loury 2014, p. 179). To this point, Loury (2014) "sees direct citizen participation in bringing charges against fellow citizens and deciding their disposition as having a crucial role in establishing, and in shaping the character of, Athenian democratic practice" (Loury 2014, p. 179). As a result of being marginalized, African Americans and Latinos are less likely to participate in direct democracy and play less of a role in shaping American democratic practice. Owen (2014) describes this marginalization as ways to sideline them from the public square. To further alienate African American and Latino ex-offenders, Owen contends, "parolees and probationers are often perceived as undeserving of citizen benefits such as food stamps, subsidized college loans, public housing and professional opportunities like licenses and contracts and deprive them of the right to vote and exercise full and free citizenship" (2014, p. 257).

Pioneering work by Weaver and Lerman (2010) and Lerman and Weaver (2014a) hypothesized that contact with the criminal justice system leads to decreased political participation because it depletes resources and increases distrust in government, which ultimately translates into reduced commitments to civic norms. Burch (2014, p. 185) stated that "[t]he criminal justice system has the power to shape not only the political participation of current and former felons but also the participation of the people who live around them because criminal justice interactions are demographically and geographically concentrated". According to Gerber et al. (2014, p. 2), "[t]here are two primary mechanisms by which spending time in prison might reduce political participation: through the effect of laws curtailing voting rights and through the effect of spending time in prison on attitudes and human and social capital". The Sentencing project found that:

> Nationally, an estimated 5.85 million Americans are denied the right to vote because of laws that prohibit voting by people with felony convictions. Felony disenfranchisement is an obstacle to participation in democratic life which is exacerbated by racial disparities in the criminal justice system, resulting in 1 of every 13 African Americans unable to vote. (The Sentencing Project 2016)

Gerber et al. (2014) also found that political participation of those formerly incarcerated is low once they become eligible to vote; of the potential explanations considered, they find that contact with the criminal justice system and incarceration is the finding with the most explanatory power. The authors contend, "there are a variety of mechanisms by which time in prison may reduce political involvement" (Gerber et al. 2014, p. 8). In the end, they "learn that they have less standing in the social and political community through this contact with the carceral state" (p. 9).

Political representation for African Americans and Latinos is also diminished as a result of imprisonment because felony disenfranchisement laws dilute the already limited political power in these communities (Mauer 2003). Gottschalk (2009) explained how impactful felony disenfranchisement laws are on African American and Latino representation; in the 2000 and 2004 presidential elections, an estimated 5 million Americans were unable to vote because of a felony conviction. Moreover, Manza and Uggen (2006, p. 10) calculated that "if Florida had not banned so many ex-felons from voting in the 2000 election, Al Gore would have carried the state by at least thirty thousand votes handily winning the White House."

An even more egregious effect of felony disenfranchisement laws on African American and Latino representation is prison-based gerrymandering. Prisoners are counted for census purposes where they are incarcerated, and because of this peculiarity in the census, "prisoners are included in the population tallies used for congressional reapportionment and for redistricting state legislatures, county governments, and city councils" (Gottschalk 2009, p. 444). Recently, "In May 2006, a federal appeals court suggested that counting tens of thousands of African American and Latino prisoners from New York City as upstate residents may be illegally diluting the voting rights of people downstate under section 2 of the Voting Rights Act" (Gottschalk 2009, p. 445; Roberts 2006).

Finally, researchers have consistently found that the devaluing experience of incarceration impacts and shapes the political behaviors and attitudes of those formerly incarcerated as well as their families (Uggen et al. 2012; Manza and Uggen 2006; Clear 2008; Travis 2005). "Ex-prisoners are less trusting of government, less likely to think they can influence politics, less engaged in political conversation, and far less likely to participate politically than those with no prior involvement in the criminal justice system" (Manza and Uggen 2006, p. 111).

In summation, based on the private prisons' business model and previous empirical work that demonstrates an adverse impact on African Americans and Latinos, we predict the new security governance in enforcing immigration, which continues to become increasingly privatized and follows a very similar business model, will result in similar negative social, political, and economic effects for racial and ethnic minorities and immigrants. We contend that securitization in its current form, tightly linked to private corporations vested in the continual growth of this industry, will affect how racial and ethnic minorities and immigrants are politically inactive and withdrawn, which will then hinder the developing and/or strengthening of social capital of these groups, and will also affect their political ideology and mobilization pattern(s).

7.9 Securitization of Immigration in the U.S., Possible by "Threat" Construction

Trump, shockingly, is no real departure from existing xenophobic and politicized rhetoric when it comes to immigrants. Historically, this harsh stance has been politically expedient for political elites and elected officials. Bigo (2002, p. 65) attributed the securitization of immigration to several factors; first, the fear by those who hold political power of losing "their" symbolic territories to foreigners and immigrants; second, securitization is facilitated by globalization of technologies of surveillance and control that exist beyond countries' borders; third, securitization of immigration exists because structural risk is embedded in neoliberal discourse as a limit to freedom. He refers to the securitization of immigration as a "transversal political technology" (p. 65) because "the framing of the state as a body endanger[ed] by migrants is a political narrative activated for the purpose of political games in ways that permit each politician to distance himself or herself from other politicians, but within the same rules of the game. It is a social construction useful for the politicization of migration" (p. 68). Indeed, security and immigration are large political opportunities for those in power, as illustrated by our opening Trump anecdote, and echoing previous "smear campaigns" against African Americans by linking them to criminality and justifying the expansion of incarceration. Bigo stated, "The relation between security and migration is fully and immediately political. The wording is never innocent" (2002, p. 71). This is problematic once democracy becomes compromised and justifiably so in light of emergency and exception.

In the U.S., immigration is framed a severe threat, a multidimensional one that endangers national identity and social cohesion (perhaps best illustrated by Huntington 2004). The complexity of this security threat became increasingly nuanced once terrorism was added to the already existing rhetoric of how immigrants bring an influx of crime, a depletion of public resources, and endanger local economies. After 9/11, immigration policy became counter-terrorist policy in the U.S., and vice versa. Chebel d'Appollonia (2012, p. 3) presents how the terms "immigrant" and "terrorist" were consistently linked in the aftermath of 9/11, which led to a new heightened security mantra and resulted in two effects: first, terrorism was portrayed as a threat not only to people's lives but also to their values, freedom, and economic and social welfare, justifying exceptional responses, outside the realm of normal democratic politics. Second, the category constituting the 'others'—those outside the mainstream of society who were considered to pose a security threat—was also broadened. Today it includes all those who threaten—or are perceived to threaten—national unity and civil security. The categories of foreigners, immigrants, and suspicious minorities have been increasingly conflated—irrespective of their actual status—because the impossibility of knowing where and against whom to fight back had led to increasing unease about the identity and the location of the enemy.

This has facilitated a number of things; first, the domestic audience in the U.S. at large has shown little to no political resistance (in fact, it is often quite the opposite) when political leaders frame immigration and security as a serious threat that must be aggressively tackled by the state; ultimately, the implementation of the policy solutions set forth by the state actively target and burden immigrants, Latinos, and Muslims in the U.S., yet are framed by the state as the only feasible solution. Secondly, it has caused the groups most vulnerable to securitization to "express strong concerns about being singled out for increased surveillance, monitoring, racial profiling, and increased discrimination" (Chebel d'Appollonia 2015, p. 3). However, because of the lack of social and political clout within the Latino and Muslim communities in the U.S., challenges to securitization by minorities are left unsaid out of fear and resentment (Moreno Saldivar 2012, 2015). This is also impacted by the fact that the domestic audience in the U.S. at large has accepted the framing of immigration as a security threat; according to a recent Pew Research study (2015), about half of Americans believe the government's anti-terrorism policies have not gone far enough to protect them and the country (Gao 2015). The culmination of these factors result in a political landscape in which the manipulation of images used in the social construction of knowledge and the sensational political rhetoric are used to justify policy responses that are punitive and burdensome, providing gains for political leaders (Schneider and Ingram 1997), while also then providing the private prison industry with the easy feat of strategically organizing their business in a way to maximize this new punitive market of detaining immigrants.

7.10 The "New" War on Terror, the Same Key Players

The same ALEC organization that spread tough on crime legislation is now involved in restrictive anti-immigrant laws, such as Arizona's S.B. 1070; ALEC designed and drafted this legislation, then sponsored and advocated it across the U.S., leading to 36 state legislatures considering these Arizona copycat bills (Moreno Saldivar and Price 2015; Hodia 2010; Sullivan 2010a, b). Most of the federal privatization in Table 7.1 can be ascribed to "an unprecedented increase in the number of detained immigrants—incarcerated pursuant to civil detention authority but housed in prison-like conditions" (ACLU 2011, p. 16). A *Huffington Post* investigation reinforces the data in Table 7.1 as it found that there is a concerted effort by the private prison industry to tilt policies favorable to increased immigration detention (Kirkham 2012). Moreover, the investigation found:

> In Washington, the industry's lobbyists have influenced policy to secure growing numbers of federal inmates in its facilities, while encouraging Congress to increase funding for detention bedspace. Here in this southern Arizona community, private prison companies share the spoils of their business with the local government, effectively giving area law enforcement an incentive to apprehend as many undocumented immigrants as they can. (Kirkham 2012)

The *Huffington Post* investigation confirms that lobbying has contributed to a doubling of immigrant detainees. The report found that immigration detainees have increased to about 400,000 a year and half are held in private prisons, up from one-fourth a decade ago according to the report which cites the Department of Homeland Security (Kirkham 2012). According to the report and as a result of the successfully lobbying, the two largest for profit prison corporations, Corrections Corporation of America (CCA) and The Geo Group, have more than doubled their immigration detention revenues since 2005.

The ACLU (2011) reported these two for-profit prison companies house nearly 50% of the more than 30,000 immigrants detained by Immigration and Customs Enforcement (ICE) at any given time. Furthermore, Moreno Saldivar and Price (2015) demonstrated that the private prison lobby funds exist overwhelmingly in states that have proposed anti-immigrant bills very similar to Arizona's, with CCA and The GEO Group spending over 90% of their lobbying dollars between 2003 and 2012 in states that proposed Arizona copycat bills. Goodkind (2013) of Yahoo Finance reports that "Private prisons bring in about $3 billion in revenue annually, and over half of that comes from holding facilities for undocumented immigrants. Private operations run between 50% and 55% of immigrant detainment facilities" (Goodkind 2013). "Seemingly ever increasing number of immigrants in the United States—and elsewhere—are incarcerated while awaiting immigration and deportation hearings, in facilities including county- and state-operated prisons and privately managed detention centers" (Colon and Hiemstra 2014, p. 335). This carceral expansion is driven by privatization, the rise of interior immigration policing, and the securitization of immigration (Colon and Hiemstra 2014).

7.11 Data and Method

Given that it has been established that private prisons are inherently involved in the passing of anti-immigrant legislation that has grown immigration detention (which they run), this study attempts to provide a portrait of how this affects those most vulnerable to the securitized immigration sector. To empirically test the current social and political standing of those most vulnerable to being affected by the securitization of immigration in the U.S. (immigrants and Latinos), this study uses secondary quantitative data from the Current Population Survey (CPS) from 2013. The CPS is a nationally representative dataset executed by the U.S. Census Bureau, with the individual respondent as the unit of analysis. The CPS uses a random sample, allowing for generalizations on the U.S. population to be made. The data used in this statistical analysis includes a sub-sample of 25,321 observations. This study relies on a hierarchical regression to illustrate the quantitative models' explanatory power as more independent variables are added to the analysis. The year of the data, 2013, is important because it means that the securitization context is well established in the United States; the U.S. had an influx of anti-immigrant legislative initiatives that began after 9/11. Notably, there was a wave of state anti-immigrant bills after Arizona passed its Senate Bill 1070 in 2010, which was sponsored and drafted by members of the private prison lobby (Moreno Saldivar and Price 2015); this caused 36 states to propose copycat legislation in their state legislatures. Because we know that securitization is in full effect by 2013, illustrated by the number of policy proposals across the country's state legislatures, we believe the 2013 dataset is appropriate for this study.

The key dependent variables included in this study are two—the social and political impact of securitization on those it is most likely to affect the most. To examine the social impact of securitization, we operationalize this variable by using a survey question that inquires on the respondent's level of trust in their community and neighborhood; respondents are asked to answer the question using a Likert scale from low to high. This variable is relevant because it is indicative of a respondents' social capital and sense of belonging in their community. Scholars of securitization have argued that the discrimination incurred by immigrants and minorities as a result of securitized immigration processes has led to alienation at both the individual and group levels; however, scholars have failed to provide empirical evidence of this. Given the complexity of studying these phenomena, this is to be expected. However, despite these limitations, we use this measure of the level of trust in the community as a proxy to compare responses between racial, ethnic groups and immigrants to address whether the data confirms discrepancies exist by groups, which can provide evidence of alienation. This social aspect can also be linked to levels of social capital, which research identifies as a determinant of civic engagement (Putnam 1996).

Additionally, to examine the political impact of securitization, we operationalize this by using two measures from the survey on political attitudes and participation, one that inquires on how often the respondent votes (using a Likert scale, low to high) and another that asks how often the respondent discusses politics with family and friends (also, using a Likert scale, low to high). The body of work on political participation is largely quantitative and focuses on conventional, or electoral, participation. This is a limiting factor when studying Latinos, who naturalize in lower numbers and at a slower pace than other immigrant groups, and immigrants in general. Therefore, our analysis includes a measure of political participation that is conventional, how often a respondent participates in electoral elections, as well as an unconventional measure, which asks how often a respondent discusses politics with family and/or friends (citizenship is not required). We use the two to get a sense of political attitudes and participation among the different groups and make comparisons.

The independent variables included in this study are race, ethnicity, immigrant and citizenship status; socio-demographic variables of education level, household yearly income, and age are included as control variables.

A three-step hierarchical multiple regression is used. Hierarchical regression uses ordinary least squares (OLS) regression in a nested format to compare explanatory power between models. This method is also appropriate because it accommodates multiple predictor variables.

The first quantitative model begins with educational attainment level, household annual income, and age as socio-demographic variables that we control for.

$\Upsilon = \beta_0 + \beta_1 X_1 + \beta_2 X_2 + \beta_3 X_3$

The second quantitative model adds race and ethnicity, allowing for comparisons to be made across whites, African Americans, and Latino respondents. This is appropriate for this study because it allows us to compare responses between racial and ethnic groups.

The third and final model adds whether the respondent is a foreign-born immigrant or native-born, as well as whether the respondent is a citizen or not, distinguishing between foreign-born respondents who have become naturalized citizens and those who are legal residents.

Unstandardized coefficients as well as standardized are reported; standard errors as well. However, since the key variables used in this data analyses exist in a variety of raw units of measurement, the beta coefficients are the most useful and indicate the strength in the weight of each variable.

7.12 Findings

This study uses hierarchical analysis to examine the social and political effects of securitization, beginning with the social impact. This first portion of the analysis used the level of trust the respondent has in his/her community and neighborhood as the main dependent variable (Table 7.2). This analysis resulted in a number of elements: first, each hierarchical model gradually increases the R^2, or the explanatory power, of each model, and each of the models are highly statistically significant, which is a positive indication of the quantitative analyses included in this study.

The first step of the model begins with control variables, which include educational attainment level, household income, and age; these socio-demographic variables that measure resources are all, unsurprisingly, highly significant. The R^2 of the first model begins with 9%, meaning 9% of the variation in explaining the predictors of level of trust in community is explained by the control variables included. This R^2 increased gradually as the hierarchical models included more independent variables. In the second model, which added race and ethnicity, the R^2 increases to 13%, and finally, in the third and last step of the hierarchical model, it is 14%. This means 14% of the variation in predicting a respondent's level of trust in their community is accounted by the full third model, which includes control

Table 7.2 Social impact

	Model 1			Model 2			Model 3		
Variable	B	SE B	Β	B	SE B	Β	B	SE B	β
Education	0.08	0.01	0.09***	0.06	0.01	0.07***	0.06	0.01	0.07***
Household income	0.04	0.00	0.18***	0.03	0.00	0.14***	0.03	0.00	0.14***
Age	0.01	0.00	0.22***	0.01	0.00	0.18***	0.01	0.00	0.18***
White				0.19	0.02	0.09***	0.15	0.02	0.06***
Black				−0.29	0.02	−0.10***	−0.33	0.03	−0.12***
Latino				−0.35	0.02	−0.12***	−30	0.02	−0.11***
Immigrant							−0.13	0.02	−0.05***
Citizenship							−0.05	0.03	0.01***
R^2	0.09			0.13			0.14		

*$p < 0.05$, **$p < 0.01$, ***$p < 0.001$
Summary of hierarchical regression analysis for variables predicting respondent's trust in their community and neighborhood (n = 25,321)

variables controlling for individual's resources of education, and income, socio-demographic variables of age, race, and ethnicity, and the last step includes variables of whether the respondent is an immigrant and a citizen (naturalized or native). All models are highly significant, indicating a good fit, and the standardized beta coefficients allow us to determine the weight and strength of each variable in comparable order to the other variables included, even though all are measured in different raw, original units. The positive or negative sign indicates the sign of the relationship. This means that the largest positive predictors of level of trust are income and age, meaning the higher the level of income and the older the respondent, then the higher level of trust reported.

The next two strongest predictors are negative, which include Black and Latino respondents. This means that race and ethnicity are negatively correlated with level of trust in their community and neighborhood. Whites are the only group with a positive relationship, indicating higher levels of trust among this population. Immigrants also show a negative relationship, meaning if a respondent is an immigrant, the level of trust in their community is lower than those respondents who are not immigrants.

This is important to consider when we think about levels of social capital, of which Blacks, Latinos, and immigrants have the lowest, and when we consider this is exactly what makes the social construction of security *against* these groups by large and powerful corporations (and the politicians whose campaigns they finance) very doable and practical, and will allow these to continue to frame immigration as a severe security threat.

This also has implications in the response to securitization by Blacks, Latinos, and immigrants—low levels of social capital indicate a lower likelihood of responding in protest by any of these groups, which results in an acquiescence response from the audience.

Table 7.3 Impact on political participation (conventional, electoral)

	Model 1			Model 2			Model 3		
Variable	B	SE B	B	B	SE B	B	B	SE B	β
Education	0.27	0.01	0.22***	0.25	0.01	0.21***	0.24	0.01	0.20***
Household income	0.04	0.00	0.12***	0.04	0.00	0.13***	0.04	0.00	0.12***
Age	0.02	0.00	0.34***	0.02	0.02	0.32***	0.02	0.00	0.31***
White				0.44	0.03	0.14***	0.18	0.03	0.06***
Black				0.71	0.03	0.18***	0.46	0.03	0.12***
Latino				−0.42	0.02	−0.11***	−0.06	0.02	−0.01*
Immigrant							−0.29	0.03	−0.08***
Citizenship							0.89	0.04	0.17***
R^2	0.19			0.22			0.26		

*$p < 0.05$, **$p < 0.01$, ***$p < 0.001$
Summary of hierarchical regression analysis for variables predicting how often a respondent votes (n = 25,321)

The next portion of the analysis (Table 7.3) distinguishes between conventional and unconventional forms of political participation as a response to securitization.

The first analysis examining conventional political participation (voting) resulted in all three steps of the hierarchical regression being highly statistically significant. The first model, which are the control variables, resulted in an R^2 of 19%, meaning 19% of the variation in explaining how often a respondent votes is explained by education, income, and age. These variables are all highly significant, which was expected based on the vast amount of literature and empirical studies around the Classic SES model (Campbell 1960) that emphasized socio-demographic and level of resources as the strongest predictors of voting. The second step of the model that includes race and ethnicity increases the R^2 to 22%, meaning this is able to explain more of the variation and means this addition is valuable to the quantitative analysis. It is important to point out that white and Black respondents have positive and highly significant relationships with voting, while Latino respondents are the *only* group to result in a negative standardized coefficient, meaning Latino respondents represent lower levels of electoral political participation.

The third step and final cumulative model which added immigrant and citizenship variables indicated that age and education carry the strongest weight as predictors of voting and increase the R^2 to 26%, meaning the variables included in this study carry substantial explanatory power and strengthen the quantitative model with each step. Also interestingly, the final model demonstrates that immigrants are highly statistically significant in a negative relationship. If the respondent is an immigrant, then within this cross section of data from 2013, this means the respondent is correlated with lower voting turnout. The immigrant variable includes respondents who are naturalized citizens and can vote in elections, as well as those who have not become naturalized. Latinos are the only other result that reflects a negative relationship, meaning lower voting turnout. White and Black respondents both had a highly significant and positive result.

This can suggest that the groups most targeted by securitization included in this dataset reflect lower levels of electoral voting, which can be by design if we consider the work by Schneider and Ingram (1997) in which they predict that political participation depends on how individuals internalize messages about their self-worth based on their exchanges with bureaucracies and government entities; if these perceive that they do not matter to government, as previous research on Latinos in Arizona following the passage of S.B. 1070 has found (Saldivar 2012, 2016, forthcoming), then these groups ultimately withdraw from formal political processes, including voting. The result is very similar to individuals who have been incarcerated. When they re-enter society, their belief in government efficacy is low and they consider forms of political participation futile; they live in marginalization and experience disenfranchisement through various means.

The last portion of the analysis (Table 7.4) examines the political effects in an unconventional method of political participation, operationalized by the measure on how often a respondent discusses politics with family and/or friends. The analysis shows the strongest predictor is continuously the respondent's education level.

The variables of Latino and immigrant, however, are the only two highly significantly negative results in this piece of the analysis. This means that Latinos and immigrants result in the lowest unconventional form of participation of discussing politics with friends and/or family. White, Black, and citizen respondents (though citizenship is not a prerequisite for discussion on politics, especially local politics that affect residents the most) all result in highly significant and positive relationships, with the control variables of education and income carrying the most weight.

Table 7.4 Impact on political participation (unconventional)

	Model 1			Model 2			Model 3		
Variable	B	SE B	B	B	SE B	B	B	SE B	β
Education	0.32	0.01	0.23***	0.30	0.01	0.21***	0.30	0.01	0.21***
Household Income	0.05	0.00	0.15***	0.05	0.00	0.14***	0.05	0.00	0.14***
Age	0.01	0.00	0.10***	0.01	0.00	0.08***	0.01	0.00	0.07***
White				0.42	0.03	0.11***	0.31	0.03	0.08***
Black				0.28	0.04	0.06***	0.18	0.04	0.04***
Latino				−0.40	0.03	−0.09***	−0.26	0.03	−0.06***
Immigrant							−0.21	0.03	−0.05***
Citizenship							0.16	0.05	0.03***
R^2	0.11			0.12			0.13		

$*p < 0.05$, $**p < 0.01$, $***p < 0.001$

Summary of hierarchical regression analysis for variables predicting how often a respondent discusses politics with friends/family (n = 25,321)

7.13 Discussion, Interpretations, and Conclusion

The findings from the quantitative analyses show that Latino and immigrant respondents have consistently negative results in *both* the social and political aspects examined here, even when accounting for citizenship status, education level, and household income. This provides evidence of a number of important things; first, citizenship is not the strongest determinant of social and political attitudes, which is in line with the literature reviewed in this paper indicating that the social construction of a security threat and "the other" it creates and perpetuates through fear and suspicion is *not* based on legal citizenship status, giving credence and providing evidence of the reality of racial profiling. This is especially alarming; securitization can potentially erode civil liberties and due process of American citizens based on the social perception that they *pose* a threat. Ultimately, this can potentially manifest in a number of problematic ways that prohibits the successful social and political integration of Latinos and immigrants in the U.S., which is an obstacle to social cohesion.

Huysmans's (2000) research concluded inclusion for immigrants became *more* difficult in a securitized immigration sector. He found (2000, p. 771) securitization of immigration negatively impacted community solidarity, integration, and cultural identity. We add to Huysmans that the negative impact on community solidarity, integration, and cultural identity is the result of the state's securitization process *in conjunction with* private corporate interests. Plainly, this means private security corporations, motivated by growing profits and safe in their political power accumulated since 9/11, are directly vested *against* the integration of immigrants and are complicit in the state's framing of them as a security threat rather than a challenge worth solving. Similar to the devastating and enduring effects from the War on Drugs, the actions of the War on Terror target those who are already in a compromised, weakened position and guarantees to keep them from building any real social and political capital.

This response, referred to by the literature as "an acquiesced response," can be expected when the large corporations involved lobby millions of dollars and push a dominant and politicized narrative; this narrative keeps America in a continual state of exception fearful of the threats to its national identity and security. This is a key detraction from African Americans' response to the previous War on Drugs, which was framed by the civil rights movement and in which they mobilized in large numbers using civil disobedience methods. Immigrants, Latinos, and Muslims all lack the opportunity structure, the social capital, the political clout, and the financial resources to publically oppose and placate public fears on national security. They have in common, however, being socially construed as "deviants" for political gain as well as being targeted by local police, bringing issues of trust, government efficacy, and community development to the forefront.

When profit motive is present among an industry made up of very strong, competitive, and global corporations, it is safe to assume that securitization will likely continue to grow in the U.S. without much political resistance, despite its erosion of due process and violation of individual civil rights and liberties. In holding our government's leadership accountable, it is imperative to include in our evaluation the role of private security companies as key actors in the securitization process. This role is made possible because politicians and the media frame a security threat and reinforce the use of anti-immigrant measures as a means to achieve national security, then privatize and use corporations to fulfill certain responsibilities. Research from the U.S. and Europe suggests that the social and political assimilation and integration of immigrants is highly dependent on the use of political discourse, symbols, and framing used by the state to justify policy responses. If these are punitive, those who experience them tend to lean towards alienation, instead of inclusiveness.

Profit will always guide private companies' behaviors and strategies; this is simply rational behavior on their part. However, instead of being objects of regulation, the U.S. witnesses private industries as *shapers* of regulation; this regulation will reflect their own private interests relevant to their bottom line (also see Carrapico and Farrand, Chap. 9; Bonfanti and Stefanucci, Chap. 11; Porcedda, Chap. 12). This is a deficiency of democracy. Our goal is not to vilify private contractors; our goal is to present existing evidence to show how private companies are inherently vested in what are critical social issues, which can result in detrimental and unequal social and political effects on American citizens. The way that the current model exists today, where dollars translate into social and political power, we can predict that marginalization and disenfranchisement of immigrants, Latinos, and Muslims (we need future research to include data on Muslims as this is incredibly difficult to acquire from existing data) will continue, leaving these groups to experience second-tier citizenship that first assumes their guilt until they prove their innocence through burdensome, strict, means-tested protocols.

If the U.S. is going to continue its reliance on the private prison industrial complex in its enforcement of immigration, then it is imperative to establish ways to include oversight and public accountability. As we see more and more neoliberal economic policies became the norm not just in the U.S. but globally, we must consider regulatory frameworks as our procedural safeguards to uphold normative values of equity, fairness, and due process over that of profits. This will prove to be a challenge as private companies have the political currency and the economic means to fund their way into the policymaking arena, and will lobby for the policies that will fill the most beds in their detention centers (as it equals to more dollars). As immigration enforcement moves in this direction, different avenues to offset the negative impact of private corporations need to be explored, such as regulatory frameworks, increased political participation and representation of racial and ethnic minorities and immigrants in the policy making arena, as well as ways in which we can strengthen political and social incorporation of minorities, potentially through developing and building their levels of social capital and their sense of belonging in their local communities.

This proves to be all the more challenging since Trump's election has already resulted in the increase of immigrant arrests by about 40% in the first 100 days alone, overloading and backlogging the immigration court system and assuring longer detainment for these immigrants. While this translates into higher profits for the corporations involved, the observable social and political effects on these families and communities are immediate. Because immigrant communities are increasingly fearful of any interaction with the state, there is a decrease in the number of crimes reported; there is a spike in the rates immigrant and/or Latino children are absent from school; there is a withdrawal from participating in social services families are entitled to (resulting in greater food insecurity); and a decrease in preventative and routine healthcare, which ultimately leads to poorer health outcomes.

We have a responsibility to build interdisciplinary research on the issues central to this particular book. Our specific study, while in pursuit of one particular research question left us at the conclusion with another key question, and that is, with the private prison industrial complex being an integral part of the immigration enforcement domain in the U.S., what procedural mechanisms can we use to ensure our government's normative values of accountability, transparency, ethics, fairness, due process, and social equity are not devalued at the expense of profit and efficiency in the hands of private entities, as well as keep these from curtailing our existing legal frameworks.

References

Ackerman, A. R., & Furman, R. (2013). The criminalization of immigration and the privatization of the immigration detention: Implications for justice. *Contemporary Justice Review, 16*(2), 251.

ACLU. (2011). Banking on bondage: Private prisons and mass incarceration. New York: American Civil Liberties Union. Retrieved October 26, 2016, from https://www.aclu.org/files/assets/bankingonbondage_20111102.pdf

Alexander, M. (2010). *The new Jim Crow: Mass incarceration in the age of colorblindness.* New York, NY: The New Press.

Aman, A. C. J., & Greenhouse, C. J. (2014, December). Prison privatization and inmate labor in the global economy: Reframing the debate over private prisons. *Fordham Urban Law Journal, 42*, 355.

Ashton, P., & Petteruti, A. (2011, June). *Gaming the system: How the political strategies of private prison companies promote ineffective incarceration policies.* Washington, DC: Justice Policy Institute.

Balzacq, T. (2005). The three faces of securitization: Political agency, audience and context. *European Journal of International Relations, 11*(2), 171–201. doi:10.1177/1354066105052960.

Beckett, K., & Sasson, T. (2005). Review of the politics of injustice: crime and punishment in America. *Journal of Criminal Justice and Popular Culture, 12*(1), 71–76.

Berg, M. T., & Huebner, B. M. (2011, April). Reentry and the ties that bind: An examination of social ties, employment, and recidivism. *Justice Quarterly, 28*(2), 382.

Biewen, J. (2002). *Part 1: corporate-sponsored crime laws, corrections Inc*. Washington, DC: American Radio Works.
Bigo, D. (2002). Security and immigration: Toward a critique of the governmentality of unease. *Alternatives, 27*(Special Issue), 63–92.
Blesset, B. (2012). Prisons for profit: The political and economic implications of private prisons. In B. E. Price & J. C. Morris (Eds.), *Prisons privatization: The many facets of a controversial industry* (pp. 9–27). Santa Barbara, CA: Praeger.
Bortolotti, B., & Siniscalo, D. (2004). *The challenges of privatization, an international analysis*. Oxford: Oxford University Press.
Bortolotti, B., Fantini, M., & Siniscalo, D. (2003). Privatization around the world: Evidence from panel data. *Journal of Public Economics, 88*, 305.
Burch, T. R. (2014). Effects of imprisonment and community supervision on neighborhood political participation in North Carolina. *The Annals of the American Academy, 651*, 450.
Burkhardt, B. C., & Conner, B. T. (2016). Durkheim, punishment, and prison privatization. *Social Currents, 3*(1), 84.
Buzan, B., Waever, O., & de Wilde, J. (1998). *Security: A new framework for analysis*. London, UK: Lynne Rienner Publishers, Inc..
Campbell, A., Converse, P. E., Miller, W. E., & Stokes, D. E. (1960). *The American voter*. Chicago: Wiley.
Chebel d'Appollonia, A. (2012). *Frontiers of fear: Immigration and insecurity in the United States and Europe*. Ithaca, NY: Cornell University Press.
Chebel d'Appollonia, A. (2015). *Migrant mobilization and securitization in the U.S. and Europe: How does it feel to be a threat?* New York, NY: Palgrave Macmillan.
Chi, K. S., & Jasper, C. (1998). *Private practices: A review of privatization in state government*. Lexington, KY: Council of State Governments.
Clear, T. (2008). The effects of high imprisonment rates on communities. *Crime and Justice, 37*(1), 97–132.
Cohen, M. (2015, April 28). How for-profit prisons have become the biggest lobby no one is talking about. *Washington Post*.
Colon, D., & Hiemstra, N. (2014). Examining the everyday micro-economies of migrant detention in the United States. *Geographic Helvetica, 69*, 335.
Doty, R. L., & Wheatley, E. S. (2013). Private detention and the immigration industrial complex. *International Political Sociology, 7*, 426.
Feely, M. J. (2002). Entrepreneurs of punishment—The legacy of privatization. *Punishment and Society, 4*(3), 321.
Fraga, L. R. (2009). Building through exclusion: Anti-immigrant politics in the United States. In J. L. Hochschild & J. H. Mollenkopf (Eds.), *Bringing outsiders in: Transatlantic perspective on immigrant political incorporation* (pp. 176–192). Ithaca: Cornell University Press.
Fulcher, P. A. (2012). Hustle and flow: Prison privatization fueling the prison industrial complex. *Washington Law Journal, 51*, 589.
Gao, G. (2015, May 29). *What Americans think about NSA surveillance, national security and privacy*. Pew Research Center. Retrieved May 18, 2016, from http://www.pewresearch.org/fact-tank/2015/05/29/what-americans-think-about-nsa-surveillance-national-security-and-privacy/
Gerber, A. S., Huber, G. A., Meredith, M., Biggers, D. R., & Hendry, D. J. (2014, December 11). *Does incarceration reduce voting? Evidence about the political consequences of spending time in prison from Pennsylvania and Connecticut*. Unpublished manuscript.
Goodkind, N. (2013). *Top 5 secrets of the private prison industry*. Message posted to http://finance.yahoo.com/blogs/daily-ticker/top-5-secrets-private-prison-industry-163005314.html
Gottschalk, M. (2009). Money and mass incarceration: the bad, the mad, and penal reform. *Criminology & Public Policy, 8*, 87–109.
Guerino, P., Harrison, P., & Sabol, W. (2011). Prisoners in 2010. U.S. Department of Justice. http://www.bjs.gov/content/pub/pdf/p10.pdf

Haney, C., & Zimbardo, P. (1998). The past and future of U.S. Prison policy twenty-five years after the Stanford prison experiment. *American Pyscologist, 53*(7), 709.
Hattery, A. J., & Smith, E. (2014, November). Families of incarcerated African American men: The impact on mothers and children. *The Journal of Pan African Studies, 7*(6), 128.
Herman, E. S., & Chomsky, N. (2002). *Manufacturing consent: The political economy of the mass media*. New York: Pantheon Books.
Hirschi, T. (1969). *Causes of delinquency*. Berkeley: University of California Press.
Hochschild, J., Chattopadhyay, C. G., & Jones-Correa, M. (2013). *Outsiders no more? Models of immigrant political incorporation*. Oxford: Oxford University Press.
Hodia, B. (2010, June 21). *Corporate con game: How the private prison industry helped shape Arizona's anti-immigrant law*. Message posted to http://inthesetimes.com/article/6084/corpo rate_con_game
Hodia, B. (2012, August 29). *Marco Rubio, GEO Group, and a legacy of corruption*. Message posted to http://www.prwatch.org/news/2012/08/11591/marco-rubio-geo-group-and-legacy-corruption
Holzer, H., Raphael, S., & Stoll, M. (2013). Employment barriers facing ex-offenders. New York University Law School. Retrieved October 26, 2016, from http://www.urban.org/sites/default/files/alfresco/publication-pdfs/410855-Employment-Barriers-Facing-Ex-Offenders.PDF
Huntington, S. (2004). *Who are we? America's great debate*. London: Simon and Schuster.
Huysmans, J. (2000). The European Union and the securitization of migration. *Journal of Common Market Studies, 38*(5), 751–777.
Huysmans, J. (2002). Defining social constructivism in security studies: The normative dilemma of writing security. *Alternatives, 27*(Special Issue), 41–62.
Jing, Y. (2010). Prison privatization: A perspective on core governmental functions. *Crime Law and Social Change, 54*, 263.
Kim, Y., & Price, B. E. (2014). Revisiting prison privatization: An examination of the magnitude of prison privatization. *Administration and Society, 46*(3), 255.
King, R. S., & Mauer, M. (2006). *Sentencing with discretion: Crack cocaine sentencing after booker*. New York: Sentencing Project.
Kirkham, C. (2012). *Private prisons profit form immigration crackdown, federal and local law enforcement partnerships*. Message posted to http://www.huffingtonpost.com/2012/06/07/pri vate-prisons-immigration-federal-law-enforcement_n_1569219.html
Laub, J., & Sampson, R. (2003). *Shared beginnings, divergent lives: Delinquent boys to age 70*. Boston: Harvard University Press.
Lee, E. (2015). *Millions spent lobbying by private prison corporations to keep a quota of arrested immigrants, report says*. Think progress. Retrieved October 26, 2016, from https://thinkprogress.org/millions-spent-lobbying-by-private-prison-corporations-tokeep-a-quota-of-arrestedimmigrants-report-c68e82916819#.omkyf85nu
Lerman, A. E., & Weaver, V. (2014a). *Arresting citizenship*. Chicago: University of Chicago Press.
Lerman, A. E., & Weaver, V. (2014b). Staying out of sight? *Annuals of the American Academy of Political and Social Sciences, 651*(1), 202.
Liedka, R. V., Piehl, M. A., & Useem, B. (2006). The crime-control effect of incarceration: Does scale matter. *Criminology & Public Policy, 5*(2), 245.
Loury, G. C. (2014). Detention, democracy, and inequality in a divided society. *The Annals of the American Academy, 651*, 178–182.
Manza, J., & Uggen, C. (2006). *Locked out: Felon disenfranchisement and American democracy*. New York: Oxford University Press.
Mauer, M. (2003). *The sentencing project, comparative international rates of incarceration: An examination of causes and trends 2*. Washington, DC: The Sentencing Project.
Mauer, M. (2016). *Felony disenfranchisement*. Retrieved April 3, 2015, from http://www.sentencingproject.org/issues/felony-disenfranchisement/

Mavelli, L. (2013). Between normalisation and exception: The securitisation of Islam and the construction of the secular subject. *Millennium: Journal of International Studies, 41*(2), 159–181.

Megginson, W., & Kay, S. J. (2000). Privatization. *Foreign Policy Journal, 118*, 14.

Meierhoefer, B. S. (1992). *The general effect of mandatory minimum prison terms: A longitudinal study of federal sentences imposed.* Washington, DC: Federal Judicial Center.

Mollenkopf, J. (2013). Dimensions of immigrant political incorporation. In J. L. Hochschild, J. Chattopadhyay, C. Gay, & M. Jones-Correa (Eds.), *Outsiders no more?* (pp. 107–118). New York: Oxford University Press.

Mollenkopf, J., & Hochschild, J. (2009). Setting the context. In J. L. Hochschild & J. H. Mollenkopf (Eds.), *Bringing outsiders in: Transatlantic perspective on immigrant political incorporation* (pp. 3–14). Ithaca: Cornell University Press.

Mollenkopf, J., & Hochschild, J. (2010). Immigrant political incorporation: Comparing success in the United States and Europe. *Ethnic and Racial Studies, 33*(1), 19–38.

Moreno Saldivar, K. (2012). *The impact of Arizona's senate bill 1070 on Latino political attitudes and participation: A mixed methods study.* https://rucore.libraries.rutgers.edu/rutgers-lib/37343/pdf/1/

Moreno Saldivar, K. (2015). A muted voice? Red tape and Latino political participation. *Public Administration Quarterly, 39*(1), 51–84.

Moreno Saldivar, K. M., & Price, B. E. (2015). Private prisons and the emerging immigrant market in the U.S.: Implications for security governance. *Central European Journal of International and Security Studies, 9*(1), 40–65.

Muller, C., & Schrage, D. (2014). Mass imprisonment and trust in the law. *The Annals of the American Academy of Political and Social Science, 651*(1), 139–158.

Pager, D. (2003, March). The mark of a criminal. *American Journal of Sociology, 108*(5), 937.

Owen, S. (2014). *The case for private prisons.* Politico magazine. Retrieved October 26, 2016, from http://www.politico.com/magazine/story/2014/02/the-real-story-about-private-prisons-104098_Page2.html#.V_mwiiMrLyV

President's private sector survey on cost control. (1983). *Report on privatization.* Washington, DC: U.S. Government Printing Office.

Price, B. E. (2006). *Merchandizing prisoners: Who really pays for prison privatization?* Santa Barbara, CA: Praeger.

Price, B. E., & Morris, J. C. (2012). Introduction. In B. E. Price & J. C. Morris (Eds.), *The environment of private prisons* (Vol. 1, p. 4). Santa Barbara: Praeger.

Roberts, Sam. (2006, May 31). *Court asks if residency follows inmates up the river.* New York Times, sec B1.

Sampson, R. J., & Laub, J. H. (1993). *Crime in the making: Pathways and turning points through life.* Cambridge, MA: Harvard University Press.

Schain, M. (2008a). Immigration policy and reactions to terrorism after September 11. In A. Chebel d'Appollonia & S. Reich (Eds.), *Immigration, integration and security: America and Europe in comparative perspective* (pp. 111–129). Pittsburgh: University of Pittsburgh Press.

Schain, M. (2008b). *The politics of immigration in France, Britain, and the United States.* New York: Palgrave Macmillan.

Schmitt, C. (2011). What drives the diffusion of privatization policy? Evidence from the telecommunications sector. *Journal of Public Policy, 31*(1), 95.

Schneider, A., & Ingram, P. (1997). *Policy design for democracy.* Lawrence: University Press of Kansas.

Seidenstat, P. (1996). Privatization: Trends, interplay of forces, and lessons learned. *Policy Studies Journal, 24*(3), 464.

Sentencing Project. (2016). *Felony disenfranchisement.* Retrieved February 23, 2015, from http://www.sentencingproject.org/template/page.cfm?id=133

Shover, N. (1996). *Great pretenders: Pursuits and careers of president thieves*. Boulder, CO: Westview.
Smith, E., & Hattery, A. (2011). Can social capital networks assist re-entry felons to overcome barriers to re-entry and reduce recidivism? *Socialization Today, 9*(1), 1.
Stritzel, H. (2007). Towards a theory of securitization: Copenhagen and beyond. *European Journal of International Relations, 13*(3), 357–383.
Sullivan, L. (2010a). *Prison economies help drive Arizona immigration law. National public radio*. Retrieved May 13, 2016, from http:www.npr.org/2010/10/28/130833741/prison-economics-help-drive-ariz-immigration-law
Sullivan, L. (2010b). *Shaping state laws with little scrutiny. National public radio*. Retrieved May 13, 2016, from http://www.npr.org/2010/10/29/130891396/shaping-state-laws--with-little-scrutiny
Travis, J. (2005). *But they all come back: Facing challenges of prisoner reentry*. Washington, DC: The Urban Institute Press.
Uggen, C. (2000). Work as a turning point in the life course of criminals: A duration model of age, employment, and recidivism. *American Sociological Review, 67*(6), 529.
Uggen, C., Shannon, S., & Manza, J. (2012). *State-level estimates of felon disenfranchisement in the United States, 2010*. Washington, DC: The Sentencing Project.
Watson, S. D. (2012). 'Framing' the Copenhagen school: Integrating the literature on threat construction. *Millennium: Journal of International Studies, 40*(2), 279–301.
Weaver, V. M., & Lerman, A. E. (2010). Political consequences of the carceral state. *American Political Science Review, 104*(4), 817.
Western, B. (2006). *Punishment and inequality in America*. New York: Russell Sage.

Chapter 8
The Sentinel and the Rebel: Multi-choice Policing in Burundi and the State-Centered Approach of Security Sector Reform

Gilles Biaumet

8.1 Introduction

As a low income, turmoiled transitional country, Burundi has faced and still faces the challenge of mastering its security sector after a protracted civil war, characterized by large-scale massacres. This chapter sheds light on several internal security arrangements in Burundi, involving 'beyond the state' security, whether they are corporate-driven or informal mechanisms of social control. Alongside a corporate security sector, which presents the peculiarity of being almost completely local, Burundi also experiences occurrences of grassroots arrangements in a multi-choice policing environment (Baker 2008; Hills 2009). These arrangements go from the use of informal sentinels in Bujumbura, to the employment of former combatants to guard palm oil plots in the countryside.

Drawing on an analysis of the above-mentioned grassroots arrangements, this chapter develops a back-to-back approach to the notions of 'security governance' and 'security sector reform' (SSR). The latter has become, in the late 2000s, a touchstone policy reference, emphasizing holistic approaches of security reforms at least on a conceptual level. The literature presented in the chapter accounts for years of debate over the progressive incorporation of non-state actors to SSR concepts and practices (Schroeder et al. 2014). On the other hand, the notion of security governance remains a shallow tool of multiple social science subfields, summoning issues of coordinated management and regulations as means for governing security through heterarchical relations between various actors (Dupont 2004; Shearing and Wood 2003). More importantly, the security governance literature varies widely in its approaches. For example, recent works on nodal

G. Biaumet (✉)
Centre de Recherche en Science Politique (CReSPo), Université Saint-Louis – Bruxelles, Boulevard du Jardin Botanique 43, 1000 Bruxelles, Belgium
e-mail: gilles.biaumet@usaintlouis.be

O. Bures, H. Carrapico (eds.), *Security Privatization*,
DOI 10.1007/978-3-319-63010-6_8

security governance have pushed an ambitious research agenda for analytical accountings of sites of security (Wood 2006). On the contrary, concerns about the rule of law, due process and general accountability, in an environment of overlapping private and public orders, have led authors to assume various normative stances over specific nodes' role in steering security (Hoogenboom 2010; Avant 2005).

Burundi is a sort of Petri dish of security arrangements and SSR practices. On the one hand, grassroots arrangements arguably reflect the unwillingness or inability of homeowners or entrepreneurs to resort to state or corporate security. On the other hand, Burundi has been a site of experimentation for some of the latest conceptualizations of SSR processes.

After contextualizing SSR processes in the country and some of their realizations, the chapter moves to the literature on security governance and underlines its moments of dialogue with the literature on SSR. In a more empirical section, insights are offered on corporate, then grassroots arrangements of security in Burundi. The use of self-policing mechanisms not only adds to the case for considering the persistence of flaws in SSR conceptualizations or implementations. It also seemingly shows how sites of security in areas of limited statehood, where different agents and normativities are intertwined in the provision of security, may remain impervious to external interventions.

The main aim of the chapter is twofold. First, it intends to strengthen empirical knowledge of the multi-choice policing environment in Burundi. Second and against this background, it questions the persisting connections and disconnections between the literature on security governance and the literature on SSR, both in their analytical and normative perspectives.

8.2 Burundi: A Tale of Needed Security Sector Reforms

Ever since 1962, Burundi's national history as an independent country has been scourged with conflicts. Whether interpreted as ethnic or political, outbursts of violence culminated on several occasions (Reyntjens et al. 2000): in 1972, massacres of unprecedented scales resulted in the death of approximately 200,000 Hutus between April and November; in 1988, around 20,000 people were killed in a new cycle of violence barely a year after Major Pierre Buyoya bloodless coup; from 1993, following the murder of the first democratically-elected president of Burundi, Melchior Ndadaye, violence settled in the country for 13–16 years (Boshoff et al. 2010). Each time, the role of the Burundian security forces had been central, and recognized as such on several occasions by national elites (Buyoya 2012). In fact, numerous attempts at turning security forces into peace vectors have failed in the past (Wilén et al. 2015).

Consequently, during the process leading to the 2000 Arusha agreement for peace and reconciliation, an exclusive committee was put in motion to negotiate the future of the Burundian security landscape as part of the broader settlement

(Nindorera 2011). Negotiators at Arusha acknowledged that the control of security forces by a fraction of the population couldn't guarantee protection for the whole population. The pre-Arusha situation was indeed very much in line with what Hills et al. (2000) has shown for other newly independent countries: as new rulers needed last resort authority to draw on if their position was to be challenged, police could provide a coercive force to back this authority. As an institution playing such an important role in power preservation, police in pre-Arusha Burundi had been able to resist transformation, precisely thanks to its entanglement with political authority.

For these very reasons, the Arusha agreement, and particularly its third protocol, explicitly identified the security institutions as the main forces behind the violence (Arusha Peace and Reconciliation Agreement for Burundi. Protocol III 2000). The agreement acknowledged that the instruments of state power in charge of public safety were directly or indirectly responsible for the massacres, precisely because they never became inclusive instruments in the service of the population, instead of a tool for authority preservation (Rumin 2012). Therefore, the Arusha agreement pursued two important goals related to national peace and security. First, the agreement addressed the delicate psychological and political equation by introducing ethnic balance through strict quotas in, among other public institutions, the defense and security forces. Second, the agreement required the separation of the 'gendarmerie' from the army through the creation of a new stand-alone national police force. Even though the project had already been proposed by President Ndadaye's administration in 1993 (Lemarchand 1996), resentment in military circles and the fear that a national police would counterbalance the army regularly overturned the project, especially after the murder of Ndadaye (Mora 2008). While the reform proposed in the Arusha agreement concerned all security actors, the agreement remarkably put forward the ambition to create three separate bodies, with specific missions. A military body: the *Force de défense nationale* (FDN); a public security body: the *Police nationale du Burundi* (PNB); and a national intelligence service: the *Service national des renseignements* (SNR). In terms of political management of these defense and security bodies, the agreement paved the way for democratic civilian oversight and clear demarcation between the political and military spheres. It mentioned the principle of accountability for these new institutions and political neutrality, along with parliamentary control of their activities.

On an implementation level, while the Arusha agreement was massively ambitious, it faced one arguably last challenge: the need to end the hostilities with the remaining main rebel movements. If the agreement was signed in 2000, it was in the notable absence of the two largest Hutu rebel groups: the *Palipehutu-Forces nationales de libération* (Palipehutu-FNL) and the *Conseil National pour la Dé fense de la Démocratie-Forces de Défense de la Démocratie* (CNDD-FDD). Following a change of direction in 2003, the CNDD-FDD signed a special cease-fire agreement with the transitional government. And while it didn't become party to the Arusha agreement, leaders of the CNDD-FDD actually started to act in its spirit (Taylor 2013). It was particularly the case from 2005, when Pierre Nkurunziza, a leader of the CNDD-FDD, was elected president and formed an inclusive government in formal compliance with the Arusha agreement. On a political level though, many authors have suggested that new commitments related to the agreement were yet to be fully implemented, which the CNDD-FDD never actually did (Vandeginste 2011). At that time, the reorganization of the PNB had already started, with a series of laws promulgated in December 2004 to shape the institution as prescribed by the Arusha agreement. These laws formed the first backbone of the mandates, missions and bodies of the PNB (Republic of Burundi 2004). For these reasons, the new ruling party had to quickly engage with the continuation of this PNB overhaul. In a relatively short period of time, the PNB thus replaced the gendarmerie to become a significantly restructured body of civilian security, with its members increasing from about 2000 officers to more than 18,000—coming from the large pool of former rebel combatants and military—in 2008 (Nindorera 2012).

It can be acknowledged on the one hand that, from 2005, Burundi has been undergoing ambitious SSR processes, along with the continuation of Disarmament, Demobilization and Reintegration (DDR) processes. Initially solely focused on ethnical and political balance in the institutions, DDR and SSR processes have permitted to achieve a first wave of reorganization of the country's defense and security forces. But on the other hand, the ambitions expressed in the Arusha agreement have met several pitfalls. For instance, the massive and heterogeneous recruitments quickly posed challenges to the professionalization of the new PNB, especially regarding its interaction with civilian population (CIGI 2009).

Several donor states and development partners have been dedicating a significant portion of their aid budgets—through both bilateral and multilateral programs (for an inventory of realizations, see DEVCO-EuropeAid 2014)—to support the police. As a result, progress has undoubtedly been made as police reform is concerned. While the formulation of the 2004 round of laws and decrees related to the PNB organization was clearly a very much prospective one—with lawmakers essentially focusing on the hypothetical future of the post-Arusha police—the following organizational vacuum has been the target of several strategic and ethical plans. For instance, the decree organizing the missions and organization of the General Directorate of the PNB—the structure in charge for the daily management of the police inside the Ministry of Public Security (MSP)—emerged in 2007 (Republic of Burundi 2007). Police staff status and ethical codes were adopted in 2010 (Republic of Burundi 2010). In the same context, new material and train-and-equip programs have also been developed to strengthen professionalism within police forces. However, and against this background, many indicators show that SSR processes regarding the PNB have produced mixed results: from 2004 onwards, corruption (Transparency International UK 2014), the question of resources (Ball 2014) and the question of accountability (Nindorera 2010) haven't been sufficiently tackled with, demonstrating insufficient progress in the development of a transparent, professional and accountable institution of public security in Burundi. This broad context sheds some light on the complexity of security governance in post-Arusha Burundi.

8.3 Notional Boundaries of Security Governance and Analytical Value

Sometimes highlighted as a key to understand the world, the notion of governance remains elusive. The history of the concept brings no comfort here: from its birth in the business world, to the prescriptive or ideological meanings that it has been and is still carrying, particularly in the development community, governance as an operational concept may have been rejected, particularly in French academia (Paye 2005).

Still, security governance has risen to prominence these last years, including as a seemingly stand-alone concept. It has indeed been used by scholars to account for the contemporary replacement of vertical, hierarchical structures of governing security affairs by horizontal networks, coordinated management and regulations between multiple and diverse actors (Webber et al. 2004; Dupont 2004). However, the analytical potential of the concept of security governance varies from one author to the other, as does the very value of the concept as an independent variable to address empirical observations. This seems to derive from the widely heterogeneous ways in which the concept of security governance has been applied in social science literatures such as International Relations (IR) and criminology.

In IR, security governance has mainly been looked at through a global lens, stressing the emergence of new transnational security architectures since the end of the Cold War (Krahmann 2003). In this fashion, the interest of the concept of global security governance lies in its ability to apprehend some of the key questions of post-Cold War security management, notably the competing approaches of multilateralism (Kirchner and Sperling 2007) and the rise of international regimes bolstered by civil society (Price 1998). Also, IR attention has recently focused on private security governance, following the growing use of military companies operating outside their home state with the potential to resort to lethal force (Chesterman and Lehnardt 2007; Singer 2011). In this context, many authors have questioned the opportunity to create new transnational normative frameworks, whether state-driven (Avant 2005) or market-driven (Cockayne 2009).

In criminology, security governance has been a way to describe a 'quiet revolution' (Shearing and Stenning 1981) in security provision. Throughout history, the centralization of social control in one single public police—a state body consisting of specialized officers of public security—lasted only a short time (Wakefield 2012). In this respect, the pluralism that characterizes the development of security arrangements was not a novelty in the 1970s. This pluralism has however accelerated even further recently. Accordingly, the criminological perspective on the post-Keynesian police gradually crystallized around the notion of policing (Mawby 2008; Brodeur 2010). In this sense, security governance in criminology amounts *de facto* to governance of policing, policing being

> '(...) those organised forms of order-maintenance, peacekeeping, rule or law enforcement, crime investigation and prevention and other forms of investigation and associated

> information-brokering—which may involve a conscious exercise of coercive power—undertaken by individuals or organisations' (Jones and Newburn 1995, p. 18–19).

In this last sense, security governance has much more to do with the management and enforcement of social control and community conflict resolution than it has with international peace and security.

Despite the utility of the many iterations it can be apprehended with, this short literature review allows to argue that the analytical concept of security governance draws from similar premises. This can be deducted not only from the common semantics of both IR and criminology but also from a close examination of their common theoretical foundations (Wood and Shearing 2013). Cited works often comprise references to Beck—on risk and the management of a 'bottomless barrel of demands' (Beck 1992) for security—and to Foucault's views on a shared and widely spread conception of power (Foucault 1990).

As a result, four overlapping characteristics of the concept of security governance can be identified, arguably forming the notional boundaries of this concept. First, the concept refers to the reconfiguration of the state position in a changing security environment, for instance in matters of international high politics or regarding social control. Second and consequently, security management and production do not fall under the exclusive purview of the state, but rather is the result of a proliferation of public, private or hybrid actors acting towards each other in various fashions. Third, the state may nevertheless retain, to a certain extent, a role in the steering of interactions between security actors, through rules and regulations for instance. But the state loses its position as highest item of a hierarchical, vertical decision and implementation structure. Fourth, there is a new orchestration of security production and management, made from multi-level, heterarchical relations in multiple security arrangements.

Within these notional boundaries, security governance can be understood as a broad analytical framework of interpretation. In this sense, security governance would be considered *a minima* as a 'general trend of research that requires the analytical look to also cover non-institutional aspects of government processes' (Paye 2005, p. 32. Trans.) in the security environment. This understanding of security governance implies that all modes of coordination between every stakeholders of security, their motivations and resources should be looked upon, from individuals to social groups, corporate security businesses, local communities and (international) institutions that collectively lead or seek to provide security services. This is very much in line with Wood and Shearing's methodological considerations on nodal security governance (Shearing and Wood 2003). The authors advocate for 'a comprehensive empirical mapping of existing governance nodes and networks within specific sites' (Wood 2006, p. 230), as a key phase for engaging in the design, implementation and diffusion of ideas and practices. This epistemological stance is ambitious, and the empirical work it suggests to undertake seems limitless. However, this research agenda has been repeatedly promoted, as it was the case in Hufty's early work on a 'governance analysis framework' (Hufty 2008). This framework aims to be a similar practical methodology and also promotes mappings of governance sites, showing networks of interacting nodes, standards and norms, actors, and processes.

Finally, it should be mentioned that this agenda has started to produce innovative and comprehensive research (Blaustein 2014). Drawing on Bourdieu's theory of capitals, Abrahamsen and Williams (2010) precisely manage to overcome Hufty's fear of the impossibility to effectively order such an amount of data. They report and analyze security assemblages in various sites of Sub-Saharan Africa to account for

> 'new practices and forms of power that cannot be neatly contained within the geographical boundaries of the nation-state (where) various security actors interact in a field of tension, structured by the opposition between the public and the private and their different forms of material and symbolic'.

Berndtsson and Stern (2011) also provide the mapping of 'complex struggles and negotiations involved in the redrawing of public–private divides and sites of authority' at another site of security: the Stockholm-Arlanda airport. It is the same analytical perspective that leads Aarstad (Chap. 4) to examine the particular site of security that is Norwegian maritime security.

Wood and Shearing's proposal, as Hufty's, invite to acknowledge and operationalize the common premises of the security governance literature. Both seem indeed particularly suited to produce analysis of security governance in given sites of security. Most of all, both projects intend to cope with the often normative persistence of the Weberian model of statehood in security environment analysis. As Wood points out:

> 'For researchers, this means that the explanatory work they carry out should not be driven by the assumption that particular nodes are more effective or, for that matter, more democratic than others' (Wood 2006, p. 219–220).

The following section presents how both first generation critiques of SSR and contemporary SSR policy concepts seem precisely to have been shaped, to a significant extent, by the idea that a particular node should be put at the center of a security network.

8.4 SSR as a Node-Centered View of Security Governance

Somehow departing from nodal security governance as sketched out above, some authors in IR and criminology have made use of the concept of security governance more as a normative tool. Those authors explicitly or implicitly emphasize how specific nodes ought to play a role or how specific nodes ought to be taken into account in the security network.

The first common bias to be considered concerns the persistence of the Weberian model of statehood. Deriving from considerations on the rule of law or democratic oversight of the security sector, strong emphasis may be put on the state, framed as a necessary steering node of security. The idea that the state should remain the central locus of security governance offers ways to cope with 'questions related to accountability and governance within this new landscape that could have profound implications for human rights, privacy and civic society as a whole' (Hoogenboom 2010, p. 7). It also offers answers as general legitimate concerns about values, trade-offs between liberties and security, etc. are concerned (see the literature review of Bures, Chap. 2). This normative viewpoint has led to strong debates precisely over nodal security governance, its use as an analytical framework and its possible—if not desirable—development into a normative one (see Wood and Dupont 2006). On a similar note, authors in IR have suggested that a regulatory framework for the private security industry ought to be state-led or at led along state parameters (Singer 2003; Avant 2005). Some authors have, since, changed their minds (Avant 2016).

The connected, second, more recent bias to be found refers to considerations on universal provision of security or the value of market-driven normative frameworks of security. Following years of prominent malpractices in the private security industry, authors may have had a tendency to emphasize the role of corporate security providers in security governance. While claiming to engage in hybrid approaches of the security environment, this may ultimately have led to the neglect of informal or multi-choice policing (Baker 2004). For instance, Abrahamsen and Williams' early work on 'bringing the private in (SSR)' (2006) was clearly fundamental in 2006. This was especially the case at that time, given the epistemological stands and the seemingly impossible look beyond statehood in SSR early concepts (Schroeder et al. 2014). However, such a focus on a single node—here the corporate security sector—is precisely one of the flaws of contemporary SSR concepts, as it will be discussed below.

Finally, issues of legitimacy in the public–private debates are still sensitive, particularly in areas of limited statehood. As Börzel and Risse argue:

> 'it goes without saying that the "horizon of legitimacy" provided by the state is equally weak. Moreover, the weak state of developing countries is usually not very democratic and the rule of law is equally deficient. As a result, we need to have a close look at the various governance processes and institutions to ascertain their legitimacy' (Börzel and Risse 2010, p. 127–128).

Focusing on the state or the corporate sector as primary nodes in the security network do not give full merits to Wood and Shearing's approach of nodal security governance. Moreover, this state or corporate-bias also seem to be at work in even recent, more inclusive SSR policies. In this respect, the literature on nodal security governance and former or recent SSR concepts arguably disconnect from one another on the issue of node-centered views.

Framed as a 'new aid paradigm' (Bellamy 2003), SSR models have been conceived as 'good scenarios' of development for state donors' action in the realm of security. This openly normative agenda (Chappuis and Hänggi 2009), tracing back to the end of the Cold War (see Schroeder and Chappuis 2014), is best found in the Organisation for Economic Cooperation and Development (OECD) policy documents. Inside the OECD, the Development Assistance Committee

(DAC) has emerged as a major organization in the elaboration of guidance for development aid. Moreover, the DAC has been, since 1997, one of the main sources for SSR guidelines. Bryden (2007) traces the conceptualization of SSR in DAC forums. He stresses how, from the creation of a dedicated network of discussion in 1995, to the elaboration of formal guidelines by state members, the OECD/DAC have been instrumental in the affirmation of the security-development nexus, offering ready-to-go conceptual framework for donors' work on development cooperation in conflict and post-conflict situations (Tschirgi 2003). SSR's approach is problem-solving and aims to realize convergence between security and development programs through new synergies. Although the DAC guidelines and policy documents have often been criticized by scholars as technical and managerial methods promoting western liberal values (Chandler 2007), many donor states have worked in line with and have implemented DAC recommendations. Therefore, many states rely heavily on DAC policy documents to design their approach to SSR. It is particularly the case for the Netherlands, which growingly aligns on the OECD/DAC Handbook on SSR (Albrecht and Stepputat 2015). The Handbook goes a step further than former DAC guidelines and constitutes one the most important document dealing with SSR concepts and implementation.

Notably, the Handbook allegedly promotes a genuine paradigm shift in the way security governance is conceptualized and SSR is to be implemented. As a matter of fact, recommendations enclosed in the Handbook explicitly stress the necessity of a holistic, hybrid, so-called 'wide' approach in SSR, nominally extending fields of intervention far beyond 'the usual suspects' of defense and social control. As it reads, the Handbook even seems to reconnect with contemporary analytical approaches of security governance:

> 'Understanding who provides security and justice is central to SSR. The reality in most countries is that these services are delivered by a large number of actors. Some are state agencies and services, but some are likely to be non-state organisations and systems. Although the state has an irreducible role in justice and security provision, effective reform across the system requires working with a broad spectrum of actors' (OECD/DAC 2008).

For instance, the Handbook largely emphasize the question of non-state corporate security actors, raising concerns over universal provision of security and accountability. These concerns have also been raised in other development policy documents, such as in the World Bank's (2011).

However, this nominal account of broadly defined actors reportedly produces mixed results. The more recent and prominent policy documents do formally include references to various actors and their interactions, and have extended the definition of the security sector to include more than the police and the armed forces. But grassroots policing mechanisms and actual encompassing mechanics of security are still on the sideline of SSR, or at least do not overcome implementations hurdles. As a matter of fact, Brzoska (2006) points out the risk that SSR, as it is currently conceived, could be met with reactive behavior on the ground and produce unintended outcomes. On a same note, numerous authors have recently accounted for situations of disconnection between SSR and local dynamics: Hills (2014), Baker and Scheye (2007), Menkhaus (2007), Lemay-Hébert (2009), etc. The 'new perspectives' on SSR promoted by Schroeder and Chappuis in this context are enlightening:

> 'Yet what is lacking in understanding the exigencies of context are generalizable insights into the nature of security governance and reform at the local, inter-personal levels of interaction. Fine-grained, micro-focused empirical data, describing security from the bottom-up, has been largely absent from studies of SSR' (Schroeder and Chappuis 2014, p. 141).

This is precisely where the literature on SSR—or rather this new critical perspective on SSR—and the literature on nodal security governance connect again. Read together, they invite to investigate local security dynamics in association with SSR concepts. In Burundi for instance, examples of grassroots policing arrangements not only tend to show that 'the future is non-state' (Baker 2010, p. 208) but also tend to confirm that the future may well be non-corporate, as investigated recently (Bures and Carrapico, Chap. 1).

8.5 Methodology and Data Collection

Given Burundi's peculiar state of bureaucracy and the consequent difficulties to effectively rely on its administration (USAid 2006), the method of data collection used for this research was open-ended. The research questions revolve around security governance, internationally backed SSR, corporate security and grassroots policing. Consequently the study mainly makes use of various publicly available documents: Burundi's laws and decrees regarding security, international guidelines issued by the OECD/DAC, evaluations conducted by donor states on security needs and on the private security sector in the country, a comprehensive evaluation of all cooperation and development policies of six European countries and the European Commission in Burundi, several reports from local and international research centers on local security initiatives, etc. While publicly available, certain documents such as Burundi's laws and decrees may not be available online. Publications of the government gazette, the *Bulletin Officiel du Burundi* are, at best, scarce and generally not available online. Numerous background interviews were also carried out. The interviews were conducted between 2011 and 2014 with various stakeholders, including officials from the MSP, police officers, representatives of the Belgian and Dutch development programs, executives of all major gardiennage companies (see for a list Bresde Consulting Group 2014) in Burundi except for one, local journalists and scholars. In total, 33 interviews were conducted in-depth but often in an informal fashion. Indeed, the general culture of secrecy surrounding domestic security as stressed by Westley (1953) remains very much at work in Burundi, and several officials and executives politely declined to be taped, although accepting 'to go on record', as long as the record was cautiously written and, on some occasions, revised.

Therefore, the methodological walkthrough for this chapter is pretty straightforward. First, it resumes the narrative initiated in the first part of the chapter, then presents the realizations of the most ambitious SSR program in Burundi, to quickly assess these realizations in the light of OECD's conceptual ambitions. Finally, the chapter moves to the analysis of grassroots, policing arrangements, as examples of security mechanisms that remain either untouched or arguably fostered by SSR processes.

8.6 Coping with the Blind Spots with Blind Spots: Examples of Grassroots Policing Mechanisms in Burundi

Quickly following the signing of the Arusha agreement for Burundi, DDR and SSR processes began with ambitions of a complete security landscape overhaul. Over time, this broad transformation process has been supported by many multilateral and bilateral donors: main donors are the World Bank through the International Development Association, the United Nations (UN) office in Burundi, the United States, the Global Fund, the United Kingdom until 2012, the European Union, Belgium, Germany, the Netherlands and France.

As mentioned above, SSR programs in Burundi have achieved several technical and governance-oriented objectives toward better functioning defense and security forces (DEVCO-EuropeAid 2014). However, train-and-equip programs have not been fully completed across the country (Journalist 1, personal communication, June 13 2012; Journalist 1, personal communication, November 14 2014) and political will has been reportedly weak as governance-oriented objectives are concerned (Diplomat 1, personal communication, June 14 2012; Diplomat 2, personal communication, June 19 2012).

Along with state-centric measures, donors in Burundi and Burundian authorities have nevertheless seemingly begun to embrace a holistic approach of security. In particular, in 2009, the Netherlands and Burundi launched a comprehensive program of 'security sector development' (DSS) (see for a description of the program Ball 2014). Initially designed as a 3-year plan, the partnership was still operational in late 2015 and has shown progressive ambitions to the transformation of Burundi security sector (Diplomat 2, personal communication, June 19 2012). Not only has the DSS program targeted the reinforcement of the PNB, it has also specifically targeted non-state actors and local dynamics in an incremental fashion. In terms of realization, the DSS has been instrumental to the enhancement of the capacities of the MSP to supervise public security as a whole (Ministère de la Sécurité Publique 2012). Several Burundian laws and decrees clearly derive from this cooperation, such as the 2009 decree on the Ministry reorganization (Republic of Burundi 2009), the 2011 decree on the creation of a division of the MSP designed to oversee and control gardiennage companies (Republic of Burundi 2011) and the 2013 decree defining the missions of this division (Republic of Burundi 2013). The creation of the division was pure pragmatism: a recent study commissioned by the DSS established the number of corporate guardians at 8878, working for 23 companies operating mainly in the capital-city, Bujumbura (Bresde Consulting Group 2014). In contrast, there are about 18,000 members of the PNB across the whole country (Boshoff and Vrey 2006). Yet, the creation of the division summons the specter of an aforementioned common problem in Burundi's SSR: as it was the case for the MSP, several years separated the creation of the division and the legal definition of its missions. Furthermore, while the 2011 and 2013 decrees are a specific national legal instrument allegedly framing democratic oversight and the activities of the corporate security sector, the division remains an empty shell, with no historical practices and background (Diplomat 2, personal communication, June 19 2012; PSC executives 1, 2, 3, 6, 7, 12, personal communications, June 18–20 2012; Representative of the Division of gardiennage oversight, personal communication, June 13 2012). Before 2013, a few gardiennage companies were actually regulated under unspecific provisions: the code of private societies, enforced by the Ministry of Trade and the Commercial Court. Other companies operated as non-profit associations (Bresde Consulting Group 2014). Moreover, the newly created division is currently dramatically understaffed and underfinanced (Representative of the Division of gardiennage oversight, personal communication, June 13 2012), and the 2013 decree lacks clarity on the methodology of concrete monitoring and control of gardiennage companies (Civil society member 1, personal communication, November 15 2014). Finally, Burundi's corporate security landscape is characterized by small, local companies. To date, one single international private security company, KK Security, is operating in the country. Other companies came mainly from initiatives of former police or military officers, or former rebels (Journalist 1, personal communication, November 14 2014), with strong connections to national authorities. Therefore, recent efforts to clarify the normative framework of corporate security across Burundi have yet to produce tangible effects, as only 9 out of the 23 companies have complied with the homologation process as of June 2014 (Bresde Consulting Group 2014). In Burundi, the local corporate security sector still resists global ethos, despite international support and the creation of institutional tools.

As Baker (2005) argues, the burden of survival and protection often transfers to individuals and their household in post-conflict settings. In such circumstances, self-policing becomes the norm, whether in the form of resorting to corporate security or grassroots arrangements. In Bujumbura, if the first form is quite visible, the latter seems favored by the population (PSC Executive 6, personal communication, June 19 2012; Journalist 1, personal communication, November 14 2014). Actually, a vast majority of home and business owners don't rely on companies focused on security. Instead, hotels, expatriates, bakeries, banks, phone operator agencies, grocery stores and home owners trust single individuals, whom they employ directly. Those individuals are usually called *zamus*—mostly by foreign nationals—or *sentinelles*. The *sentinelle* is part of the day to day life of the Burundians, and while the phenomenon is hardly quantifiable, sentinels dressed with the famous blue, sometimes brown, uniform are to be seen everywhere in the street. On Singer's (2011) metaphoric spear for a private security typology, sentinels would likely add a bottom ladder. They indeed represent providers of security excluding almost any use of force. Sentinels are rather elements of dissuasion focused on alarm-triggering and door-opening, when they don't act as chauffeur. They, in fact, could sometimes qualify as 'hotel concierge' or 'handyman' (Journalist 1, personal communication, June 13 2012; Journalist 1, personal communication, November 14 2014). Informality is the norm here, as it is the case in other documented occurrences of informal security in urban settings (Blaauw and Bothma 2003; Fabiyi 2010), and in contrast with partially formalized instances elsewhere in the world (Gooptu 2013).

The sentinel phenomenon may be looked upon as untouched by both the state and SSR processes. In post-colonial Burundi, the burden of crime control has remained for large parts on communities, even in rapidly transforming Bujumbura (Civil society member 1, personal communication, November 15 2014; PSC Executive 12, personal communication, June 20 2012). Moreover, the phenomenon doesn't derive from an explicit governmental policy or strategy, adopted to progressively focus on core security tasks and actively solicit corporate actors or the general public (Garland 1996). As a matter of fact, Burundian strategy documents on security tend to emphasize the exact opposite and conceptually promote a state-led security environment:

> 'The security policy will be comprehensive and will refer to a wide notion of security. Police will expand all its services to the population. Besides its traditional tasks of internal security, it will further develop prevention and emergency first line. The security policy will integrate all security actors: organizations related to control and management of security, judicial institutions, risk prevention and disaster management agencies, private security services, civil society and the population' (Ministère de la Sécurité Publique 2012, p. 17).

While the Arusha agreement may have started new dynamics between society and the state, reforms have so far produced mixed outcomes as empowerment of population-oriented public policing is concerned. From its independence until today, Burundi remains a country where the police is seen as an instrument of domination or preservation of power rather than an institution operating under public accountability and democratic control. Major remnants of corruption, politicization, human rights violation, or simply lack of professionalism are to be found on a daily basis (CENAP 2012). Recent crackdowns on dissent in the country have come as a confirmation of this observation (Cumming-Bruce 2016). Therefore, while wide programs have been put in motion since 2005, SSR processes have yet to realize their ambitions of state-centered, population-oriented security governance.

Most home or business owners in Bujumbura don't rely on corporate private security either. In a multi-choice policing environment, this new choice seems to be welcomed with skepticism by the population. First, the corporate security sector is fairly young, with the creation of the first gardiennage company dating back to 1992. Second, gardiennage companies are seeking high-capital customers, such as diplomatic representations, non-governmental organizations, agencies of the UN system and foreign nationals (PSC Executives 1, 2, 3, 4, 6, 9, 11, personal communications, June 18–20 2012). This is understandable, as those institutions and individuals often prefer corporate services to those of the state, reportedly for the reason that the latter is not civilly responsible and rarely pays damages for the defects of its services (Bresde Consulting Group 2014). Accordingly, the market for security in Burundi is marginally oriented towards the general population. Third, and consequently, corporate security remains expensive (Business Owner 2, personal communication, November 10 2014). In contrast, sentinels remain cheap and flexible, as they enjoy a small salary often completed by informal modes of remuneration, such as the possibility of being housed, fed or dressed.

For the above-mentioned reasons, the sentinel phenomenon has so far resisted international and state ambitions towards state-centered reorganizations of security governance. This grassroots mechanism has seemingly been untouched by changes in the Burundian formal security architecture. More importantly, it should be noted that, so far, the use of informal sentinels has been completely overlooked as rules and regulations are concerned, both by the state and internationally backed SSR programs. For these reasons, the use of informal sentinels in Bujumbura remains a blind spot, untouched by both state-centered and corporate-centered approaches on security governance.

About 70 km south of Bujumbura is the city of Rumonge, located in the province of the same name, formerly the Bururi Province. Along with the city of Nyanza-Lac, Rumonge concentrates more than 10,000 hectares of oil palm groves, scattered in hundreds of small plantations (see Carrere 2010). The Rumonge region is affected by at least two sources of insecurity. First, the civil war has become root for numerous land ownership conflicts (Douma et al. 2010). In return from exile, part of the local population found that many of the properties changed owners, new owners often being close to local circles of power (Musahara et al. 2005). The Clingendael Institute reports that there are over 3000 cases of unresolved land disputes in Rumonge alone (Scheye 2013). While the redistribution of land was supposed to be carried out by the state through the National Land and Asset Commission, issuances of ownership titles have been controversial over the time. In fact, the Commission is more and more seen as a tool to impose an unequal partition of land between returnees and new owners. In this fertile region, the problem of land ownership is felt acutely and occasionally leads to violent dispute (Civil society member 1, personal communication, January 15 2011). Second source of insecurity is the general poverty and unemployment in a wealthy area. In Rumonge, the theft of palm oil crop—the source of wealth—was a recurring problem for the cooperatives stocking them (Diplomat 2, personal communication, June 19 2012). Moreover, plot owners were not used to go to the police to signal the theft of their product. Testimonies gathered by Scheye are, as this matter is concerned, self-explanatory:

> 'It is not the role of the police to patrol in the fields. Here, the police responsibility is to protect us in our homes' (. . .) 'people have to organize themselves to protect themselves' (. . .) Another said that the police stay on the roads and that what happens off the roads is the concern of the citizenry' (Scheye 2011, p. 14).

For these reasons, 2000 owners and tenants of palm groves, joining in the Palm Oil Guard Association (POGA), turned to another source of security than the police: 'jobless, thieves, street kids and ex-combatants' (Derks 2011).

Directly recruiting from the pool of those who otherwise would have probably been the one stealing from them, owners of palm oil plots came in contract with former combatants, willing to join the POGA as guards. The POGA guards receive palm oil rations as remuneration. The association also serves as facilitator on the market (CENAP 2011). Little to not equipped, the responsibility of the POGA guards is mainly to dissuade thieves to act at night, or to catch them. The guards' behaviors have sometimes been questioned and, formations have been dispensed these last years by local partners, backed by the DSS to improve collaboration between the guards and local authorities (CTB Burundi 2014). As a consequence, cases of torture and beatings are being progressively replaced with surrendering to proper authorities. Furthermore, the POGA now promotes a peculiar reconciliation process between the owner of the stolen palm oil plot and the thief (Scheye 2011). It should also be noted that the POGA provides its guards with insurances, in case of injury in the line of duty.

The POGA constitutes another example of grassroots policing. The first rationales behind this mechanism are similar than those accounting for the sentinel phenomenon. First, the PNB presence is scarcer than in Bujumbura and more prone to abuse (CENAP 2012). Second, corporate security sector presence is limited, as most foreign institutions and nationals are concentrated in the capital-city.

The POGA case calls for two interesting observations. First, the POGA is a local grassroots policing arrangements occasionally backed by a state donor's SSR program, namely the DSS. Second, the case nevertheless raises important questions regarding early SSR in Burundi. DDR processes may have appeared successful in terms of quantitative goals towards the reduction of state armed forces. However, three elements should be noted. First, although some stability has been found in Burundi after the implementation period of DDR processes, socio-economic development is still very low. The country remains one of the poorest in the world, leaving few job opportunities for ex-combatants: even under favorable conditions, the DDR process reinstated in poverty in major part of the countryside (Kleingeld and van Leeuwen 2010). Furthermore, the poverty has also been aggravated by flaws in the reintegration phase. This phase has been achieved with little to no regards for the acquisition of new skills, vocational training and general guidance (Member of the CNDDR, personal communication, June 16 2012; Journalist 1, personal communication, November 2014). Second, the reintegration into new public security institutions dismissed many: disabled or invalid, older, undisciplined candidates, and those whose education level was too low to follow a professionalizing military or police training. Third and finally, the lack of implementation of transitional justice mechanisms in Burundi, the provisional immunity of ex-combatants under the various cease-fire agreements, and the little emotional support during DDR processes raise debates over the relationship ex-combatants have to violence. By hiring background-checked former combatants, the POGA thus not only provides security, it also embraces social considerations.

In this respect, the POGA case underlines two elements: occasional consideration from certain state donors for local dynamics of security on the one hand; major flaws in international and national efforts towards the reintegration of weakened population on the other hand.

8.7 Concluding Remarks: on the Nodal Security Governance Research Agenda in Multi-choice Policing Environment

Both examples of the sentinels and the POGA guards provide interesting insights on grassroots policing in Burundi. Three short sets of conclusions can be drawn from these examples. First, it is clear that these arrangements arise from a certain degree of distrust in public security institutions. It is also clear that the persistence of the sentinel model has not been mitigated by the growth of a corporate security sector. Second, both arrangements have been almost completely overlooked by Burundian authorities so far. Yet, as highlighted in the chapter, the sentinels and the POGA guards actively engage in order-maintenance and prevention, with various degree of coercive power. On the one hand, they could be considered as policing actors. On the other hand, it remains doubtful that the sentinels and the POGA guards' employers themselves—home or business owners—consider provision of security as their key purpose, given their primary social role. However, the outcome remains the same: local businesses and individuals have engaged, for various reasons sketched out in this chapter, in security-related functions at their own benefits, at the benefits of their customer or, incidentally, at the benefits of the general public. In this respect, these security actors to contribute to multi-choice policing. Third, the most recent SSR policy documents and implementations fail to grasp the full extent of security governance on a given site. More importantly, the POGA guards case shows that grassroots policing arrangements may appear as a consequence of shortcomings and pitfalls of international interventions. The chapter shows how the notable failure of DDR to reintegrate weakened former combatants have contributed to situations of insecurity that have been addressed by the creation of the POGA. While some grassroots policing may have been around for some time, the formalization of this specific mechanism adds new layers of complexity to security governance in Burundi.

This last insight raises many questions regarding security governance and the way SSR research operationalizes it. At first sight, security governance could be framed as fragmented into separated, non-collaborative agents. On one side, state-centered security governance is backboned by donors' discourses on local empowerment and caution vis-à-vis the corporate security sector. On the other side, grassroots security mechanisms, as observed here, could appear or could be framed as untouched by global discourses and norms. The empirical findings regarding the POGA guards show the exact opposite: palm oil plot sites of security involve donor states, local authorities, plot owners, criminals, former rebel groups etc. in a complex security architecture.

It seems clear that SSR researchers and policy-makers could benefit from the nodal security governance perspective. For example, the sentinel case continues to raise many questions, to be addressed with a full mapping of the security network. In this chapter for instance, collected data is insufficient to assess mutual relations between the sentinels, gardiennage companies, the PNB, the MSP and external interventions. However, many hypotheses should be addressed as this site is concerned: are sentinels symbolically influenced by the new corporate sector regulations? Would this alleged influence derive from the fact that these regulations are internationally-sponsored? Has the sentinel phenomenon been fostered by a general sense of security/insecurity in Bujumbura? Is this sense of security/insecurity somehow related to the growth of the corporate security sector? Does any of these propositions make sense?

In his review of *Democracy, Society and the Governance of Security*, Haggerty discusses Wood's methodological considerations on nodal security governance, stressing that:

> 'The sheer scope of this epistemological project suggests that nodal governance seeks to be omniscient. Unfortunately, even with a small army of highly coordinated researchers such 'preliminary' research would likely take years to accomplish, and would culminate in a voluminous but unprioratized archive' (Haggerty 2006).

Researchers that engage in this type of work in sites of international interventions or more generally in sites of limited statehood must be prepared to face unparalleled uncertainty when gathering empirical evidence. Put in other words, they should be prepared to face a bottomless barrel of data.

References

Abrahamsen, R., & Williams, M. C. (2006). Security sector reform: Bringing the private in. *Analysis. Conflict, Security & Development, 6*(1), 1–23.

Abrahamsen, R., & Williams, M. C. (2010). *Security beyond the state: Private security in international politics*. Cambridge: Cambridge University Press.

Albrecht, P., & Stepputat, F. (2015). The rise and fall of security sector reform in development. In P. Jackson (Ed.), *Handbook of international security and development*. Cheltenham: Elgar.

Arusha Peace and Reconciliation Agreement for Burundi. Protocol III. Peace and Security for All. 28 August 2000.

Avant, D. (2005). *The market for force: The consequences of privatizing security*. Cambridge: Cambridge University Press.

Avant, D. (2016). People (including me) used to think that the private military industry couldn't govern itself. We were wrong. *The Washington Post*. Retrieved from https://www.washingtonpost.com

Baker, B. (2004). Multi-choice policing in Africa: Is the continent following the South African pattern? *Society in Transition, 35*(2), 204–223.

Baker, B. (2005). Who do people turn to for policing in Sierra Leone? *Journal of Contemporary African Studies, 23*(3), 371–390.
Baker, B. (2008). *Multi-choice policing in Africa*. Uppsala: Nordiska Afrikainstitutet.
Baker, B. (2010). The future is non-state. In M. Sedra (Ed.), *The future of security sector reform*. Waterloo: CIGI.
Baker, B., & Scheye, E. (2007). Multi-layered justice and security delivery in post-conflict and fragile states: Analysis. *Conflict, Security & Development, 7*(4), 503–528.
Ball, N. (2014). Putting governance at the Heart of Security Sector Reform: Lessons from the Burundi-Netherlands Security Sector Development Programme. *CRU Report*. The Hague: Clingendael.
Beck, U. (1992). *Risk society: Towards a new modernity*. London: Sage.
Bellamy, A. J. (2003). Security sector reform: Prospects and problems. *Global Change, Peace & Security, 15*(2), 101–119.
Berndtsson, J., & Stern, M. (2011). Private security and the public–private divide: Contested lines of distinction and modes of governance in the Stockholm-Arlanda security assemblage. *International Political Sociology, 5*(4), 408–425.
Blaauw, P. F., & Bothma, L. J. (2003). Informal labour markets as a solution for unemployment in South Africa – A case study of car guards in Bloemfontein. *SA Journal of Human Resource Management, 1*(2), 40–44.
Blaustein, J. (2014). The space between: negotiating the contours of nodal security governance through 'Safer Communities' in Bosnia–Herzegovina. *Policing and Society, 24*(1), 44–62.
Börzel, T. A., & Risse, T. (2010). Governance without a state: Can it work? *Regulation & Governance, 4*(2), 113–134.
Boshoff, H., & Vrey, W. (2006). *A case study for Burundi: Disarmament, demobilisation and reintegration during the transition in Burundi: A technical analysis*. Pretoria: Institute for Security Studies Monographs.
Boshoff, H., Vrey, W., & Rautenbach, G. (2010). *The Burundi peace process*. Pretoria: Institute for Security Studies.
Bresde Consulting Group. (2014). *Étude sur les acteurs non étatiques fournisseurs de sécurité au Burundi: Cas des sociétés privées de gardiennage et de surveillance (SPGS)*. Bujumbura: DSS.
Brodeur, J. P. (2010). *The policing web*. Oxford: Oxford University Press.
Bryden, A. (2007). From policy to practice: the OECD's evolving role in security system reform. *DCAF Policy Paper, 22*. Geneva: Centre for Democratic Control of Armed Forces.
Brzoska, M. (2006). Introduction: Criteria for evaluating post-conflict reconstruction and security sector reform in peace support operations. *International Peacekeeping, 13*(1), 1–13.
Buyoya, P. (2012). *The inter-burundian negotiations: A long walk towards peace*. Paris: L'Harmattan.
Carrere, R. (2010). Oil palm in Africa: Past, present and future scenarios. *World Rain Forest Movement Series on Tree Plantations, 15*, 111.
CENAP. (2011). *Renforcement des capacités des cellules de sécurité communautaire de Rumonge*. Bujumbura: CENAP.
CENAP. (2012). *Étude sur les besoins de sécurité au Burundi*. Bujumbura: CENAP.
Chandler, D. (2007). The security–development nexus and the rise of 'anti-foreign policy'. *Journal of International Relations and Development, 10*(4), 362–386.
Chappuis, F., & Hänggi, H. (2009). The interplay between security and legitimacy: Security sector reform and state-building. *Facets and Practices of State-Building*, 31–56.
Chesterman, S., & Lehnardt, C. (2007). *From mercenaries to market: The rise and regulation of private military companies*. Oxford: Oxford University Press.
CIGI (Centre for International Governance Innovation). (2009). *Security Sector Reform Monitor: Burundi, 1*.
Cockayne, J. (Ed.). (2009). *Beyond market forces: Regulating the global security industry*. New York: International Peace Institute.

CTB Burundi. (2014). *Quels sont les problèmes locaux de sécurité au Burundi ? Recueil d'expé rience menées dans 11 communes pilotes*. Bujumbura: CTB Burundi.

Cumming-Bruce, N. (2016). Burundi is torturing prisoners in crackdown on dissent, United Nations Says. *The New York Times*. Retrieved from http://www.nytimes.com

Derks, M. (2011). *Safety from below: Is non-state security the way forward?* The Hague: Clingendael.

DEVCO-EuropeAid. (2014). *Évaluation conjointe de la coopération de l'Allemagne, de la Belgique, de la Commission européenne, de la France, des Pays-Bas, du Royaume-Uni et de la Suède avec le Burundi*. Brussels: European Commission.

Douma, P., Briscoe, I., & Gasana, J.-M. (2010). *Peace in idle hands: The prospects and pitfalls of economic recovery in Burundi*. The Hague: Clingendael.

Dupont, B. (2004). Security in the age of networks. *Policing and Society, 14*(1), 76–91.

Fabiyi, S. (2010). Community building in response to insecurity in enclosed neighborhoods: A comparative perspective, Johannesburg-Ibadan. In C. Bénit-Gbaffou, O. Fabiyi, & E. Peyroux (Eds.), *Sécurisation des quartiers et gouvernance locale: Enjeux et défis pour les villes africaines (Afrique du Sud, Kenya, Mozambique, Namibie, Nigeria)*. Paris: Karthala.

Foucault, M. (1990). *The history of sexuality, vol. I: An introduction*. New York: Vintage Books.

Garland, D. (1996). The limits of the Sovereign state strategies of crime control in contemporary society. *British Journal of Criminology, 36*(4), 445–471.

Gooptu, N. (2013). Servile sentinels of the city: Private security guards, organized informality, and labour in interactive services in globalized India. *International Review of Social History, 58* (01), 9–38.

Haggerty, K. (2006). [Review of the book Democracy, Society and the Governance of Security, by Jennifer Wood, Benoît Dupont, eds.]. *Canadian Journal of Sociology Online*.

Hills, A. (2009). *Policing post-conflict cities*. London: Zed Books.

Hills, A. (2014). Security sector or security Arena? The evidence from Somalia. *International Peacekeeping, 21*(2), 165–180.

Hills, A., Siperstein, G. N., Wieseler, N. A., & Hanson, R. H. (2000). *Policing Africa: Internal security and the limits of liberalization*. London: Lynne Rienner Publishers.

Hoogenboom, B. (2010). *The governance of policing and security*. Palgrave Macmillan UK.

Hufty, M. (2008). La gouvernance est-elle un concept opérationnel? Proposition pour un cadre analytique. *Fédéralisme régionalisme, 7*(2). Trans.

Jones, T., & Newburn, T. (1995). How big is the private security sector? *Policing and Society: An International Journal, 5*(3), 221–232.

Kirchner, E. J., & Sperling, J. (Eds.). (2007). *Global security governance: Competing perceptions of security in the twenty-first century*. New York: Routledge.

Kleingeld, J., & van Leeuwen, M. (2010). *Connecting community security and DDR: Experiences from Burundi*. Netherlands: Peace, Security and Development Network.

Krahmann, E. (2003). Conceptualizing security governance. *Cooperation and Conflict, 38*(1), 5–26.

Lemarchand, R. (1996). *Burundi: Ethnic conflict and genocide*. Cambridge: Cambridge University Press.

Lemay-Hébert, N. (2009). Statebuilding without nation-building? Legitimacy, state failure and the limits of the institutionalist approach. *Journal of Intervention and Statebuilding, 3*(1), 21–45.

Mawby, R. I. (2008). Models of policing. In T. Newburn (Ed.), *Handbook of policing*. London: Willan.

Menkhaus, K. J. (2007). Governance without Government in Somalia: Spoilers, state building, and the politics of coping. *International Security, 31*(3), 74–106.

Ministère de la Sécurité Publique. (2012). *Plan Stratégique du Ministère de la Sécurité Publique 2013–2016*. République du Burundi.

Mora, S. (2008). *La réforme du secteur de la sécurité au Burundi*. New York: International Center for Transitional Justice.

Musahara, H., Kamungi, P. M., Oketch, J. S., & Vlassenroot, K. (2005). *Conflict in the Great Lakes Region: How is it linked with land and migration*. London: Overseas Development Institute.
Nindorera, W. (2010). *Des principaux défis de la Police Nationale pour une meilleure sécurité publique et le renforcement démocratique*. Bujumbura: CENAP.
Nindorera, W. (2011). La police nationale, le renforcement démocratique et la consolidation de la paix au Burundi. *Canadian Journal of Development Studies/Revue canadienne d'études du dé veloppement, 32*(1), 79–93.
Nindorera, W. (2012). The CNDD-FDD: The Path from Armed to Political Struggle, *Berghof Transitions Series, 2*.
OECD/DAC. (2008). *The OECD DAC handbook on security system reform: Supporting security and justice*. Paris: OECD.
Paye, O. (2005). La gouvernance: D'une notion polysémique à un concept politologique. *Études internationales, 36*(1), 13–40.
Price, R. (1998). Reversing the gun sights: Transnational civil society targets land mines. *International Organization, 52*(03), 613–644.
Republic of Burundi. (2004). Law n°1/020 of 31 December 2004 on the creation, organization, missions, composition, and functioning of the National Police.
Republic of Burundi. (2007). Decree n°1/100/276 of 27 September 2007 on the organization, missions and functioning of the General Direction of the National Police.
Republic of Burundi. (2009). Decree n°100/18 of 17 February 2009 on the missions and organization of the Ministry of Public Security.
Republic of Burundi. (2010). Law n°1/16 of 31 December 2010 on the status of PNB constables; Law n°1/17 of 31 December on the status of PNB brigadiers; Law n°1/18 of 31 December 2010 on the status of PNB officers.
Republic of Burundi. (2011). Decree n° 100/298 of 21 November 2011 on the organization of the Ministry of Public Security.
Republic of Burundi. (2013). Decree n°100/186 of 20 July 2013 on the reglementation of the activities of private gardiennage and surveillance companies in Burundi.
Reyntjens, F., & Minority Rights Group. (2000). *Burundi: Prospects for peace*. London: Minority Rights Group.
Rumin, S. (2012). Burundi. In A. Bryden & V. Scherrer (Eds.), *Disarmament, demobilization and reintegration and security sector reform: Insights from UN experience in Afghanistan, Burundi, the Central African Republic and the Democratic Republic of the Congo*. Münster: LIT Verlag.
Scheye, E. (2011). *Local justice and security development in Burundi: Workplace associations as a pathway ahead*. The Hague: Clingendael.
Schroeder, U. C., & Chappuis, F. (2014). New perspectives on security sector reform: The role of local agency and domestic politics. *International Peacekeeping, 21*(2), 133–148.
Schroeder, U. C., Chappuis, F., & Kocak, D. (2014). Security sector reform and the emergence of hybrid security governance. *International Peacekeeping, 21*(2), 214–230.
Shearing, C., & Stenning, P. (1981). Modern private security: Its growth and implications. *Crime and Justice, 3*, 193–245.
Shearing, C., & Wood, J. (2003). Nodal governance, democracy, and the new 'denizens'. *Journal of Law and Society, 30*(3), 400–419.
Singer, P. (2003). War, profits, and the vacuum of law: Privatized military firms and international law. *Columbia Journal of Transnational Law, 42*, 521–535.
Singer, P. (2011). *Corporate warriors: The rise of the privatized military industry*. Cornell University Press.
Taylor, D. (2013). "We Have No Influence": International discourse and the instrumentalisation of transitional justice in Burundi. *Stability: International Journal of Security and Development, 2* (3): 47, 1–10.

Transparency International UK. (2014). *Étude sur les aspects de l'intégrité de la Police Nationale du Burundi*. London: Transparency International UK.

Tschirgi, N. (2003). *Peacebuilding as the link between security and development: Is the window of opportunity closing?* New York: International Peace Academy, Studies in Security and Development.

USAID. (2006), *Reconstruction for development in Burundi: Guiding criteria and selected key issues*. Washington, USA.

Vandeginste, S. (2011). Bypassing the prohibition of amnesty for human rights crimes under international law: Lessons learned from the Burundi peace process. *Netherlands Quarterly of Human Rights, 29*(2), 189–211.

Wakefield, A. (2012). *Selling security*. New York: Routledge.

Webber, M., Croft, S., Howorth, J., Terriff, T., & Krahmann, E. (2004). The governance of European security. *Review of International Studies, 30*(01), 3–26.

Westley, W. A. (1953). Violence and the Police. *American Journal of Sociology, 59*(1), 34–41.

Wilén, N., Ambrosetti, D., & Birantamije, G. (2015). Sending peacekeepers abroad, sharing power at home: Burundi in Somalia. *Journal of Eastern African Studies, 9*(2), 307–325.

Wood, J. (2006). Research and innovation in the field of security: A nodal governance view. In J. Wood & B. Dupont (Eds.), *Democracy, society, and the governance of security*. Cambridge: Cambridge University Press.

Wood, J., & Dupont, B. (Eds.). (2006). *Democracy, society, and the governance of security*. Cambridge: Cambridge University Press.

Wood, J., & Shearing, C. (2013). *Imagining security*. New York: Routledge.

World Bank. (2011). *World Development Report 2011. Conflict, security and development*. Washington, DC: World Bank.

Part III
The Privatization of Security in an Expanding Digital World

Chapter 9
Blurring Public and Private: Cybersecurity in the Age of Regulatory Capitalism

Benjamin Farrand and Helena Carrapico

9.1 Introduction

Despite being one of the most recent fields of European Union (EU) governance, Network and Information Security (NIS) has also become one of its key priorities. NIS, briefly put, ensures the security of computer networks operating within critical infrastructures such as waste management systems and electricity grids, and the data they contain, through ensuring the resilience of those systems to attacks. The protection of networks and information systems has become essential in a society that is as connected and as dependent on technology as the European one—indeed, the European Commission considers the Internet and digital communications to be "the backbone" of social and economic prosperity, with NIS being the armour preventing it from breaking (Commission 2014). The recent examples of cyber attacks on the Yahoo accounts (the biggest data breach in history, which took place in September 2016) and on Tesco Bank (November 2016) are representative of the challenges posed to operators of Internet-based services, now generally understood by the EU to constitute a form of Critical Information Infrastructure (CII). In the case of the Janet Computer Network attack, British academic institutions found their internal and external network access brought down by a concerted Distributed Denial of Service attack, making university network servers inaccessible (JISC

The authors of this chapter would like to sincerely thank Oldrich Bures, as well as all the participants in the BISA 2015 workshop on 'Security Privatization beyond PMSCs', for their useful comments, advice and support.

B. Farrand (✉)
Warwick School of Law, University of Warwick, Coventry CV4 7AL, UK
e-mail: h.farrand-carrapico@aston.ac.uk

H. Carrapico
Department of Politics and International Relations, School of Languages and Social Sciences, Aston University, Birmingham, UK

O. Bures, H. Carrapico (eds.), *Security Privatization*,
DOI 10.1007/978-3-319-63010-6_9

2015). In the case of TalkTalk, an Internet Service Provider offering high-speed broadband Internet access, its servers were not only attacked, making websites slow to respond, but a significant volume of consumer data, including unencrypted personal information, was also accessed and allegedly shared online (Gibbs 2015). The cost of this intrusion, according to some estimates, could reach as high as £60 million, and has resulted in the loss of 100,000 subscribers (Farrell 2016). Given that approximately 78% of EU citizens actively use the Internet (European Commission 2006, p.6), the breakdown of Internet communications presents significant economic costs, and the unauthorised access to personal data may pose both economic and social costs, including loss of confidence in the security of online transactions (European Commission 2010a). Yet, given that these infrastructures, whether in the form of Internet access providers such as Virgin Media or the Spanish Telefónica S.A. or online service providers such as eBay, Google or Facebook (see Farrand 2016 for more on this distinction), known collectively as Internet service providers, are privately operated, how best to ensure their security? The dominant view, at least in the EU, is that this is best achieved by bringing in the technical knowledge and expertise of the private actors themselves; after all, who better to identify the challenges that market operators face than those market operators themselves? Within the context of liberalisation and privatisation, as the State has stepped back from the provision of goods and services, the private sector has filled this ostensible gap, and is perceived as being best placed to identify and respond to regulatory challenges.

The present chapter aims to contribute to the topic of this special issue on how private actors, working in non-private military and security fields, are participating in security governance, by exploring the case study of Internet service providers. As mentioned in the introductory chapter (Bures and Carrapico, this issue), there is a clear gap in the literature in terms of exploring the function and the extent to which private companies, whose main activity is not related to security, are involved in security governance. The present chapter wishes to contribute to reducing this gap by asking how Internet service providers have been incorporated into and have contributed to shaping the governance of NIS in the EU. The chapter argues that Regulatory Capitalism and Network Governance frameworks can contribute to answering this research question by bringing to light how current economic theories based on liberalisation and privatisation have led to the normalisation of a rationale according to which the private sector should be further involved in the regulatory process, as it is associated not only with a higher level of efficiency, but also to greater capacity, expertise and knowledge. Such a rationale has resulted in the delegation of regulatory functions to independent bodies, as well as the transfer of the provision of goods and services to the private sector. However, this chapter argues that there has been a further important shift that has led the private sector working in fields considered as NIS-related critical information infrastructures to evolve along the following three stages: (1) Private actor as a passive object of regulation; (2) Private actor becomes responsible for adopting regulation; (3) Private actor becomes an active participant in the shaping of that regulation (please see Tables 9.1 and 9.2 for further detail).

Table 9.1 'The Transformation of Governance and the nature of regulatory capitalism' (source: Levi-Faur 2005)

	Laissez Faire capitalism (1800s–1930s)	Welfare capitalism (1940s–1970s)	Regulatory capitalism (1980s–)
Steering	Business	State	State and agencies
Rowing	Business	State	Business
NIS stages	0	0	1 and 2

Table 9.2 Adapted table 'The Transformation of Governance and the nature of regulatory capitalism' (source: Levi-Faur 2005; Braithwaite 2005)

	Laissez Faire capitalism (1800s–1930s)	Welfare capitalism (1940s–1970s)	Regulatory capitalism (1980s–)	Networked regulatory capitalism
Steering	Business	State	State and agencies	State, agencies, business
Rowing	Business	State	Business	Business
NIS stages	0	0	1 and 2	3

The authors propose to pursue this argument by, firstly, undertaking documentary analysis to uncover how the role of the private sector is being framed in NIS, and, secondly, by using process tracing, to map the evolution of the private sector role along the above-mentioned three stages and identify key turning points.[1] The chapter starts by discussing the theoretical frameworks of Regulatory Capitalism and of Network Governance, which it then uses to guide us through the evolution of public–private relations in NIS. This evolution is the object of analysis in the second section of the chapter, which uses the above-mentioned NIS 3 stage approach to understand how private actors in this field have shifted from being framed as victims in need of protection to being considered as actors responsible for adopting regulation, and in a final stage to being perceived as participating in the shaping of such regulation. To further clarify the dynamics at play within this last stage, the third section focuses on the specific case study of the Telecoms Package and how private actors in NIS have become actively involved in shaping regulatory standards. The final section of the chapter explores how this governance trend has

[1]We use process tracing here in an interpretive sense; not as a means of identifying causal mechanisms that explain outcomes (Bennett and Checkel 2014; George and Bennett 2005), but as a means of tracing the development of keys ideas and themes by analysing the meanings that actors ascribe to their actions and policies (Hall 2013: 24). In the way that Schimmelfennig has used process tracing methods to analyse the way that the conceptualisation and internalisation of liberal democracy impacted upon the way in which enlargement decisions were taken by the former communist Member States (Schimmelfennig 2003), this chapter seeks to understand how conceptualisations of how best to regulate and internalised understandings of the expertise held by private sector actors then influences NIS-focused regulatory decisions taken by the Commission.

become further accentuated with an expansion of the role of private actors and of the definition of critical information infrastructures.

9.2 Conceptualising the Role of Private Actors in Network and Information Security Regulation

As mentioned in the introduction, the chapter seeks to understand the growing role of the private sector within NIS and its increased influence as policy-shapers, reconceptualised through the lenses of Regulatory Capitalism (Braithwaite 2008; Gilardi 2008; Levi-Faur 2005) and of Network Governance (Börzel 1998). Regulatory Capitalism provides a general framework for understanding the current forms of governance in NIS, by highlighting the increased role of the private sector in the State/Public–Private sector division of labour, and by pointing out the resulting reliance on businesses' expertise. Network Governance complements Regulatory Capitalism by conceptualising the growing influence of the private sector as policy shapers and by articulating the existing relations between public and private actors (for more on Public Private partnerships see Bures, Chap. 1, and Bossong and Wagner, Chap. 10).

When 'neoliberal' economic thought became a mainstream approach to economics at the end of the 1970s and beginning of the 1980s, Western governments quickly moved in the direction of cuts to public spending and deregulation, underscored by a belief that the private sector was best placed to achieve the market efficiencies that such an understanding of economic activity entailed. For the purposes of this chapter, we consider that Neoliberalism is a political economy theory that proposes that individuals' interests are more efficiently achieved in a context of free markets, free trade, strong private property rights and reduced State intervention (Harvey 2007). Since the 1980s, efficient governance has become intimately tied with privatisation and de-regulation (Fourcade-Gourinchas and Babb 2002). As argued by Vogel, however, the *theory* of Neoliberalism is rather different from the *practices* of Neoliberalism (1996), which have also been described as 'actually existing neoliberalism' (Cahill 2015). In fact, rather than the expected deregulation and retreat of the state resulting from this paradigm shift, we have observed a reregulation process, which Gilardi (2008), Braithwaite (2008) and Levi-Faur (2005) have described as contrary to the theory of neoliberalism; instead of markets becoming unregulated akin to a *laissez-faire* approach to economic activity, regulatory bodies and ensuing regulations have in fact proliferated (Levi-Faur and Jordana 2005; Braithwaite 2008). Given the exponential increase in non-State regulation, these authors consider that we should, instead, refer to this process as Regulatory Capitalism.

In a rather neofunctionalist approach, in order for the free market to function adequately and for privatisation processes to be implemented and overseen, the creation of independent regulatory bodies was perceived as necessary (Haas 1968).

The latter included regulatory agencies, regulatory networks, and regulatory instruments, such as public–private partnerships (Braithwaite 2008). In a study by Braithwaite and Jordana (referred to in Braithwaite 2008, p.vii), which looks at 49 countries from 1920 to 2002, we can observe how the number of regulatory agencies being created leaped from 5 per year between the 1960s and the 1980s, to 40 per year in the period between 1994 and 1996. Numerous examples can be provided of this reregulation process. Where quality standardisation and certification is concerned, for instance, most of the industry is now being regulated by international standards. The International Organisation for Standardisation (ISO), an independent non-governmental organisation, creates international standards for goods and services, including things as different as toy safety, waste management, the work of private security services, and critical infrastructure protection. The standards, which are defined by technical committees comprised of industry bodies, research and testing organisations, local and central government, and consumers, are then voluntarily adopted by industry and public bodies in an attempt to keep a competitive edge and boost their reputation (Ponte et al. 2011). This global shift has led not only to radical changes in the way the State engages with the economy, but also to a major transformation in the way the economy itself is organised (Gilardi 2008; Majone 1996). Considering the chapter's interest in how the private sector is participating in security governance, it is important to discuss the role of regulatory bodies in this reregulation process. As the empirical sections of the chapter will point out, although the private sector is traditionally not included in the list of regulatory bodies, it has gradually come to take part in the reregulation process, namely through the encouragement of the State and of regulatory agencies.

As mentioned previously, the decision to create regulatory agencies, networks and instruments is related to the perceived need to efficiently pursue a liberalisation and privatisation agenda. The emergence of regulatory agencies is intimately related to two elements: firstly, the State apparatus, which was understood as too dependent on electoral results and varying political interests, was considered to be too politically uncertain to serve as a solid base for economic development (Moe 1990). In order to provide a more coherent and continuous approach, which the markets could rely on, it was decided that efficiency could only be achieved in an apolitical context by professional regulators (Lægreid and Verhoest 2010). Secondly, the process of privatisation also led to public demand for regulation of the private sector and its capacity to provide society with goods and services (Braithwaite 2005). As a result, regulatory bodies emerged as the ideal operational solution to regulate liberalisation, in a way that is autonomous from the political system. Their main functions are to collect and process information, as well as to produce efficient solutions to practical regulatory problems (Rittberger and Wonka 2012; Dehousse 1997).

Although the degree of efficiency of Neoliberalism has often been questioned (Bourdieu 1998; Castells 1996; Chomsky 1998), there is little doubt regarding the hegemonic character of its discourse, with the consequent reregulation having become (1) the norm in most countries; and (2) transversal to most sectors of the economy. As we will see throughout the chapter, the efficiency of neoliberal discourse was particularly instrumental in the development of new sectors, in particularly technology-intensive sectors such as the NIS, where private actors' input has been prioritised based on their perceived expertise. As announced in the introduction, it allowed for private actors in the field of NIS, namely Internet Service Providers, to evolve along three stages: (1) Passive role as object of regulation; (2) Actors responsible for adopting and implementing regulation; (3) Active participants in the shaping of that regulation.

Let us start by focusing on the first stage. As Table 9.1 indicates, Levi-Faur and Braithwaite consider that the economic governance paradigm of the nineteenth century and early twentieth century, which was based on private initiative or *laissez-faire*, was replaced with the mid-twentieth century State-based regulatory model (named Welfare Capitalism in Table 9.1). In the latter, the State is both responsible for organising the economy (steering) and for providing citizens with a considerable amount of goods and services (rowing). The role of the private actors in the second model is limited to areas open to private initiative and competition. According to these authors, the Regulatory Capitalism model (from the 1980s onwards) would be a further evolution, where the State maintains the direction of the economy and oversight over the content of produced regulations, delegating powers to independent agencies to implement and enforce those regulations (steering), with the private sector being responsible for a much larger provision of goods and services (rowing). The privatization of traditional State sectors, such as the electric grid or the management of nuclear power plants are good examples of Regulatory Capitalism model changes. This model corresponds to both stages 1 and 2 of our analytical framework. In the first stage, the private sector adopts a passive role as a 'rower' and as an object of regulation by the State and, in the second stage, it becomes responsible for adopting regulation. Although still in the context of a hierarchical relation, where the regulatory adoption has a mandatory character, the private sector begins to emerge as a more active actor.

This re-emergence of the private sector in the regulatory process is interpreted by Braithwaite (2005), Bevir and Rhodes (2003) and Castells (1996) as transforming what used to be, up until the 1970s/1980s, a single actor system of governance into a form of network governance, characterized by the presence of multiple actors with different functions being brought together (see also Lazer 2005). Although Regulatory Capitalism authors make substantial references to the growing importance of the private sector, the majority of this body of literature has two limitations: (1) it is mainly focused on regulatory agencies and their geographical and multilevel diffusion (Gilardi 2008; Jordana and Levi-Faur 2004), and, more importantly, (2) it depicts the private sector as subservient to State or agency regulation. As a result, the role of industry is generally understood as limited to that of a provider of goods and services that requests and implements regulation (Braithwaite 2005). As the empirical sections of this chapter will point out, however, there are sectors of activity, such as NIS, where the private sector is not only rowing, but also steering.

On this basis, the present chapter aims to contribute to the Regulatory Capitalism literature by proposing that the shift from a regulatory State to regulatory capitalism paved the way for a greater presence of the private sector, not only as a service provider, but also as an actor within the regulatory process itself, including through self-regulation, and through participation in regulatory bodies. As such, the chapter proposes a new phase to Levi-Faur's conceptualisation of governance and its transformation. As can be seen in Table 9.2, the authors propose that a fourth phase be introduced to reflect the private sectors' current role in steering regulation. This arrangement corresponds to stage 3 of our analytical framework, where the private sector is an active participant in the shaping of regulation.

This is an idea that already features in the Network Governance literature (Börzel 1998) and that more adequately represents the role of the private sector in the NIS field, an understanding that can complement and expand the Regulatory Capitalism framework as a way for conceptualising governance within the current economic system. Within this literature, Risse and Börzel (2005) analysed current regulation as being the result of four different relations between public and private entities: (1) 'State-led regulation with consultation of the private sector'; (2) 'State delegation of powers to independent agencies and bodies'; (3) 'Co-regulation between the public and private sectors as equal partners'; and (4) 'Private self-regulation that is sanctioned by the State'. In the remainder of the chapter, we will see that all these different relations between the public and private sectors have existed at some stage within the European governance of NIS, leading to an understanding of a much more active role of the private sector in the production of regulation than that implied in Regulatory Capitalism. In fact, if we apply the insights of the Network Governance literature to Braithwaite's regulatory networks, we can begin to identify what is actually a more hybrid form of governance (Calliess and Zumbansen 2010; Picciotto 2006), in which public-private relations are collaborative, rather than competitive. Network Governance also provides some insights into the organisational rationale of these regulatory networks, allowing us to understand how the private sector managed to achieve such a key position within the production of regulation of NIS. The transnational networks are not formed around formal power and institutional design, but rather around technical knowledge and expertise. Control over the expertise is essential to the capacity to exert control over the regulatory process (Cohen 2011). As a result, depending on the field, expertise could be located within different actors. Within the current economic framework, 'expertise' is closely linked to business practice, based as it is in the belief that private market actors are efficient and best placed to understand their regulatory needs (see for example Culpepper 2011).

As will be argued throughout the chapter, in the case of NIS, as in most emerging areas, the State and independent regulatory agencies do not have adequate technical knowledge to regulate this field. To protect critical information infrastructures, it is considered necessary to be aware of the most recent cyber threats and how to appropriately respond to them. Even if security is not the main business of a great deal of information and technology companies, such as Internet service providers, they are considered to be better placed to understand, and subsequently minimise the risks within NIS (Farrand and Carrapico 2013). When Regulatory Capitalism draws insight from Network Governance, it can serve to better understand *how* private actors are involved in regulation of specific sectors, as well as *why* they are brought into these regulatory networks. In the next section of this article, the development of the role of private actors in NIS will be further explored, highlighting the European Commission's developing of NIS policy. It will demonstrate the shifting perception of the private sector from being potential victims of cyber-attacks, to commercial actors bearing responsibility for the adoption of regulatory standards for system resilience, identified by a regulatory agency.

9.3 NIS Stages 1, 2 and 3: Private Actors as Objects of Regulation, as Regulation Adopters, and as Regulation Shapers

Dedicated European Commission efforts in the field of cyber-security and NIS can be traced at least as far back as the 2001 initiative, 'NIS: Proposal for A European Policy Approach', which discussed the protection of networks and information systems in security terms (European Commission 2001). Prior to 2001, States were presented as being responsible both for implementing Network and Information Security legislation and for combating criminal activities affecting NIS. Although the private sector was starting to be present in the area, a considerable part of the services was still provided by the public sector. The 2001 Communication, however, marks an important turning point in the division of labour between the public sector and businesses, as it finds a new role for the private sector, more characteristic of the 'regulatory capitalism' model.

9.3.1 Stage 1: The Emergence of EU Cyber-Security and the Emphasis Upon the Private Sector

In the 2001 Communication, the Commission states that "security is becoming a key priority because communication and information have become a key factor in economic and societal development" (2001, p.2). NIS, for the purposes of this Communication, was considered as constituting "the ability of a network or an information system to resist, at a given level of confidence, accidental events or malicious actions" (2001, p.3). Such actions include the interception of communications data, unauthorised access to a computer system for the purposes of copying, modifying or destroying information, disruptive attacks such as Distributed Denial of Service attacks (DDoS) and the spreading of malware or other forms of virus (European Commission 2001, pp.3–4). While, prior to the 2001 initiative, there had been indirect EU concerns over illicit activities taking place online, they were not necessarily conceptualised in terms of 'security' of systems themselves, but instead in terms of combatting 'cybercrime' (see for example Porcedda 2011).

Furthermore, emphasis was placed upon the types of data that may be subject to unauthorised access or use, such as personal or private data (European Commission 1990), resulting in Directive 1995/46/EC on the Protection of Personal Data, and copyrighted works available on the Internet (European Commission 1995), in Directive 2001/29/EC on Copyright in the Information Society. At the same time, at the international level, States concluded the Council of Europe's Convention on Cybercrime, intended to facilitate a common approach to computer-based crimes such as the illegal access or interception of data, data interference, systems interference and content related offences such as the distribution of materials depicting child abuse, or intellectual property infringements (Council of Europe 2001; see also Clough 2012). Again, however, this Convention focused on the combatting of criminal acts and on the requirement of criminal sanctions, rather than focusing upon attacks on information systems in terms of security and resilience. In this respect, early initiatives in this field view the private sector as largely being the *victims* of such attacks, rather than having a responsibility to anticipate and resist such attacks. Whereas previously, telecommunications networks were operated by the public sector, a liberalised, decentralised market open to competition resulted in "many private operators and service providers [acting...] increasingly on a European and global level" (European Commission 2001, p.2). This, the Commission acknowledged, made the regulation of this sector somewhat complex (2001, p.2), and dependent upon *cooperation* between undertakings (2001, p.19). While the State was continuing to do the 'steering', the 'rowing' of service provision was being conducted by the private sector; what was needed was regulatory oversight.

9.3.2 *Stage 2: From Passive to Active Actors Responsible for Adopting Regulation*

To facilitate this oversight, the EU established the European Union Agency for Network and Information Security (ENISA) through Regulation No 460/2004 in 2004. Becoming operational in 2005, ENISA was initially given a mandate to "assist the Commission and the Member States, and in consequence cooperate with the business community, in order to help them meet the requirements of NIS" (Regulation No 460/2004, Article 1(2)). Through this framing in the Regulation, it becomes clear that the Commission views the private sector operators not only as the target for potential cyber-attacks, but in fact as an active stakeholder that should form part of the regulatory structure. Recital 3 of the ENISA Regulation, for example, refers to "the huge number of private and public actors that bear their own responsibility". However, it would also appear from the Regulation that the role of private sector actors is predominantly that of passive recipients of information intended to improve their NIS policies; Article 3(c) refers to the role of ENISA in enhancing cooperation between different actors cooperating in NIS through organising consultations with industry and establishing working groups for private sector and consumer bodies. While Recital 24 refers to receiving input and expertise from the private sector, the emphasis in Article 3 is upon the use of private sector actors to adopt and diffuse NIS policies, akin to the traditional regulatory capitalism approach.

9.3.3 Stage 3: The Development of a Multi-Stakeholder Governance Model: From Regulation Adopters to Regulation Shapers?

In 2006, the Commission began to lay down the foundations for a larger mandate for ENISA and further legislation in the field of NIS with its Communication 'A Strategy for a Secure Information Society' (European Commission 2006). The document stated that "the availability, reliability and security of networks and information systems are increasingly central to our economies and to the fabric of society" (2006, p.3). NIS as currently understood by the Commission expands upon the 2001 Communication definition, while reiterating the emphasis on resilience. NIS is, according to this Communication,

> [T]he ability of a network or an information system to resist, at a given level of confidence, accidental events or malicious actions that compromise the availability, authenticity, integrity and confidentiality of stored or transmitted data and the related services offered by or accessible via these networks and systems (European Commission 2006, p.3).

As will be demonstrated through discussion of later Commission initiatives, the need to protect the Internet is hereafter closely associated with issues of growth and economic development as specific security issues; as the Commission states, "ICT is a critical component of innovation and is responsible for nearly 40% of productivity growth [. . .] According to Eurostat, 89% of EU enterprises actively used the Internet in 2004" as did approximately 50% of EU consumers (2006, p.5), numbers that had increased by 2013 to 90% (Eurostat 2013) and 81% respectively (Eurostat 2014). Given the near-ubiquitous use of information systems by both enterprise and individuals, a breach of NIS can result in severe consequences beyond the purely economic, with potential repercussions for other forms of critical infrastructure, such as loss of energy supplies or failure of transport networks (2006, p.5). Indeed, as Knowles et al. indicate, corporate networks and the Internet increasingly form part of industrial control systems, presenting potential risks to physical industrial systems through the misuse or attack of computer systems (2015). However, and of direct relevance to this paper, the 2006 Commission Communication proposes a strategy for ensuring NIS that goes beyond the initial discussions in the 2001 Communication and the previously limited role of the private sector under the 2004 ENISA Regulation, through direct interaction and engagement with private stakeholders, based on "dialogue, partnership and empowerment" (2006, p.6). The Commission views the roles of private and public sectors regarding NIS as complementary, necessitating policies based on multi-stakeholder dialogue (2006, p.6), facilitating the private sector actors as regulation shapers, rather than 'mere' regulation adopters or diffusers. This would reflect the proposed 'networked regulatory capitalism' phase of Regulatory Capitalism, in which 'steering' is conducted through the cooperation of state, agency and private sector in determining the content of regulation. In this phase, the private sector does not only act as an adopter of regulation, but can also be actively involved in shaping policy responses and the resulting regulation.

In the case of NIS, the effective methods of ensuring the resilience of information systems are considered by the Commission to be through benchmarking of national NIS policies, the identification of best practices, and stakeholder debates on how to use existing regulatory instruments, as well as ensuring private actors work *with* ENISA to collect data on cyber-security incidents (2006, p.8). Finally, the Commission invited private sector firms to "develop an appropriate definition of responsibilities for software producers and Internet service providers in relation to the provision of adequate and auditable levels of security" (2006, p.9), leaving the choice of policy definition to these private actors, as well as the choice of whether to engage with this process. This would appear to indicate a shift of the private sector from a victim of cyber-attacks to be protected by national legislation, to a self-regulator with an imposed duty to ensure that it responds effectively to ENISA-identified security threats, and thereafter to an active participant in shaping regulations applicable to NIS. This last shift will be discussed further in the next section.

9.4 The Telecoms Package as a Stage 3 Case Study

The formalisation of the role of private sector actors as one of being actively involved in shaping NIS resilience standards beyond engagement with ENISA, rather than 'merely' adopting and diffusing such standards begins with the passing of Directive 2009/140/EC in November 2009, known as the 'Telecoms Package' (see for example Reestman and Eijsbouts 2009). While previous legislative initiatives, as discussed in the preceding section, focused upon the criminalisation of attacks on information systems, with the Telecoms Package comes both a requirement of system resilience, as well as an active role in regulatory standard-setting. This again demonstrates the usefulness of extending the regulatory capitalism framework from its focus on 'state' (the EU) and 'agency' (ENISA) to include 'business' (private sector ISPs). While a substantial body of the academic discussion on the Telecoms Package has been dedicated to the politics of intellectual property law-making (Coudert and Werkers 2010; Horten 2011; Reestman and Eijsbouts 2009 for example), comparatively little attention has been paid to the impact upon NIS. Directive 2009/140/EC (amongst other things) amends Directive 2002/21/EC on a common regulatory framework for electronic communications networks and services, inserting two new Articles on the security and integrity of networks and services. Article 13a requires that Member States ensure that "undertakings providing public communications networks or publicly available electronic communications services take appropriate technical and organisational measures to appropriately manage the risks posed to security of networks and services". Furthermore, under subsection 3, Member States should also ensure that "undertakings providing public communications networks or publicly available electronic communications services notify the competent national regulatory authority of a breach of security or loss of integrity that has had a significant impact on the operation of networks or services".[2]

While Article 13a is addressed to Member States and National Regulatory Authorities (NRAs), giving the appearance that private stakeholders such as ISPs play no role in dictating the terms of regulation or shaping policy in this area, their actual position is not so clear cut. In a Communication on Critical Information Infrastructure Protection (CIIP) published in March 2009, approximately 6 months before the adoption of the Telecoms Package, the Commission referred to the new regulatory regime as including "new provisions on security and integrity, in particular to strengthen operators' obligations to ensure that appropriate measures are taken to meet identified risks, guarantee the continuity of supply of services and notify security breaches" (2009, p.3). Reiterating the need to ensure NIS due to the social and economic importance of computer networks for business and individuals and the potential impact of cyber-attacks (2009, p.4), the Commission admitted the governance problems arising from the need to protect CIIs. While Member States are considered as retaining the ultimate responsibility for defining CII-related policies, "their implementation depends on the involvement of the private sector, which owns or controls a large number of CIIs" (2009, p.5). The Commission expressed hope that a multi-stakeholder governance model, facilitated by ENISA, could "foster the involvement of the private sector in the definition of strategic public policy objectives as well as operational priorities and measures" (2009, p.6), linking national policy-making to operational expertise, and putting the private sector at the centre of the regulatory process, 'steering' as well as 'rowing'. The role of ENISA as facilitator is highlighted in the preamble to Directive 2009/140/EC, where it is stated at recital 44 that ENISA "should contribute to the enhanced level of security of electronic communications by, among other things, providing

---

[2]The basis for this obligation can be found in the Communication on Electronic Communications Regulation (2007a), in which the Commission states that NIS is gaining in importance, and greater efforts to counter security threats were needed "given the significant social and economic impact of illicit activities in this area" (2007a: 18). In order to achieve the goal of improving the resilience of computer systems, the Commission concluded that "close cooperation between enforcement authorities, network operators and ISPs at national level is also needed" (European Commission n. d.: 71), which would be tackled through amendment of the existing telecommunications regulations. The original Directive 2002/21/EC made no mention of network or information security, and neither did the Commission Communication upon which the Directive was based (2000). The decision by the Commission to impose such obligations upon ISPs appears instead to have its origins in the above-stated 2006 Communication, as mentioned explicitly in the Proposal for the Telecoms Package, which states that the NIS-related amendments to Directive 2002/21/EC are "designed to strengthen the resilience of current electronic communications networks and systems" (2007b: 3).

expertise and advice, and promoting the exchange of best practices". To contribute toward the facilitation of these new policy approaches, ENISA was newly empowered under Regulation No 526/2013 to actively engage in the development of policies concerning NIS under Article 2(2), in addition to upholding its coordinating and consultative roles. These policies were to be designed through analysing publicly available NIS strategies and promoting their publication, as well as identifying best practices in industry, as indicated in Article 3. To achieve this facilitation of coordinated policy action and identification of best practices, ENISA has set up the Article 13a Expert Group, comprising representatives from the NRAs, as well as "experts working in the electronic communications sector via ENISA's electronic communications reference group" (ENISA 2014, p.ii). This electronic communications reference group has met three times so far, the first time in Rome in 2013. While ENISA does not provide a list of members of the reference group, it does nevertheless state that it comprises experts from the national telecoms providers (including mobile and ISPs) (ENISA 2013, 2015a). Working through a multi-stakeholder process, ENISA, the NRAs and telecoms providers have developed a single harmonised framework for the interpretation of Article 13a, intended as "a tool *for authorities* supervising the electronic communications sector, to be used as a structure for creating guidance or recommendations for providers" (ENISA 2014, p.iv). Yet what are these standards based on? Are they 'top-down' standards imposed by NRAs and ENISA? The answer to this question, it would appear, is 'no'. Returing to the 2009 Communication on CIIP, it is understood by the European Union institutions and ENISA that private sector involvement is essential to the creation of a well-functioning NIS regime. As a document published by ENISA in 2012 demonstrates, the standards applied to ensuring information security and integrity are based heavily upon a set of twenty industry standards in use in the EU telecommunications market (2012, p.4), including ISO 27001 on the governance of information security, used by all respondents to ENISA's surveys and interviews (ENISA 2012, p.5). In response to the interview question asking what standard should be used for an EU-wide information security good practice requirement, all respondents answered that it should be based upon the ISO 27001 standard (2012, p.14). Through the identification of standards of best practice, as well as the perceived position of experts in the field of telecoms, although the Commission has imposed binding legislation upon them, they have nevertheless been able to influence the standards by which the legislation is applied and interpreted by feeding into the multi-stakeholder process. It is likely that the private sector will be as actively involved in such activities in the future; according to ENISA's 2016 Work Programme, it is stated that ENISA will continue to work with NRAs and the private sector to "analyse the national reports [. . .and] identify new trends and develop good practices and lessons learned" (ENISA 2015b, p.30). Furthermore, ENISA states that it will work with the private sector (in addition to the public sector) to both develop and disseminate recommendations, good practices and new initiatives (2015b, p.31). In this way, private industry can shape both the current NIS policies developed by and applied throughout the EU, as well as being well placed to contribute to their development in the future.

9.5 An Expansion of the 3rd Stage? The Current Trend Towards a More Comprehensive Role for a Larger Number of Private Sector Actors in Critical Information Infrastructures

As discussed, the above security and incidence reporting requirements were imposed upon telecoms operators solely, including ISPs. However, as the use of web-based services such as online document storage, social media tools and databases has become more widespread, so too has the understanding amongst EU institutions that these *online service providers* could also constitute CII, not only the ISPs acting as *access providers*, and should therefore also ensure NIS through resilience to attack. Through this, we see that the Commission's approach to regulation in this field is to draw a larger range and number of private sector stakeholders into this regulatory sphere, based on perceptions of industry know-how, and allowing for these actors to actively 'steer' regulatory standards. In December 2009, just 1 month after the passing of the Telecoms Package, the Council passed a Resolution reiterating the growing importance of NIS, as well as the importance of collaboration between the private sector and governments. In the Resolution, the Council stated that the multi-stakeholder approach is important in mitigating "identified risks where such an approach delivers added value in helping to ensure a high level of network resilience" (Council of the European Union 2009, p.IV(7)) and reiterated the "vital role providers play in providing robust and resilient electronic communication infrastructures to society" (2009, p. IV(8)). The document proposed the expanding of ENISA's mandate, as well as the facilitating of a larger role for the private sectors in NIS protection (2009, p.VII(6)). Interestingly, the private sector is invited to "continue to work on standardisation of NIS to strive to find harmonised and interoperable solutions" (2009, p.IX(4)), indicating that the Council perceives the expertise held by private sector actors in their fields of activity to be an efficient and effective means of regulating NIS, reinforcing the position of these private actors as policy-shapers, albeit indirectly through the setting of standards rather than directly influencing legislation.

Cyber-security and NIS forms part of the EU's Digital Agenda, which is part of the Europe 2020 initiative. Europe 2020, shaped by concerns over the significant impact of the Global Financial Crisis upon EU economic growth and stability (European Commission 2010b, p.6; see also Farrand 2014), proposed a number of initiatives intended to restore the EU to economic strength (2010b, p.8). The 2010 Digital Agenda Communication stated with regard to cyber-security that the "cooperation of relevant actors needs to be organised at global level to be effectively able to fight and mitigate security threats" (European Commission 2010a, p.17). The Commission stated it would pursue a renewed and reinforced NIS policy, and would "foster multi-stakeholder dialogue and self-regulation of European and global service providers (e.g. social networking platforms, mobile communications providers)" (2010a, p.17–18), indicating both that the understanding that private sector actors are best-placed to tackle security threats, allowing for them to be involved in the shaping of cyber-security responses, as well as expanding the focus of NIS efforts from telecoms (i.e. access providers) to online service providers. Pillar III of the Digital Agenda Strategy, named 'Trust and Security' provides a series of actions for the European Commission to undertake, including Action 28: A Reinforced Network and Information Security Policy. This Action included the extending of ENISA's mandate and position as the 'fulcrum' for EU expertise and information exchange, as well as serving as the basis for an additional Action Point 123: a proposed Directive on NIS (European Commission 2013a).

The proposed NIS Directive was preceded by the Cyber-security Strategy of the European Union published in February 2013, in which it was again affirmed that cyber-security is seen as a multi-stakeholder effort with a significant role for the private sector (European Commission and High Representative of the European Union for Foreign Affairs and Security Policy 2013, p.4). In the legislation as proposed, the European Parliament et al. state that the involvement of the private sector in both facilitating resilience in NIS, as well as defining the standards for NIS, is essential. The proposal was intended to:

> Improve preparedness and engagement of the private sector. Since the large majority of network and information systems are privately owned and operated, improving engagement with the private sector to foster cybersecurity is crucial. The private sector should develop, at technical level, its own cyber resilience capacities and share best practices across sectors. (2013, p.6)

The Commission subsequently released an Impact Assessment, creating "a strong incentive [for public administrators and private actors] to manage and dimension [*sic*] security risks effectively" by imposing a regulatory regime facilitating private stakeholder involvement (2013b, p.6). The resulting Proposal indicated that upon consultation with the private sector, as with the Telecoms Package security amendments, standard setting for resilience would be best based upon industry standards, placing the private sector not only in the 'steering' category of the networked regulatory capitalism phase, but at its helm. Recital 32 of the proposed Directive states that the "standardisation of security requirements is a market-driven process. To ensure a convergent application of security standards, Member States should encourage compliance or conformity with specified standards to ensure a high level of security at Union level". The relevant private actors, according to the Proposal, are information society providers as defined by Directives 98/34/EC Article 1(2) and 2000/31/EC Article 2(a), namely "any service normally provided for remuneration, at a distance, by electronic means and at the individual request of a recipient of services", which would cover all Internet services such as Google, Facebook or Twitter, but not the ISPs themselves, as they are already covered by the amendments made to the above-discussed Directive 2002/21/EC (as stated in the proposed Directive Article 1(3). Article 14(1) states that Member States should "ensure that public administrations and market operators take appropriate technical and organisational measures to manage the risks posed to the security of the networks and information systems which they control and use in their operations", with Article 16(1) stating that Member States should "encourage the use of standards and/or specifications relevant to networks and information security". These standards would presumably be those used by private actors providing online services.

Indeed, this would appear to be the view of the Commission; in a 'Frequently Asked Questions' document released pertaining to the proposed Directive, the Commission stated that it did not see itself as a standard setting body, instead providing a minimal legislative requirement that would facilitate ENISA to "work with standardisation bodies and all relevant stakeholders to develop technical guidelines and recommendations for the adoption of NIS benchmarks and good practices" (European Commission 2013c). On this basis, a High-Level Conference held by the Commission took place on 28 May 2015, with over 200 public and private sector representatives, including representatives from service providers such as Blackberry, Amazon, IBM, Microsoft and Symantec. The purpose was "exploring the way forward regarding the Commission proposal for a Directive laying down measures to ensure a high level of NIS across the Union" (European Commission 2015). Subsequent to the political agreement between the European Parliament and Council (European Parliament 2015) on the Commission's proposal, achieved through an informal trilogue in December 2015 (Council of the European Union 2016), the NIS Directive (2016/1148) was formally adopted in July 2016. What is particularly interesting is the way in which the Directive was revised in trilogue to further establish the role of private sector actors in protecting NIS. While not legally binding, some of the recitals indicate a clear intent for the regulation of NIS to incorporate the private sector; reiterating that "cooperation between the private and public sector is essential", the Directive specifies that informal cooperation should be encouraged between market operators to ensure NIS at Recital 35. Furthermore, ENISA is regarded as having an essential role in disseminating best practices and expertise (Recital 36), and is also specifically tasked with providing advice and guidelines to Member States regarding market-driven standards (Recital 66). The revised Directive provides more concrete definitions of the relevant private actors in Article 4, which as well as including operators of essential services such as airlines (a list of essential services being included in Annex II appended to the Directive), states that it applies to 'digital service providers' (Article 4(6)), including operators of online marketplaces (Article 4(17)), online search engines (Article 4(18)) and cloud computing services (Article 4(19)). Again, highlighting the nature of NIS as a sector in which regulatory networks comprising public and private actors are deemed most effective, Article 11 establishes a Cooperation Group, comprising representatives of the Commission, ENISA and the Member States, which may "invite representatives from the relevant stakeholders to participate in its work". The relevant work, as indicated in Article 11(2), is to include establishing work programmes, as well as exchanging best practices on incident notification, capacity building, training, and research and development, as well as identifying best practices in national NIS practices and policies through periodic evaluations. The role of private actors is significant; whereas Article 14(1) is largely untouched in the revision to the Directive, Article 19 on standards is significantly modified, stating that Member

States should "encourage the use of European or internationally accepted standards and specifications" for NIS, and adding a clause that "ENISA, in collaboration with Member States, shall draw up advice and guidelines regarding the technical areas to be considered in relation to paragraph 1 as well as regarding already existing standards, including Member States' national standards, which would allow for those areas to be covered". These standards, as discussed above, constitute those best practices established by existing private actors in these fields. ENISA, as indicated in its 2016 Work Programme, foresees itself as having a guiding and coordinating role in the implementation of the Directive, stating that "ENISA will leverage its existing knowledge and expertise in stakeholder engagement with the public and/or private sector" (2015b, p.35). The Work Programme refers to ENISA's previous successes in achieving this regarding other sectors, such as the establishment of minimum security measures for smart grids. Through engagement with its existing working groups, it can quickly and effectively identify relevant sectoral actors, engage with them on identifying best practices and, subsequently, how best to implement them (2015b, p.35). This ultimately means that, as with the amendments produced through the Telecoms Package, while private sector actors may not necessarily be dictating the wording of the legislation *per se*, they will nevertheless be able to shape the regulatory approaches dictated *by* legislation through using their industries' standards and best practices, as well as the way in which they will be implemented. The development of the NIS Directive demonstrates that the expansion of the role witnessed in the Telecoms Package is not an unusual development in this field, but in fact was the first step in the development of a more holistic approach to NIS protection, incorporating a wider body of private sector actors in the identification and dissemination of industry best practices as regulatory tools. In January 2017, as part of the 2017 Work Programme, the Commission launched a public consultation into the effectiveness of ENISA's operation. Commissioner Ansip, Vice-President for the Digital Single Market stated in relation to this consultation that "cooperation is key for successful responses to [. . .] new security challenges" (European Commission 2017a). The consultation itself, which closes in mid-April, asks for interested parties to consider, amongst other issues, whether there is overlap between the function of ENISA and other cyber-security bodies, as well as to identify what they consider to be the key priorities for future initiatives in this field, with "stronger public–private cooperation" being one of the possible options (European Commission 2017b). Given the perceptions of industry expertise, and that industry is best placed to combat these security threats, the importance of such cooperation is likely to be reinforced, rather than dismissed.

9.6 Conclusion

This chapter has sought to provide a case study in how private actors who are not considered security actors have nevertheless been incorporated into security-related regulatory structures, based on the knowledge and expertise they are perceived to possess. Based on the Regulatory Capitalism and Network Governance frameworks, the chapter has sought to provide a better understanding not only of *how* these private actors become involved in security governance, but also of *why* they are brought into the regulatory structure not only as policy adopters, but policy shapers. Through application of the proposed theoretical framework, the chapter develops a 3-stage analysis that explores the evolution of the private sector in NIS from objects of regulation, to regulation adopters and, at a later stage, to regulation shapers. This adds to the existing Regulatory Capitalism framework by demonstrating the ways in which private actors can take on an active 'steering' function in regulation by the shaping of regulatory responses, rather than a more passive role of adopting or diffusing regulation (i.e. 'rowing'). The understanding that Internet service providers have technical knowledge and expertise not possessed by the State or regulatory agencies has resulted in technical standards developed by private industry actors being adopted as resilience standards for NIS by bodies such as ENISA; furthermore, through active engagement in working groups and expert committees, these industry actors are able to shape regulatory responses through the coordinated and cooperative identification of best practices that serve as the basis for the EU's resilience strategies. Current developments in this field indicate that this trend is likely to continue, if not accelerate, particularly in areas of technological complexity. The private sector may not serve only to steer the ship; instead, it may determine its ultimate destination.

References

Bennett, A., & Checkel, J. T. (2014). Process tracing: From philosophical roots to best practices. In A. Bennett & J. T. Checkel (Eds.), *Process tracing: From metaphor to analytic tool* (pp. 3–37). Cambridge: Cambridge University Press.

Bevir, M., & Rhodes, R. A. (2003). *Interpreting British Governance*. London: Routledge.

Börzel, T. A. (1998). Organizing Babylon – On the different conceptions of policy networks. *Public Administration, 76*(2), 253–273.

Bourdieu, P. (1998). The essence of neoliberalism. *Le Monde diplomatique*.

Braithwaite, J. B. (2005). *Neoliberalism or regulatory capitalism*. Accessed February 22, 2016, from http://papers.ssrn.com/abstract=875789

Braithwaite, J. (2008). *Regulatory capitalism: How it works, ideas for making it work better*. Cheltenham: Edward Elgar.

Cahill, D. (2015). *The end of Laissez-Faire?: On the durability of embedded neoliberalism*. Cheltenham: Edward Elgar.

Calliess, G.-P., & Zumbansen, P. C. (2010). *Rough consensus and running code: A theory of transnational private law*. Oxford: Hart Publishing.

Castells, M. (1996). *The rise of the network society: Economy, society, and culture*. Oxford: Blackwell.
Chomsky, N. (1998). *Profits over people: Neoliberalism and the global order*. New York: Seven Stories Press, U.S.
Clough, J. (2012). The council of Europe convention on cybercrime: Defining 'crime' in a digital world. *Criminal Law Forum, 23*(4), 363–391.
Cohen, E. (2011). Assessing the impact of the global financial crisis on transnational financial law and regulation. *Finnish Yearbook of International Law, 22*, 51–84.
Coudert, F., & Werkers, E. (2010). In the aftermath of the promusicae case: How to strike the balance? *International Journal of Law and Information Technology, 18*(1), 50–71.
Council of Europe. (2001). *Convention on cybercrime*, CETS No.185, Budapest 23 November 2001.
Council of the European Union. (2009). *Council resolution of 18 December 2009 on a collaborative European approach to Network and Information Security*, Brussels.
Council of the European Union. (2016). *Proposal for a directive of the European Parliament and of the Council concerning measures to ensure a high common level of network and information security across the Union – Political agreement.*
Culpepper, P. D. (2011). *Quiet politics and business power: Corporate control in Europe and Japan*. Cambridge: Cambridge University Press.
Dehousse, R. (1997). Regulation by networks in the European community: The role of European agencies. *Journal of European Public Policy, 4*(2), 246–261.
ENISA. (2012). *Shortlisting network and information security standards and good practices*. Heraklion, Crete.
ENISA. (2013). 1st Meeting of ENISA's electronic communications reference group in Rome. Accessed June 11, 2015, from http://www.enisa.europa.eu/media/news-items/1st-meeting-of-enisa2019s-electronic-communications-reference-group-in-rome
ENISA. (2014). *Technical guideline on security measures for Article 4 and Article 13a*. Heraklion, Crete.
ENISA. (2015a). Information sharing in focus at ENISA's 3rd Electronic Communications Reference Group Meeting. Accessed June 11, 2015, from http://www.enisa.europa.eu/media/news-items/information-sharing-in-focus-at-enisa2019s-3rd-electronic-communications-reference-group-meeting
ENISA. (2015b). *Work Programme 2016.*
European Commission. (1990). *Protection of individuals in relation to the processing of personal data in the Community and information security.*
European Commission. (1995). *Green Paper: Copyright and related rights in the information society*. Brussels: European Commission.
European Commission. (2000). *Proposal for a directive of the European Parliament and of the Council on a common regulatory framework for electronic communications networks and services*. Brussels.
European Commission. (2001). *Network and information security: Proposal for a European policy approach*. Brussels.
European Commission. (2006). *A strategy for a secure information society: "Dialogue, partnership and empowerment,"* Brussels.
European Commission. (2007a). *European electronic communications regulation and markets (12th Report)*. Brussels.
European Commission. (2007b). *Proposal for a directive amending Directives 2002/21/EC on a common regulatory framework for electronic communications networks and services, 2002/19/EC on access to, and interconnection of, electronic communications networks and services, and 2002/20/EC on the authorisation of electronic communications networks and services*. Brussels.

European Commission. (2009). *Critical information infrastructure protection: "Protecting Europe from large scale cyber-attacks and disruptions: enhancing preparedness, security and resilience."*
European Commission. (2010a). *A digital agenda for Europe*, Brussels.
European Commission. (2010b). *Europe 2020: A strategy for smart, sustainable and inclusive growth*. Brussels.
European Commission. (2013a). Action 28: Reinforced network and information security policy. *Digital Agenda for Europe*. Accessed June 12, 2015, from ec.europa.eu/digital-agenda/en/pillar-iii-trust-security/action-28-reinforced-network-and-information-security-policy
European Commission. (2013b). *Commission staff working document: Impact assessment accompanying the document: Proposal for a Directive of the European Parliament and of the Council Concerning measures to ensure a high level of network and information security across the Union*, Brussels.
European Commission. (2013c). *Proposed Directive on Network and Information Security – frequently asked questions*. Brussels. Accessed June 12, 2015, from http://europa.eu/rapid/press-release_MEMO-13-71_en.htm
European Commission. (2015). EU Cybersecurity Strategy – 2nd High Level Conference. *Digital Agenda for Europe*. Accessed June 12, 2015, from ec.europa.eu/digital-agenda/en/news/eu-cybersecurity-strategy-2nd-high-level-conference
European Commission. (2017a). Commission launches a public consultation for the review of the European Union Agency for Network and Information Security (ENISA). *Digital Single Market*. Accessed April 8, 2017, from https://ec.europa.eu/digital-single-market/en/news/commission-launches-public-consultation-review-european-union-agency-network-and-information
European Commission. (2017b). Questionnaire on the evaluation and review of the European Union Agency for Network and Information Security. *EUSurvey*. Accessed April 8, 2017, from https://ec.europa.eu/eusurvey/runner/ENISA_review
European Commission. *Commission staff working document annex to the European electronic communications regulation and markets (12th Report)*, Brussels.
European Commission & High Representative of the European Union for Foreign Affairs and Security Policy. (2013). *Cybersecurity strategy of the European Union: An open, safe and secure cyberspace*. Brussels.
European Parliament. (2015). MEPs close deal with Council on first ever EU rules on cybersecurity. *European Parliament News*. Accessed February 22, 2016, from http://www.europarl.europa.eu/news/en/news-room/20151207IPR06449/MEPs-close-deal-with-Council-on-first-ever-EU-rules-on-cybersecurity
Eurostat. (2013). *Enterprises with fixed broadband access*. Brussels.
Eurostat. (2014). *Percentage of households who have internet access at home*. Brussels.
Farrand, B. (2014). The digital agenda for Europe, the economy and its impact upon the development of EU copyright policy. In I. A. Stamatoudi & P. Torremans (Eds.), *Copyright Law in the European Union*. Cheltenham: Edward Elgar.
Farrand, B. (2016). The future of copyright enforcement online: Intermediaries caught between formal and informal governance in the EU. In I. A. Stamatoudi (Ed.), *New Developments in EU and International Copyright Law*. Alphen aan den Rijn: Kluwer Law International.
Farrand, B., & Carrapico, H. (2013). Networked governance and the regulation of expression on the internet: The blurring of the role of public and private actors as content regulators. *Journal of Information Technology & Politics, 10*(4), 357–368.
Farrell, S. (2016). TalkTalk counts costs of cyber-attack. *The Guardian*. Accessed February 29, 2016, from http://www.theguardian.com/business/2016/feb/02/talktalk-cyberattack-costs-customers-leave
Fourcade-Gourinchas, M., & Babb, S. L. (2002). The rebirth of the liberal creed: Paths to neoliberalism in four countries. *American Journal of Sociology, 108*(3), 533–579.

George, A. L., & Bennett, A. (2005). *Case studies and theory development in the social sciences*. Cambridge, MA: MIT Press.
Gibbs, S. (2015). TalkTalk criticised for poor security and handling of hack attack. *The Guardian*. Accessed February 29, 2016, from http://www.theguardian.com/technology/2015/oct/23/talktalk-criticised-for-poor-security-and-handling-of-hack-attack
Gilardi, F. (2008). *Delegation in the regulatory state: Independent regulatory agencies in Western Europe*. Cheltenham, UK; Northampton, MA: Edward Elgar.
Haas, E. B. (1968). *The Uniting of Europe: Political, social and economic forces, 1950–57*, 2nd Revised ed. Stanford University Press.
Hall, P. A. (2013). Tracing the progress of process tracing. *European Political Science, 12*(1), 20–30.
Harvey, D. (2007). *A brief history of neoliberalism*, New ed. Oxford; New York: OUP Oxford.
Horten, M. (2011). *The copyright enforcement enigma: Internet politics and the "Telecoms Package."* New York: Palgrave Macmillan.
JISC. (2015). DDoS attack disrupting Janet network. *JISC News*. Accessed February 29, 2016, from https://www.jisc.ac.uk/news/ddos-attack-disrupting-janet-network-08-dec-2015
Jordana, J., & Levi-Faur, D. (2004). The politics of regulation in the age of governance. In J. Jordana & D. Levi-Faur (Eds.), *The politics of regulation: Institutions and regulatory reforms for the age of governance*. Cheltenham: Edward Elgar.
Knowles, W., et al. (2015). A survey of cyber security management in industrial control systems. *International Journal of Critical Infrastructure Protection, 9*, 52–80.
Lægreid, P., & Verhoest, K. (2010). Introduction: Reforming public sector organizations. In P. Lægreid & K. Verhoest (Eds.), *Governance of public sector organization: Proliferation, autonomy and performance*. Hampshire: AIAA.
Lazer, D. (2005). Regulatory capitalism as a networked order: The international system as an informational network. *The Annals of the American Academy of Political and Social Science, 598*(1), 52–66.
Levi-Faur, D. (2005). The rise of regulatory capitalism: The global diffusion of a new order. *The Annals of the American Academy of Political and Social Science, 598*(1), 12–32.
Levi-Faur, D., & Jordana, J. (2005). Globalizing regulatory capitalism. *The Annals of the American Academy of Political and Social Science, 598*(1), 6–9.
Majone, G. (Ed.). (1996). *Regulating Europe*. London: Routledge.
Moe, T. M. (1990). Political institutions: The neglected side of the story. *Journal of Law, Economics, & Organization, 6*, 213–253.
Picciotto, S. (2006). *Regulatory networks and global governance*. Institute of Advanced Legal Studies: University of London.
Ponte, S., Gibbon, P., & Vestergaard, J. (Eds.). (2011). *Governing through standards: Origins, drivers and limitations*, 2011 ed. Houndmills, Basingstoke, Hampshire; New York: AIAA.
Porcedda, M. G. (2011). Translantic approaches to cybersecurity and cybercrime. In P. Pawlak (Ed.), *The EU-US security and justice agenda in action*. Chaillot Papers.
Reestman, J.-H., & Eijsbouts, W. T. (2009). Internet policy and the European political and legal orders. *European Constitutional Law Review, 5*(2), 169–172.
Risse, T., & Börzel, T. A. (2005). Public-private partnerships: Effective and legitimate tools of international governance. In E. Grande & L. W. Pauly (Eds.), *Complex sovereignty: Reconstituting political authority in the twenty-first century*. Toronto: University of Toronto Press.
Rittberger, B., & Wonka, A. (Eds.). (2012). *Agency governance in the EU*. Routledge.
Schimmelfennig, F. (2003). *The EU, NATO and the Integration of Europe: Rules and Rhetoric*. Camberidge; New York: Cambridge University Press.
Vogel, S. K. (1996). *Freer markets, more rules: Regulatory reform in advanced industrial countries*. Ithaca: Cornell University Press.

Chapter 10
A Typology of Cybersecurity and Public–Private Partnerships in the Context of the European Union

Raphael Bossong and Ben Wagner

10.1 Introduction

Current discussions on security on the Internet mostly revolve around the necessity and limits of *public* action in the face of a decentralised and privately owned or operated space (Radu et al. 2014; Eriksson and Giacomello 2009). Unsurprisingly, the question of public authority particularly comes to the fore in matters of security. The original vision of an entirely self-regulated as well as resilient, decentralised Internet has come under severe stress due to structural vulnerabilities beyond the reach of any individual actor (Mueller et al. 2013). These vulnerabilities are increasingly exploited by a growing number of harmful actors, which are also increasingly putting their services and malware products on sale and wide access. This calls for more multi-faced and coordinated governance approaches to improve security on the Internet that is typically termed 'cybersecurity' (Von Solms and Van Niekerk 2013).[1] In short, to provide cybersecurity public and private actors clearly need to engage with each other (Tropina 2015). This is reflected in a growing number of policy initiatives and public declarations that underline the value of Public Private Partnerships (PPP) for increasing or providing cybersecurity (Min et al. 2015). Such partnerships are also critical site to translate broad or ambiguous conception of cybersecurity, which may have reinforced the trend towards an ever

[1] One should, however, that there are alternative framings of technical IT security and problems with the general label of "cyber", which will be briefly taken up below.

R. Bossong (✉)
German Institute for International and Security Affairs (SWP), Ludwigkirchplatz 3-4, 10719 Berlin, Germany
e-mail: Raphael.Bossong@swp-berlin.org

B. Wagner
Institute for Management Information Systems, Vienna University of Economics and Business, Vienna, Austria

O. Bures, H. Carrapico (eds.), *Security Privatization*,
DOI 10.1007/978-3-319-63010-6_10

more encompassing securitisation of contemporary Western societies, into daily practices.

However, the interaction or partnership between public and private actors for cybersecurity can take many institutional shapes and forms (also see Bures, Chap. 2; Bonfanti and Stefanucci, Chap. 11; and Porcedda, Chap. 12 in this volume), which remain obscured by an overly encompassing and ambitious political rhetoric (Carr 2016). One can point to considerable gaps between public rhetoric and practice of security cooperation with private actors (Dunn-Cavelty and Suter 2009)—or see this cooperation as comprehensive "dataveillance" (van Dijck 2014), whereby public actors access a hitherto unimaginable depth of information that consumers are structurally inclined to provide in exchange for free online services and software applications. For instance, the NSA scandal has revealed substantial evidence for public–private collaboration, whereas the current debate on the legitimacy of strong commercial encryption underlines that the relationship between "national security" and private authorities is at least as often fraught with tension and confrontation.

Even more broadly speaking, this relates to a fundamental conceptual and political debate on the evolving nature of security governance (see Bures and Carrapico, Chap. 1), which has challenged conventional understandings of modern statehood and foundations of public authority (Bevir 2014; Hameiri and Jones 2015). In particular, the provision of security has been traditionally understood as the first-and-foremost responsibility of the state, as the legitimate bearer of the monopoly on the use of legitimate violence, but increasingly involves a much wider array of actors, be they companies, private individuals, civil society organisations or international organisations. Networks of security governance can be considered a functional adaptation to increasingly networked and transnational risks and threats, such as terrorism or critical infrastructure failure, while also balancing some of the problematic tendencies of state security apparatus by including a wider range of voices and perspectives (Nance and Cottrell 2014). At the same time, security governance that moves away from public authorities generates multiples challenges and critical questions (Kennedy 2016; Ehrhart et al. 2014; Crawford 2006), be it with regard to the sheer number of actors at multiple levels (compare Aarstad, Chap. 4 and Biaumet, Chap. 8 in this volume) or the exercise of coercive powers for profit (compare Saldivar, Chap. 7 in this volume).

Against this complex background, this chapter does not stake out a clear position for or against public–private cooperation for cybersecurity. It does not appear feasible or realistic to disentangle the level functional interdependence and geographical extension of security governance networks, especially in the area of information communication technologies (ICT). Rather, it pursues a more modest, but—in our view—nonetheless essential aim, namely to clarify our understanding and conceptualisation of the varied forms and kinds of PPPs in the area of cybersecurity, especially in so far as it concerns more regular and publicly known forms of cooperation.[2] It then applies this understanding to the case of the EU that

[2]In contrast to informal working arrangements for security and intelligence agencies.

arguably constitutes a representative, relatively transparent and significant case for such regular kinds of PPPs for cybersecurity.

These steps reflect in two parts of the chapter. First, we argue that ideal-typical PPPs focus on operational provision or delivery of services—or policy implementation in a broad sense—, in contrast to other forms of policy consultation, shared regulation and interest representation. Furthermore, PPPs likely to benefit from formalised agreements that specifies intended benefits or profits as well as the risks of the venture. Yet we also note that the ICT sector exhibits some distinct characteristics, which may explain some of the confusion about the possible meaning of PPPs. In particular, "cyberspace" and the respective manifestations of "cybersecurity" play out at multiple levels and among varied communities of practice, ranging from infrastructural issues to the management of online content. A corresponding typology helps to map different actor incentives as well as normative concerns with regard to the range of possible public–private interactions for cybersecurity. However, such an abstract representation necessarily glosses over many important nuances and still needs to be situated in particular empirical context.

With these considerations in mind, the second part of this chapter applies this heuristic framework to survey the EU's efforts to develop PPPs for cybersecurity (Procedda 2014; Christou and Simpson 2006). It has to be underlined that EU member states remain mainly responsible for the provision of "internal security", which can include cyberspace, following the example of technologically advanced North-Western European states, such as the UK, Germany or the Netherlands. One can also point to wide variety of platforms, alliances and initiatives for cybersecurity at European national as well as wider global levels,[3] so that the EU does not necessarily take a central position in wider transnational governance efforts for cybersecurity. Yet the EU is building a wide transnational regulatory regime on cybersecurity (Fahey 2014) and can exercise significant influence with regard to the large number of European states that have yet to formulate respective policies, processes and structures. In particular, the EU cybersecurity strategy extensively stresses the importance of public private interactions for cybercrime and cybersecurity (EU 2013), while the EU's recent agenda on internal security (European Commission 2015, p. 20) argues that "cooperation with the private sector is also of critical importance, with public-private partnerships to structure a common effort to fight online crime."

Moving beyond these official declarations, the second part of this chapter reviews the internal differentiation and diversity of EU PPPs for cybersecurity. The EU has doted itself with two agencies or centres that can participate in more regular administrative or operational aspects of cybersecurity, namely the European Network Information Security Agency (ENISA) and the EC3 cybercrime centre in EUROPOL. ENISA seeks partnerships for improving the technical reliability and resilience of cyberspace or critical information infrastructures, which are in private hands (compare Farrand and Carrapico, Chap. 9; Bonfanti and Stefanucci,

[3]For instance, https://www.icspa.org/ or https://www.ncia.nato.int/NewsRoom/Pages/140918-NATO-launches-Industry-Cyber-Partnership.aspx

Chap. 11; and Porcedda, Chap. 12 in this volume). In contrast, the EC3 seeks out more operational exchanges with IT security companies in order to address cybercrime and complex threats, such as botnets, in a more proactive manner. In addition, the EC3 and its host institution EUROPOL seek to extend voluntary mechanisms for Internet content control with private actors, which has recently given rise to the so-called Internet Referral Unit. Related content control measures have given rise to a particularly critical discussion in its own right, but may also be usefully be thought of as a variant of wider patterns of PPPs for cybersecurity. In conclusion, the proposed typology of public–private interactions helps to develop more systematic and analytical arguments about the development or relative stagnation of different kinds of PPPs for cybersecurity. It also underlines the need to focus normative critiques on specific cooperation dynamics, such as information sharing and active assistance, which need to be evaluated against wider legal and political principles that the EU officially endorses. Finally, the conclusions also return to the argument for more contractual or formalised PPPs, which should be evaluated in further research on the dynamically evolving relationships between public and private actors in the cyber realm.

10.2 Towards a More Structured Conceptualisation of PPPs in Cybersecurity

10.2.1 Public Private Partnerships in ICT

The rise of public private partnerships—as one component of the so-called New Public Management and more neoliberal models of the role of the state—initially grew out the privatisation of public infrastructure and as a means for attracting private resources for further public construction projects (Grimsey and Lewis 2007). As the next logical step, PPPs spread to the management and general provision of public services that are based on these infrastructures, such as hospitals, schools or even prisons (Schneider 1999). Over the last two decades this development has led to an extensive international debate on the merits and drawbacks of PPPs (Bovaird 2004). For instance, opinions diverge on how far economic efficiency should remain the main standard for assessing the merits of PPPs, or whether other values, such as fairness and equity in access to public services can also be enhanced or at least maintained in such contexts (Hodge and Greve 2007; Reynaers and De Graaf 2014). Further critical questions are asked about the accountability of both public and private actors, and the transparency of their mutual agreements beyond formal administrative structures (Forrer et al. 2010; Willems and Van Dooren 2011). Finally, one must also recognise that different state traditions, or political cultures, influence respective assessments (Hodge and Greve 2005). Alongside efforts for standardisation by international organisations (European Commission 2004; United Nations Economic Commission for Europe

2008), one continues to observe major cross-national differences in PPPs, including government support, dedicated institutions or agencies, laws, technical expertise (Van den Hurk et al. 2015) as well as more informal norms, historically grown economic structures and societal values (Roumboutsos 2015).

This level of empirical diversity as well as debate about relative merits may explain why the term PPP is still often used without precision (Linder 1999). Nevertheless, mainstream PPPs are typically based on an explicit or formalised agreement, which tasks private actors with the provision of a public service, maintenance of infrastructure or new construction project. Such PPPs should also specify matching responsibilities, profit and risk sharing arrangements (Bovis 2015), which follows conventional economic reasoning on the need for calibrated (financial) incentives and control instruments to align the interests of self-interested rational actors (Hans Voordijk et al. 2016). However, standard commercial contracts cannot address all potential problems of PPPs, especially in high-risk projects or with regard to long-term partnerships agreements, so that there is a need for flexibility, learning and adaptability over time (Van Den Hurk and Verhoest 2016). Some analysts emphasise further demanding and intangible standards for PPPs, whereby a shared sense of objectives, trust-based relations and synergetic use of the capacities of both public and private actors beyond cost considerations are the most central feature (Brinkerhoff and Brinkerhoff 2011).

However, the main driver for the formation of typical PPPs are cost and efficiency considerations—or related policy beliefs—among public authorities. As summed up by Bovis (2013, p. xiii): “A common definition on public–private partnerships does not exist. However, ... [t]he method of financing and the risk transfer from public to the private sector are common features in different jurisdictions across the world ... The principal benefit from involving the private sector in the delivery of public services through a public-private partnership format has been attributed to the fact that the public sector does not have to commit its own capital resources ... and that substantial transfer of risks to the private sector offers value for money.”

Yet in the contemporary ICT sector the relations between public and private actors exhibit distinct features (Gómez-Barroso and Feijóo 2010). Unlike many other key economic and societal infrastructures, the internet is a dominantly private construct, at least since its extremely dynamic spread and development since the early 1980s (Townes 2012; Braman 2011). This means that classic PPPs for construction and service provision are comparatively rare—at least in non-rural areas, advanced economies or with regard to standard infrastructures for telecommunications (LaRose et al. 2014; Narayanan et al. 2005). Instead, PPPs serve as broad rhetorical instruments to influence private actors that operate, underpin and provide cyberspace, its logical interfaces and content, tying in with wider political discourses on innovation, competitiveness as well as national security (Carr 2016). This has given rise to the situation whereby an extremely wide range of policy initiatives, forums and consultation platforms in the ICT sector have been labelled as PPPs (ENISA 2011a), which adds to, or surpasses, the existing definitional problems with conventional PPPs as outlined above.

In fact, when approaching the problem of security and safety in other infrastructure and industrial sectors one would expect classic debates on the need for binding regulations or liability rules versus considerations about economic competitiveness (Héritier 2001). The wide range of voluntary and private governance instruments—which go under multiple labels, such as corporate social responsibility or, in the EU-context, the open of method of coordination—are frequently reviewed as a potential alternative to hierarchical regulation due to speed, flexibility, range and support from stakeholders in implementation processes (Harcourt 2013; Graz and Nölke 2007). And as mentioned in the introduction, this corresponds to general arguments about the benefits of security governance that breaks out of the mould of the hierarchical security state. The classic counter-argument is to highlight the necessary "shadow of hierarchy" to make soft law effective (Börzel 2010; Wagner 2014)—or to trace the evolution of soft law to increasingly hard regulation over time, as it becomes evident that not all private actors make the necessary "non-productive" investments into security (Wiater 2015).

Such familiar debates currently play out in the ICT sector, where the growing regulatory ambitions of public authorities competes with long-standing private approaches to self-governance (Bauer 2010). Most recently, this can be illustrated by the European directive for Network Information Security (European Commission 2013), which emulates and advanced various related national provisions on mandatory security standards and reporting among relevant infrastructure providers and dependent operators (see Farrand and Carrapico, Chap. 9).[4] However, the ICT sector continues to present particular challenges in terms of technical complexity, speed of change, diversity of participants and transnational interdependence, so that conventional policy-making remains constrained or needs to be complemented by alternative processes. Here one can refer the dynamically growing literature on "internet co-regulation" between public and private actors (Tropina and Callanan 2015; Marsden 2011) as well as the related notion of "multi-stakeholder governance" (Carr 2015; Chenou 2014; Bendiek and Porter 2013), which is as often conflictual as cooperative. Therefore, we cannot rule out, or delimit, the term PPP at this level of generality, but first need to disentangle the specific institutional relationship involved as well as the characteristics of cybersecurity that should be advanced to clarify the forms of cooperation in the context.

[4]At the time of writing, the legislative proposal had gained political agreement from all EU institutions, but was not formally concluded yet. See: https://ec.europa.eu/digital-single-market/en/news/network-and-information-security-directive-co-legislators-agree-first-eu-wide-legislation

10.2.2 Public–Private Cooperation and Governance Tasks for Cybersecurity

Just as the notion of PPPs, “cybersecurity” is characterised by a lack of specificity—especially when moving beyond technical understandings of information security that focus on the confidentiality, integrity and availability of computer system.[5] Arguably, the cyber label has opened a discursive door that provides an ever more expansive understanding of the shape and scope of the object to be secured, which may empower public security authorities (Hansen and Nissenbaum 2009; Dunn Cavelty 2013) and affect the wider conduct of international relations (Wagner forthcoming). Precisely for this reason, it is useful to take a step back from high-level debates and to sketch out a more applied perspective on cybersecurity that takes multiple levels or dimensions of cyberspace into account.[6] These levels and dimensions are relevant to the analysis of PPPs as they are constituted by different actors or professional communities with different incentives for cybersecurity. For instance, a security engineer in a private company may rather consider himself part of a transnational community for a specific aspect of information security than responsible for national cybersecurity (Schmidt 2014), which—in turn—shapes the possible range or format for respective partnerships.

To delineate the possible diversity of these communities, Choucri and Clark (2012) provide a useful heuristic, which extends technical notions of IT network and internet architecture to broader social and information dimensions. Thus, cyberspace is constituted by, and cybersecurity plays out at,

1. the physical infrastructures layer (cables, IXP, etc.) the layer of logical interfaces that are used to run and connect these infrastructures
2. the layer of content/information flowing across or being stored on these networks and the layer of users (individual as well as corporate) that operate or depend on these systems.

The first two technical layers are critical to systemic cybersecurity, but are not necessarily reliant on public intervention (DeNardis 2012). Due to economic interests in business continuity, private companies that own, provide, manage or operate infrastructures for cyberspace can be expected to make considerable investments in network reliability and resilience. At the same time, information security experts and engineers have long developed close networks for cooperating on

---

[5]Information and computer scientist tend to prefer other more technical and precise concepts, such as information security, which is composed of definable attributes of integrity, availability and confidentiality. Security scholars, in contrast, have highlighted the dangers of “securitizing” the digital communications or simply just ‘cyber’ and merging distinct issues of cybercrime, cyber-assisted crime with more state-centred notion of security, which can legitimate “offensive” methods and the involvement of the military.

[6]Again, we cannot go into the question whether cyberspace is a suitably precise analytical concept. For a widely cited official definition, see http://www.dhs.gov/sites/default/files/publications/Cyberspace_Policy_Review_final_0.pdf

technical issues that underpin the global internet infrastructure on a global scale (Mathew 2014). This explains why the respective efforts of states and international organisations to regulate the infrastructural dimension of the internet (DeNardis 2014) continues competes with strong self-governance mechanisms by these private actors[7]—at least in liberal states that publicly refrained from direct control, while Western companies take on a matching central role (Ruiz and Barnett 2014).

The situation is at least as complex with regard to the second layer of applications. Private and largely confidential expert networks have long exchanged information on vulnerabilities and coding errors, not least as there is also a considerable reputational issue towards customers. Users are thus being provided with free software updates and vulnerability patches on a regular basis, even if the frequency with which this happens—and the growing commodification of vulnerabilities—also fuels a critical discourse on structural weaknesses and vulnerabilities of the commercial software market (Anderson and Moore 2006; August and Tunca 2011).[8] The most fundamental approach to full self-regulation in this area is the open source movement that aims to provide better and more secure software on the basis of voluntary, transparent and largely non-remunerated collaboration of programmers around the globe. Conversely, there are also growing public efforts for certification and regulation that establish product liability and security standards for software providers (Brown and Marsden 2013; Edwards et al. 2014). In a nutshell, the early catch-phrase that "code is law", which can be interpreted to mean that software code directly constitutes its own binding set of rules and behavioural constraints, is being complimented by complex legal frameworks for product regulation, especially when it comes to increasingly autonomous and interdependent software-based systems.

When moving to the content and user layer, Internet Service and especially Content Providers and Social Media Companies and other public-private interaction dynamics move centre-stage (Kleinschmidt 2010). A standard assumption is that these actors do not have a direct commercial interest in public definitions of "security" beyond their service continuity and expanding the range of users (Rowe and Wood 2013; Usman 2013). This can, but does not have to, imply protecting their platforms and services from malicious actors, as far as these threaten to highjack bandwidth or related technical service capacities, as in the case of botnets and spam (Van Eijk 2013). However, it is economically costly and technologically challenging to implement more rigorous controls on exchanged content, while a conventional understanding of the internet would emphasise its "end-to-end" nature, i.e. the primary responsibilities of senders and receivers rather than intermediaries of information, and the corresponding "neutrality" or equality of data

---

[7]For instance, http://www.ix-f.net/ixp-models.html. See also Farrand and Carrapico, Chap. 9, for a more detailed discussion on the historical development from public to private management of critical infrastructures.

[8]An especially controversial response to this challenge has been to create separate market incentives through programs such as 'bug bounties.'

packages that flow across network (Clark et al. 2014). Furthermore, monitoring problematic (non-verbal) internet content cannot be fully automated at this stage, and therefore tends to require comparatively costly human resources for reviewing flagged items. At the same time, it is clear that liberal political systems require some degree of cooperation from these providers to maintain legal norms about the limits of expression and the respect for human dignity (Cohen-Almagor 2015).[9] This has led to complex trade-offs and variants between legal and voluntary governance arrangements for content control (Horten 2015; Wagner 2014; Parti and Marin 2013), which briefly returned to in the second part of this chapter.

Finally, the fourth layer of users encompasses actor-centred, rather than technical or data-driven, dynamics in cyberspace. This is necessarily a very broad residual category where one cannot clearly separate security-conscientious actors from the supposedly rather passive and security-insensitive mass of (corporate or individual) users (August et al. 2014; Camp 2011).

Building on this layering and heuristic parsing of communities for cybersecurity, we propose a cross-cutting differentiation between five broad areas or tasks of public private interactions for cybersecurity. According to a descriptive functionalist logic[10] these tasks are: (1) the reliable *provision* of internet/ICT access; (2) the co-*regulation* of technical security as well as of data handling; (3) the *exchange of information* on threats and vulnerability; and (4) *mutual assistance* in addressing known threats or illegal content in cyberspace. These tasks can be related to the previous critical discussion on the possible meaning of PPPs. In particular, these tasks need to be applied across various considerations of cybersecurity until here.

Concerning provision of service, it has already been mentioned that access to ICT infrastructures and the internet (in the West) has largely been provided by the private sector without formal requests from public actors, which limits the classic uses of PPPs for construction. As also referred to above, market regulation, that deals with possible externalities of economic activities, such as pollution, risks of accidents, eroding social security, etc., can involve various forms of hard law and soft governance. This could be likened to coordination in PPPs, but should—in our view—better be categories as other forms of soft governance, such as co-regulation or corporate social responsibility. In any case, in the area of ICT the initial bottom-up and non-governmental patterns of self-regulations that characterised the early days of the internet are increasingly replaced or complemented by national and

[9]Such as "hate" speech, weapons instructions, child sexual abuse material, etc.

[10]These functionally differentiated tasks or processes have been inductively derived by the authors from the diverse social science literature on cybersecurity referred above. For reasons of space this differentiation cannot be systematically related to wider theories of public (economic) regulation and security governance here, but this may prove a worthwhile research agenda for the future. On the one hand, one could test whether the proposed tasks are truly exhaustive and comprehensive in the area of cybersecurity. On the other hand, more elaborate formal reasoning on collective action dynamics, such as with regard to the public good qualities of information or reliable access, could be explored beyond the cursory remarks made below.

international legal instruments,[11] which will also be illustrated in the second part of the chapter.

The third task of information exchange between public and private actors, in contrast, is closer to the notion of an implementation or service-oriented partnership. Both public and private organisations should profit from up-to-date assessment of specific cyber threats and vulnerabilities, while strategic data aggregation should help to address more structural problems of under-investments in IT security. Such threat awareness should alert potential targets of the substantial level of risk, even if they lack specific experience with cyberattacks and consider themselves an unlikely target (Suter 2007; Kaijankoski 2015; Hare 2010). Systems and processes for information sharing between public and private actors should also cut down on response times to cyber incidents, which is especially significant when moving beyond data-losses or -thefts towards potential outages of major services (e.g. banking) and infrastructures (e.g. energy).

Nevertheless, public–private information sharing on cyber threats and incidents is beset by various cooperation problems and challenging externalities (Dourado and Castillo 2015; Bauer and Van Eeten 2009). Among other issues, it is mistaken to assume a general positive impact for all participants of information-sharing exercises. Many actors apparently fear the reputational costs of, or possible liabilities deriving from, breaches of their cybersecurity more than desiring the rather diffuse benefits of strategic threat awareness (Nolan 2015). This explains the trend away from partnership towards mandatory public regulation and regulated institutional processes for a "duty to notify" in cases of major ICT incidents (Kesan and Hayes 2015).

Alternatively, the general risks of cyberattacks may not dominate over the specific and costs for up-to-date mechanisms of protection. This can lead to collective problems (Rosenzweig 2011), such as free-riding behaviour where individual actors may see themselves as too small to affect the wider level of IT security, so that they hope that other public players or dedicated IT companies will address the most serious threats. In any case, public and private actors are obviously extremely diverse, including global corporations, small and medium enterprises, local governments, non-technical line ministries or dedicated cyber units in defence ministries, just to name a few examples. As such, these actors have very different levels of human resources and technical capacities for engaging in cybersecurity (e.g. Prince and King 2013). This explains why PPPs for information exchanges on cybersecurity mostly remain limited to comparatively exclusive clubs between major companies, be they infrastructure providers or global IT players, and dedicated cybersecurity authorities. In the US, this most clearly reflects in formalised and sector-specific centres for cyber-information sharing.[12]

[11]If one applies a broad or multi-level understanding of cybersecurity, this can range from questions of rights management, privacy and data protection to secure communication protocol standards or product safety and security.

[12]http://www.nationalisacs.org/#!member-isacs/jnog6

The fourth area of active collaboration in addressing cyber-threats concerns an even smaller range of actors, but constitutes the most significant area for operational partnerships. Specialised IT security companies have an active commercial interest to buttress their visibility in the field, or may directly be tasked by public authorities for the provision of cybersecurity. This will be illustrated further below with regard to the EU cybercrime centre EC3, and may be conceptually related to the wider debate on privatised security governance and policing (Crawford 2006). Yet other corporate actors beyond IT security firms may have a specific interest in operational cooperation with public authorities. For example, financial services experience particular exposure to cyberattacks and virtual thefts and therefore have a direct stake in respective criminal investigations (Lagazio et al. 2014). Internet providers and social media companies provide another sector, where reputational costs of hosting extremist content has increasingly led them to partner with public authorities for monitoring and take-downs.[13]

Yet such proactive forms of assistance can create several normative problems. On the one hand, it is not clear in how far private actors have been drawn into 'pragmatic' cooperation that falls short of legal certainty and accountability for citizens, customers and users. For instance, it may be easier for private providers to block reported content than to develop a balanced assessment merit of each such request according to a different national and international legal standards (Brown and Cowls 2015). On the other hand, public actors may be unduly empowered by drawing on private capacities to collect information that may then be used in criminal prosecutions or other executive actions (Nolan 2015).

10.2.3 A Heuristic Typology of PPPs for Cybersecurity

To summarise these various considerations, we propose to a heuristic typology on public–private interactions in cybersecurity. It has been argued, albeit briefly that PPPs in cybersecurity centre on information-sharing and active assistance, whereas basic service provision mostly remains in private hands.[14] At the same time, processes of internet co-regulation already constitute a highly complex issue are and should, at least for analytical purposes, be kept apart from the notion of PPPs. Furthermore, different layers of cyberspace reflect in different communities and incentives or disincentives for public–private cooperation across these tasks. While infrastructural and technical levels should not be excluded by definition, they tend

[13]http://www.wired.com/2015/11/facebook-and-twitter-face-tough-choices-as-isis-exploits-social-media/

[14]This point can be unlined by the fact that PPPs for a more secure internet provision at the infrastructural level have not yet been funded in Europe, as illustrated by the failed idea of a "Schengen-net" for secure data transfers in Europe.

to gravitate to the task of co-regulation with public actors, as general rule-setting is most significant for structural cybersecurity.

As can be read from the following Table 10.1, it is, therefore, the layers of content and users, and the functions of information-sharing and active assistance, that constitute the core of operational PPPs for cybersecurity. The table also indicates that other interactions as well as partnerships are possible. For instance, the NSA scandal highlighted that active assistance and access provided by infrastructural providers has been a key instrument for extensive intelligence collection. However, for reasons of space we cannot discuss every possible typological field, while it is also one of the core aims of the chapter to provide more focus to the discussion on PPPs in cybersecurity. For these reasons, we consider it justifiable to limit the following discussion and empirical illustration to the identified "core" fields of PPPs for cybersecurity. But different reading and critique of the heuristic framework for focussing the link between PPPs and cybersecurity are certainly possible and deserve further attention.

10.3 Surveying EU Cybersecurity and Public Private Partnerships

The two EU agencies ENISA and EUROPOL are the main public operational or executive actors in the area of EU cybersecurity. Both actors are heavily dependent on cooperation with private actors for their organisational success, and are supposed to cooperate increasingly with each other. At the same time, they clearly have different mandates and respective relationships with private actors. The following overview therefore uses the typological differentiation with regard to the central tasks of PPPs, namely information-sharing and active assistance, and sets in relation to the different audience or layers that the two agencies appeal to.[15] By providing a structured overview of the types of relationships these organisations engage in, we hope to provide a clearer picture of what cybersecurity partnerships in this area actually look like in practice.

10.3.1 ENISA

ENISA, the European Union Agency for Network and Information Security, is the main organisation for structural cybersecurity, i.e. at the infrastructural and technical/logical level. ENISA was founded in 2004 and has gradually established itself as a leading provider of technical advice in Europe (see Farrand and Carrapico, Chap. 9). In particular, the agency produces a large volume of conceptual papers

[15]The typological fields are referred to in the respective subheadings of the different sections.

Table 10.1 A heuristic typology of PPPs for cybersecurity

Function Layer (communities)	Provision	Co-regulation	Information-sharing	Active assistance
Physical infrastructure (Private owners)	PPPs for physical installation and service provision	Rules for internet exchange points and cable operators	Exchanges on mainly physical vulnerabilities	Allowing access to ICT infrastructures by security services
Logical interface (IT expert community and software providers)	Publicly supported research for privately provided security standards	Technical standard-setting for network communication protocols and reliability of applications	Regular exchanges on code errors, exploits and vulnerabilities	Public–private cooperation to address vulnerabilities and incidents (CERT)
Content/data (Internet service providers, social media)	Voluntary hosting of public messages/propaganda/counter-narratives by private service providers	Multiple regulatory issues on content management, data protection, privacy protection, "regulated" access for security services, etc.	**Reporting of problematic content to public authorities (e.g. radical websites)**	**Active filtering and take-down of content beyond formal regulatory requirements**
Other actors that use or proactively defend ICT systems	Commercial provision of cybersecurity products and systems to public authorities	Definition of users with higher security and reporting requirements (e.g. other ICT-supported infrastructures)	**Reporting on attacks and malignant actors, strategic threat awareness**	**Active collaboration in take-downs and prosecution of malignant actors**

and organises exercises,[16] workshops and expert meetings on cybersecurity. In 2013, ENISA was given an expanded and permanent legal basis, which defined its organisational mandate as follows (European Union 2013, p. 43): "The Agency should contribute to a high level of network and information security, to better protection of privacy and personal data, and to the development and promotion of a culture of network and information security for the benefit of citizens, consumers, businesses and public sector organisations in the Union, thus contributing to the proper functioning of the internal market."

In light of this, regular interactions across the public–private divide are clearly essential to the work of ENSIA. At a very general level, this can be illustrated by the inclusion of private representatives in the so-called permanent stakeholder group,

[16]ENISA has organised several annual major ICT incident exercises for EU member states that were triggered official EU conclusions in the aftermath of the 2009 Estonian cyber-attacks. Assessments of these exercises are limited to official document, where the large number of participants (500+) and positive resonance had highlighted.

which should assist the management of ENISA after the last revision of its mandate.[17] But already well before, ENISA conducted extensive research on different models and potential of PPPs in the ICT sector (ENISA 2011b), which supports several arguments made in the first part of this chapter. Thus, the agency underlines that private actors are often unwilling to share information on a voluntary basis and that formal agreements or structures are necessary to ensure the operational usefulness of PPPs to both private and public actors.

At the same time, the focus of ENISA on more infrastructural layers of cybersecurity suggests that public–private interactions are more likely to take the form of co-regulation for general standard setting or security certification.[18] This reflects in a range of multi-stakeholder governance forums overseen by ENISA, such as the "ENISA Internet infrastructure security and resilience reference group",[19] and the "Electronic Communications Reference Group (ECRG)"[20] These groups interact with other forums for technical self-regulation, mainly the International Standards Organisation (ISO), the European Electronic Standards Institute (ETSI, with MoU) and CEN CELENEC for further industrial standards.[21]

ENISA also engages in a range of wider educational and awareness raising activities that should stimulate greater cybersecurity investments among both public and private actors. Aside from a so-called awareness raising community of ENISA—which seems to have been discontinued after 2010—,[22] the largest coordinated effort is the so-called cybersecurity awareness month, which includes various private organisations.[23] However, these educations activities cannot be considered as sustained and substantial PPPs, since its target audience is diffuse and participants are not expected to enter into more regular relationships with ENISA.

10.3.1.1 PPPs for Information Sharing (Logical and User Layer)

For more substantial PPPs for cybersecurity, one can instead turn to private forums for sector-specific information sharing and which have contacts to ENISA. Examples are the so-called European Financial Institutes—Information Sharing and Analysis Centre[24] (EU-FISAC), or the so-called European Cyber Security

[17]See https://www.enisa.europa.eu/about-enisa/structure-organization/psg

[18]See also Art. 3 of the EU regulation establishing ENISA (revised 526/2013).

[19]https://resilience.enisa.europa.eu/internet-infrastructure-security-and-resilience-reference-group

[20]https://resilience.enisa.europa.eu/ecrg

[21]https://www.enisa.europa.eu/publications/articles/standards-for-cyber-security

[22]https://www.cscan.org/openaccess/?id=213

[23]http://www.enisa.europa.eu/activities/stakeholder-relations/nis-brokerage-1/european-cyber-security-month-advocacy-campaign

[24]https://www.enisa.europa.eu/activities/cert/support/information-sharing/european-fi-isac-a-public-private-partnership. This has been modelled on a corresponding US Forum with global reach. http://www.fsisac.com/

Protection Alliance (CYSPA),[25] which united both business and research institutions. A somewhat confusing array of additional private initiatives and platforms, such as the Internet Security Alliance for Europe and the Security Alliance for Europe, also interact with ENISA and comment on EU policy.[26]

However, the main PPP officially led by ENISA has been the so-called "European Public + Private Partnership for Resilience" (or *E3PR*). This initiative emerged in the context of a larger EU policy programme to increase the security of Critical Information infrastructures (CIIP) (Commission of the European Communities 2009). The E3PR format generated a number of thematic working and expert groups that should exchange information on relevant vulnerabilities and define policy options (compare Farrand and Carrapico, Chap. 9).[27] However, the E3PR failed to generate tangible results due to the diversity of stakeholders and avenues for action that could be considered before the EU proposed a more specific legislative agenda (Irion 2013). Information sharing channels for CIIP issues remained highly fragmented in Europe,[28] particularly when aiming to address the cross-sectoral vulnerabilities of infrastructures. A later official evaluation report of the E3PR underlined that that multiple conflicts of interests with regard to the confidentiality of data or prospect of costly mandatory security measures further hampered the emergence of the desired partnership (ENISA 2015).

By 2013, the EU already debated the aforementioned NIS directive (European Commission 2013), which should extend mandatory information sharing on cybersecurity incidents from telecommunications providers[29] to other critical infrastructure providers. Even before the directive has been politically agreed on in December 2015, ENISA created the so-called NIS platform to succeed the E3PR. By mid-2015, the NIS platform listed more than 200 members—with approx. 110 of them representing business interests—,[30] and had met at least five times. This indicates a substantial effort of public-private networking.

Yet the terminological change from a *partnership* to a *platform* for private industry is telling. Rather than promoting regular operational or administrative

[25]http://www.cyspa.eu/default.aspx?page=home

[26]http://www.scmagazineuk.com/internet-security-alliance-to-launch-european-spinoff/article/382265/

https://ec.europa.eu/futurium/en/system/files/ged/safe_-_nis_and_the_dsm_07042015.pdf

[27]ENISA, 2012a. European Public + Private Partnership for Resilience. Activity Report 2012. Available at: https://resilience.enisa.europa.eu/ep3r/2012-activity-report

[28]Compare also for an incomplete survey of information-sharing platforms across EU member states https://resilience.enisa.europa.eu/nis-platform/shared-documents/wg2-documents/wg2-outcome-draft/at_download/file

[29]This would hitherto be limited to some cases that are covered by the 2009 EU telecommunications regulation (Directive 2009/140/EC). See https://resilience.enisa.europa.eu/article-13

[30]Public authorities from 18 member state are taking part, while the rest is constituted by academic institutions or experts See full list of members http://ec.europa.eu/transparency/regexpert/index.cfm?do=groupDetail.groupDetail&groupID=2920&NewSearch=1&NewSearch=1

cooperation, as we would expect in a classic PPP, the NIS Platform has worked on a clearer agenda for co-regulation and related policy options. For these purposes, ENISA created three working groups, namely on risk management, information exchange and incident coordination and, finally, secure ICT research and innovation. Clearly, these tasks may also apply to operational PPPs, but at the time of writing, the NIS platform has not reached beyond several conceptual papers that were intended to prepare the implementation of the upcoming NIS directive.[31] This stakeholder consultation should also be viewed in wider international processes, as reflected in a recent and first EU US meeting in that format.[32] In sum, the NIS platform should mainly be regarded as a supporting process of regulatory governance of critical infrastructures.

10.3.1.2 Active Assistance (Logical and User Layer)

Yet one point to another area where ENISA may take on a more operational role for cybersecurity with private actors already, namely via its support for Computer Emergency Response Teams (CERTs). CERTs[33] have been developed since 2006 onwards. At the time, a few member states had started to create such units in emulation of the US, which pioneered this instrument already in 1990s (Morgus et al. 2015). By 2012, a separate EU CERT has been created,[34] while regular network activities and standardization of procedures to coordinate the work of national CERTs were underway.[35] The web presence of the EU CERT further includes regular news items on cyber threats and vulnerabilities of various applications.

These CERTs arguably constitute of boundary case for PPPs as defined for the purposes of this chapter. The leading US model is mainly public organisation, which maintains close contacts with private business.[36] Various national CERTs in Europe clearly have strong ties with the private sector[37]—or conversely, CERTs of

[31] See https://resilience.enisa.europa.eu/nis-platform. Especially the second working group provide the most detailed recommendations on how to differentiate, improve and link up the variety of information-sharing initiatives for CIIP, see https://resilience.enisa.europa.eu/nis-platform/shared-documents/5th-plenary-meeting/chapter-3-wg2_final-for-discussion-may-27-2015/at_download/file

[32] https://resilience.enisa.europa.eu/nis-platform/shared-documents/eu-us-preliminary-workshop-comparing-approaches

[33] Or computer security incident response teams in alternative European parlance (CSIRT), see https://www.enisa.europa.eu/activities/cert/support/guide2/introduction/what-is-csirt

[34] http://cert.europa.eu/cert/plainedition/en/cert_about.html

[35] For instance, one could point to frameworks for data sharing or best practice collection, see http://www.enisa.europa.eu/activities/cert/support/data-sharing

http://www.enisa.europa.eu/activities/cert/support/fight-against-cybercrime/the-directive-on-attacks-against-information-systems

[36] https://www.us-cert.gov/about-us

[37] http://cybersecurity.bsa.org/assets/PDFs/study_eucybersecurity_en.pdf

leading IT providers, such as the German Telecom, maintain close contacts with the public sector, including the EU level.[38] The EU CERT Mechanism similarly lists various private companies and internet providers as "partners"[39] for regular information sharing. However, public authorities also increasingly seek to provide their own cyber response capacities without having to partner with, or to rely on, private assistance.[40] For instance, the so-called European Governmental Cert Group[41] and officially listed partners of the EU-CERT are purely made up of public authorities,[42] while a recent analytical paper uses the added qualifier of national CSIRTs (nCSIRTs), even if there remain significant interfaces with private actors (Morgus et al. 2015). So formalised governance networks can only be made out among public sector CERTs. This interpretation of CERTs as moving away from PPP should be tested in further comparative empirical research.

In sum, ENISA expresses strong support for public private partnerships for cybersecurity, but mainly acts as a facilitator for technical co-regulation and certification with private actors (at the logical and infrastructure layer). ENISA organises stakeholder consultations in relevant EU regulation on cyber and critical infrastructure, as in the NIS Platform, and supports general awareness raising on cybersecurity among both public and private actors. Yet there is limited evidence for more operational PPPs, as official CERTs increasingly focus on the specific internal or defensive needs of public actors.

10.3.2 The EC3 and Its Public Private Partnership Activities

In contrast, operational PPPs for serious cybercrime seem to be the quickly growing domain of the EC3. As the EC3 has only been created in 2013, it does not surprise that there is no academic literature on it yet. To date, one can only refer to a preparatory feasibility study by the RAND consultancy (2012) that highlighted the challenges, but also the need for more coherent approach across European states in the fight against cybercrime. The EC3 was also created in a climate of austerity and thus with a tightly delimited budget, allegedly cutting into the human resource base of EUROPOL. Nevertheless, the EC3 quickly emerged as a significant actor in various international operations against botnets and serious cybercrime.[43] This is

---

[38]https://www.telekom.com/verantwortung/sicherheit/136918

[39]https://www.enisa.europa.eu/activities/risk-management/events/enisa-workshop-on-eu-threat-landscape/05PresentationStavrosLingris p-15

[40]https://www.enisa.europa.eu/activities/cert/support/information-sharing/detect-share-protect-solutions-for-improving-threat-data-exchange-among-certs

[41]http://www.egc-group.org/index.html

[42]https://cert.europa.eu/cert//plainedition/en/cert_partners.html

[43]http://www.nttdata.com/global/en/insights/it-briefings/2015022401.html

underpins, and is reinforced by, its intensive efforts to engage and partner with private actors.

10.3.2.1 Information Sharing (Users)

The EC3 has been flanked from the outset with two advisory groups, which included private corporate actors. One group is constituted by representative from security specialists, whereas the other gives a platform to the specific concerns of the financial sector. According to the initial terms of reference for the security-focused group,[44] the advisory group should, among other tasks, influence the strategic priorities of the new centre, inform various standards and define possible pilot projects for cooperation between the Centre and private IT security companies. This kind of private–public sector collaboration is not unusual in the IT security community and constitutes a relatively common form of cross-sectoral engagement beyond institutional boundaries (Reitano et al. 2015). Notably creation of these advisory groups does seem to be bearing fruit and there is evidence of regular and intense cooperation between the EC3 and financial service providers. A recent example is the cooperation of all major credit card providers in an EC3 led global operation against fraudulent air tickets sales.[45]

Building on its advisory groups, the EC3 has signed numerous Memoranda of Understanding (MoU) with private actors in the two sectors. To date at least four MoUs have been signed with financial actors or organisations,[46] adding to a larger number of agreements with IT security companies, such as Kaspersky,[47] McAfee,[48] Mnemonic,[49] Microsoft (security branch),[50] FireEye,[51] Group IB,[52]

[44]https://www.europol.europa.eu/sites/default/files/publications/ec3_programme_board_-_tor_-_terms_of_reference_and_mandate_of_the_advisory_group_on_internet_security.pdf

[45]http://www.computerweekly.com/news/2240235526/Over-a-hundred-cyber-criminals-arrested-in-global-operation

[46]Barclays, ING Group, Citibank, the European Banking Federation, and the association for ATM Security (EAST). See https://www.europol.europa.eu/category/news-category/agreements?page=1 and https://www.european-atm-security.eu/tag/ec3/ and http://www.finextra.com/news/fullstory.aspx?newsitemid=27536

[47]http://www.kaspersky.com/about/news/business/2014/Kaspersky-Lab-Broadens-Cooperation-with-Both-INTERPOL-and-Europol

[48]http://news.softpedia.com/news/Intel-and-Europol-Sign-Agreement-on-Fight-against-Cybercrime-465520.shtml

[49]http://www.eurosecglobal.de/europols-european-cybercrime-centre-ec3-and-mnemonic-co-operate.html

[50]http://iq-media.com/category/cybercrime/

[51]http://www.thepaypers.com/digital-identity-security-online-fraud/europol-s-ec3-joins-forces-with-fireeye-to-better-detect-cybercrime/761040-26

[52]https://www.europol.europa.eu/latest_news/europol-signs-agreement-group-ib-cooperate-fighting-cybercrime

AnubisNetworks,[53] and the Shadowserver Foundation.[54] The practice of such MoUs seems to reflect a wider trend in international cooperation, as evidenced by comparable agreements of INTERPOL with Kaspersky.[55] Microsoft, for its part, embedded the signing of MoUs with a global effort and networking, including the US and Latin America[56] and invested in a corporate cybercrime centre.[57] While the MoUs of the EC3 are not public, they seem to follow a common template that covers the exchange of "strategic" threat information, wider statistical information on security trends and of professional expertise. As far as can be inferred from public news items, the MoUs are limited to "non-operational" information.[58] These exchanges should help private actors to enhance their preparedness, while keeping the EC3 up-to-date on the latest security threats.

10.3.2.2 Active Assistance (Users)

The increasing formalisation of cooperation, such as in the form of a MoU, could be expected in light of the general characteristics of PPPs discussed above, which pointed to the use of explicit profit and risk-sharing arrangements. From an empirical perspective, this development could be related to current consultations by the European Commission on the value of further contractual arrangements for PPPs in the area of research for cybersecurity (General Secretariat of the Council 2015). But this does not mean that the nascent EU arrangements for more operational assistance and partnerships in addressing cyber threats are already well specified or mature. In particular, the distinction between general information exchange, which the MoU are supposed cover, and further operational cooperation is maintained in practice. There is increasing number of publicised cases of direct cooperation of the

[53]https://www.europol.europa.eu/newsletter/ec3-and-anubisnetworks-initiate-cooperation-fighting-malware-threats

http://www.so-co-it.com/post/368648/anubisnetworks-and-europol-s-european-cybercrime-centre-sign-memorandum-of-understanding-to-fight-international-malware-threats.html/

[54]https://www.europol.europa.eu/latest_news/shadowserver-foundation-steps-cooperation-europol-combat-cybercrime

[55]http://www.kaspersky.com/about/news/business/2014/Kaspersky-Lab-Broadens-Cooperation-with-Both-INTERPOL-and-Europol

http://www.informationsecuritybuzz.com/kaspersky-lab-broadens-cooperation-interpol-europol/

See on the joint EUROPOL INTERPOL MoU http://www.threatmetrix.com/interpol-has-new-nerve-centerand-more-muscle/

And conference http://www.interpol.int/News-and-media/Events/2014/INTERPOL-Europol-Cybercrime-Conference-2014/INTERPOL-Europol-Cybercrime-Conference-2014

[56]http://iq-media.com/category/cybercrime/

[57]http://news.microsoft.com/presskits/dcu/

[58]https://www.european-atm-security.eu/tag/ec3/

https://www.european-atm-security.eu/tag/ec3/

mentioned IT companies with various European public authorities in criminal investigations, takedowns of botnets[59] and eliminations of Trojans.[60] It is conceivable that general threat and vulnerability information provided by private actor sufficed for a technical shutdown, but it is equally more than probable that personal information of owners of IP addresses or computers would have been uncovered in the process.

This ties in with the formation of the so-called J-CAT task force, which unites the EC3, seven European national partners,[61] the US, Canada, Australia and Colombia. The task force founded in autumn 2014 as a pilot project for transnational cybercrime investigations.[62] Although it is official constituted by public actors, participants also highlight the contribution of IT security companies, such as Anubis, Symantec and Microsoft, during operations (Reitano et al. 2015). The initial successes of the task force have created a momentum to put this flexible forum on a permanent basis.[63] Yet to date, there has been no clarification on the legal framework and respective powers of the task force and its associated private actors. Participants suggest that national legal frameworks and the use of 'lead states' for specific investigations provide a pragmatic solution (ibid, p. 145). This clearly reflects the perspective of security authorities that are interested in cross-national prosecutions, but needs to be critically evaluated by other judicial or civil society actors. Data protection issues or decisions on the appropriate legal basis for persecuting individual actors remain to be addressed based on transparent and consistent rules, rather than by ad hoc decisions which state, legal framework or cooperation arrangement with private actors could be brought to bear in a given instance.

---

[59] http://blogs.microsoft.com/on-the-issues/2015/02/25/europol-takes-down-servers-used-by-cybercriminals-to-steal-financial-data/

[60] http://www.2uzhan.com/police-security-firms-team-up-and-take-down-shylock-malware/ This particular action even seems to have involved the British signals intelligence service GCHQ

[61] Austria, France, Germany, Italy, Spain, the Netherlands and the UK

[62] http://sgocnet.org/site/wp-content/uploads/2014/06/08_ReitanoEtAl_pp142-154.pdf

http://www.theguardian.com/technology/2014/sep/01/europol-taskforce-cybercrime-hacking-malware

https://www.europol.europa.eu/content/expert-international-cybercrime-taskforce-launched-tackle-online-crime

http://www.scmagazineuk.com/europol-plans-more-malware-takedowns/article/396089/

https://www.clearswift.com/blog/2014/07/25/why-joint-cybercrime-action-taskforce-positive-europe

http://www.computing.co.uk/ctg/news/2348940/europol-cybercrime-head-international-public-private-collaboration-the-one-true-way-to-stop-cyber-criminals

[63] http://www.scmagazineuk.com/j-cat-operations-to-continue/article/422464/

10.3.2.3 Information Sharing and Active Assistance (Content)

The final and perhaps most controversial development of public–private cooperation and partnership for cybersecurity equally falls between the cracks of information-exchanges and active assistance on internet content (also see Bonfanti and Stefanucci, Chap. 11; Porcedda, Chap. 12). In 2015 EC3 has been flanked by the so-called "internet referral unit" (EU IRU) at Europol, in order to "combine the expertise of both EC3 and Europol's counter terrorism unit ... to support the Member States in their endeavour to tackle online terrorism propaganda" (Council of the European Union 2015, p. 4). The unit should identify extremist online content, coordinate with national authorities on the respective recommended course of action (monitor or takedown), and make corresponding suggestions to private internet service providers and social media companies. The first months of operation of the new unit appear to have been comparatively successful, with a reported cooperation rate of 88% of private industry with regard to flagged problematic content.[64] Officially, the EU maintains that the decision to take down content remains with the respective private company that hosts the content.[65] Yet the high rate of compliance, as well as the related national experience of similar units, most notably the UK Counterterrorism Internet Referral Unit—which served as the organisational model for the IRU—suggest that the respective partnership with private industry is increasingly structured.[66] For instance, UK authorities have been awarded so-called "super-flagger" status by platforms such as YouTube, which exemplifies the regularisation of this kind of cooperation.[67]

The IRU is already connected to the wider "EU-level Forum with IT companies", which since late 2015 unites major players, such as Google, Facebook, Microsoft and Twitter to improve their cooperation with content control measures, but has been criticized by NGOs for a lack of transparency and wider participation.[68] These initiatives also build on the previous European efforts, the so-called "Check-the-Web" portal hosted at Europol since 2008 and the 2010 'CleanIT' project that sought to build links between the private sector and public sector and to draft shared 'best practices' in addressing 'terrorist use of the internet'.[69] This led to the so-called European Joint Initiative on Internet Counter Terrorism (EJI-ICT) to develop another network of national contact points for content monitoring. However, already the CleanIT project drew heavy criticisms from civil rights organizations[70] that highlighted the extremely vague and encompassing proposals for delegating tasks of internet filtering and monitoring to private companies.

---

[64]EU DOC 6785/16, p. 35

[65]http://www.adjacentgovernment.co.uk/ict/european-union-internet-referral-unit-europol/23582/

[66]https://wiki.openrightsgroup.org/wiki/Counter_Terrorism_Internet_Referral_Unit

[67]http://www.ft.com/intl/cms/s/0/b5b03bb4-a87b-11e3-b50f-00144feab7de.html

[68]https://edri.org/european-internet-forum-untransparent-and-dangerous/

[69]http://www.cleanitproject.eu/about-the-project/

[70]https://edri.org/CleanIT-evaluation/

Already since the mid-2000s, the EU funded various Internet contact points for the takedown of content as part of the EU Safer Internet programme, which mainly focus on child sexual abuse. This Programme officially already addressed material that is "celebratory, trivializing or inhumane representations of violence [and] material inciting violence for racial or national reasons and glorifying war, propaganda material of unconstitutional organisations."[71] Moreover, the EU Safer Internet Program was intended as a means for private sector organisations to take responsibility and engage with civil society in supporting the police and ensuring a swift takedown of content. Yet instead of clarifying the legal basis or the precise partnership model for such kind of PPPs for content controls, the current focus on online terrorist activities has led to a further period of experimentation with new initiatives such as the IRU, where mutual responsibilities and risks remain unclear.

10.4 Conclusion

This chapter has aimed to provide a nuanced, more focused, yet nonetheless critical reading of PPPs for cybersecurity. To begin with, it is clearly necessary to sharpen our conceptual language and to map the diversity of public–private interactions with regard to the complex notion of cybersecurity. The resulting heuristic typology showed, firstly, that *partnerships* only constitute one part—albeit a key one—of the wider governance processes in this field. In particular, it is helpful to distinguish general policy coordination and shared rule-setting for cybersecurity between public and private actor, which may be termed co-regulation, from other forms of cooperation that are rather focused on implementation or operational tasks, such as information exchange and mutual assistance with regard to specific threats. Secondly, the proposed typology underlined the diversity of private stakeholders or communities of practice that contribute to cybersecurity at different technical or logical levels. While it is obvious that owners of critical information infrastructures differ from IT security companies or internet service providers, it has been instructive to compare these different communities across the varied task of public–private interactions for cybersecurity. Such a crosscutting overview underlines that PPPs for cybersecurity often remain at the level of rhetoric and do not correspond to the interest of many private entities. Due to a variety of conflicting interest, blame shifting and cost considerations, one can rather see a trend to more regulatory governance, which is a familiar feature from other economic sectors. Overall, the heuristic typology helped to categorise and differentiate different forms of PPPs for cybersecurity, and to formulate some basic expectations about their prospects, obstacles and possible normative concerns.

The second empirical part of this chapter applied this heuristic framework about PPPs for cybersecurity to the case of the EU. At the technical and infrastructural

[71] http://www.fsm.de/hotline

levels, we could identify an extension of consultation and co-regulation processes under the leadership of ENISA, whereas broader and more operational notions of PPPs for cybersecurity revealed their limits. Aside from the discontinuation of the so-called E3PR public private partnership for resilience, CERTs have rather moved in the direction of stand-alone *public* capacities for operational cybersecurity. However, the activities of EUROPOL demonstrate that other forms public–private cooperation and partnership for cybersecurity are expanding fast. In particular, the areas of information exchange on illegal content, as undertaken via the new Internet Referral Unit, and of operational assistance with regard to cybercrimes and -threats, as undertaken via the EC3, are currently ill understood.

While one can refer to a wider a debate on the problems of "voluntary" content control, or filtering, on the internet, we have almost no insights into other forms of PPPs for addressing cybercrimes. The mentioned J-CAT Task Force in the EC3 is explicitly designed to take on criminal prosecutions, but also regularly exchanges information with private actors. This underpins the recent statement in the European Agenda on Security, where PPPs are linked with the ambition to develop a "new approach to law enforcement in the digital age" (European Commission 2015, p. 20). But despite its evident sensitivity, this "new approach" is nowhere debated in public and rather emerges from diffuses practice of security authorities, supported by private companies that have a direct commercial interest in touting their security expertise and products. While the unavoidability of such collaboration is persistently repeated, it is entirely unclear whether this is actually the case or whether this new approach masks shifts in law enforcement operation and collaboration that would otherwise be impossible.

In sum, flexible and operational PPPs for cybersecurity may have their constructive uses, such as in the case actions against transnational botnets, but the generally ill-defined forms of cooperation should us give pause—even if this chapter has sought to provide some more focus on the use of the term PPP. One fundamental problem is that the terms 'cyber' and 'security' can be defined to encompass most areas of human life. Therefore, it needs to be spelt out more precisely how PPPs for cybersecurity can be combined and balanced with other normative principles on transparency, accountability, privacy and other civil and human rights that the EU officially endorses with regard to internet governance (European Commission 2012; Wagner et al. 2014).

In particular, many of the highlighted developments and initiatives for PPPs can be seen as piecemeal policy developments in relation to different crises, perceived security threats and stakeholder communities. On the one hand, the proposed typology underlines the use for a functional differentiation and tailored instruments for different aspects of cybersecurity. On the other hand, it remains essential for public authorities to keep a wider perspective on the overarching orientation, attribution of responsibilities and legitimate bases for security provision. This concerns, for instance, more hidden, but dynamic developments within professional communities and specialised agencies, as in the case of the EC3.

Aside from general normative debates, we need deeper operational insights into operational cybersecurity PPPs to disentangle the respective power-relations and problems. Conventional PPPs often include contractual arrangements on profit and economic risk sharing, while there are wider debates on appropriate standards for public accountability. In the area of cybersecurity, other forms of risks and responsibilities beyond timely construction or reliable service provision have to be considered. Governments are also increasingly able to exert pressure to obtain 'voluntary' cooperation from business, as illustrated in the controversial area of content control, where various commentators suspect a deliberate blame-shifting strategy of public actors (Walker and Conway 2015). But when dealing with new or advanced cyber threats, public actors often enter these partnerships as the weaker partner, reliant on specialised IT companies to define the level of vulnerability and appropriate countermeasures. The mentioned Memoranda of Understanding of the EC3 can provide a focal point to test this assumption, as well as to discern the solidity of public criminal prosecution in pragmatic cooperation networks. These memoranda and other related contractual arrangement for PPPs for cybersecurity should be made public as far as possible, which—in light of their general framework nature—should be possible without endangering specific operations against cyber threats. Finally, we would argue that the proposed typology may also be applied beyond the case of the EU, and prepare the ground for more systematic and comparative analyses of appropriate governance frameworks for public private interactions and partnerships for cybersecurity.

References

Anderson, R., & Moore, T. (2006). The economics of information security. *Science, 314*(5799), 610–613.

August, T., & Tunca, T. I. (2011). Who should be responsible for software security? A comparative analysis of liability policies in network environments. *Management Science, 57*(5), 934–959.

August, T., August, R., & Shin, H. (2014). Designing user incentives for cybersecurity. *Communications of the ACM, 57*(11), 43–46.

Bauer, J. M. (2010). Changing roles of the state in telecommunications. *International Telecommunications Policy Review, 17*(1).

Bauer, J. M., & Van Eeten, M. J. G. (2009). Cybersecurity: Stakeholder incentives, externalities, and policy options. *Telecommunications Policy, 33*(10), 706–719.

Bendiek, A., & Porter, A. L. (2013). European cyber security policy within a global multistakeholder structure. *European Foreign Affairs Review, 18*(2), 155–180.

Bevir, M. (2014). The rise of security governance. In M. Bevir, O. Daddow, & I. Hall (Eds.), *Interpreting global security* (pp. 17–34). London: Routledge.

Börzel, T. (2010). European governance: Negotiation and competition in the shadow of hierarchy. *JCMS: Journal of Common Market Studies, 48*(2), 191–219.

Bovaird, T. (2004). Public–private partnerships: From contested concepts to prevalent practice. *International Review of Administrative Sciences, 70*(2), 199–215. doi:10.1177/0020852304044250.

Bovis, C. (2013). *Public-private partnerships in the European Union*. Routledge.

Bovis, C. H. (2015). Risk in public-private partnerships and critical infrastructure. *European Journal of Risk Regulation, 6*(2).

Braman, S. (2011). The framing years: Policy fundamentals in the internet design process, 1969–1979. *The Information Society, 27*, 295–310.

Brinkerhoff, D. W., & Brinkerhoff, J. M. (2011). Public–private partnerships: Perspectives on purposes, publicness, and good governance. *Public Administration and Development, 31*(1), 2–14.

Brown, I., & Cowls, J. (2015). Check the web: Assessing the ethics of politics of policing the internet for extremist material. *Voxpol Report.* http://voxpol.eu/category/publications/vox-pol-publications/

Brown, I., & Marsden, C. T. (2013). *Regulating code: Good governance and better regulation in the information age*. Cambridge: MIT Press.

Camp, L. J. (2011). Reconceptualizing the role of security user. *Daedalus, 140*(4), 93–107.

Carr, M. (2015). Power plays in global internet governance. *Millennium – Journal of International Studies, 43*(2), 640–659. doi:10.1177/0305829814562655.

Carr, M. (2016). Public–private partnerships in national cyber-security strategies. *International Affairs, 92*(1), 43–62.

Chenou, J.-M. (2014). From cyber-libertarianism to neoliberalism: Internet exceptionalism, multi-stakeholderism, and the institutionalisation of internet governance in the 1990s. *Globalizations, 11*(2), 205–223.

Choucri, N., & Clark, D. D. (2012). Integrating cyberspace and international relations: The co-evolution dilemma. In *Explorations in cyber-international relations: Who controls cyberspace?* Cambridge, MA: MIT.

Christou, G., & Simpson, S. (2006). The Internet and public–private governance in the European Union. *Journal of Public Policy, 26*(01), 43–61.

Clark, D., Berson, T., & Lin, H. S. (2014). *At the nexus of cybersecurity and public policy: Some basic concepts and issues*. Washington, DC: National Academies Press.

Cohen-Almagor, R. (2015). Internet architecture, freedom of expression and social responsibility: Critical realism and proposals for a better future. *Innovation: The European Journal of Social Science Research, 28*(2), 147–166.

Commission of the European Communities. (2009). Communication from the commission.. on critical information infrastructure protection. "Protecting Europe from large scale cyber-attacks and disruptions: enhancing preparedness, security and resilience". COM(2009) 149 final.

Council of the European Union. (2015). "EU Internet Referral Unit at Europol – Concept note." *7266/15*.

Crawford, A. (2006). Networked governance and the post-regulatory state? Steering, rowing and anchoring the provision of policing and security. *Theoretical Criminology, 10*(4), 449–479.

DeNardis, L. (2012). Hidden levers of internet control: An infrastructure-based theory of Internet governance. *Information, Communication & Society, 15*(5), 720–738.

DeNardis, L. (2014). *The global war for internet governance*. New Haven, CT: Yale University Press.

Dourado, E., & Castillo, A. (2015). "Information Sharing": No panacea for American cybersecurity challenges. *Mercatus Center Policy Paper, George Mason University*. http://mercatus.org/publication/information-sharing-no-panacea-american-cybersecurity-challenges

Dunn Cavelty, M. (2013). From cyber-bombs to political fallout: Threat representations with an impact in the cyber-security discourse. *International Studies Review, 15*(1), 105–122.

Dunn-Cavelty, M., & Suter, M. (2009). Public–private partnerships are no silver bullet: An expanded governance model for critical infrastructure protection. *International Journal of Critical Infrastructure Protection, 2*(4), 179–187.

Edwards, B., Locasto, M., & Epstein, J. (2014). Panel Summary: The Future of Software Regulation. Proceedings of the 2014 workshop on New Security Paradigms Workshop. http://dl.acm.org/citation.cfm?id=2683478

Ehrhart, H.-G., Hegemann, H., & Kahl, M. (2014). Putting security governance to the test: Conceptual, empirical, and normative challenges. *European Security, 23*(2), 119–125.

ENISA. (2011a). Cooperative models for effective public private partnerships. *http://www.enisa.europa.eu/activities/Resilience-and-CIIP/public-private-partnership/national-public-private-partnerships-ppps/copy_of_desktop-reserach-on-public-private-partnerships/at_download/fullReport*

ENISA. (2011b). *Cooperative models for effective public private partnerships. Desktop Research Report.* http://www.enisa.europa.eu/activities/Resilience-and-CIIP/public-private-partnership/national-public-private-partnerships-ppps/copy_of_desktop-reserach-on-public-private-partnerships/at_download/fullReport ENISA.

ENISA. (2015). EP3R 2009–2013 Future of NIS Public Private Cooperation. https://www.enisa.europa.eu/activities/Resilience-and-CIIP/public-private-partnership/european-public-private-partnership-for-resilience-ep3r/ep3r-2009-2013/at_download/fullReport

Eriksson, J., & Giacomello, G. (2009). Who controls the internet? Beyond the obstinacy or obsolescence of the State. *International Studies Review, 11*(1), 205–230.

EU. (2013). Joint communication on the cybersecurity strategy of the European Union: An Open, Safe and Secure Cyberspace. *JOIN(2013) 1 final.* http://eeas.europa.eu/policies/eu-cyber-security/cybsec_comm_en.pdf

European Commission. (2004). Green paper on public-private partnerships and community law on public contracts and concessions. *COM (2004) 327 final.*

European Commission. (2012). Internet policy and governance Europe's role in shaping the future of internet governance. *COM/2014/072 final.*

European Commission. (2013). Proposal for a directive of the European Parliament and of the Council concerning measures to ensure a high common level of network and information security across the Union. *COM(2013) 48 final.* http://ec.europa.eu/newsroom/dae/document.cfm?doc_id=1666

European Commission. (2015). The European Agenda on Security. *COM* (2015) 185. http://eur-lex.europa.eu/legal-content/en/HIS/?uri=celex%3A52015DC0185

European Union. (2013). Regulation (EU) No 526/2013 of the European Parliament and of the Council of 21 May 2013 concerning the European Union Agency for Network and Information Security (ENISA) and repealing Regulation (EC) No 460/2004 Text with EEA relevance. *OJ L 165*, 41–58.

Fahey, E. (2014). 'EU's cybercrime and cyber-security rulemaking: Mapping the internal and external dimensions of EU security, The. *Eur. J. Risk Reg.* 46.

Forrer, J., Kee, J. E., Newcomer, K. E., & Boyer, E. (2010). Public–private partnerships and the public accountability question. *Public Administration Review, 70*(3), 475–484.

General Secretariat of the Council. (2015). Friends of the Presidency Group on Cyber Issues. *15059/15.*

Gómez-Barroso, J. L., & Feijóo, C. (2010). A conceptual framework for public-private interplay in the telecommunications sector. *Telecommunications Policy, 34*(9), 487–495.

Graz, J.-C., & Nölke, A. (2007). *Transnational private governance and its limits.* London: Routledge.

Grimsey, D., & Lewis, M. (2007). *Public private partnerships: The worldwide revolution in infrastructure provision and project finance.* Cheltenham: Edward Elgar.

Hameiri, S., & Jones, L. (2015). *Governing borderless threats: Non-traditional security and the politics of state transformation.* Cambridge: Cambridge University Press.

Hansen, L., & Nissenbaum, H. (2009). Digital disaster, cyber security, and the Copenhagen School. *International Studies Quarterly, 53*(4), 1155–1175.

Harcourt, A. (2013). Participatory gains and policy effectiveness: The open method of co-ordination information society. *JCMS: Journal of Common Market Studies, 51*(4), 667–683. doi:10.1111/jcms.12022.

Hare, F. (2010). The interdependent nature of national cyber security: Motivating public action for a private good. PhD, George Mason University. http://digilib.gmu.edu:8080/dspace/bitstream/1920/6312/1/Hare_dissertation_2010.pdf

Héritier, A. (2001). Market integration and social cohesion: The politics of public services in European regulation. *Journal of European Public Policy, 8*(5), 825–852. doi:10.1080/13501760110083536.

Hodge, G. A., & Greve, C. (2005). *The challenge of public-private partnerships: Learning from international experience*. Cheltenham: Edward Elgar.

Hodge, G. A., & Greve, C. (2007). Public–private partnerships: an international performance review. *Public Administration Review, 67*(3), 545–558.

Horten, M. (2015). The policy challenge of content restrictions: How private actors engage the duties of states. *Media@LSE Working Paper* 34. http://www.lse.ac.uk/media@lse/research/mediaWorkingPapers/pdf/WP34-FINAL.pdf

Irion, K. (2013). The Governance of Network and Information Security in the European Union: The European Public-Private Partnership for Resilience (EP3R). In J. Krüger, B. Nickolay, & S. Gaycken (Eds.), *The Secure Information Society* (pp. 83–116). London: Springer.

Kaijankoski, E. A. (2015). Cybersecurity information sharing between public private sector agencies. http://oai.dtic.mil/oai/oai?verb=getRecord&metadataPrefix=html&identifier=ADA620766: DTIC Document.

Kennedy, D. (2016). *A world of struggle: How power, law, and expertise shape global political economy*. Princeton: Princeton University Press.

Kesan, J. P., & Hayes, C. M. (2015). Creating a "Circle of Trust" to further digital privacy and cybersecurity goals. *Michigan State Law Review, 2014*(5), 1475.

Kleinschmidt, B. (2010). An international comparison of ISP's liabilities for unlawful third party content. *International Journal of Law and Information Technology*:eaq009.

Lagazio, M., Sherif, N., & Cushman, M. (2014). A multi-level approach to understanding the impact of cyber crime on the financial sector. *Computers & Security, 45*, 58–74.

LaRose, R., Bauer, J. M., DeMaagd, K., Chew, H. E., Ma, W., & Jung, Y. (2014). Public broadband investment priorities in the United States: An analysis of the broadband technology opportunities program. *Government Information Quarterly, 31*(1), 53–64. doi:10.1016/j.giq.2012.11.004.

Linder, S. H. (1999). Coming to terms with the public-private partnership a grammar of multiple meanings. *American Behavioral Scientist, 43*(1), 35–51.

Marsden, C. T. (2011). *Internet co-regulation: European law, regulatory governance and legitimacy in cyberspace*. Cambridge: Cambridge University Press.

Mathew, A. J. (2014). *Where in the world is the internet? Locating political power in internet infrastructure*. http://gradworks.proquest.com/3685949.pdf. University of California, Berkeley.

Min, K.-S., Chai, S.-W., & Han, M. (2015). An international comparative study on cyber security strategy. *International Journal of Security and Its Applications, 9*(2), 13–20.

Morgus, R., Skierka, I., Hohmann, M., & Maurer, T. (2015). National CSIRTs and their role in computer security incident.

Mueller, M., Schmidt, A., & Kuerbis, B. (2013). Internet security and networked governance in international relations. *International Studies Review, 15*(1), 86–104.

Nance, M., & Cottrell, P. (2014). A turn toward experimentalism? Rethinking security and governance in the twenty-first century. *Review of International Studies, 40*(02), 277–301. doi:10.1017/S026021051300017X.

Narayanan, A., Jain, A., & Bowonder, B. (2005). Providing rural connectivity infrastructure: ICT diffusion through private sector participation. *International Journal of Services Technology and Management, 6*(3–5), 416–436.

Nolan, A. (2015). Cybersecurity and information sharing: Legal challenges and solutions. *Congressional Research Service 7–5700*. http://a51.nl/sites/default/files/pdf/R43941.pdf

Parti, K., & Marin, L. (2013). Ensuring freedoms and protecting rights in the governance of the Internet: A comparative analysis of blocking measures of illegal Internet content and the liability of ISPs. *Journal of Contemporary European Research, 9*(1), 138–159.

Prince, D., & King, N. (2013). Small business cyber security workshop 2013: Towards digitally secure business growth. http://eprints.lancs.ac.uk/65265/

Procedda, M. (2014). Public-private partnerships: A soft approach to cybersecurity? Views from the European Union. In G. Giacomello (Ed.), *Security in Cyberspace: Targeting Nations, Infrastructures, Individual*. New York, London: Bloomsbury Academic.

Radu, R., Chenou, J.-M., & Weber, R. H. (2014). *The evolution of global internet governance: Principles and policies in the making*, vol. 56. Springer Science & Business Media.

RAND Europe. (2012). Feasibility study for a European cybercrime centre. http://www.rand.org/pubs/technical_reports/TR1218.html

Reitano, T., Oerting, T., & Hunter, M. (2015). Innovations in international cooperation to counter cybercrime: The joint cybercrime action taskforce. *The European Review of Organised Crime, 2*(2), 142–154.

Reynaers, A.-M., & De Graaf, G. (2014). Public values in public–private partnerships. *International Journal of Public Administration, 37*(2), 120–128.

Rosenzweig, P. (2011). Cybersecurity and public goods. The public/private "partnership". In P. Berkowitz (Ed.), *Emerging threats in national security and law*. Stanford: Hoover Institution, Stanford University.

Roumboutsos, A. (2015). *Public private partnerships in transport: Trends and theory*. Routledge.

Rowe, B., & Wood, D. (2013). Are home internet users willing to pay ISPs for improvements in cyber security? In *Economics of information security and privacy III* (pp. 193–212). Springer.

Ruiz, J. B., & Barnett, G. A. (2014). Who owns the international Internet networks? *Journal of International Communication, 21*(1), 38–57.

Schmidt, A. (2014). Open security. Contributions of networked approaches to the challenge of democratic internet security governance. In R. Radu, J.-M. Chenou, & R. H. Weber (Eds.), *The evolution of global internet governance* (pp. 169–187). Berlin, Heidelberg: Springer.

Schneider, A. L. (1999). Public-private partnerships in the US prison system. *American Behavioral Scientist, 43*(1), 192–208.

Suter, M. (2007). Improving information security in companies: How to meet the need for threat information. In M. D. Cavelty, V. Mauer, & S. F. Krishna-Hensel (Eds.), *Power and security in the information age: Investigating the role of the state in cyberspace* (pp. 129–150). Aldershot: Ashgate.

Townes, M. (2012). The spread of TCP/IP: How the Internet became the Internet. *Millennium-Journal of International Studies, 41*(1), 43–64.

Tropina, T. (2015). Public–private collaboration: Cybercrime, cybersecurity and national security. In *Self-and co-regulation in Cybercrime, cybersecurity and national security* (pp. 1–41). Springer.

Tropina, T., & Callanan, C. (2015). *Self-and co-regulation in cybercrime, cybersecurity and national security*. Heidelberg: Springer.

United Nations Economic Commission for Europe. (2008). Guidebook on promoting good governance in public private partnerships. *ECE/CECI/4*.

Usman, S. H. (2013). A review of responsibilities of internet service providers towards their customer network security. *Journal of Theoretical and Applied Information Technology, 49*(1), 70–78.

Van Den Hurk, M., & Verhoest, K. (2016). The challenge of using standard contracts in public–private partnerships. *Public Management Review, 18*(2), 278–299.

Van den Hurk, M., Brogaard, L., Lember, V., Petersen, O. H., & Witz, P. (2015). *National varieties of Public–Private Partnerships (PPPs): A comparative analysis of PPP-supporting units in 19 European countries* (pp. 1–20). Research and Practice: Journal of Comparative Policy Analysis.

van Dijck, J. (2014). Datafication, dataism and dataveillance: Big Data between scientific paradigm and ideology. *Surveillance & Society, 12*(2), 197–208.

Van Eijk, N. (2013). Duties of care on the Internet. In *The secure information society* (pp. 57–81). Springer.

Von Solms, R., & Van Niekerk, J. (2013). From information security to cyber security. *Computers & Security, 38*, 97–102.

Voordijk, H., Sarmento, J. M., & Renneboog, L. (2016). Anatomy of public-private partnerships: their creation, financing and renegotiations. *International Journal of Managing Projects in Business, 9*(1), 94–122.

Wagner, B. (2014). The politics of internet filtering: The United Kingdom and Germany in a comparative perspective. *Politics, 34*(1), 58–71.

Wagner, B. (forthcoming). Constructed "cyber" realities & international relations theory. In R. Marlin-Bennett & J. P. Singh (Eds.), *Technology and international relations theory*. Cambridge: CUP.

Wagner, B., Gollatz, K., & Calderaro, A. (2014). Internet & Human Rights in Foreign Policy: Comparing narratives in the US and EU Internet Governance agenda. *Robert Schuman Centre for Advanced Studies Research Paper No. RSCAS* 86.

Walker, C., & Conway, M. (2015). Online terrorism and online laws. *Dynamics of Asymmetric Conflict, 8*(2), 156–175. doi:10.1080/17467586.2015.1065078.

Wiater, P. (2015). On the notion of "partnership" in critical infrastructure protection. *European Journal of Risk Regulation, 6*(2), 255–262.

Willems, T., & Van Dooren, W. (2011). Lost in diffusion? How collaborative arrangements lead to an accountability paradox. *International Review of Administrative Sciences, 77*(3), 505–530.

Chapter 11
Exploring the New Frontiers of Security Privatisation: Web-Based Social Networking Services and Their Challenging Contribution to Foster Security and Public Safety

Matteo E. Bonfanti and Piergiorgio Stefanucci

11.1 Introduction

Social media platforms and services are used by an increasing number of individuals, as well as private or public organisations for pursuing a wide range of goals that span various sectors.[1] Like many other technologies and services, social media were not formally conceived as tools to be employed for safeguarding or enhancing security, or promoting public safety and order.[2] They were ideated and crafted to

[1]According to *Digital in 2017*, there were 2.79 billion (out of 3.77 billion internet users) active social media users in the world in January 2016; 21% more than in January 2016 (WeAreSocial 2017, p. 5–6).

[2]There is no agreed definition of social media in the literature and among practitioners. In plain language, the expression refers to both the Internet-based technologies and the techniques/practices that allow users to generate and share content in different formats (video, audio, textual). In everyday life, the expression social media is often used interchangeably with that of social network, which is employed to refer to both a group of individuals that interact among themselves on the basis of a shared interest and to websites devoted to the building up and development of a virtual social web. From this latter point of view, a social network represents a virtual space in which the individuals-users share information and establish relations among them. In general, the lack of a clear common definition of "social media" seems to be ascribed also to a close dependence of its notion on: the applied technologies/software, their continuous development and update, as well as the different kind of social interactions users can establish among themselves. These elements seem to contribute, in a dynamic perspective, to constantly refine the concept of social media and prevent the "crystallisation" of a notion. In addition, it seems also hard to proceed with a coherent classification of the plethora of existing social media platforms (e.g. *Twitter*, *Facebook*, *LinkedIn*, *MeetUp*, *Wikipedia*, *Flickr*, *YouTube*, *Vimeo*, *Slideshare.net*, *Second Life*, etc.) even if part of the academic literature has tried to do so. See for instance Kaplan and Haenlein (2010), who identify different social media categories according to: the main goal which is pursued through their use (bi/multi-directional communication among individuals-users,

M.E. Bonfanti (✉) • P. Stefanucci
ETH Center for Security Study, Haldeneggsteig 4, 8092 Zurich, Switzerland
e-mail: matteo.bonfanti@sipo.gess.ethz.ch; pstefanucci@yahoo.it

O. Bures, H. Carrapico (eds.), *Security Privatization*,
DOI 10.1007/978-3-319-63010-6_11

allow Internet users to create, share through their networks, and consume information, to establish or develop social relationships among them, and to participate in the on-line (and off-line) community life.[3] Along with the securitisation of the Internet and, in a larger perspective, of the cyberspace, social media have nowadays become both the object and the instrument of security-oriented initiatives. Their capabilities are exploited by law enforcement, security, and public safety agencies for managing crisis and emergencies, policing, and/or conducting intelligence activities in the field of counter-terrorism, crime or other threat prevention and response. These agencies resort to social media for engaging with different individual users or groups of users; enforcing the law; and/or producing knowledge on selected safety-security related phenomena that occur both on-line and off-line.

The legitimacy of these initiatives has yet to be carefully discussed. To what extent is the contribution of social media service providers to fostering security regulated by law or defined by policy or other instruments? To what extent are providers accountable for achieving security goals or liable for any ascertained failure or abuse in their conducts? Is there any formal or informal oversight mechanism put in place? Has the impact generated by the employment of social media for security purposes been (*ex ante* or *ex post*) assessed in relation to society as a whole, and individuals' fundamental rights specifically? And does the applicable policy or regulatory framework acknowledge the results of such assessment? The above questions point to some of the governance implications that the use of social media platforms and services for security raise. Answering these questions is not a straightforward process; neither is it to clearly identify the role and responsibilities of social media platforms and service providers in offering their—proactive or passive, informed or not-informed—support to security. And it is not only a matter of being transparent about what providers actually (should) do or do (should) not do. Indeed, there are several cases where the actions taken by social network providers to foster security are publicly reported by these entities themselves. This is for example the case when they contribute to fighting hate-speech, extremist and terrorist propaganda by deleting user accounts and removing offensive information. Nevertheless, one may wonder on what normative or other kind of basis they are taking these actions, and what legal implications this may have.

---

independently from their object or aim; the collaboration among them in more or less circumscribed fields and for more or less pre-determined purposes; the sharing of multimedia content and entertainment); the type of content which is shared (textual, image, video, audio) and, last but not least, the degree of personal involvement and participatory expectation of the individual-user.

[3]Internet represents an important vector of the globalisation process and since its very beginning has had the role of main generator and, at the same time, of main collector of information in almost all areas (Ivan et al. 2014, p. 505). In particular, within the Internet, social media embody a new kind of private/public space in which individual users or groups interact and generate, share, obtain information.

The present chapter has a circumscribed scope and does not cover all the questions mentioned above. Furthermore, it investigates the topic by adopting a broad perspective. Nevertheless, it provides food for thought about some of the most relevant governance implications concerning the employment of social media platforms and services for security and safety purposes. It considers the policy frameworks adopted at both the European Union (EU) and Italian levels, and tries to identify evident discrepancies in the way the topic is governed at the supranational and domestic levels.

Where the supranational level is concerned, the chapter looks at how the European Union is governing the growing security-related use of social media, and at how the EU sponsored initiatives in the field are being implemented by the involved stakeholders, in particular by platform and service providers. Indeed, it has to be noted that the employment of social media services and users' generated content for security purposes has resulted in large political debates and advocacy campaigns for the adoption of consistent policies, strategies and programmes aimed at dealing with the issue. Debates and campaigns have tackled different items. Much attention has been—and is presently—paid to privacy and data protection implications (European Parliament 2013a, p. 7–11; 2013b, p. 5–6; Art. 29WP 2014, p. 2; EDPS 2015, p. 12; 2016, p. 3). Discussions have also considered the broad normative and policy framework regulating the cooperation between national authorities and social media providers in policy sectors like counter-terrorism and contrast to serious crimes.[4] Sometimes discussions have led to the promotion of policy initiatives by governments and supranational bodies like the European Union.

In general, the initiatives promoted at the EU level and their outcomes exhibit some critical flaws. As it is further discussed below, initiatives are overall fragmented in their scope and reach, meaning that they do not cover comprehensively the security sectors in which social media are increasingly employed. For example, most of the steps the EU has taken in the field addresses the practices of preventing/countering online radicalisation, violent extremism and hate speech through social media; few of them concern the use of these platforms and their services for disaster/risk management, security intelligence gathering, and intelligence-led policing. This is partially due to the 'national security exemption' that rules out the EU competence on matters falling within the scope of Member States' exclusive national jurisdiction (European Union 2010).[5] Security

---

[4]*See* infra in the text.

[5]The Union competences are a complex set of rules separating policy areas and specifying levels of Union and Member State involvement in those areas. Under Article 3 TFEU, the EU has exclusive supranational competence in the areas of the customs union, Eurozone financial matters, establishing competition rules for the internal market and conservation of marine resources under the common fisheries policy. It has a shared competence with Member States in areas such as wider internal market policy, the environment, the area of freedom, security and justice, energy policy and consumer protection. In policies areas such as health, industry, culture and tourism the EU can only support national governments. The EU has no competence with regards to matters falling within Member States' national security (see next footnote).

intelligence related activities fall within that scope.[6] However, the national security exemption does not fully cover matters like Member States' initiatives in crisis management even if this field of policy-making is primarily the responsibility of Member States. The EU level action should be developed in accordance with two principles: *national responsibility* and *EU solidarity* (Council of the European Union 2008, p. 4). In effect, this means that the EU should only promote coordination among individual Member States, i.e. support the sharing of national resources or best-practices, or foster interoperability among procedures or tools adopted at the national level. Until now, the EU has not led any initiative aimed at harmonising the way social media are used for crisis and disaster management across the Member States. As per the employment of social media for law enforcement and policing purposes, the policy initiatives promoted at the EU level have not resulted in the adoption of any specific binding instrument. In general, the concerned initiatives have endorsed the adoption of self or voluntary regulations, e.g. code of conducts or guidelines. These instruments have little if any enforceability and are amenable to "flexible" implementation by addressed stakeholders. Codes of conduct are, nevertheless, not negative *per se* as they can help in building robust trust among interested parties.

With regard to Italy, it seems there are neither general nor sectorial *ad hoc* policies and legislation addressing the employment of social media platforms and services for security and safety goals. Nevertheless, there are some over-arching binding rules that apply to such an employment and define the duties and rights of the involved parties, i.e. national authorities, providers, and—in general—individual users. The rules cover policing and intelligence activities in general, and address the use of the Internet and social media because they fall within the reach of these activities. The lack of comprehensive policies or legislation covering the use of social media for security and safety reasons seems conflicting with the demand for an all-encompassing governance that comes from national institutions and sectors of civil society (Garante per la protezione dei dati personali 2014, p. 176; p. 197; 2015, p. 16; 2016, p. 3–4).

Starting from a short presentation of the security discourse concerning the use of social media platforms, technologies, and services at the EU level and in Italy, the chapter reviews the potential applications of these tools in specific security fields, namely: emergency and crisis management, policing, and intelligence gathering. Applications are clustered according to the engagement, enforcement, or intelligence/surveillance goals they serve. Then, the chapter discusses some of the relevant governance implications arising from these applications. It examines the EU (supranational) and Italian (domestic) adopted policies that foresee the security-oriented employment of social media platforms and services. In particular, it considers the extent to which such an employment is comprehensively governed

[6]Art. 4(2) of the TEU reads as follows: "The Union shall respect the equality of Member States (...) as well as their national identities (...) It shall respect their essential state functions, including (...) safeguarding national security. In particular, national security remains the sole responsibility of each Member State".

i.e. regulated by law or covered by general or sectorial policy instruments. Special attention is paid to the study of the envisaged role, responsibilities and functions of social media providers. The chapter concludes by acknowledging that improvements in the governance of the security-related employment of social media can be achieved through the adoption and implementation of a more coordinated, coherent, comprehensive, and effectively inclusive approach to the matter.

11.2 Social Media in the EU and Italian Security Discourse

11.2.1 EU Security Policies and the Role of the Internet and Social Media

Social media and, in general, the Internet lie at the heart of several policy initiatives promoted by the EU in order to enhance the European internal security and safety.[7] These initiatives have been taken within the EU supranational cooperation framework to prevent and fight terrorism, organised crime (in particular cybercrime) and—to a lesser extent—emergency and crisis management. They address the Internet and social media because these are: (i) the places/dimensions where threats to the EU and its Member States' security may arise or further develop; (ii) the instruments for conducting malevolent activities that jeopardize the European security; iii) the tools to be employed by public authorities to prevent and counter these activities or to reach other security-related goals. A common element of the EU sponsored initiatives in the field of security that concerns the Internet and social media is the request for close and harmonised collaboration between national (and European) public authorities, platforms and service providers, and the civil society. Indeed, these are the main actors who are encouraged to take action.

The fight against terrorism has been one of the driving factors for the adoption of measures addressing the use of the Internet and social media in the EU. In the aftermath of the Madrid (2004) and London (2005) terrorist attacks, the Council of the EU adopted the *EU Counter-Terrorism Strategy* through which it invited Member States to impede the communication and dissemination of terrorists' technical knowledge, especially via the Internet (Council of the EU 2005, p. 8–9). Five years later, the *EU Internal Security Strategy* reiterated that the Internet is a powerful instrument for the dissemination of extremist propaganda, radicalisation and recruitment of aspiring terrorists. It invited Member States to remove illegal internet content and to counter terrorists' on-line narratives. It recommended Member States to adopt coherent approaches in dealing with the subject matter, and supported the establishment of harmonised cooperation between

[7]Please see below.

Internet service providers, law enforcement authorities, and civil society organisations (Council of the EU 2010, p. 21). The same endeavour was reaffirmed in the *Draft Council Conclusions on the Renewed European Union Internal Security Strategy 2015–2020* (Council of the EU 2015a, p. 6).

Due to the increasing malevolent use of the Internet and social media by terrorists—as well as by criminals—the 2015 *EU Agenda on Security* called for the establishment of the European Union Internet Referral Unit (EU IRU) to be embedded within Europol's European Counterterrorism Centre (ECTC) (European Commission 2015a, p. 13).[8] Established in July 2015 but operating within the ECTC as of 1 January 2016, the EU IRU has "the role to anticipate and pre-empt terrorist abuse of online tools, as well as to play a pro-active advisory role towards EU Member States and the private sector in this field" (Europol 2016, p. 3).[9] The *EU Agenda on Security* also foresaw the launch of the EU Internet Forum (active as of 3 December 2015), namely a platform bringing together EU Ministers of Interior, representatives of major Internet and social media providers (e.g. Facebook, Google/YouTube, Twitter, Microsoft and Ask.fm), Europol, the European Counter Terrorism Coordinator and the European Parliament (European Commission 2015b, p. 13–14). The aim of the forum is to propose measures for countering terrorists and violent extremists on the Internet, for example by providing alternative online narratives to terrorist propaganda. The Forum supports the implementation of the current voluntary referral process, and promotes the sharing of best practices and expertise.[10]

[8]Europol is the EU's agency whose main goal is to support and enhance Member States' competent authorities action and their mutual cooperation in preventing and combating organised crime, terrorism and other forms of serious crime affecting two or more Member States (Council of the European Union 2009). Starting from May 2017, a new legal instrument will govern Europol activities (European Union 2016).

[9]In particular, the EU IRU has the following tasks: (1) to coordinate and share the flagging of terrorist and violent extremist content online with relevant partners (i.e. Member States LEAs and social media providers); (2) to carry out referrals in close cooperation with the industry; (3) to support competent authorities, by providing both strategic and operational analysis; (4) to act as a hub of expertise in these fields (for further operational details see *infra* paragraph 11.3.2). The EU IRU builds upon another Europol promoted initiative. It is the "Check-the-Web" (CTW) which aimed at strengthening cooperation on monitoring and evaluating open Internet sources on a voluntary basis. CTW has led to the creation of an electronic reference library of jihadist terrorist online propaganda, accessible by the competent authorities of EU Member States and associated third Parties (Council of the European Union 2007, p. 4–5).

[10]In practical terms, within the EU Internet Forum, Europol EU IRU contributes to flag and refer terrorist content online in cooperation with LEAs from EU Member States and the Internet industry whereas civil society is engaged in designing alternative narratives with the support of the Internet industry. In the framework of the EU Internet Forum, civil society has been so far represented by the Radicalisation Awareness Network, a EU sponsored network of practitioners. In addition, it is within the EU Internet Forum that a number of projects have been developed and launched such as the recent *shared database of digital "hashes"* to help identify potential terrorist content on social media and prevent its reappearance on other platforms, or the *Civil Society Empowerment Programme*, a 10 million Euros financial support to civil society actors to develop alternative narratives to combat terrorism online which will be distributed mainly through social media channels.

The need for dealing with the increasing use of the Internet and social media for terrorist purposes gained further attention after the attacks that took place in Paris and Brussels in 2015/2016. The *Conclusions of the Justice and Home Affairs Council of the European Union* adopted in November 2015 invited Member States' authorities to improve cooperation with internet service providers in order to address the phenomena of on-line hate speech and terrorist radicalisation (Council of the EU 2015b, sect. 3). Similarly, the *Joint statement of the EU Ministers for Justice and Home Affairs and representatives of EU institutions*—issued during the 24 March 2016 Extraordinary meeting of EU Ministers for Justice and Home Affairs and representatives of EU institutions—insisted on continuing the development of "preventive measures to guarantee early detection of signs of *(on-line)* radicalisation by requiring the Commission to intensify work with IT companies in the framework of the EU Internet Forum to counter terrorist propaganda and to develop by June 2016 a Code of conduct against hate speech online" [emphasis added]. The cited Code of conduct was officially presented by the European Commission together with Facebook, Microsoft, Twitter and YouTube on 31 May 2016.[11] The Joint statement also underlined the need "to secure and obtain more quickly and effectively digital evidence by intensifying cooperation with third countries and service providers" (Council of the EU 2016a).

Collaboration on collecting and sharing digital evidence is required not only to fight terrorism but also organised crime and, in particular, cybercrime (European Commission 2015a, p. 19–20; 2016c, p. 8–9). In its *Conclusions on improving criminal justice in cyberspace* of 9 June 2016 the Council asked for a commonly agreed legal framework governing this form of cooperation (Council of the EU 2016b, p. 3–4).[12] However, cooperation between public authorities and Internet service providers in the fight against cybercrime goes beyond mere digital evidence gathering and sharing. The 2013 *EU Cybersecurity Strategy* prompts the European Network and Information Security Agency (ENISA) to identify, in cooperation with Europol's European Cybercrime Centre (EC3) "emerging trends and needs in view of evolving cybercrime and cybersecurity patterns in order to develop adequate digital forensic tools and technologies" (European Commission 2013, p. 14).[13] Within the EC3 operates the Cyber Intelligence Team, which collects

[11]For further details on its content and implementation see *infra* in paragraph 11.4.

[12]In general, the EU put great emphasis on the need to safeguard individuals' privacy and the principle of due process with regard to the disclosure of digital evidence, in order to ensure that the Internet and social media service providers do not become a 'choke-point' for investigations (European Commission 2015a, p. 19–20).

[13]The EC3 was launched in January 2013 as a specialised centre within Europol to strengthen the law enforcement response to cybercrime in the EU. In particular, EC3 focuses on cybercrimes: (1) committed by organised criminal groups, generating large criminal profits; (2) seriously harming victims such as online child sexual exploitation; (3) affecting critical infrastructure and information systems in the EU. The European Cybercrime Centre serves as a central hub for criminal information and intelligence. It provides EU Member States and Third partner countries' law enforcement agencies with strategic analysis products as well as highly specialised technical

and process cybercrime-related information from public, private and open sources (including social media) and identifies emerging threats and patterns (Europol 2013, p. 10).

It is worth reporting that in August 2016 the French Minister of Interior and his German counterpart met in Paris and presented a *Franco-German Initiative on the key challenges of EU cooperation in the field of Internal Security* to the European Commission. Among other things, the initiative called for a series of measures to deal with encryption of terrorist communications, cybercrime and Internet referrals (Ministère de l'intérieur de la République Française 2016, p. 3–4). A few months later, the concerned Ministers asked the Council Presidency for the adoption of legislation aimed at enhancing cooperation with Internet—and social media—service providers in the field of security (Council of the European Union 2016c, p. 3–4). They asked for norms (binding rules!) aimed at enhancing cooperation between governmental authorities and electronic communication service providers, particularly those that are not based within the Union. They also advocated the definition of a stricter and binding timeframe for providers to enforce requests (e.g. the removal of illicit content promoting terrorism) from national authorities.[14] On 20 February 2017, the two Ministers asked again the Commission for action.

To a very limited extent, social media platforms and services are the object of policies adopted by the EU to foster its Member States' public safety against natural or man-made disasters. The Emergency Response Coordination Centre (ERCC) established within the EU mechanism for Civil Protection has the mandate to collect and process open source data including data extracted from social media.[15] Apart from this, it seems that no EU specific policy or other instrument address the topic extensively.[16]

11.2.2 The Case of Italy

Like in many other EU Member States, social media have become the object of security-oriented activities in Italy. These activities represent the operational implementation of legal and policy instruments that generally deal with the prevention of

and digital forensic support capabilities to investigations and operations. (Europol 2013, p. 4). See also https://www.europol.europa.eu/about-europol/european-cybercrime-centre-ec3

[14]In order to facilitate the process, the Ministers called for the establishment of a point of contact within each of the service providers to directly respond to legal requisitions from the competent authorities.

[15]See the EU Civil Protection Mechanism. http://ec.europa.eu/echo/what/civil-protection/mechanism_en. Accessed 19 December 2016.

[16]See also the European Flood Alert System, developed by the European Commission's Institute for Environment and Sustainability (IES), the European Forest Fire Information System (EFFIS) and the Global Disaster Alerts and Coordination System (GDACS) which can gather and process data extracted from social media (European Commission 2016).

and response to crime, terrorism and, more recently, the protection of cyber-space. The concerned instruments were partially adopted as follow up of EU-driven initiatives concerning Member States' cooperation in the field of security and justice. However, especially when national security is at stake, they mainly represent the outcome of decisions adopted within the Italian domestic jurisdiction.

As per cybersecurity, the *Piano Nazionale per la Protezione Cibernetica e la Sicurezza Informatica* (National Plan for Cyber Protection and IT Security) invites "institutional subjects and private operators involved in cyber security, including those operating outside the national territory, to monitor constantly social media as well as other ICT systems and platforms to guarantee early detection of cyber vulnerabilities which might be the object of cyber-attacks" (Presidenza del Consiglio dei Ministri 2013b, p. 7–8; Presidenza del Consiglio dei Ministri 2013a, p. 3).

With regard to counter terrorism, the Law Decree No. 374 of 18 October 2001—converted into Law No. 438 of 15 December 2001 on *Disposizioni urgenti per contrastare il terrorismo internazionale* (Urgent measures to contrast international terrorism) authorised the Italian judiciary police and public prosecutors to get access to Internet data (Parlamento Italiano 2001). This Law was partially amended by Law No. 155 that further introduces the possibility for the Director of intelligence services, upon mandate of the President of the Council of Ministers, to request authorisation of the General Prosecutors' Offices in the Courts of Appeals to carry out preventive wiretapping of Internet data as well as asking Internet service providers for phone/Internet data (Parlamento Italiano 2005). The Law Decree No. 7 of 18 February 2015, converted into Law No. 43 of 17 April 2015 on *Misure urgenti per il contrasto del terrorismo, anche di matrice internazionale* (Urgent measures to contrast terrorism also of international nature) criminalises the use of the web for terrorist purposes (e.g. recruiting foreign fighters or advocating foreign fighting in the name of jihad). According to the Law, Internet providers must shut down websites and social media profiles that support terrorism (Parlamento Italiano 2015).

Similarly to the EU, the prevention and fight against terrorism are key drivers for the adoption of national policies and legislation that focus on Internet and social media from a security perspective. With regard to the use of social media for crises and emergency prevention and response, the Italian Civil Protection Department—that is based in the offices of the Presidency of the Council of Ministers—has established a community of users that contributes to crisis communication.[17] Launched in 2013, *#socialProCiv: la rete social di protezione civile* is a network of institutions, authorities, associations of volunteers and media operators. Also ordinary citizens can give their contribution to the network by sharing information that they find in #socialProCiv. Associations and individuals who join the network commit themselves to comply with and implement a set of guidelines in order to guarantee both a streamlined and trustworthy flow of relevant information (Dipartimento della Protezione Civile 2016, p. 1–2).

[17]The Department coordinates the response to natural disasters, catastrophes or other events.

11.3 Social Media and Their Security-Related Activities: Engagement, Enforcement and Intelligence

The employment of social media platforms and services for security and safety (e.g. crisis management) is a common trend across Europe. The modalities of employment vary according to the concerned Member State, in particular to its relevant authorities' nature and interests, responsibilities, remits and capabilities, and the general contexts and purposes for resorting to social media as tools for promoting security. As far as purposes and modalities are concerned, they generally consist in: engaging with different individual users or groups of users; enforcing the law; and/or producing intelligence concerning selected safety-security related phenomena that occur both on-line and off-line. The use of social media for "engagement" is generally aimed at getting different types of audience (members of local communities, selected organisations or the wide population) involved and contributing to the management of specific situations. Expected contributions can vary significantly and range from the action of sharing/spreading relevant information to the compliance with communicated instructions or recommendations. When employed for "law enforcement" purposes, social media becomes the instrument and the object of measures or actions taken by national authorities for ensuring the observance of, or obedience to, established legal provisions. A third employment of social media is for "generating intelligence" goals, i.e. for crafting actionable knowledge on specific events or phenomena (Bonfanti 2015, p. 11–12).[18] Engagement, enforcement, and intelligence are all goals and modalities for the use of social media in the fields of security, public safety and crisis management.

With regard to the latter field, social media have been employed in crisis and emergency management for some years (Chan 2012, p. 1; Jennex 2012, p. 2). They are nowadays used by safety agencies for both gathering and disseminating information (in the form of alerts, instructions, recommendations, news, etc.) to selected recipients before, during, and/or after a crisis or emergency. They also serve as communication tools for improving coordination among different crisis managers and other stakeholders (Wendling et al. 2013, p. 11).[19] From this point of view, social media

[18]The security intelligence community worldwide acknowledged the different advantages in crafting knowledge from social media data. These are: the low cost of gathering and analysing data, the huge quantity and great variety of available information, as well as the speed with which data can be accessed and collected (often at real-time). These advantages are noticeable especially when compared with more traditional techniques of data gathering (e.g. telephone tapping, application of hidden microphones, undercover operations, just to mention some). There are of course constraints and disadvantages that cannot be underestimated (Bonfanti 2015, p. 19–20; Omand et al. 2012b, p. 51–61).

[19]It is worth noting that the application of social media in crisis and emergency management has offered a change of perspective in what affected populations can do in these critical situations. In fact, individuals have gradually become active users of official recommendations and advice coming from rescue agencies, as well as active contributors of relevant information through their social media profiles (Wendling et al. 2013, p. 8).

platforms and their related services—combined with the use of specific technological applications—have enhanced/enlarged the existing set of instruments that can be deployed by first responders for managing critical or emergency situations.[20]

Social media platforms and services have also become valuable tools for policing activities, especially for crime prevention and response (Mateescu et al. 2015, p. 1–2).[21] They are presently employed by police forces for both action and relational purposes. As per the former, social media platforms support policing operations either through the dissemination or acquisition of relevant information. Through social media, law enforcement agencies can detect, prevent and investigate offences or criminal activities and take coercive measures in the context of such activities. In particular, they can track public comments and scrap criminal profiles and posts, discover criminal behaviour and obtain probable cause for a search warrant, collect evidence for court hearings, pinpoint the location of criminals, manage volatile situations, witness identification and solicit tips from the public (Mateescu et al. 2015, p. 2–3; Bayerl et al. 2015, p. 198–200). Some of the above described actions may require access to users' private information which is stored and processed by social media providers in encrypted fashion. Access to such information by law enforcement agencies should in principle be granted by the providers upon request made by judiciary authorities.[22] Social media generated and collected information could also be analysed with the goal of understanding certain events or phenomena, as well as their short-mid-term developments. Police resorts to social media also for keeping the public accurately informed during major critical events or disorders.[23] In a broader sense, the police uses these tools for community outreach and public relations' initiatives (Bayerl et al. 2015, p. 199).

[20]Among the existing applications used in disaster management that generate knowledge from social media data, see for example the Slándáil System (http://slandail.eu/) i.e. a software which collects social media data, as texts, images and videos (including sensitive data like names) during a natural disaster. It then aggregates these data and provides outputs in the form of actionable information for rescuers (e.g. key places under particular threat, identities and numbers of missing people and casualties) (Jackson et al. 2015, p. 168).

[21]In order to investigate the extent to which social media data are used by law enforcement agents, the US business research company LexisNexis carried out an online survey on more than 1200 US federal, state and local law enforcement professionals. The result is quite clear as 81% of the interviewed people confirmed to utilise social media as an investigative and intelligence gathering tool and, more in particular, 63% used social media for crime investigation, whereas 51% used them for crime anticipation purposes (LexisNexis 2014, p. 4). This trend may be justified by both the lower cost of social media tools compared to more classical forms of surveillance and, in particular, as a response to public pressure for the police to investigate crimes online after a number of violent attacks occurring at world level revealed to have been anticipated on social media with several warning signs (Mateescu et al. 2015, p. 1).

[22]In some European countries (e.g. France, Germany, United Kingdom) Governmental authorities have recently asked providers of social media as well as of services of instant messaging (e.g. WhatsApp) to make any relevant encrypted information "readable" and directly accessible to law enforcement authorities for investigation purposes (Sparrow 2017).

[23]For instance, during the investigations carried out in the aftermath of the Boston Marathon bombings, the Boston Police Department used Twitter to communicate with the population. They

As discussed above, social media users generate and share a great variety and quantity of data and metadata (textual, video, images, etc.). If properly collected and analysed, these data can create intelligence to be consumed to detect, predict and counter threats to public order and national security (e.g. terrorism, organised criminal activities, major public disorders and other kinds of subversive events). The process of deriving intelligence from social media information/data is known as Social Media Intelligence (or by its acronym—SOCMINT).[24] SOCMINT consists of two phases: data search/access/mining; and data analysis. Both phases are generally implemented through the deployment of technological applications/software. As per the data analysis, it is usually carried out through IT tools known as "social media analytics" that assist human analysts in interpreting the gathered data (Omand et al. 2012a, p. 804; Bonfanti 2015, p. 7). European intelligence and security agencies had the chance to appreciate the value of social media intelligence, for instance, on the occasion of the 2009 Iranian green movement protests or the 2011 Arab spring revolutions. At that time, it became clear that Twitter and Facebook could offer a significant repository of information to be collected and examined in order to understand what was happening in those countries and identify main trends. Since then, several agencies have intensified the monitoring of social media generated data, as well as acquired the technical and human capabilities to analyse collected information and produce intelligence. As it was reported, there are some intelligence agencies that are developing *ad hoc* social media analysis centres (Leavey 2013, p. 5–6). In addition, a new generation of data mining tools to be applied to social media have been developed.[25] It is worth noting that intelligence agencies are social media users too; they employ these tools for engaging with the public (Landon-Murray 2015, p. 67).

provided updates on police activities and the status of the investigation, announced traffic diversions, and requested public assistance as eye witnessing/statements. Furthermore, Twitter proved to be a timely source of direct observations of, and immediate reactions to events, such as turmoil like the 2011 London riots (Glasgow 2015, p. 40).

[24]The term SOCMINT does not only refer to a process but also to the product that results from such process (Bonfanti 2015, p. 12).

[25]For example, the US Defence Intelligence Agency (DIA) has also developed an instrument that scans social media for individual faces by analysing millions of postings for images of a single person. As reported in an interview released by Gen. Flynn, the previous DIA Director, this technique proved useful during the Crimean annexation by Russia in the beginning of 2014 (Barnes 2014).

11.4 The Policy Framework(s) in the EU and Italy: Making Room for Improved Governance

The employment of social media platforms and services for security purposes generates several governance implications at different levels (e.g. operational, tactical, strategic; procedural, normative, policy). These implications vary according to the specific security or safety sector social media are used in—though there are some horizontal issues, e.g. privacy and data protection (Hadjimatheou et al. 2016, p. 5). They also vary according to the considered domain, i.e. the supranational or domestic. In general, the exploitation of social media platforms and services by law enforcement, security and safety agencies, as well as the role played by social media providers in contributing to public security and safety goals, do not appear to be consistently and thoroughly governed. At least, this seems to be the case of the EU, and—to a different extent—of the Italian context.

For instance, the efficient and effective use of social media during crises requires a certain degree of coordination/cooperation between, on the one side, private social media platforms and service providers and, on the other, public safety authorities and rescue agencies. Coordination and mutual engagement should occur at both the design and implementation stages of the selected solutions that involve the use of social media. A lack of coordination is likely to result in inefficient management, which is counterproductive. This is one of the major criticisms moved against some of the existing social media emergency tools e.g. the Facebook Safety Check or Google Crisis Response.[26] In fact, it seems there was limited coordination with the national public safety stakeholders who are responsible for people's safety in the design and implementation of these tools (Quadling and Potter 2014). Public safety authorities should have undisputed leadership in disaster management, e.g. being effectively granted with the capacity to supervise and "control" the information that is circulated through social media during a disaster or other critical situations (Di Paolo 2015). In extreme cases and when necessary, they should have the capacity to get information either timely removed from social media or further propagated depending on the specific context at stake. This requires high coordination and synergies between social media providers and governmental authorities. It also requires the definition of a clear procedural framework governing this kind of collaboration. A framework that should consist of provisions who also acknowledge the need to safeguard freedom of expression and prevent unjustified censorship even during a critical situation. Such a framework does not yet seem to be in place either at the EU level or in its Member States. With regard to Italy, the Italian Civil Protection Department has

[26] *Safety Check* is an app launched by Facebook which allows people to quickly share with friends and family that they are safe and helps them connect with close people. In particular, during a disaster, *Safety Check* allows: to acknowledge friends and family that a person is safe; control on friends and family in the affected area and connect with them and share what a person knows regarding a friend or family member's status. See https://www.facebook.com/help/695378390556779/. See also Google (2016) and https://www.google.org/crisisresponse/about/

drafted a policy document and guidelines to be adopted and applied by social media users adhering to the community who contributes to crisis communication.[27] Nevertheless, it does not address the role and responsibilities of providers and how they should coordinate their actions with those enacted by public authorities.

With regard to the employment of social media for policing purposes, it is worth noting that the interplay between law enforcement and social media providers is particularly complex. The latter (and Internet providers in general) hold subscriber information, some connection logs, location information, and communication content, all of which can represent critical electronic evidence of an offence. Data retention obligations and disclosure policies vary widely by country, industry, and type of data. Law enforcement authorities most often use court orders to obtain evidence from service providers established within their jurisdiction or abroad. This is for example the case of Italy where national providers are entitled to retain traffic data for investigating purposes up to 24 months (Parlamento Italiano 2015).[28] In other countries, however, public agencies may be able to obtain stored subscriber data, traffic data, and even content data, "directly". In this respect, although providers generally adopt and implement the policy of requiring due legal process for data disclosure, there are some cases where they might voluntarily comply with direct law enforcement requests. Informal relationships between law enforcement and service providers seem to assist the process of information exchange and trust-building in several cases (UNODC 2013, p. 144).

A good example of the complex interplay between law enforcement and social media providers in the field of policing terrorism is provided by the case of illegal content referral at the EU (supranational) level. The referral is a practice consisting in the reporting/flagging of terrorist and extremist online content from special police units to the concerned online service provider. It is a practice carried out by many Member States' authorities on the basis of national regulations.[29] In Italy, for example, the Law No. 43 of 17 April 2015 prescribes Internet providers to shut down websites and social media profiles that support or exalt terrorism within 48 hours following a referral by the competent law enforcement authority. If providers do not comply with the request, the Internet domain is blocked with the exception of the webpages not involved in the illicit conduct. The latter provision concerns social media platforms whose services might be used for disseminating terrorist propaganda. At the EU supranational level, a referral mechanism is established too. The EU Internet Referral Unit, embedded within Europol's European Counterterrorism Centre, regularly monitors the web (including social media platforms), assesses online materials (including posts and data shared on social media platforms) and, if their content is flagged as suspicious and/or

---

[27]The policy document and guidelines are available at http://www.protezionecivile.gov.it/jcms/it/view_dossier.wp?contentId=DOS52445

[28]See *supra*.

[29]See also the case of the UK Counterterrorism Internet Referral Unit (National Police Chiefs' Council 2016).

dangerous for public security (e.g. websites providing terrorist propaganda material, extreme-right forums inciting to religious/ideological hatred, etc.), it reports it to the online service providers.[30] It then asks providers to remove the on-line content. Actually, it should be noted that providers do not "have" an all-encompassing duty to remove the content, and are often not liable if they do not comply with the request for removal. The lack of liability is the result of some provisions established by the e-Commerce Directive (Directive 2000/31/EC) that regulates Internet providers' conduct in this respect. These provisions grant service providers a sort of large exemption from the obligation to follow up requests from the IRU. Indeed, they cannot be held liable for the information they store, transmit, and host temporarily if they are a "mere conduit", "caching" or "hosting" provider.[31] According to the Europol Report on the activity of the EU IRU, "a referral activity . . . does not constitute an enforceable act. Thus the decision and removal of the referred terrorist and extremist online content is taken by the concerned service providers under their own responsibility and accountability (in compliance with their Terms of Reference)" (Europol 2016, p. 4). In fact, despite the results achieved by Europol as per the activity carried out by its IRU,[32] few paradoxical situations occurred, namely that the material under scrutiny was removed only after sometime or that the referred online material was not removed at all by some service

[30]The EU IRU acts according to the rules set out in the Europol Council Decision (which will be substituted by the Europol Regulation starting from 1 May 2017). This means that research for information is performed in compliance with Europol data processing rules and for the purpose of determining whether the information is relevant for Europol tasks. Therefore, Europol identifies terrorist and extremist online content based on its mandate. An expert evaluation of the content is performed in accordance with the principles set up in Council Framework Decision 2008/919/JHA on combating terrorism. The Council Framework Decision 2008/919/JHA on combating terrorism (amending the Council Framework Decision 2002/475/JHA) sets out a definition on what is to be considered as "public provocation to commit a terrorist offence".

[31]European Union 2000. See art 12–14 of Directive 2000/31/EC, setting out a number of exemptions from liability. See also art. 42–45 that further clarify the conditions according to which service providers can benefit from the concerned exemptions. These are: "the activity of the information society service provider is limited to the technical process of operating and giving access to a communication network not having knowledge of or control over the information which is transmitted or stored" (art. 42); "the service provider is in no way involved with the information transmitted by, for example, deliberately collaborating with one of the recipients of its service in order to undertake illegal acts" (art. 43–44). It is worth highlighting that the exemptions from liability of service providers "do not affect the possibility of injunctions of different kinds" (e.g. orders by courts or administrative authorities requiring the removal of illegal information or the disabling of access to it). It should be noted that there is a growing debate among Governmental bodies and, in general, the public opinion about making social media providers responsible and liable for their users' activities. Extending providers' responsibility would imply a significant change in the "nature" and core activities of social media: from enabling communications to publishing content—a crucial distinction which presently means that they are not liable for trolling or abuse.

[32]In 2016 the EU Internet Referral Unit has taken 20,548 decisions for referral to internet service providers (82% of which resulted in removals by the companies) (Europol 2017).

providers. The latter situations prompted calls for making Europol IRU's requests for removals mandatory.

As a consequence of the requests coming from both the EU and US administrations on social media providers to commit more proactively and efficiently to curb spread of online terrorist content, on 5 December 2016 Facebook, Microsoft, Twitter and YouTube announced the establishment of a shared industry database of "hashes". These are digital fingerprints (sequences) of online contents (images, videos, etc.) that providers have removed from their services because of their association to terrorism. By sharing the hashes, providers aim at increasing their capacity to detect potential terrorist content on their platforms. The removal and subsequent sharing of images, videos, etc. will be carried out in compliance with each provider's internal procedure. The database of ashes will be open to any social media provider willing to join. The creation of this shared database—which is expected to be implemented by 2017—can be considered a first step towards a voluntary but more effective contribution of social media providers to countering on-line terrorism propaganda and recruitment (Facebook 2016; Pennisi 2016).

As one may understand, effective cooperation and engagement from social media providers are paramount to the enforcement of the law. In the lack of specific obligations, cooperation and engagement can be achieved only on a voluntary basis. This is for example what happens with regard to the contribution of providers in combating on-line hate speech and xenophobia. In May 2016 the EU Commission presented the above-mentioned "Code of conduct on countering illegal hate speech online."[33] According to the Code, IT companies commit to: "(1) Have in place clear and effective processes to review notifications regarding illegal hate speech on their services so they can remove or disable access to such content; (2) Review the removal notifications against their rules of procedure, guidelines and, where applicable, national laws transposing the Framework Decision 2008/913/JHA; (3) Review the majority of valid notifications for removal of illegal hate speech in less than 24 h and remove and disable such content, if necessary, besides creating counter-narratives to confront the problem" (EU Commission 2016b, p. 2–3). However, as shown by the "6 month activity report on the Code of conduct" published in December 2016 (European Commission 2016a), the Code has not been properly implemented by social media providers; its main limit lies in the lack of enforceability because it is not a binding legal instrument.[34] Further to this limit,

[33]See *supra* paragraph 11.2.1.

[34]In the aftermath of the publication of the progress report regarding the level of commitment of Internet companies to the "Code of Conduct" showing disappointing results (40% of recorded cases reviewed within 24 h, 80% after 48 h with other contents not being removed at all), Věra Jourová, EU Commissioner for Justice, Consumers and Gender Equality, stated during an interview to the Financial Times that "If Facebook, YouTube, Twitter and Microsoft want to convince me and the ministers that the non-legislative approach can work, they will have to act quickly and make a strong effort in the coming months", therefore casting doubts on the effectiveness of self-regulation, speculating instead on the application of a hard law approach (Beesley 2016).

one may argue that the definition and implementation of the technical aspects of the procedures could be challenging too.

In light of the above, it is quite evident that the cooperation between social media providers and national or EU relevant law enforcement, security and safety agencies is regulated in a fragmented way across the EU. For example, as per the referral mechanism in place at the EU level, this is mainly enacted on the basis of "voluntary arrangements" (Hadley et al. 2016, p. 3). Although not negative *per se*, voluntary arrangements or codes of conduct should at least be aligned with fundamental principles or rules to be established by an EU consistent regulatory scheme, which would make the contribution of social media providers to fostering security more accountable and in compliance with some basic prescriptions.

As for the use of social media for intelligence gathering or intelligence-led policing, there are nowadays concerns for the risk of "mass surveillance" the above initiatives may bring about.[35] From their perspective, social media platforms and service providers (e.g. Twitter, Slack) do not seem comfortable with the security-oriented use of SOCMINT. They are concerned that the implementation of this practice will make their users feel routinely monitored in their on-line activities and make them abandon or decrease their use of social media.[36] For these reasons, some providers declared their intention to limit the possibility of exploiting users' data for security intelligence or intelligence-led policing.[37] The lack of specific policies and legal provisions regulating these activities on social media platforms is nowadays a matter of major concern in many countries (Mateescu 2015, p. 4; Omand et al. 2012b, p. 26).[38] In Italy, for example, the Data Protection Authority (DPA) has already raised this concern. By posing a special emphasis on the protection of individuals' fundamental rights and the safeguard of the principle of the rule of law and democratic values, the Italian

[35]These concerns increased after the revelations made in May 2013 by Edward Snowden, a former contractor at the US National Security Agency (NSA). Snowden revealed the existence of internet and phone mass surveillance programmes that were carried out by the NSA and other intelligence agencies with the cooperation of telecommunication companies. (Greenwald Glenn et al. 2013).

[36]According to the June 2015 Eurobarometer survey on data protection, 81% of Europeans feel that they do not have complete control over their personal data online; 69% would like to give their explicit consent before the collection/processing of their data and only 24% of Europeans trust online platforms (including social media providers).

[37]Twitter has recently terminated the agreement with the US intelligence community to use Dataminr. This data mining service partially owned by Twitter (5% stake) was the only authorised one to accessing the real-time stream of public tweets. Dataminr's software is able to detect patterns in hundreds of millions of daily tweets, traffic data, news wires and other sources and matches the data with market information and geographic coordinates to determine what information is credible. It seems that this service proved useful to detect unfolding terroristic attacks (Stewart and Maremont 2016).

[38]Documents from the Chicago Cook County Sheriff's Office revealed the increasing use by law enforcement personnel of undercover online operations carried out with very little clarity both in terms of frequency and legal framework. Sometimes, the implementation of these actions has been left up to the discretion of police officers themselves and without prior *ad hoc* training (Joseph 2016).

DPA called for rules governing SOCMINT and intelligence-led policing practices through social media (Garante per la protezione dei dati personali 2015, p. 168).[39] There is a general lack of accountability that can nevertheless be ensured by putting in place *ad hoc* policies and control systems that guarantee compliance and provide relevant evidence in particular to independent supervisory authorities. Debates and research on this topic have recently started to emerge, especially at the academic and industry level as proved by the launch of several thematic projects co-financed by the EU.[40]

On top of the risk of mass surveillance, the exploitation of social media for gathering intelligence on some serious threats such as terrorism is likely to pose a specific governance issue. This issue stems from the different goals pursued by intelligence agencies—as well as their needs, interests and *modus operandi*—and by law enforcement's implemented initiatives, namely the above described referral mechanisms. As discussed, referrals are aimed at removing social media profiles and webpages who are flagged as providing illegal content. The removal should occur quickly. This can conflict with the interest of some security agencies to keep the illegal content online for longer in order to gathering further information and intelligence on users, networks, contents. In other words, there is a dilemma that could only be addressed by the definition of policies and/or procedures providing for effective coordination and cooperation between intelligence, law enforcement agencies, and social media platforms and services providers.

11.5 Conclusions

This chapter reviewed some of the most relevant governance implications concerning the employment of social media platforms and services for security and safety purposes. It examined the main policies adopted in this field at both the EU and Italian domestic level, and identified significant issues that should be dealt with in order to make room for better governance. These issues vary according to

[39]It is worth noting that the Law Decree No. 7 of 18 February 2015, converted into Law No. 43 of 17 April 2015 on *Misure urgenti per il contrasto del terrorismo, anche di matrice internazionale* originally foresaw a provision on remote monitoring of data stored in suspected individuals' computers, other devices and their applications - including those related to social media accounts—by law enforcement and intelligence agencies. The provision was amended upon request from the former Italian Prime Minister, Matteo Renzi, during the parliamentary debate of the bill within the Committee on Justice at the Chamber of Deputies (Innamorati 2015).

[40]One recent example of thematic research on the use of social media for public security is the MEDIA4SEC project, presented by a consortium including academia, private companies and public stakeholders. It focuses on enhancing the understanding of the opportunities, challenges and ethical considerations of social media use for public security. The project began on 1 July 2016 and will run for 30 months. It is financed under the EU Horizon 2020 Research Framework Programme. More info are available on http://media4sec.eu/about/)

the specific security or safety sector social media are used in—though there are some horizontal questions, e.g. privacy and data protection implications.

With regard to the EU, its adopted policies and initiatives do not cover comprehensively the security sectors in which social media are increasingly employed. This is partially due to the Union's established areas of competence. Mainly, EU policies focus on online radicalisation, violent extremism and hate speech and considers the contribution social media providers can give to prevent/counter these phenomena; few or no initiatives concern the use of these platforms and their services for disaster/risk management and security intelligence gathering. As per the latter, there is of course an on-going institutional debate on the privacy and data protection implications originating from mining the Internet and social media for security reasons. The EU is also trying to set up more uniform and clearer standards informing the contribution social media service providers can offer to the policing of on-line terrorism and extremism. Standards are provided by soft law instruments like voluntary arrangements or codes of conduct. Although these instruments could, in principle, be more suitable to shape the collaboration between public authorities and providers than binding tools—because they afford a flexible application to different contexts and situations, the lack of enforceability limits their actual reach.[41] This is the main reason why Member States like Germany and France claimed for norms (binding rules!) aimed at enhancing cooperation between the Governmental authorities and providers in the field of security.

With regard to Italy, the national adopted policies and legislation consider the employment of social media platforms and services for security within the context of the prevention of and fight to terrorism and organised crime. These national instruments have been generally adopted to follow-up EU-driven initiatives and actions. In some cases, they provide for binding rules that define the duties and rights of the involved parties, including social media providers. The rules cover policing and intelligence-led policing activities in general, and address the use of the Internet and social media because they fall within the scope of these activities. In particular, the use of social media for crises and emergency management and for gathering security related intelligence is far from being adequately governed.

In conclusion, the pursuit of security and safety through the employment of social media platforms and services is a growing practice in the EU and its Member States. The role assigned to social media providers by public policies, developed practices, and public expectations about their contribution in this field are increasing. This picture is confronted with a fragmented and, to a certain extent, weak governance framework that needs to be improved. Improvements can be achieved through the adoption and implementation of a more coordinated, coherent, comprehensive, and effectively inclusive approach to the matter. From this perspective, it seems for instance more important to define how to deal with the challenges of

[41]It is worth noting that the adoption and implementation of soft law instruments could also be seen as an approach that acknowledges the essence of the Internet and social media that are based on freedom of expression and right to participation.

governing the employment of social media for security, rather than decide on the actual content of a future governance framework. Any attempt to govern the use of social media for security should endorse the above-cited approach. This approach should be: (1) coordinated i.e. centrally driven or based on a mutually agreed roadmap establishing clear duties, time-frames, and accountability mechanisms; (2) coherent, meaning that it has to acknowledge and deal with the different implications the use of social media for security-related goals are likely to raise, as well as strike a balance between the different (public/private) interests and goals that are at stake; (3) comprehensive i.e. consider the diverse applications of social media in different security and safety-related sectors; and finally (4) inclusive, in the sense that it should engage substantially with relevant stakeholders, in particular, social media providers and get their effective commitment. Adopting the recommended approach seems to be the first necessary step in the process of governing the use of social media.

As a very final remark, it should be considered that the adoption of social media platforms and services for security tend to destabilize existing norms, institutions and power relationships. The problem is also exacerbated by the rapid pace social media and their applications develop, the uncertainties surrounding the outcome of their development, as well as their possible utilisation. In a context of great uncertainty, governing the security applications of social media is a great challenge; but it is one that is worth being taken in order to legittimately benefit from the opportunities social media can offer in terms of enhancing security.[42]

References

Article 29 Working Party. (2014). Working Document on surveillance of electronic communications for intelligence and national security purposes. Accessed January 24, 2017, from http://ec.europa.eu/justice/data-protection/article-29/documentation/opinion-recommendation/files/2014/wp228_en.pdf

Barnes, J. E. (2014). U.S. Military Plugs Into Social Media for Intelligence Gathering. *The Wall Street Journal* (online edition), August 6. Accessed November 22, 2016, from http://www.wsj.com/articles/u-s-military-plugs-into-social-media-for-intelligence-gathering-1407346557

Bayerl, P. S., Akhgar, B., Brewster, B., Domdouzis, K., & Gibson, H. (2015). Social media and its role for LEAs: Review and applications. In B. Akhgar, A. Staniforth, & F. Bosco (Eds.), *Cyber crime and cyber terrorism investigator's handbook* (pp. 197–220). Amsterdam: Elsevier.

Beesley, A. (2016). Brussels urges US social media sites to act swiftly on hate posts. *The Financial Times* (online edition), December 4. Accessed December 16, 2016, from https://www.ft.com/content/b3163cca-ba32-11e6-8b45-b8b81dd5d080

[42]The present chapter was conceived by Dr. Matteo E. Bonfanti who elaborated and drafted all the sections it consists of. Mr. Piergiorgio Stefanucci assisted in the collection of relevant documentation, drafted the preliminary version of sections 11.2 and 11.3, as well as compiled the reference list of the present chapter. The authors would like to thank those national law enforcement officers who provided useful insight on the topic discussed by the chapter.

Bonfanti, M. E. (2015). *Social Media Intelligence* a Salvaguardia dell'Interesse Nazionale: Limiti e Opportunità di una Pratica da Sviluppare. In U. Gori & L. Martino (Eds.), *Intelligence e Interesse Nazionale* (pp. 231–262). Roma: Aracne editrice.

Chan, J. C. (2012). The role of social media in crisis preparedness, response and recovery. Rahs Think Centre. Accessed November 20, 2016, from http://www.oecd.org/governance/risk/The%20role%20of%20Social%20media%20in%20crisis%20preparedness,%20response%20and%20recovery.pdf

Council of the European Union. (2005). The European Union Counter-Terrorism Strategy. Accessed December 17, 2016, from http://register.consilium.europa.eu/doc/srv?l=EN&f=ST%2014469%202005%20REV%204

Council of the European Union. (2007). Council conclusions on cooperation to combat terrorist use of the Internet ("Check the Web"). Accessed March 20, 2017, from https://register.consilium.europa.eu/doc/srv?l=EN&f=ST%208457%202007%20REV%203

Council of the European Union. (2008). Council conclusions on reinforcing the union's disaster response capacity – Towards an integrated approach to managing disasters. Accessed March 20, 2017, from http://www.eu2008.si/si/News_and_Documents/Council_Conclusions/June/0616_GAERC-Disaster_Response.pdf

Council of the European Union. (2009). Council decision 2009/371/JHA of 6 April 2009 establishing the European Police Office (Europol). Accessed April 27, 2017, from https://www.europol.europa.eu/publications-documents/council-decision-of-6-april-2009-establishing-european-police-office-europol

Council of the European Union. (2010). Internal security strategy for the European Union – Towards a European security model. Accessed December 17, 2016, from http://www.consilium.europa.eu/uedocs/cms_data/librairie/pdf/qc3010313enc.pdf

Council of the European Union. (2015a). Draft Council Conclusions on the Renewed European Union Internal Security Strategy 2015–2020. Accessed February 11, 2017, from http://data.consilium.europa.eu/doc/document/ST-9798-2015-INIT/en/pdf

Council of the European Union. (2015b). Conclusions of the Council of the European Union and of the Member States meeting within the Council on enhancing the criminal justice response to radicalisation leading to terrorism and violent extremism. Accessed December 18, 2016, from http://www.consilium.europa.eu/en/press/press-releases/2015/11/20-conclusions-radicalisation/

Council of the European Union. (2016a). Joint statement of EU Ministers for Justice and Home Affairs and representatives of EU institutions on the terrorist attacks in Brussels on 22 March 2016. Accessed February 11, 2017, from http://www.consilium.europa.eu/en/press/press-releases/2016/03/24-statement-on-terrorist-attacks-in-brussels-on-22-march/

Council of the European Union. (2016b). Council conclusions on improving criminal justice in cyberspace. Accessed December 18, 2016, from www.consilium.europa.eu/en/meetings/jha/2016/06/cyberspace--en_pdf

Council of the European Union. (2016c). German-French letter concerning cooperation between law enforcement agencies and electronic communication service providers. Accessed December 18, 2016, from http://data.consilium.europa.eu/doc/document/ST-14001-2016-INIT/en/pdf

Di Paolo, F. (2015). Social media per le crisi. Accessed November 19, 2016, from https://www.linkedin.com/pulse/social-media-per-le-crisi-ferruccio-di-paolo

Dipartimento della Protezione Civile. (2016). Manifesto #socialProCiv. Accessed December 19, 2016, from http://www.protezionecivile.gov.it/resources/cms/documents/manifesto_socialProCiv.pdf

European Commission. (2015a). Communication from the Commission to the European Parliament, the Council, the European Economic and Social Committee and the Committee of the Regions: The European Agenda on Security. Accessed December 17, 2016, from https://ec.europa.eu/anti-trafficking/sites/antitrafficking/files/eu_agenda_on_security_en.pdf

European Commission. (2015b. EU Internet Forum: Bringing together governments, Europol and technology companies to counter terrorist content and hate speech online (press release). Accessed December 18, 2016, from http://europa.eu/rapid/press-release_IP-15-6243_it.htm

European Commission. (2016a). Fighting illegal online hate speech: first assessment of the new code of conduct. Accessed April 16, 2017, from http://ec.europa.eu/newsroom/just/item-detail.cfm?&item_id=50840

European Commission. (2016b). Code of Conduct on countering illegal hate speech online. Accessed December 16, 2016, from http://ec.europa.eu/justice/fundamental-rights/files/hate_speech_code_of_conduct_en.pdf

European Commission. (2016c). Communication from the Commission to the European Parliament, the European Council and the Council – Delivering on the European Agenda on Security to fight against terrorism and pave the way towards an effective and genuine Security Union. Accessed December 18, 2016, from https://ec.europa.eu/home-affairs/sites/homeaffairs/files/what-we-do/policies/european-agenda-security/legislative-documents/docs/20160420/communication_eas_progress_since_april_2015_en.pdf

European Commission and High Representative of the European Union for Foreign Affairs and Security Policy. (2013). Joint Communication to the European Parliament, the Council, the European Economic and Social Committee and the Committee of the Regions. Cybersecurity Strategy of the European Union: An Open, Safe and Secure Cyberspace. Accessed April 8, 2017, from https://ec.europa.eu/digital-single-market/en/news/eu-cybersecurity-plan-protect-open-internet-and-online-freedom-and-opportunity-cyber-security

European Data Protection Supervisor (EDPS). (2015). Opinion 4/2015 – Towards a new digital ethics: Data, dignity and technology. Accessed January 22, 2017, from https://secure.edps.europa.eu/EDPSWEB/webdav/site/mySite/shared/Documents/Consultation/Opinions/2015/15-09-11_Data_Ethics_EN.pdf

European Data Protection Supervisor (EDPS). (2016). Opinion 9/2016 – EDPS Opinion on Personal Information Management Systems: Towards more user empowerment in managing and processing personal data. Accessed March 20, 2017, from https://secure.edps.europa.eu/EDPSWEB/webdav/site/mySite/shared/Documents/Consultation/Opinions/2016/16-10-20_PIMS_opinion_EN.pdf

European Parliament. (2013a). Study on National Programmes for mass surveillance of personal data in EU Member States and their compatibility with EU law. Accessed March 20, 2017, from http://www.europarl.europa.eu/RegData/etudes/etudes/join/2013/493032/IPOL-LIBE_ET(2013)493032_EN.pdf

European Parliament. (2013b). LIBE Committee Inquiry on electronic mass surveillance of EU citizens – Protecting fundamental rights in a digital age: Proceedings, Outcome and Background Documents. Accessed March 20, 2017, from http://www.europarl.europa.eu/document/activities/cont/201410/20141016ATT91322/20141016ATT91322EN.pdf

European Police Office (Europol). (2013). European Cybercrime Centre (EC3) – First year report. Accessed April 8, 2017, from https://www.europol.europa.eu/publications-documents/european-cybercrime-center-ec3-first-year-report

European Police Office (Europol). (2017). One year of the European Counter Terrorism Centre (ECTC) at Europol. Accessed February 11, 2017, from https://www.europol.europa.eu/newsroom/news/information-sharing-counter-terrorism-in-eu-has-reached-all-time-high

European Union. (2000). Directive 2000/31/EC of the European parliament and of the council of 8 June 2000 on certain legal aspects of information society services, in particular electronic commerce, in the Internal Market (Directive on electronic commerce). Accessed March 20, 2017, from http://eur-lex.europa.eu/legal-content/EN/TXT/PDF/?uri=CELEX:32000L0031&from=EN

European Union. (2010). Consolidated treaties and charter of fundamental rights. Accessed January 24, 2017, from https://europa.eu/european-union/sites/europaeu/files/eu_citizenship/consolidated-treaties_en.pdf

European Union. (2016). Regulation (EU) 2016/794 of the European Parliament and of the Council of 11 May 2016 on the European Union Agency for Law Enforcement Cooperation (Europol) and replacing and repealing Council Decisions 2009/371/JHA, 2009/934/JHA, 2009/935/JHA, 2009/936/JHA and 2009/968/JHA. Accessed January 22, 2017, from https://www.europol.europa.eu/publications-documents/regulation-eu-2016/794-of-european-parliament-and-of-council-of-11-may-2016

Facebook. (2016). Partnering to Help Curb Spread of Online Terrorist Content. Accessed December 17, 2016, from http://newsroom.fb.com/news/2016/12/partnering-to-help-curb-spread-of-online-terrorist-content/

Garante per la protezione dei dati personali. (2014). Relazione 2014. Accessed January 24, 2017, from http://194.242.234.211/documents/10160/2148177/Relazione+annuale+2014.pdf

Garante per la protezione dei dati personali. (2015). Relazione 2015. Accessed April 26, 2017, from http://www.corrierecomunicazioni.it/upload/images/06_2016/160628134834.pdf

Garante per la protezione dei dati personali. (2016). Audizione di Antonello Soro Presidente del Garante per la protezione dei dati personali presso le Commissioni riunite I e II della Camera dei Deputati (22 settembre 2016) in merito alla Comunicazione della Commissione al Parlamento europeo, al Consiglio europeo e al Consiglio recante "Attuare l'Agenda europea sulla sicurezza per combattere il terrorismo e preparare il terreno per l'Unione della sicurezza" (COM(2016) 230). Accessed April 26, 2017, from http://www.garanteprivacy.it/web/guest/home/docweb/-/docweb-display/export/5447549

Glasgow, K. (2015). Big data and law enforcement: Advances, implications, and lessons from an active shooter case study. In B. Akhgar, G. B. Saathoff, H. Arabnia, R. Hill, A. Staniforth, & P. Bayerl (Eds.), *Application of Big Data for National Security. A practitioner's Guide to Emerging Technologies* (pp. 39–54). Oxford: Butterworth-Heinemann.

Google. (2016). Google crisis response: Making critical information more accessible in times of disaster. Accessed April 27, 2017, from https://www.google.org/our-work/crisis-response/

Greenwald, G., MacAskill, E., & Poitras, L. (2013). Edward Snowden: The whistleblower behind the NSA surveillance revelations. *The Guardian* (online edition), June 11. Accessed April 27, 2017, from https://www.theguardian.com/world/2013/jun/09/edward-snowden-nsa-whistleblower-surveillance

Hadjimatheou, K., Roosendaal, A., & Vermeulen, P. (2016). Ethics and legal issues inventory: Positive and negative societal impacts of the adoption of social media across the public security community. Media4SEC. Accessed January 24, 2017, from http://media4sec.eu/downloads/d1-3.pdf

Hadley, A., Khan, S., Ruiz, D., Sestito, M., & Wilson, K. (2016). Private sector engagement in responding to the use of the internet and ICT for terrorist purposes. Strengthening Dialogue and Building Trust. ICT for peace foundation and UNCTED. Accessed January 21, 2017, from https://www.un.org/sc/ctc/wp-content/uploads/2016/12/Private-Sector-Engagement-in-Responding-to-the-Use-of-the-Internet-and-ICT-for-Terrorist-Purposes.pdf

Innamorati, G. (2015). Terrorismo: Renzi, via norma su computer. *ANSA*, March 25. Accessed March 20, 2017, from http://www.ansa.it/sito/notizie/flash/2015/03/26/renzi-fa-stralciare-da-antiterrorismo-norme-su-computer_1e3e819f-ff70-4d3d-a9e8-853560b927f2.html

Ivan, A. L., Anamaria, C., Iov, R. C., Lutai, G., & Nicolae, M. (2014). Social media intelligence: opportunities and limitations. *CES Working Papers, 7*(2A), 505–510.

Jackson, D., Aldovrandi, C., & Hayes, P. (2015). Ethical framework for a disaster management decision support system which harvests social media data on a large scale. In N. B. B. Saoud, C. Adam, & C. Hanachi (Eds.), *Information systems for crisis response and management in mediterranean countries – Second international conference, ISCRAM-med 2015, Tunis, Tunisia, October 28–30, 2015, proceedings* (pp. 167–180). Zurich: Springer.

Jennex, M. (2012). *Managing crises and disasters with emerging technologies: Advancements.* Hershey: IGI Global Group.

Joseph, G. (2016). How police are watching you on social media. *CityLab*, December 14. Accessed December 17, 2016, from http://www.citylab.com/crime/2016/12/how-police-are-watching-on-social-media/508991/?utm_source=atlfb

Kaplan, A., & Haenlein, M. (2010). Users of the world, unite! The challenges and opportunities of Social Media. *Business Horizons, 53*(1), 59–68.

Landon-Murray, M. (2015). Social media and U.S. intelligence agencies: Just trending or a real tool to engage and educate? *Journal of Strategic Security, 8*(5), 67–79. doi:10.5038/1944-0472.8.3S.1476.

Leavey, J. (2013). Social media and public policy, What is the evidence? Alliance for Useful Evidence. Accessed November 22, 2016, from https://www.alliance4usefulevidence.org/assets/Social-Media-and-Public-Policy.pdf

LexisNexis. (2014). Social media use in law enforcement. Accessed November 22, 2016, from https://www.lexisnexis.com/risk/downloads/whitepaper/2014-social-media-use-in-law-enforcement.pdf

Mateescu, A., Brunton, D., Rosenblat, A., Patton, D., Gold, Z., & Boyd, D. (2015). Social media surveillance and law enforcement. Data & Society, Data & Civil Rights Conference. Accessed November 22, 2016, from http://www.datacivilrights.org/pubs/2015-1027/Social_Media_Surveillance_and_Law_Enforcement.pdf

Ministère de l'intérieur de la République Française et Ministère de l'intérieur de la République Fédérale d'Allemagne. (2016). Initiative franco-allemande sur les enjeux clés de la coopération européenne dans le domaine de la sécurité intérieure. Accessed December 18, 2016, from http://www.interieur.gouv.fr/Archives/Archives-ministre-de-l-interieur/Archives-Bernard-Cazeneuve-avril-2014-decembre-2016/Interventions-du-ministre/Initiative-franco-allemande-sur-la-securite-interieure-en-Europe

National Police Chiefs' Council (NPCC). (2016). The Counter Terrorism Internet Referral Unit. Accessed November 27, 2016, from http://www.npcc.police.uk/NPCCBusinessAreas/PREVENT/TheCounterTerrorismInternetReferralUnit.aspx

Omand, D., Bartlett, J., & Miller, C. (2012a). Introducing Social Media Intelligence (SOCMINT). *Intelligence and National Security, 27*, 801–823. doi: 10.1080/02684527.2012.716965 .

Omand, D., Bartlett, J., & Miller, C. (2012b). "A balance between security and privacy online must be struck.... " #INTELLIGENCE. Demos. Accessed November 20, 2016, from https://www.demos.co.uk/files/_Intelligence_-_web.pdf?1335197327

Parlamento Italiano. (2001). Legge 15 dicembre 2001 n. 438 - Conversione in legge, con modificazioni, del decreto-legge 18 ottobre 2001 n. 374, recante disposizioni urgenti per contrastare il terrorismo internazionale. Published on the Official Journal of the Italian Republic No. 293 of 18 December 2001. Accessed December 19, 2001, from http://www.camera.it/parlam/leggi/01438l.htm

Parlamento Italiano. (2005). Legge 31 luglio 2005, n. 155 – Conversione in legge, con modificazioni, del decreto-legge 27 luglio 2005, n. 144, recante misure urgenti per il contrasto del terrorismo internazionale. Published on the Official Journal of the Italian Republic No. 177 of 1 August 2005. Accessed December 19, 2001, from http://www.camera.it/parlam/leggi/05155l.htm

Parlamento Italiano. (2015). Legge 17 aprile 2015, n. 43 – Conversione in legge, con modificazioni, del decreto-legge 18 febbraio 2015, n. 7, recante misure urgenti per il contrasto del terrorismo, anche di matrice internazionale, nonché proroga delle missioni internazionali delle Forze armate e di polizia, iniziative di cooperazione allo sviluppo e sostegno ai processi di ricostruzione e partecipazione alle iniziative delle Organizzazioni internazionali per il consolidamento dei processi di pace e di stabilizzazione. Published on the Official Journal of the Italian Republic No. 91 of 20 April 2015. Accessed December 19, 2016, from http://www.gazzettaufficiale.it/atto/serie_generale/caricaDettaglioAtto/originario?atto.dataPubblicazioneGazzetta=2015-04-20&atto.codiceRedazionale=15A02961&elenco30giorni=false

Pennisi, M. (2016). Google, Facebook, Twitter e Microsoft contro il terrorismo online. *Il Corriere della Sera* (online edition), December 5. Accessed December 17, 2016, from http://www.corriere.it/tecnologia/social/16_dicembre_06/google-facebook-twitter-microsoft-contro-terrorismo-online-4ac67432-bb8b-11e6-a857-3c2e3af6f0b6.shtml

Presidenza del Consiglio dei Ministri. (2013a). Decreto del Presidente del Consiglio dei Ministri del 24 gennaio 2013. Direttiva recante indirizzi per la protezione cibernetica e la sicurezza informatica nazionale (13A02504). Published on the Official Journal of the Italian Republic No. 66 of 19 March 2013. Accessed February 11, 2017, from http://www.gazzettaufficiale.it/eli/id/2013/03/19/13A02504/sg

Presidenza del Consiglio dei Ministri. (2013b). Piano nazionale per la protezione cibernetica e la sicurezza informatica. Accessed December 19, 2016, from http://www.agid.gov.it/sites/default/files/leggi_decreti_direttive/piano-nazionale-cyber_0.pdf

Quadling, A., & Potter, H. E. (2014). Is social media responsible for your safety during a disaster? *The Conversation*, November 10. Accessed November 26, 2016, from http://theconversation.com/is-social-media-responsible-for-your-safety-during-a-disaster-33138

Sparrow, A. (2017). WhatsApp must be accessible to authorities, says Amber Rudd. *The Guardian* (online edition), March 26. Accessed April 9, 2017, from https://www.theguardian.com/technology/2017/mar/26/intelligence-services-access-whatsapp-amber-rudd-westminster-attack-encrypted-messaging

Stewart, C. S., & Maremont, M. (2016). Twitter bars intelligence agencies from using analytics service. *The Wall Street Journal* (online edition), May 8. Accessed November 22, 2016, from http://www.wsj.com/articles/twitter-bars-intelligence-agencies-from-using-analytics-service-1462751682

United Nations Office on Drugs and Crime (UNODC). (2013). Comprehensive study on cybercrime. Accessed March 20, 2017, from https://www.unodc.org/documents/organized-crime/UNODC_CCPCJ_EG.4_2013/CYBERCRIME_STUDY_210213.pdf

WeAreSocial. (2017). Digital in 2017. Accessed April 25, 2017, from https://wearesocial.com/uk/blog/2017/01/digital-in-2017-global-overview

Wendling, C., Randish, J., & Jacobzone, S. (2013). The use of social media in risk and crisis communication. *OECD Working Papers on Public Governance, 24*, 1–41. Accessed April 26, 2017, from http://www.oecd-ilibrary.org/docserver/download/5k3v01fskp9s-en.pdf?expires=1493215945&id=id&accname=guest&checksum=27FB2BE608839D837DB59E3276DEB1F0

Chapter 12
Regulation of Data Breaches in the European Union: Private Companies in the Driver's Seat of Cybersecurity?

Maria Grazia Porcedda

12.1 Introduction

"It's not a question if you...will be breached, the only question is when" (http://breachlevelindex.com/data-breach-mindset). While this may simply be the slogan of a security firm trying to attract customers, the truth is that data breaches are a daily occurrence. Data breaches often result from hacking and data exfiltration, which correspond to the cybercrimes 'illegal access' and 'data interference' contained in Directive 2013/40/EU on attacks against information systems. Fighting against cybercrimes is one of the goals of cybersecurity, and indeed one of the three pillars of the EU Cybersecurity Strategy (European Commission and High Representative of the European Union for Foreign Affairs and Security Policy 2013). As a result, addressing data breaches has cybersecurity relevance. Since network and information systems, as well as data, are (or better, have become) for the greatest part privately owned, the achievement of cybersecurity, including dealing with data breaches, rests in the hands of such private actors. Thereby, private companies overseeing data, information systems and networks, influence the pursuit of (cyber)security, even if security is not their (primary) business focus. The purpose of this chapter is to illustrate how the EU law on data breaches de facto acknowledges private companies as agents of cybersecurity. In metaphorical terms, we could say that it is as if EU law accepts that private companies sit in the driver's seat of the cybersecurity car, whilst at the same time trying to dictate the car's route and fit it with emergency breaks. The overall purpose of the chapter is achieved by addressing three sub-objectives—reflecting the wider objectives of this book—which are pursued with a mix of legal-descriptive and legal-argumentative analysis. The first sub-objective is to describe the rules on the notification and management

M.G. Porcedda (✉)
School of Law, The Liberty Building, University of Leeds, Leeds LS2 9JT, UK
e-mail: M.G.Porcedda@leeds.ac.uk

O. Bures, H. Carrapico (eds.), *Security Privatization*,
DOI 10.1007/978-3-319-63010-6_12

of data breaches, thereby showing their rationale. The first rules originate from the Citizens' Rights Directive (2009/136/EC) and the Better Regulation Directive (2009/140/EC) (a.k.a Telecom Package), which introduced a double regime on the notification and mitigation of data breaches. The first regime, enshrined in the revised e-Privacy Directive (2002/58/EC), concerns the protection of personal data. The rationale was to create legal and reputational incentives for companies managing or profiting from (personal) data to implement both security and privacy measures, incentives that were hitherto missing. The second regime, included in the Framework Directive (2002/21/EC), relates to breaches of security that do not concern personal data, arguably to increase the level of network and information security.

In the space of 8 years, the scope of such a double regulatory regime has broadened beyond Telecommunications (hereafter Telcos) and e-Privacy law. Rules on personal data breaches are now enshrined in the General Data Protection Regulation (2016/679/EU) (hereafter GDPR), whereas 'breaches of security' are mentioned in the electronic identification and assurance services (hereafter eIDAS) Regulation (910/2014/EU), and the Network and Information Security (hereafter NIS) Directive (2016/1148/EU). In line with the expansion of its scope, legislation on data breaches has come to embrace a broader spectrum of companies than Telcos. Describing the evolving legal lands cape allows me to pursue the second sub-objective of this chapter, namely to show that legislation on data breaches formally acknowledges the cybersecurity role played by private companies that profit from the Information and Communication Technologies (hereafter ICTs) services they offer, and the data they process, but nonetheless are not private military and/or security companies (PMSCs, see Chap. 1).

In fact, in addition to Telecommunications networks and services providers, addressees of data breaches legislation now include Information Society Services (including, but not limited to, online marketplaces, cloud services and online search engines), providers of e-signatures, e-seals, e-stamps, electronic registered delivery services and certificates, and e-certificates for website authentication, providers of internet exchange points (IXPs), and domain name systems and servers (DNS).

My third sub-goal consists in unequivocally showing the cybersecurity import of the management of both regimes of data breaches, i.e. personal data breaches and security incidents. This becomes possible by considering the matter not only from the perspective of cybercrime, but also from that of Network and Information Security (hereafter NIS), which is another pillar of the aforementioned EU Cybersecurity Strategy. All instruments, in fact, are informed by a logic of risk management and assessment aimed at securing information and data, which substantially overlap in NIS. Going back to the car metaphor, the cybercrime dimension of data breaches, which consists in their notification and mitigation, is akin to fitting the car with emergency breaks. Conversely, the NIS dimension of data breaches, which is the adoption of measures aimed at preventing data breaches, is akin to setting the car's route. The fact that the law has the effect of putting private companies in the drivers' seat of cybersecurity does not mean that they will drive down the desired route, without crashing. This ultimately depends on the effectiveness of the incentives and obligations embedded in the law, which may be badly conceived, or wrongly implemented, and which must be discussed as a separate research objective.

The three sub-goals are not addressed in order, but rather are interwoven in the different sections of the chapter, which develops as follows. The first two sections, 12.2 and 12.3, address the two data breaches regimes. In Sect. 12.2, I recount the rules laying down personal data breaches notification and mitigation obligations, thereby describing the different practices that private companies should adhere to. In Sect. 12.3, the most substantial of this chapter due to the breadth of the instruments covered, I illustrate the legislation on security incidents, thereby also describing the practices that private companies have to follow. The illustration of the two regimes of data breaches is necessary to compare (more than to contrast) those regimes. Accordingly, in Sect. 12.4, I show the commonalities between both regimes—and the relevance of their common goals for cybersecurity—through the role played by the European Network and Information Security Agency (hereafter ENISA). The descriptive account contained in Sects. 12.2 and 12.3 is also necessary in order to unpack the notion of data breaches as defined in EU law, the correspondence between 'data' and information', and to appreciate the security role of private companies processing data (and profiting from the processing thereof) which should be shielded from breaches. On this basis, in Sect. 12.5 I demonstrate that the duty to manage any data breach is an open acknowledgment of the role of private companies as cybersecurity agents. This finding is independent from both private companies' willingness to take up the role of cybersecurity agent, as well the effectiveness of their actions *viz.* the pursuit of cybersecurity, which I address in the conclusions.

12.2 The Regime on Personal Data Breaches

This section addresses the provisions on personal data breaches. In Union law, the notion of personal data, laid down in article 2(a) of Directive 95/46/EC, is composed of four cumulative elements (Article 29 Data Protection Working Party 2007), which have been maintained in the GDPR (article 4.1). First, personal data refers to 'information,' regardless of its degree of sensitivity, format (paper, electronic, audio) and truthfulness. Secondly, such information is 'personal' in that it must be either (directly or indirectly) about an individual, or used for the purpose of affecting an individual, or resulting in affecting an individual.[1] Thirdly, the person must be 'identified or identifiable' (through so-called 'identifiers'), i.e. it must be possible to distinguish such person from all other members of the group, through means that are likely to be used (recital 26 of Directive 95/46 and 26 of the GDPR). The means are conceived of in evolutionary terms: a dynamic test should be applied to technological developments, in order to assess the potential capability

[1]Know-how is excluded from the notion of personal data. Deceased individuals do not enjoy the protection of the GDPR (recital 27).

of a technology to 'identify' individuals.[2] Article 4(1) of the GDPR broadens the notion of identifiers, and includes online identifiers, location data, and factors relating to mental identity. Fourthly, the individual must be a "natural person" (data subject), that is, a human living being, regardless of residence and nationality (article 1(2) and recital 14).

In the following, after describing the regime of data breaches enshrined in Directive 2002/58/EC and the relating Regulation 2013/611, I illustrate the provisions contained in the GDPR (but not the Police Directive[3]), as well as the innovations contained in the proposed Regulation amending the e-Privacy Directive. For each instrument I highlight the addressees, the scope of application, the objectives, and the broader context of application of the data breaches regime.

12.2.1 The e-Privacy Directive (Telcos)

The e-Privacy Directive is the *lex specialis* of the Data Protection Directive (95/46/EC), i.e. it lays down the regime of protection of personal data and confidentiality of one's communications in the context of electronic communications. It is therefore addressed to providers of publicly available "electronic communications services", which are defined in article 2 (c) of the Framework Directive as "a service normally provided for remuneration which consists wholly or mainly in the conveyance of signals on electronic communications networks, including telecommunications services and transmission services in networks used for broadcasting, but exclude services providing, or exercising editorial control over, content transmitted using electronic communications networks and services".

'Communications' is defined in article 2 (d) as "any information exchanged or conveyed between a finite number of parties by means of a publicly available electronic communications service." Broadcasted communications (e.g. TV or radio) do not fall within this definition, unless "the information can be related to the identifiable subscriber or user receiving the information". Typically, communications by means of a publicly available electronic communication service would take place on a public communications network (defined *infra*, Sect. 12.3). In terms of addressees of these rules, the e-Privacy Directive applies to Telcos over electronic networks that are available to the public (i.e. not private), but concerns

[2]For instance, "identification should include the digital identification of a data subject, for example through authentication mechanism such as the same credentials, used by the data subject to log-in to the on-line service offered by the data controller" (recital 57 of the GDPR).

[3]The GDPR was accompanied by the adoption of Directive 2016/680, which substitutes the much-criticized Council Framework Decision 977/2008/JHA, and addresses what has long been a legal grey area. It will apply to the prevention, investigation, detection and prosecution of criminal offences, but not to national security, which is the sole responsibility of Member States (article 72 TFEU). Since it concerns public bodies, which are beyond the scope of this discussion, I will not perform an analysis of the provisions on data breaches contained therein.

neither content providers, nor Information Society Services, a category embracing many web-based businesses, as I will address below (*infra*, in relation to GDPR).

Let us now look into the practices foreseen by legislation. Private companies providing electronic communications services have specific obligations with respect to personal data breaches, which are defined as "a breach of security leading to the accidental or unlawful destruction, loss, alteration, unauthorised disclosure of, or access to, personal data transmitted, stored or otherwise processed in connection with the provision of a publicly available electronic communications service" in the Union. Pursuant to article 4.3, the providers of e-communications services must always inform the competent authority, typically the National Data Protection Authority (hereafter NDPA), of any breach of personal data relating to an individual(s) or subscriber(s) (i.e. in theory, even just one). Moreover, the communications service providers must also inform the subscriber(s) or individual(s) "when the personal data breach is likely to adversely affect the personal data or privacy of a subscriber or individual ... without undue delay." Such an obligation is lifted only when the service provider satisfactorily demonstrates "that it has implemented appropriate technological protection measures, and that those measures were applied to the data concerned by the security breach." According to art. 4 of Commission Regulation 2013/611 on data breaches (611/2013/EU),[4] data controllers do not have to notify a data breach if it has taken measures that render the data unintelligible to unauthorised parties. Such measures, which are not to be considered *per se* exhaustive of the security obligations of data controllers, are laid down in the second paragraph: encryption with standardized key (letter a), or replacement of data by its hashed value calculated with a standardised cryptographic keyed hash function (letter b). Yet, the national competent authorities can still demand service providers to notify the breach if it has come to identify "the likely adverse effects" for the data subjects (the individuals/subscribers to whom data concern). Paragraph 3 further lists the type of information to be provided to the national data protection authority and to the affected subscribers/individuals. Moreover, pursuant to article 4(4), providers are under the obligation to maintain an 'inventory' of breaches occurred.

In accordance with paragraph 4, the Article 29 Working Party issued an Opinion on criteria to understand the potential adverse effect of data breaches, e.g. even if service providers have adopted technical solutions to protect the data of subscribers/individuals (Article 29 Data Protection Working Party 2011). The same Working Party has released reports on the notification of data breaches in collaboration with ENISA (European Network and Information Security Agency 2012, 2014).

The obligation for electronic communications service providers to notify personal data breaches is strongly related to the obligation to "take appropriate technical and organisational measures to safeguard *(sic)* security of its services, if

[4]Adopted pursuant to article 5(5) and 14a(2) of the e-Privacy Directive, the Commission Regulation lays down "technical implementing measures concerning the circumstances, format and procedures applicable to the information and notification requirements referred to" (recital 3) in Directive 2002/58/EC.

necessary in conjunction with the provider of the public communications network with respect to network security. Having regard to the state of the art and the cost of their implementation, these measures shall ensure a level of security appropriate to the risk presented" (article 4 (1)). Paragraph 2 of article 4 obliges e-communications providers to inform subscribers to their services of any risks of "a breach of the security of the network" over which the services are provided, whether remedying those risks is within the communications providers' reach, and the potential solutions available to subscribers. Recital 20 clarifies that "such risks may especially occur for electronic communications services over an open network such as the Internet or analogue mobile telephony."

Moreover, article 5(1) imposes on Member States the obligation to ensure the confidentiality of communications and the related traffic data "by means of a public communications network and publicly available electronic communications services, through national legislation". Accordingly, Member States have to "prohibit listening, tapping, storage or other kinds of interception or surveillance of communications and the related traffic data by persons other than users, without the consent of the users concerned" (except when legally authorised to do so, or for technical storage necessary for the conveyance of a communication).

There was a fierce political fight as to the desirability of limiting legislation to the (public) electronic communications sectors (Barcelo 2009), and the will to expand it is codified in recital 59 of the Directive amending the e-Privacy Directive, which states "the interest of users in being notified is clearly not limited to the electronic communications sector." Reiterated in two Communications (European Commission 2010a, b) in relation to achieving a successful digital internal market, broad notification requirements were enshrined in the GDPR repealing the Data Protection Directive, to which I turn now.

12.2.2 The GDPR (includes Information Society Services)

The GDPR was adopted in response to article 16.2 of the Treaty on the Functioning of the European Union (Lisbon Treaty 2010), which engenders the positive obligation for Union institutions to adopt comprehensive rules on the protection of personal data (and the free flow thereof), which is a right enshrined in article 8 of the Charter of Fundamental Rights of the European Union (2007). The Regulation was also justified by the impact on data protection of the combination of advances in technological applications and the changing nature of international data flows, as well as the divergence of approaches in the Member States (Article 29 Data Protection Working Party & Working Party on Police and Justice 2009; Buttarelli 2012; Reding 2011). When the GDPR enters into force, it will repeal Directive 95/46/EC and it will represent the most comprehensive legislation on the protection of personal data.

As for the material scope, the Regulation applies to all data controllers, i.e. to those natural or legal persons (*viz.* private companies), that process personal data wholly or partly by automated means, or process by non-automated means personal data that form part of a filing system or are intended to form part of a filing system (art. 2). The GDPR applies to the processing of whosoever personal data "in the context of the activities of an establishment of a controller or a processor in the Union, regardless of whether the processing takes place in the Union or not" (art. 3 (1)). It also applies to the processing of personal data of individuals who are in the Union by a controller or processor not established in the Union, where the processing activities are related either to the offering of goods or services, also for free, to such data subjects in the Union, or the monitoring of their behaviour as far as their behaviour takes place within the Union (art. 3(2)). As a result, the GDPR applies also to data controllers who are Information Society Services, which, pursuant to the e-Commerce Directive as amended in 2015 (2015/1535/EU), are "any service normally provided for remuneration, at a distance, by electronic means and at the individual request of a recipient of services".[5] As a result, while the definition of 'personal data breaches' contained in the GDPR corresponds to that of the e-Privacy Directive, it extends the scope of the rules beyond providers of e-communications services, to include providers of content online and digital services (see Sect. 12.3.3).

The data breaches appear in several provisions of the GDPR, but the most important ones are contained in its Chaps. 4 and 8. Article 33 concerns the notification of data breaches to the competent authority, typically the NDPA. The data controller must notify the personal data breach to the NDPA, within 72 h after having become aware of it, or later with due justification, "unless the personal data breach is unlikely to result in a risk to the rights and freedoms of natural persons."

Article 34 concerns the communication of a personal data breach to the data subject, which is due, without delay, when the breach "is likely to result in a high risk to the rights and freedoms of natural persons" (art. 34 (1)). Communication to individuals is not due in any of the following cases (art. 34 (3)): (a) the personal data affected by the personal data breach were protected with appropriate technical and organisational protection measures, such as encryption; (b) the controller has adopted mitigation measures whereby the high risk is no longer likely to materialize; and (c) direct communication to the data subjects would be disproportionate: the controller must instead communicate the breach to the public, or take "equally effective" measures. The NDPA has the last word on the likelihood of adverse consequences for data subjects, and can thus still request data controllers to communicate the data breach to affected individuals irrespective of the conditions illustrated above (art. 34 (4)). Interestingly, notification is determined by the notion of risk: notification to the national competent authority is due whenever there are

[5]For the purposes of this definition: (1) 'at a distance' means that the service is provided without the parties being simultaneously present; (2) 'by electronic means' means that the service is sent initially and received at its destination by means of electronic equipment for the processing (including digital compression) and storage of data, and entirely transmitted, conveyed and received by wire, by radio, by optical means or by other electromagnetic means; (3) 'at the individual request of a recipient of services' means that the service is provided through the transmission of data on individual request.

(unqualified) risks to the rights and freedoms of natural persons, whereas individuals must be notified if there are high risks to their rights and freedoms.

To be sure, it is important to notice upfront that the rationale of (the right to) the protection of personal data is that all personal data deserve protection irrespective of the immediate danger posed by their processing. However, the notion of the (known) risk posed by the processing serves the purpose of accommodating legitimate processing operations (which "should be designed to serve mankind", recital 4 of the GDPR). The GDPR refers to generic risks, significant or high risks[6] to the rights and freedoms of natural persons, which may lead to physical, material or non-material damage (recital 75), as well as data security risks (recital 83). If fully anonymised data are not considered personal data any longer, pseudonymised data (article 4(5) of the GDPR) pose low risk. So-called sensitive data pose significant risks (recital 51), whereas high risks are those that follow a specific assessment, e.g. in relation to data breaches or new technologies (see Chaps. 4 and 7). Recital 85 of the GDPR lists the risks that could ensue where a personal data breach is not addressed in an appropriate and timely manner, in the guise of "loss of control over their personal data or limitation of their rights, discrimination, identity theft or fraud, financial loss, unauthorised reversal of pseudonymisation, damage to reputation, loss of confidentiality of personal data protected by professional secrecy or any other significant economic or social disadvantage to the natural person concerned."

Protection is substantiated in the adoption of technical, organizational and legal measures, such as those contained in article 32 on the security of processing (and 24 on the obligations of the controller), whose stringency and severity will be based on the anticipated level of risk, based on a well-established risk-based approach (Article 29 Data Protection Working Party 2014).

As a result, and as noted in the case of the e-Privacy Directive, a breach of personal data is intimately related to a breach of security measures, which can cause differing degrees of risks to the rights and freedoms of natural persons. In this guise, Chap. 4 of the GDPR foresees the possibility to impose penalties and potentially heavy administrative fines on data controllers; according to recital 148, the calculation of penalties, including administrative fines, depends on elements of import for the management of data breaches, such as "the nature, gravity and duration of the infringement, the intentional character of the infringement, actions taken to mitigate the damage suffered, degree of responsibility or any relevant previous infringements, the manner in which the infringement became known to the supervisory authority, compliance with measures ordered against the controller or processor, adherence to a code of conduct and any other aggravating or mitigating factor."

[6]A closer reading of the relevant provisions seems to favour an understanding of 'high' risks as very likely ones, whereas 'significant' risks seems to relate to the intensity of the potential damage suffered by individuals.

Finally, the GDPR implies the revision of Directive 2002/58/EC. The Commission's proposal for a Regulation repealing the e-Privacy Directive (European Commission 2017) was adopted in January 2017. The proposed Regulation does not contain any references to personal data breaches. This is because the proposal is *lex specialis* for the GDPR, which contains exhaustive rules concerning data breaches across all sectors. I therefore move to analysing the second regime.

12.3 The Regime on Breaches of Security

What I term the "second regime" of data breaches relates to incidents that do not affect personal data. As I will show in part 3, such a "breach of security or loss of integrity" is closely linked to "personal data breaches". The new article 13a of the Framework Directive, concerning the security of networks and services, lays down rules on the obligation, for providers of public electronic networks (defined in part 2), or publicly available electronic communications services, to notify a "breach of security or loss of integrity". This provision represents the blueprint for subsequent provisions dealing with data breaches (European Network and Information Security Agency 2012), namely articles 10 and 19 of the eIDAS Regulation, and articles 14 and 16 of the Network and Information Security (hereafter NIS) Directive. As I did for the first regime, in the following, after describing the provisions on data breaches contained in the Framework Directive, I illustrate the articles of the eIDAS Regulation and the NIS Directive. For each instrument I highlight the addressees, the scope of application, the objectives, and the broader context of application of the data breaches regime.

12.3.1 The Framework Directive (Telcos)

The Framework Directive is the umbrella directive for the Union's Telecommunications legislation ("electronic communications services, electronic communications networks, associated facilities and associated services, and certain aspects of terminal equipment to facilitate access for disabled users", article 1). It concerns publicly available electronic communications services, described above, and public electronic communications networks, which, pursuant to article 2(a) and (d), are "transmission systems and, where applicable, switching or routing equipment and other resources, including network elements which are not active, which permit the conveyance of signals by wire, radio, optical or other electromagnetic means, including satellite networks, fixed (circuit- and packet-switched, including Internet) and mobile terrestrial networks, electricity cable systems, to the extent that they are used for the purpose of transmitting signals, networks used for radio and television broadcasting, and cable television networks, irrespective of the type of information conveyed"; and "used wholly or mainly for the provision of electronic communications services available to the public which support the transfer of information between network termination points". The Framework Directive does not concern Information Society Services (as defined *supra*).

The amendment to the Framework Directive effected by the Telecom Package in 2009 introduced data breaches-specific legislation, namely article 13 (a) (3), whereby "Member States shall ensure that undertakings providing public communications networks or publicly available electronic communications services notify the competent national regulatory authority of a breach of security or loss of integrity that has had a *significant* impact on the operation of networks or services." In turn, and if appropriate, the national regulatory authority can inform regulatory authorities of other Member States, as well as ENISA. In addition, if the national regulatory authority believes knowledge of the breach is in the public interest, it may inform the public of the breach, or otherwise ask or require the undertakings to do so. Similarly to what is foreseen in the e-Privacy Directive, pursuant to article 13 (a)(4), combined with article 22(3), the Commission is empowered to adopt appropriate harmonising technical implementing measures, which "shall be based on European and international standards to the greatest extent possible".

The provision on data breaches is contained in Chapter IIIa on Security and Integrity of Networks and Services. Earlier paragraphs of article 13 (a) discipline the measures that undertakings providing communications networks and services must take to ensure the security of networks and services, particularly to "prevent and minimise the impact of security incidents on users and interconnected networks". Measures should be proportionate to the level of envisaged risk, and be in line with the state of the art (art. 13 (a) (1)). Undertakings providing communications networks must also be made to guarantee the integrity of their networks and ensure the continuity of supply. Hence, the notification of data breaches is intimately linked with the maintenance of security. I must note that, in the implementation phase, privilege has been given to ensuring 'integrity' understood as continuity of service, rather than security of service, to the detriment of the latter goal (European Network and Information Security Agency 2017).

Note that the Telecommunications framework will be overhauled by the Directive establishing the European Electronic Communications Code (European Commission 2017). The Code will apply to communications services such as "voice telephony, messaging services and electronic mail conveyance services" (proposed recital 11). The proposed article 40 innovates on article 13 (a) on data breaches, in that it lists the parameters determining the significance of the impact of a security breach (which should reddress the imbalance between continuity of service, and security thereof). The proposed article 41 further refers to the adoption of measures of mitigation, Computer Security Incident Response Teams (hereafter CSIRTs), and cooperation with authorities such as NDPAs. Those additions take inspiration from the content of the NIS Directive. Before listing them, however, I analyse the eIDAS Regulation.

12.3.2 The eIDAS Regulation (e-trust services)

The eIDAS Regulation was adopted in 2014 to repeal Directive 1999/93/EC on electronic signatures, because the latter failed to deliver "a comprehensive cross-border and cross-sector framework for secure, trustworthy and easy-to-use electronic transactions" (recital 3). The purpose of the eIDAS Regulation is, in line with articles 1 and 4 ('internal market principle'), the free movement as well as 'an adequate level of security' of e-identification and trust services, which are key to e-administration and financial transactions respectively. Providing an adequate level of security is the main focus of the Regulation because, as clarified in the opening recitals, the uncertain level of security determined by the lack of a proper regulatory framework hampers the free circulation of such services (recitals 1 and 2).

The eIDAS Regulation applies to e-identification schemes notified by Member States, and to trust service providers established in the Union, with the exclusion of trust services that are "used exclusively within closed systems resulting from national law or from agreements between a defined set of participants" (art. 2). Here I focus on trust services only, because the data breach provisions concerning e-identification services are mainly addressed to Member States.

A trust service is "an electronic service normally provided for remuneration which consists of: (a) the creation, verification, and validation of electronic signatures, electronic seals or electronic time stamps, electronic registered delivery services and certificates related to those services, or (b) the creation, verification and validation of certificates for website authentication; or (c) the preservation of electronic signatures, seals or certificates related to those services." (art. 3 (16)).[7] Furthermore, services that meet the applicable requirements laid down in the Regulation are 'qualified' trust service providers (art. 3 (17)).

The Regulation does not provide a general definition of 'breaches' or 'loss of integrity', but addresses "notification of security breaches and security risk assessments" which are "essential with a view to providing adequate information to concerned parties in the event of a breach of security or loss of integrity" (recital 38).

Pursuant to article 19 (2), both qualified and non-qualified trust service providers must "within 24 h after having become aware of it, notify the supervisory body and, where applicable, other relevant bodies, such as the competent national body for information security or the data protection authority, of any breach of security or loss of integrity that has a significant impact on the trust service provided or on the personal data maintained therein." In case the breach were to "adversely affect a natural or legal person to whom the trusted service has been provided" then the trust

[7]The Regulation does not explicitly qualify the nature of the services as information society services (ISSs). It can be argued that eIDAS would not fall under the definition of ISS because they do not operate entirely by electronic means, in that they need a physical support (i.e. hardware) to work.

service provider must "notify the natural or legal person ... without undue delay". If the incident concerns two or more Member States, then trust service providers should inform the national authority of the Member States concerned and ENISA. If the "disclosure of the breach of security or loss of integrity is in the public interest", then the notified supervisory authority shall either inform the public, or ask the trust provider to do so. Qualified trust services accept to be audited at least every two years (at their own costs, article 20 (1)).

The Regulation further establishes supervisory authorities for trust service providers, which should "cooperate with data protection authorities", particularly with regards to suspected breaches of personal data protection rules, in particular in relation to security incidents and personal data breaches (Recital 31).

Similarly to the e-Privacy Directive and the Framework Directive, pursuant to the combination of articles 19 (4) and 48 (2), the Commission is empowered to adopt implementing acts to specify the measures contained in article 19 (2). Also similarly to the e-Privacy and the Framework Directive, provisions on data breach notification are laid down in the context of, and complement, security measures. For instance, article 19 (1) concerns the obligation, for any trust service providers, to "take appropriate technical and organisational measures" commensurate to the degree of "risks posed to the security of the trust services they provide", having regard to the state of the art. "In particular, measures shall be taken to prevent and minimise the impact of security incidents and inform stakeholders of the adverse effects of any such incidents." The relationship between notification and security requirements is further reinforced by the clear security objective of the Regulation.

12.3.3 The NIS Directive (essential and digital services)

After three years of debate, the Parliament and Council adopted the NIS Directive in 2016. The purpose of the Directive is to achieve "a high level of security of networks and information systems", *inter alia* by establishing "security and notification requirements for operators of essential services and for digital service providers" (article 1 (d)).

Before describing the nature of the services just mentioned, I must clarify that the NIS Directive relies on the definition of networks contained in the Framework Directive (art 4 (1) (a)), but applies only to networks that are not public (recital 7 and article 1 (3); nor does it apply to trust service providers just discussed). As for information systems, they are defined in art. 4 (1) (b) of the Directive as "any device or group of interconnected or related devices, one or more of which, pursuant to a program, perform automatic processing of digital data." Alternatively, information systems are also to be understood as "(c) digital data stored, processed, retrieved or transmitted by elements covered under points (a) and (b) for the purposes of their operation, use, protection and maintenance." The definition underlines the interrelatedness, and almost indivisibility, between network and information systems, in that there is a mutually vital relationship between the two. Although the different instruments revised in this chapter insist on the validity of definitions solely within the scope of their remit, there seems to be convergence on the understanding of 'networks' and 'information systems' (and data, as addressed later).

I can now provide the definition of the entities concerned by norms on data breaches. Operators of essential services are public or private entities which meet three cumulative criteria (arts. 4 (4) and 5 (1)): the service is 'essential for the maintenance of critical societal and/or economic activities', its provision 'depends on network and information systems', and would be highly disrupted by 'an incident', meaning "any event having an actual adverse effect" (art. 4 (7)). Operators of essential services are those in the wide sectors of energy, transport, banking, financial market infrastructures, health sector, the drinking water supply and distribution, and digital infrastructure (Annex II of the NIS Directive). The latter include Internet exchange points (IXPs), domain name system (DNS) service providers[8] and Top Level Domain name registries, which are of immediate relevance for this research.

Digital services (art. 4 (5)) are one of the following three types of Information Society Services (defined in Sect. 12.2.2): search engines, online marketplaces and cloud computing. 'Online marketplace' "allows consumers and/or traders ... to conclude online sales or service contracts with traders either on the online marketplace's website or on a trader's website that uses computing services provided by the online marketplace" (17). Online search engine "allows users to perform searches of, in principle, all websites or websites in a particular language on the basis of a query on any subject in the form of a keyword, phrase or other input, and returns links in which information related to the requested content can be found" (18). 'Cloud computing service' "enables access to a scalable and elastic pool of shareable computing resources" (19). Data breaches norms concern digital service providers that are not micro or small enterprises (article 16 (11)).

Operators of essential services and digital service providers are subject to different levels of harmonization (recital 57). Since operators of essential services have a direct link with physical infrastructure, therefore Member States "should ... impose stricter requirements than those laid down in this Directive". Instead, digital service providers have "cross-border nature". Yet, the NIS Directive seeks to "ensure a high level of harmonisation for digital service providers with respect to security and notification requirements ... in a manner proportionate to their nature and the degree of risk which they might face".

---

[8]Defined in article 4 as follows: (13) 'internet exchange point (IXP)' means a network facility which enables the interconnection of more than two independent autonomous systems, primarily for the purpose of facilitating the exchange of internet traffic; an IXP provides interconnection only for autonomous systems; an IXP does not require the internet traffic passing between any pair of participating autonomous systems to pass through any third autonomous system, nor does it alter or otherwise interfere with such traffic; (14) 'domain name system (DNS)' means a hierarchical distributed naming system in a network which refers queries for domain names; (15) 'DNS service provider' means an entity which provides DNS services on the internet.

The Directive uses the word breach but does not define it. Instead, it offers a definition of "incident" as "any event having an actual adverse effect on the security of network and information systems (art. 4 (7)). Note that recital 63 acknowledges that "personal data are in many cases compromised as a result of incidents". I will reason on the definitions used in the various instruments dealing with data breaches later on, but for the time being let us assume that 'breach' is coterminous with 'incident'. The NIS Directive also contains a definition of risk, understood "as any reasonably identifiable circumstance or event having a potential adverse effect on the security of network and information systems" (art. 4 (9)). In the light of the difference between operators of essential services and digital service providers, the NIS Directive provides two different notification requirements.

Operators of essential services have to swiftly notify the competent authority or the CSIRT of incidents having a "significant impact on the continuity of the essential services they provide" (article 14 (3) NIS Directive). As mentioned earlier, the NIS Directive follows the blueprint of the Framework Directive, but innovates in a way which is then positively affecting the Framework Directive in the recast Communications Code. Article 14 (4) lists the parameters that are relevant to assess the significance of the impact of an incident (and hence the obligation to notify it). Such parameters are: (a) the number of users affected by the disruption of the essential service; (b) the duration of the incident; and (c) the geographical spread with regard to the area affected by the incident. Competent authorities, acting together with the cooperation group (art. 4 (7)), can further clarify these guidelines.

Unlike personal data breaches legislation, the purpose of notification is not to 'name and shame'. Notification should not lead to increased liability for the notifying party (art. 14 (3)). Whenever notified, the CSIRT or the competent authority shall "preserve the security and commercial interests of the operator of essential services, as well as the confidentiality of the information provided in its notification" (art. 14 (5)). Rather, whenever possible the notified bodies must provide "information that could support the effective incident handling". Notification to the public is not mandatory. It can take place, "after consulting the notifying operator of essential services ... where public awareness is necessary in order to prevent an incident or to deal with an ongoing incident" (art. 4 (6)). Article 15 lays down strict rules to enable competent authorities to implement and enforce the rules.

Operators of essential services must swiftly notify the competent authority or the CSIRT of incidents affecting digital service providers when the latter offer their services to essential service operators (art. 16(5) NIS Directive). Digital service providers are responsible to notify all other incidents, provided two cumulative requirements are fulfilled: the incident must have a "substantial impact on the provision of a service" (art. 16 (3)), and the provider has "access to the information needed to assess the impact of an incident against the parameters" established by the Directive (art. 16 (4)). In addition to the parameters identified for operators of essential services, the article lists two further criteria of the impact of an incident:

"(d) the extent of the disruption of the functioning of the service; and (e) the extent of the impact on economic and societal activities". These parameters must be clarified by the Commission, pursuant to the combined reading of articles 16 (8) and 22 (2).

Such rules may reflect the reality of a market composed of mostly extra EU service providers. Article 16 (10) clarifies that Member States cannot impose additional "security or notification requirements on digital service providers". Similarly, supervisory measures should take place *ex post facto* (article 17). Recital 60 clarifies that "digital service providers should be subject to light-touch and reactive ex post supervisory activities justified by the nature of their services and operations. The competent authority concerned should therefore only take action when provided with evidence ... that a digital service provider is not complying with the requirements of this Directive, in particular following the occurrence of an incident".

Similarly to the case of essential services, notification of the incident has to "preserve the digital service provider's security and commercial interests as well as the confidentiality of the information provided." (art. 16 (6)). Likewise, disclosure of the incident suffered by digital services to the public is not mandatory but, differently from the case of operators of public services, dissemination can nonetheless be decided "where disclosure of the incident is otherwise in the public interest" (art. 16 (7)).

As noted in relation to the data breaches provisions analysed in previous sections, notification requirements are part of a wider security approach also in the case of the NIS Directive. Paragraph two of both articles 14 and 16 clarifies, with minor differences,[9] that service providers must take measures to prevent and minimise the impact of incidents affecting the security of the network and information systems used for the provision of such services, with a view to ensuring service continuity. Paragraph one of both articles 14 and 16 clarifies, with some differences,[10] that service providers must take appropriate and proportionate technical and organisational measures to manage the risks posed to the security of network and information systems which they use in their operations. As in the case of the eIDAS Regulation, the connection between rules on the notification of incidents and the broader security requirements should be stronger due to the clear security objective of the NIS Directive.[11] Moreover, recital 63 clarifies that

---

[9]Measures must be 'appropriate' in the case of essential services; the obligation concerns digital services referred to in Annex III that are offered within the Union.

[10]Digital service providers must identify measures; the obligation concerns operators in the Union; moreover, "having regard to the state of the art, those measures shall ensure a level of security of network and information systems appropriate to the risk posed, and shall take into account the following elements: (a) the security of systems and facilities; (b) incident handling; (c) business continuity management; (d) monitoring, auditing and testing; (e) compliance with international standards." (article 16 (1)).

[11]It is not possible to predict whether 'continuity' of the service will be given more weight than 'security' in the national rules transposing the articles on the notification of breaches, but shoud this happen, it would represent a betrayal of the spirit of the NIS Directive.

incidents may be connected to cybercrime, and encourages notification to law enforcement authorities. The European Cybercrime Centre (EC3) and ENISA could in this case facilitate coordination between competent authorities and law enforcement authorities. The role of ENISA is pivotal not just in relation to cybercrime activities, but also to data protection authorities (with whom article 63 recommends cooperation to tackle any personal data breaches resulting from incidents.)

12.4 Commonalities Between the Two Data Breaches Regime, and the Role of ENISA

The analysis just performed distinguished between incidents that relate to personal data, and incidents that do not relate to personal data. To be sure, there are some differences between the two regimes. First, each regime is managed by different responsible authorities. Secondly, not all addressees of data breaches have to maintain an inventory of the breaches occurred (a difference seemingly unrelated to the question as to whether data is (im)personal). Thirdly, and perhaps more importantly, the two regimes differ as to liability. While the personal data regime tends to have homogeneous rules for finding liability and accountability, and the GDPR has introduced a harmonized system of administrative fines, the impersonal data regime stresses the importance of defining liability (art. 13 eIDAS), and identifying effective and dissuasive penalties (art. 16 eIDAS Regulation, art. 21 NIS Directive, art. 21 Framework Directive), but leaves the matter in the hands of the Member States. I will come back to the question of liability and fines in the conclusions.

Yet, the differences between regulatory regimes seem to be trumped by their commonalities. It should be manifest that the different instruments just revised follow, with some variation, the same blueprint, composed of the following steps. The first is prevention: the adoption of appropriate technical and organizational measures proportionate to risks to prevent and minimize the impact of incidents. The second step, which is mandatory in most cases, is notification of the breach to the competent authorities to receive guidance, and ensure the mitigation of the damage. As seen, obligations vary in respect of the importance of the service, the impact of the damage, and the expected degree of control Member States have on service providers. The third step, which is not always mandatory, is that of informing the public, especially if there can be 'public interest' to this effect. Depending on the gravity of the breach, and the liability of the breached party, this could be akin to 'naming and shaming', in that the breached party may have to notify the breach to affected individuals/entities, thus attracting negative publicity.

Such similarities between the two regimes are not accidental, as can be demonstrated by analysing the bridging role of ENISA. In fact, most of the revised instruments rely on ENISA, either as an expert body for the adoption of more detailed regulation on data security and breaches (art. 4.5 of the e-Privacy Directive), as a body for reporting incidents (e-privacy, art. 19.3 eIDAs Regulation, art. 13 (a) (3) Framework Directive), or for preparedness in the face of incidents (Nis Directive).

ENISA's mandate is currently defined by Regulation 526/2013/EU[12] and includes assisting the Union and the Member States in the prevention, detection and response to incidents (art. 2 (4)). The recitals of Regulation 526/2013 clarify the interrelation between the two regimes (in force by 2013, thus excluding the eIDAS Regulation, the GDPR and the NIS Directive). Recital 14 mentions the security obligations and breach notifications contained in the Framework Directive. In a similar vein, recital 15 recounts the norms contained in the e-Privacy Directive on the adoption of appropriate technical and organisational measures to safeguard security, on the confidentiality of the communications and related traffic data, and on personal data breach information and notification. It further mentions the security obligations contained in the Data Protection Directive 95/46/EC (repealed by the GDPR), "in particular where the processing involves the transmission of data over a network and against all other unlawful forms of processing". Recital 16 synthesizes both points, in that "the Agency should contribute to a high level of network and information security, to better protection of privacy and personal data, and to the development and promotion of a culture of network and information security".

In this respect, ENISA acts as the contact point between agencies dealing with various aspects of NIS, understood as "the ability of a network or an information system to resist, at a given level of confidence, accidental events or unlawful or malicious actions that compromise the availability, authenticity, integrity and confidentiality of stored or transmitted data and the related services offered by or accessible via those networks and systems." (article 1 (3)). Note that this definition is very similar to that contained in article 4 (2) of the NIS Directive (not reported here), and in the proposed article 2 (22) of the Communications Code (keeping aside the scope of the different instruments[13]). What the bridging role of ENISA shows is that both data breaches regimes deal with the two facets of the same problem, i.e. network and information security (NIS), which is one of the three pillars of the EU cybersecurity strategy (European Commission and High Representative of the European Union for Foreign Affairs and Security Policy 2013). Otherwise said, NIS can be achieved thanks to the combination of all the instruments just analysed, and hence all addressees of data breaches legislation become potential agents of NIS, and hence cybersecurity, as I further discuss in the next section.

---

[12] Codified Directive 2015/1535/EU on Information Society Services.

[13] The differences between the definitions concern the following: the scope of threats to security, which may include natural disasters (ENISA's definition); the scope of data which can include further operations on top of transmission and storage (NIS and Framework Directive); and the explicit ambit of application.

12.5 The Management of Data Breaches as the Discharge of Security Functions

The obligation to manage all data breaches, including those of personal data, implicitly turns private companies that are not PMSCs into agents of cybersecurity. In this section I intend to substantiate this claim, by showing the common security goal of the instruments, the relevance of such a goal for cybersecurity, and the correspondence between 'data' and information'.

12.5.1 Data Breaches Notification as Instrumental to Data/ Information Security

Articles 4 and 5 of the e-Privacy Directive, articles 14 and 16 of the NIS Directive, article 13(a) and (b) of the Framework Directive, Articles 33 and 34 of the GDPR, article 19 (and 10) of the eIDAS Regulation, and article 2(4) of the ENISA Regulation, and all related recitals, express similar principles. All instruments are predicated on the same paradigm, that of risk assessment and management: all instruments aim at detecting risks (i.e. vulnerabilities to threats) and avoiding them (Porcedda, 2017). In addition to the articles mentioned above, pursuant to article 3 (d) of its Regulation, ENISA should facilitate the establishment and take-up of European and international standards for risk management and for the security of electronic products, networks and services; the related recital 33 stresses that "efficient network and information security policies should be based on well-developed risk assessment methods, both in the public and private sector ... Promoting and developing best practices for risk assessment and for interoperable risk management solutions ... will increase the security level of networks and information systems" (see also recitals 19 and 24). The notification of data breaches is intimately tied to the degree of risk entailed by the breach.

Moreover, and as I have illustrated *supra*, Sects. 12.2 and 12.3, common provisions express a logic of prevention: they aim at protecting information in relation to the seriousness of the threat and the likelihood of the risk incurred (Porcedda 2017). Accordingly, all instruments mandate the adoption of appropriate technical and organizational measures to avoid breaches in the first place. The notification of data breaches is indissolubly linked to security requirements; there would be no notification obligation without the corresponding security duties. To go back to the cybersecurity car metaphor, security requirements (i.e. NIS) represent the attempt to set the route for private companies, while notification requirements (i.e. once cybercrime has happened) are akin to fitting the car with emergency breaks.

The notification of data breaches can also be seen as the reporting of the failure to maintain the security of one's services. In this sense, reporting is the only 'stick' available to the state to ensure that private companies offer the level of security that the state itself, before privatizing Telcos and the sector of ICTs at large, used (or aspired to offer) to offer.

12.5.2 The Cybersecurity Import of (Personal) Data Breaches

The duty imposed upon private companies to guarantee the security of their services, and report any failure thereof, has immediate relevance for cybersecurity in the Union, which is composed of NIS, fighting against cybercrime, and cyberdefence (European Commission and High Representative of the European Union for Foreign Affairs and Security Policy 2013; Porcedda 2017).

The link is manifest in the case of the Framework and the NIS Directives. Both instruments impose on the providers of the infrastructure of Telecommunications, Internet Exchange Points, Domain Name System, and Domain Name Servers, online marketplaces, online search engines and cloud computing services the security of the networks they operate in (whether available to the public or not), and of the 'information' they enable to transport. The Framework Directive's 'breach of security or loss of integrity', and the NIS Directive's 'incident which have an effect on security' refer to the same objective, i.e. network and information security. It should be noted that the 'integrity' which may be lost following a breach is an information security canon[14] (expressing the objective that the data transmitted, or stored, are unchanged and complete), and hence the prevention of security breaches should be considered part of the notion of 'information security' at large. Both Directives fulfil an important critical information infrastructure protection function (though the NIS Directive clarifies that it does not prejudice the identification of critical infrastructures at large, which is the objective of Directive 2008/114/EC instead).

The link between the e-IDAS regulation and cybersecurity may seem more tenuous. Yet, it can be argued that "a breach of security or loss of integrity that has a significant impact on the trust service provided or on the personal data maintained therein" concerns the securing of information systems in the sense of article 4 (1) (c) of the NIS Directive, "i.e. digital data stored, processed, retrieved or transmitted by elements covered under points (a) and (b) for the purposes of their operation, use, protection and maintenance" in that they oversee the authenticity and integrity "of stored or transmitted or processed data" (whether personal identity, or documents) as defined by article 4 (2) of the NIS Directive. In this sense,

[14]As discussed in Sect. 12.3.1, in the implementation phase integrity has been interpreted as availability of the service (European Network and Information Security Agency 2017). However, this betrays the intention of maintaining security. A more authentic interpretation would require taking into account both meanings, i.e. available and secure.

providers of services that are crucial, among others, to financial transactions (hence critical infrastructure) perform a clear cybersecurity function.

Moreover, *supra* I noted how recital 63 of the NIS Directive suggests the potential cybercrime relevance of security incidents. In the case of all instruments revised, incidents could be caused by illegal access or (large-scale) system interference, and lead to illegal interception and data interference, which are all cybercrimes (when the conditions are met) pursuant to Directive 2013/40/EU on attacks against information systems. In the case of trust services, incidents could also lead to fraud pursuant to Council Framework Decision 2001/413/JHA. In this respect, the task or duty of 'mitigating' breaches or incidents appears fundamental for the sake of limiting the damage of cybercrime and restoring NIS, i.e. achieving cybersecurity.

Private companies managing data breaches perform cybersecurity functions even when they are dealing with personal data breaches. The link between the protection of personal data from breaches and cybersecurity can be shown both by reasoning on the meaning of information systems, and the 'risks' which data controllers, i.e. private companies overseeing the processing of personal data, should avoid by means of technical and organizational measures.

Let us begin with information systems. The secondary instruments of EU law taken into account in this chapter do not define the notion of signals, which is crucial for the definition of networks over which electronic communications, i.e. "information between network termination points" is transferred. In the NIS Directive, information systems are a device (i.e. a single computer, mobile phone, tablet, satellite etc.) or group of interconnected or related devices that automatically process data (which can be personal). Alternatively, the information system can also coincide with the data necessary for its own functioning (which would arguably be impersonal), as per art. 4 (1) (c) of NIS Directive. Following the applicable law, the closest proxy to information is data, which warrants the equivalence between 'information' and 'data'. The analogy between information and data can be found, or demonstrated, for other instruments. For instance, it can be argued in the case of the e-IDAS Regulation's 'person identification data' (Art. 3 (3), where identity is information expressed in the form of data. The link between information and data can also be argued for communications, the confidentiality of which represents an information security canon. The definition of communications found in art. 2 (d) of the e-Privacy Directive reads "any information exchanged or conveyed between a finite number of parties by means of a publicly available electronic communications service." Information should be ultimately understood as data, not least because, to be transmitted, it must be expressed in the form of digital signals, hence digital/computer data. The link between signals, information, and data is also clear in the case of the GDPR (as discussed in Sect. 12.2.2). Pursuant to its article 4 (1), 'personal data' means any information relating to an identified or identifiable natural person ('data subject'); an identifiable natural person is one who can be identified, directly or indirectly, in particular by reference to an identifier.

In sum, information can be data of an indefinite nature when looked at as electromagnetic signals, which represent information's 'physical' nature and encompass all existing (e-)information. Such data can be impersonal, i.e. carrying information that does not necessarily concern an individual but rather, say, the state of a network or information collected from environmental sensors. Conversely, such data can be personal, i.e. concerning an individual, which represents a sub-category of all e-information. Hence, pursuing the security of information systems means pursuing the security of systems of data, whether they are personal or not. The measures adopted to protect personal and impersonal data typically converge (European Network and Information Security Agency 2014).

This leads to the issue of the risks (damage) private companies should avert. As seen for impersonal data, the loss of security can both originate from, and result in, cybercrimes. This is also the case of breaches of personal data. The NIS Directive recognizes that very often breaches concern personal data; the breach of a cloud computing service, for instance, may aim at the personal data contained therein. Compromising a domain name server could also have the final objective of attacking personal data. The abovementioned recitals 75 and 85 of the GDPR mention risks to personal data (in general and if breaches are not immediately mitigated) that correspond to cybercrimes as defined in Union law, such as identity theft (an aggravating circumstance in Directive 2013/40) fraud, financial loss of confidentiality of personal data protected by professional secrecy, or unauthorised reversal of pseudonymisation. The e-Privacy Directive aims at maintaining the confidentiality of information (an information security canon), the loss of which corresponds to illegal interception within telecommunication systems (critical information infrastructures). In other words, the prevention and mitigation of personal data breaches corresponds to the prevention and mitigation of cybercrime, which are a clear cybersecurity objective.

In conclusion, a breach of security or loss of integrity of an information system concerns data, the protection of which is an integral goal of cybersecurity. The security, mitigation and notification requirements put private companies whose profits come from the processing of (personal) data, rather than the provision of security, in the driver's seat of cybersecurity. The extent to which private companies are taking up this role, however, is a completely different matter. Eurostat data relating to 2015 shows that only 60% of enterprises in the field of information and communications had a security policy in place, a figure dropping to 40% in the area of essential services; on average, less than a third of EU-28 enterprises had a formally defined IT security policy in 2015.[15] Those statistics were collected before the approval of the eIDAS Regulation, the NIS Directive, and the GDPR. The new round of data analysis, to be released in 2019, will act as the litmus test on the extent to which the obligations on data breaches and related security policies are matched by practice, or whether companies try to pass the buck for security on to the next in line (typically the end user).

[15]Statistics are available at: http://ec.europa.eu/eurostat/statistics-explained/index.php/ICT_security_in_enterprises (last accessed 12 June 2017).

12.6 Conclusions

This chapter demonstrated that managing data breaches puts private companies that are not PMSCs in the driver's seat of a metaphorical cybersecurity car. Such a role was spurred by EU regulation, following the privatization of Telcos, which at the same time tried to influence the metaphorical cybersecurity car's route and fit it with emergency breaks. The argument was broken down into three sub-objectives: describing the double regime of data breaches and their rationale; stressing the fact that addressees are not private military and/or security companies; and unequivocally showing the cybersecurity import of the management of both regimes of data breaches.

Hence, I began the chapter by analysing the applicable law as divided into a double regime, depending on whether the breach concerns personal or impersonal data. For each instrument I highlighted the addressees, the scope of application, the objectives, and the broader context of application of the data breaches regime. The analysis led to identifying some differences between the two regimes, but more importantly a number of commonalities. I noted how commonalities were not casual, and referred to the role played by ENISA, which acts as the contact point for data breaches in both regimes, to introduce the convergence of the instruments analysed in the common pursuit of network and information security (NIS). To begin with, I noted how the instruments concerning both data breach regimes are informed by similar logics, i.e. that of risk management and assessment, as well as prevention of security incidents. Said logics frame the norms on data breaches notification and mitigation, which appear part of a wider infrastructure of security, rather than, or on top of, dry regulatory obligations. Seen in this light, actually, data breaches notification appear as the (only?) 'stick' available to the state to ensure that private companies do not take all the gains of the information society, while endangering critical (information) infrastructure.

I then observed the direct link of each instrument with the first two pillars of cybersecurity as understood in the Union's 2013 Strategy: NIS and cybercrime. After a closer reading of the notion of information security, and the 'risks' entailed by personal data breaches, I demonstrated that the management of all data breaches, whether personal or impersonal, bestows upon private companies processing personal data, and profiting from such a role, the role of cybersecurity providers in the guise of pursuing NIS (implementing security measures) and addressing cybercrime (notification and mitigation of a breach). I also noted that the pivotal role in which private companies are finding themselves does not, on its own, trigger private companies' willingness to start the cybersecurity engine.

This will depend, in fact, on a number of factors, which I am currently researching as part of additional scholarship. The first is whether notification of data breaches is sufficient to ensure that private companies perform their role as desired: data relating to 2015 cast doubts as to companies' readiness to invest in higher security. Moreover, notification requirements may only be implemented in part, as in the case of the interpretation of the notion of 'integrity' in the Framework

Directive (and possibly 'continuity of service' in the NIS Directive). In this respect, extending to the addressees of the Framework and NIS Directives (but also the eIDAS Regulation) a harmonized liability and sanctioning regime akin to that of the GDPR may engender a more effective incentive, in the light of the cross-border relevance of the services provided by the addressees. This also begs the questions of the adequacy, for the sake of cybersecurity, of (currently) five different instruments on data breaches (which will become four, after the approval of the e-Privacy Regulation). A comparative study of the success and failures of each regime, supported by adequate data, would possibly shed some light on this point. A final question concerns the technical, yet no less important, issue of who decides the relevant security standards (Farrand and Carrapico, Chap. 9). Several of the mentioned instruments refer to the relevance of the market, yet the question will have important bearing on the likelihood of breaches, and ultimately the achievement of a high level of cybersecurity.

Acknowledgment The completion of this chapter has been supported by the EPSRC-funded project CRITiCaL—Combatting cRiminals In The CLoud.

References

Article 29 Data Protection Working Party. (2007). Opinion 4/2007 on the Concept of Personal Data (WP 136). Brussels.

Article 29 Data Protection Working Party. (2011). Working Document 01/2011 on the Current EU Personal Data Breach Framework and Recommendations for Future Policy Developments (WP 184). Brussels.

Article 29 Data Protection Working Party. (2014). Statement on the Role of a Risk-based Approach in Data Protection Legal Frameworks (WP 218). Brussels.

Article 29 Data Protection Working Party, & Working Party on Police and Justice. (2009). The Future of Privacy: Joint Contribution to the Consultation of the European Commission on the Legal Framework for the Fundamental Right to Protection of Personal Data (WP 168). Brussels.

Barcelo, R. (2009). EU: Revision of the ePrivacy Directive. *Computer Law Review International, 31*(5), 31.

Buttarelli, G. (2012). *Latest Developments in Data Protection.* Paper presented at the meeting of the Heads of Agencies, Stockholm, 19 October 2012.

Charter of Fundamental Rights of the European Union, OJ C 303/1 (2007).

Commission Regulation 611/2013/EU of 24 June 2013 on the Measures Applicable to the Notification of Personal Data Breaches under Directive 2002/58/EC of the European Parliament and of the Council on Privacy and Electronic Communications (Commission Regulation on Data Breaches) (2013).

Consolidated versions of the Treaty on European Union (TEU) and the Treaty on the Functioning of the European Union (TFEU), OJ C 83/01 (Lisbon Treaty).

Council Directive 2008/114/EC of 8 December 2008 on the Identification and Designation of European Critical Infrastructures and the Assessment of the Need to Improve their Protection, OJ L 345.

Council Framework Decision 2001/413/JHA of 28 May 2001 combating fraud and counterfeiting of non-cash means of payment, OJ L 149.

Directive 95/46/EC of the European Parliament and of the Council of 24 October 1995 on the Protection of Individuals with regard to the Processing of Personal Data and on the Free Movement of such Data (Data Protection Directive) OJ L 281.
Directive 2002/21/EC of the European Parliament and of the Council of 7 March 2002 on a Common Regulatory Framework for Electronic Communications Networks and Services (Framework Directive), OJ L 108.
Directive 2002/58/EC of the European Parliament and of the Council of 12 July 2002 Concerning the Processing of Personal Data and the Protection of Privacy in the Electronic Communications Sector, OJ L 201 (e-Privacy Directive), OJ L 201.
Directive 2009/136/EC of the European Parliament and of the Council of 25 November 2009 Amending Directive 2002/22/EC on Universal Service and Users' Rights relating to Electronic Communications Networks and Services, Directive 2002/58/EC Concerning the Processing of Personal Data and the Protection of Privacy in the Electronic Communications Sector and Regulation (EC) No 2006/2004 on Cooperation between National Authorities Responsible for the Enforcement of Consumer Protection Laws, OJ L 337 (Citizens' Rights Directive).
Directive 2009/140/EC of the European Parliament and of the Council of 25 November 2009 amending Directives 2002/21/EC on a common regulatory framework for electronic communications networks and services, 2002/19/EC on access to, and interconnection of, electronic communications networks and associated facilities, and 2002/20/EC on the authorisation of electronic communications networks and services, OJ L 337 (Better Regulation Directive).
Directive 2013/40/EU of the European Parliament and the Council of 12 August 2013 on Attacks against Information Systems and Replacing Council Framework Decision 2005/222/JHA, OJ L 218.
Directive 2015/1535/EU of the European Parliament and of the Council of 9 September 2015 Laying down a Procedure for the Provision of Information in the Field of Technical Regulations and of Rules on Information Society services (codification), OJ L 241.
Directive 2016/1148/EU of the European Parliament and of the Council of 6 July 2016 Concerning Measures for a High Common Level of Security of Network and Information Systems across the Union, OJ L 194.
European Commission. (2010a). A Digital Agenda for Europe. *(Communication) COM (2010) 245 final.*
European Commission. (2010b). A Comprehensive Approach on Personal Data Protection in the European Union *(Communication) COM (2010) 609 final.*
European Commission. (2017). Proposal for a Regulation of the European Parliament and of the Council concerning the respect for private life and the protection of personal data in electronic communications and repealing Directive 2002/58/EC (Regulation on Privacy and Electronic Communications) *(Communication) COM (2017) 10 final, 2017/0003(COD).*
European Commission and High Representative of the European Union for Foreign Affairs and Security Policy. (2013). Cyber Security Strategy: An Open, Safe and Secure Cyberspace *(Joint Communication) JOIN (2013) 01 final.*
European Network and Information Security Agency (ENISA). (2012). Recommendations on Technical Implementation Guidelines of Article 4.
European Network and Information Security Agency (ENISA). (2014). Technical Guideline on Security measures for Article 4 and Article 13a. Crete, Greece.
European Network and Information Security Agency (ENISA). (2017). *Annual incident reports 2016*. Analysis of Article 13a annual incident reports in the telecom sector, Crete, Greece.
Porcedda, M. G. (2017). *Cybersecurity and privacy rights in EU Law. Moving beyond the trade-off model to appraise the role of technology.* (PhD Thesis), European University Institute.
Reding, V. (2011). The Review of the EU Data Protection Framework, SPEECH/11/183.
Regulation 526/2013/EU of the European Parliament and the Council of 21 May 2013 Concerning the European Union Agency for Network and Information Security (ENISA) and Repealing Regulation (EC) No 460/2004, OJ L 165.

Regulation 910/2014/EU of the European Parliament and Council of 23 July 2014 on Electronic Identification and Trust Services for Electronic Transactions in the Internal Market and Repealing Directive 1999/93/EC, OJ L 257.
Regulation 2016/679/EU of the European Parliament and of the Council of 27 April 2016 on the Protection of Natural Persons with Regard to the Processing of Personal Data and on the Free Movement of such data, and Repealing Directive 95/46/EC (General Data Protection Regulation), OJ L 119.

Lightning Source UK Ltd.
Milton Keynes UK
UKHW01n0027120718
325594UK00009B/469/P

9 783319 630090